ORGANIZATIONAL BEHAVIOR
AND
PERSONNEL PSYCHOLOGY

**The Irwin Series in Management
and
The Behavioral Sciences**

Consulting Editors
L. L. Cummings *and* E. Kirby Warren

John F. Mee   *Advisory Editor*

ORGANIZATIONAL BEHAVIOR AND PERSONNEL PSYCHOLOGY

Kenneth N. Wexley, Ph.D.
Associate Professor of Psychology
University of Akron

and

Gary A. Yukl, Ph.D.
Associate Professor of Management
Bernard M. Baruch College
The City University of New York

 1977

RICHARD D. IRWIN, INC. Homewood, Illinois 60430
Irwin-Dorsey Limited Georgetown, Ontario L7G 4B3

© RICHARD D. IRWIN, INC., 1977

All rights reserved. No part of this publication may be
reproduced, stored in a retrieval system, or transmitted,
in any form or by any means, electronic, mechanical,
photocopying, recording, or otherwise, without the prior
written permission of the publisher.

First Printing, January 1977

ISBN 0-256-01884-7
Library of Congress Catalog Card No. 76–15738
Printed in the United States of America

for our sons
MATTHEW, DAVID, GREGORY, *and* STEVEN

PREFACE

THE PURPOSE of this book is to introduce the reader to the study of work behavior in organizations. The contents are drawn primarily from two distinct areas: organizational behavior and personnel psychology. Both areas are directly relevant to the understanding and improvement of the effectiveness of work behavior in organizational settings.

The book was designed as a primary text for courses in industrial-organizational psychology at the undergraduate level or beginning graduate level. It is also appropriate for use as a supplementary text in related courses such as organizational behavior, personnel administration, and management. Although we have covered in considerable detail the major theories and concepts of organizational behavior and personnel psychology, we have not included the endless series of minute details and obscure facts that are found in so many other books. Thus, we have been able to limit both the size and the cost of the book to allow maximum flexibility of use. It can be used by itself, or together with another general text, a readings book, a book of cases and experiential learning exercises, or with paperbacks on specialized topics.

We have included chapters on the following subareas of organizational behavior: communication, employee motivation, employee attitudes, group processes, leadership, conflict management, organization structure, organization design, and organization development. In addition, we have included chapters on measuring employee proficiency, personnel selection, equal employment opportunity, design of training programs, and management development. Although many management-oriented books on organizational behavior fail to include these personnel topics, they are clearly important for managers. It is frequently necessary for a manager to select, train, and evaluate the performance of subordinates, and some general knowledge on how these functions should be performed can be highly useful.

More than other currently available textbooks, we have tried to show the practical implications of theory for improving work behavior. We have attempted to write the book in simple, clear language with a minimum of scholarly ambiguity and technical jargon. Concrete examples are frequently provided to clarify concepts for the reader. Review and discussion questions are presented at the end of each chapter to stimulate thought about the important concepts and their implications. Finally, we have ordered the material and defined terms in such a way as to preclude the need for a background in statistics, psychology, or business administration.

We are grateful for the helpful comments made by Richard Koppelman, Michael Campion, and Joseph Keblish on an earlier draft of this manuscript. In addition, our families deserve special thanks for their understanding and patience throughout the completion of the text.

East Windsor, New Jersey   KENNETH N. WEXLEY
December 1976   GARY A. YUKL

CONTENTS

xi

ership Behavior. Importance of the Situation. Leadership Influence and Power: *Bases of Power. Position Power and Personal Power. Bilateral Power and Situational Constraints. Power and Leader Effectiveness.* Leader-Situation Interaction Models: *Fielder's Contingency Model of Leadership. The Vroom and Yetton Model of Leadership. Path-Goal Theory of Leadership.* Improving Leadership in Organizations.

part two   PERSONNEL PSYCHOLOGY

INTRODUCTION

OUR SOCIETY is composed of many different kinds of organizations. There are military, health, religious, political, industrial, governmental, social, and educational organizations to name just a few. These organizations affect our lives in important ways. Our health, well-being, education, security, and standard of living depend upon how effectively these organizations achieve their objectives. Further, these organizations provide the setting in which most persons spend a large part of their time working. Realizing the pervasiveness of organizations in our lives, it is not surprising that behavioral and social scientists (e.g., psychologists, sociologists, anthropologists, economists, political scientists) have exerted a great deal of effort in the study of organizations and their processes.

The purpose of this book is to review available theory and research relating to work behavior in organizations. Behavioral scientists are concerned with studying the behavior of individuals and groups in organizations, as well as the organization in its entirety. They hope to further their understanding of these complex phenomena so as to enhance organization effectiveness and the satisfaction of organization members. In order to accomplish this objective, they must address themselves to a wide spectrum of problems that arise in work organizations such as maximizing employee motivation, coordinating the activities of various groups, providing appropriate leadership, selecting the best employees, and so on.

Since the information presented in the remainder of this book is based on the research performed by behavioral scientists, it would prove of value to consider briefly how this research is conducted. We make no attempt in this chapter to teach the reader how to conduct organizational research. Instead, we are concerned with developing an appreciation and feel for what rigorous research *is* and *is not*. First, we shall discuss what is commonly referred to as "the scientific approach" to gaining knowledge. Following this, we shall briefly discuss three scientific methods used for studying organizations. Finally, we shall present some of the problems and difficulties that scientists encounter when conducting research in organizational settings.

THE SCIENTIFIC APPROACH

There are many different methods that behavioral scientists use to gain knowledge about organizations. Although these methods differ from one another in various ways, they have certain common features which make them a part of "the scientific approach." More will be said about these specific scientific methods in the next section. Let us now look at some of the essential characteristics of the scientific approach.

1. *The scientific approach is self-correcting.* This is one of the characteristics that no other method of attaining knowledge possesses. There are built-in checks all along the way to obtaining scientific knowledge. These checks are used to continually verify the scientist's activities and conclusions. Even if a study seems to confirm a certain hypothesis, the scientist will continue to test alternative hypotheses which may cast doubt on the first results (Kerlinger, 1973).

2. *Scientific investigation is empirical.* If scientists believe something to be true, they must somehow put those beliefs to a test outside themselves. The scientist's perceptions, beliefs, and attitudes are not taken as truisms, but are carefully checked against objective reality.

3. *Scientific investigation is open to public inspection.* Every scientist writing a research report has other scientists in the field reading what he writes. The report contains a complete description of the purpose of the research, the procedures followed, the variables measured, the results obtained, and the conclusions reached. Although it is possible for a scientist to exaggerate his findings, this is not likely since the exact procedures can be replicated and the results tested by other qualified researchers.

4. *Scientific investigation is objective and statistical.* Bias does not enter into the scientist's data collection procedures. These data are usually analyzed statistically thus allowing the scientist to arrive at a certain level of confidence in the results obtained.

5. *Scientific investigation is controlled and systematic.* The research situation is tightly disciplined so that the researcher can have substantial confidence in the outcomes obtained. The scientist tries to systematically rule out possible causes for the results he is studying other than the variables he has hypothesized to be the causes.

6. *Scientific investigations generate theories.* A theory is a synthesis or conceptual framework for organizing and explaining phenomena previously observed by scientists while conducting research on a particular

topic. These scientific theories direct future research by specifying the salient characteristics of the variables studied and the interrelationships among the set of variables (Zedeck and Blood, 1974). In doing so they suggest new hypotheses to be tested.

7. *Scientific investigations test hypotheses.* After thinking about a problem, a scientist usually tries to formulate a hypothesis to be tested. A hypothesis is "a conceptual statement, a tentative proposition, about the relation between two or more observed . . . phenomena or variables." Our scientist will say "If such-and-such occurs, then so-and-so results" (Kerlinger, 1973, p. 12).

8. *The aim of scientific investigation is to explain, understand, predict, and change.* The scientist attempts to explain and understand human behavior in organizations. One might, for example, want to understand and explain the processes underlying worker motivation. Only through explanation and understanding could the scientist hope to improve the behavior of poorly motivated workers.

RESEARCH METHODS USED BY BEHAVIORAL SCIENTISTS

There are various methods that scientists use to study organizational processes. In this section we shall examine three of the most widely used techniques: the laboratory experiment, the field experiment, and correlational research. The reader should note that research programs sometimes involve more than one approach. For instance, to better understand how job enrichment affects employee motivation and productivity, a scientist may employ a combination of laboratory and field experimentation. Before proceeding any further, the reader should become familiar with the terms *independent* variable and *dependent* variable. The independent variable is the factor that is usually manipulated in some way by the scientist, such as leadership behavior, organizational structure, or method of pay. The dependent variable (sometimes referred to as a criterion) is a measure of the effects of the independent variable, such as productivity, absenteeism, or satisfaction.

In a laboratory experiment, the scientist has the most control over whatever phenomenon is being studied. Typically the scientist systematically varies a certain independent variable (e.g., group size) while holding constant or "controlling" certain extraneous variables. In this way, any consequent effects on the dependent variable (e.g., an increase in productivity) can be attributed to the independent variable. Many social and behavioral scientists in universities conduct laboratory research using students primarily as subjects. Much of what we know today about areas such as organizational leadership, small group behavior, motivation, and organizational conflict result from laboratory experimentation. Many of the theories presented throughout this text were initially investigated in the laboratory and, in some cases, later replicated in field settings. The major drawback of laboratory experimentation is the possibility that the findings cannot be generalized to real organizational settings. Often, laboratory results have limited generalizability because of their artificiality. The behavior of a sophomore volunteering for a three hour laboratory experiment can be quite different from the work behavior of an experienced employee.

In a field experiment the scientist attempts to manipulate variables in an actual organization instead of a laboratory. Since the scientist is operating in a complex environment, he has less control over certain extraneous variables which can affect the dependent variables he is interested in measuring. This often creates ambiguous results since the scientist cannot be certain whether the changes in the dependent variables are caused by the independent variables or some other factors. The major advantage of this method is its realism and, thus, the generalizability of results to other organizations. An example of a field experiment is a study comparing the impact of two pay incentive plans on employee attendance. In one condition the incentive plan is imposed on work groups by company management while in the other condition the incentive plan is developed by the employees themselves. Employees are randomly assigned to the two conditions, and perhaps also to a control group with no incentive plan.

There is always the question of whether field experimentation is better or worse than laboratory experimentation. Campbell and Stanley (1963) distinguish between internal validity and external validity. Internal validity deals with the question: Did the experimental treatments really make a difference in this specific experimental instance or was it caused by certain extraneous variables? External validity asks the question of generalizability: To what populations, settings, treatment variables, and measurement variables can this effect be generalized? Both types of validity are obviously important to any experiment even though they are frequently at odds with one another. Field experimentation usually maximizes external validity at the expense of internal validity. The opposite is true about laboratory experimentation. The relative importance of both types of validity will depend on the problem being investigated. For instance, investigations of theoretical issues are often more suited to laboratory experimentation while investigations designed to solve practical problems are usually more suited to field experimentation.

The third method, correlational research, is one in which the scientist determines the relationship between two variables as they exist in an actual organizational setting. No attempt is made here to manipulate one of the variables to see if changes in it cause changes in another variable. The scientist simply collects data about two or more variables in order to examine their relationship. For example, information may be gathered from employees or other groups regarding their beliefs, opinions, attitudes, motivations, and behaviors. These data are usually obtained by means of questionnaires or interviews or from organization records. The relationship among variables is usually measured by the use of a coefficient of correlation to be discussed later in the book. Even if a sizeable relationship exists, cause-and-effect inferences are impossible to make since one cannot be sure whether variable A caused B, B caused A, or they both were caused by some third variable (C) or combination of other variables (C, D, and E). Despite this weakness, correlational research is used frequently in the study of organizations since there are many situations in which behavioral scientists are unable to manipulate variables.

DIFFICULTIES IN CONDUCTING ORGANIZATIONAL RESEARCH

The primary function of behavioral scientists in dealing with organizational problems is to bring to bear knowledge that can be used in solving these problems. Without scientific research, there would be no sound knowledge to apply in solving problems. Knowledge based merely on intuition and common sense would prevail. What then are some of the difficulties and obstacles that scientists encounter when performing their important research function in organizational settings?

Organizational problems such as interdepartmental conflict and ineffective management rarely develop overnight. In fact, such problems may take years to become evident. By the time the scientist is contacted, immediate solutions are not possible. Nevertheless, scientists are frequently handicapped in their attempts to resolve organizational problems by some managers who insist on quick results. For example, one of the authors was called into an organization as a consultant to reduce what management felt was excessive turnover, absenteeism, and sabotage. An analysis of survey data revealed that the problem was the result of poor supervision, defective raw materials, and ineffective selection procedures. Plant management expected this complex problem to be completely resolved within three months.

Management often decides in advance what is wrong and then calls in a scientist to solve "our selection problem" or "our communication problem." The consultant, like the physician, cannot prescribe a cure on the basis of the patient's self-diagnosis. The scientist must take the time to make a personal examination since often the problem may be something other than what management thinks it is. This, of course, takes time and may even embarrass the very managers who contacted the consultant in the first place. As an example, one company with a high turnover rate decided their selection procedure was to blame. Careful review of the situation by a consultant revealed that a large percentage of the employees who were terminating were women whose husbands were called back to work after being laid off for quite some time at a nearby steel mill.

Behavioral science has made large contributions to solving many organizational problems. These contributions can be expressed in such terms as increased productivity, reduced absenteeism, reduced training time, better quality products, and so on. No matter how impressive these contributions have been, it must be realized that scientists cannot solve all of the problems of today's organizations. We have no "bag of tricks" or "special powers" that will make all problems disappear. There is still much we do not know and much we cannot handle. After all, our measuring instruments (e.g., tests, rating scales, questionnaires) are far from perfect and we can only partially explain or predict human behavior in organizations. It is important for managers to realize these limitations as well as our contributions. Otherwise, it will be easy for managers to become the prey of unscrupulous individuals who sell their services to organizations, make their money, and get away before the company realizes that it has been promised something the consultant could not possibly deliver.

AN OVERVIEW OF THE BOOK

The contents of the book are drawn primarily from two distinct areas, namely, organizational behavior and personnel psychology. Both areas are directly relevant for understanding and improving the effectiveness of organizations. The next eight chapters of this book (Part One) are concerned with the study of organizational behavior. Chapters 2 and 3 discuss the nature and design of effective organizations. Chapter 4 presents some of the key concepts and research findings on communication processes within organizations. Chapters 5 and 6 review the theoretical and empirical literature on employee motivation, attitudes, and satisfaction. Chapter 7 provides a general understanding of group processes. Chapter 8 looks at the nature of effective leadership, theories of leadership, and the practical implications of leadership research for improving this vital process in organizations. Chapter 9 examines interpersonal and intergroup conflict in organizations with suggestions for the effective management of conflict.

In Part Two of the book (Chapters 10 through 15) we have covered what we believe are the most useful topics for managers from the area of personnel psychology. Chapter 10 sets the stage for the remaining chapters by discussing the challenging task of measuring employee proficiency. Chapters 11 and 12 are devoted to one of the most important functions of any organization, the selection and placement of personnel. Among the topics we cover in these two chapters are selection methods, approaches for making hiring decisions, and equal employment opportunity. Chapters 13 and 14 are devoted to the problems, methods, and research literature dealing with the ways in which we can identify training needs, design training and management development programs, and evaluate them properly.

Finally, in Chapter 15, we discuss "organization development" which involves change programs broader in scope than the training methods discussed in earlier chapters. We examine the process of organizational change as well as some of the more popular intervention strategies being used today.

REFERENCES

Campbell, D. T., & Stanley, J.C. *Experimental and quasi-experimental designs for research*. Chicago: Rand McNally, 1963.

Kerlinger, F. N. *Foundations of behavioral research*. New York: Holt, Rinehart & Winston, 1973.

Zedeck, S., & Blood, M. R. *Foundations of behavioral science research in organizations*. Monterey, Calif.: Brooks/Cole, 1974.

part one
ORGANIZATIONAL BEHAVIOR

2

NATURE OF ORGANIZATIONS

AN ORGANIZATION can be defined as the patterned relationships among people who are engaged in mutually dependent activities with a specific objective. Formal organizations such as business firms, hospitals, schools, prisons, labor unions, government agencies, and so forth occupy a dominant position in today's highly specialized and technologically advanced society. The study of organizations is an interdisciplinary effort involving diverse fields such as anthropology, economics, management, political science, psychology, and sociology. Behavioral scientists from these various fields have contributed toward the development of theories to describe and explain the structure and processes of organizations. In this chapter we will examine the essential features of organizations, including organization structure. In the next chapter, we will discuss various prescriptive theories and their implications for the design of effective organizations.

ORGANIZATIONS AS OPEN SYSTEMS

The best available conceptual framework for describing an organization is in terms of an "open system." A "system" is the arrangement and relationships among component parts that operate together as a whole (Katz and Kahn, 1966). Each component is a subsystem that has some system properties of its own. There is usually an elaborate web of causal connections among the components of a system. When a change occurs in one component, it will set off a chain of reactions in other components. Because of the complexity of the relationships, it is sometimes difficult to predict the eventual state of each component, including the one that was originally changed.

11

Input-Transformation-Output Cycle

A system is "open" if it has transactions with the environment in which it exists. Transactions between an organization and its environment involve "inputs" and "outputs." Inputs are usually in the form of information, energy, money, personnel, materials, and equipment that are received by the organization from the environment. Outputs from the organization to the environment can take many forms, depending on the nature of the organization. Most of the outputs are derived from inputs that have been transformed by the organization. For example, manufacturing firms transform raw materials into industrial or consumer products. Educational institutions transform uneducated persons into more educated ones. Hospitals transform unhealthy persons into more healthy ones. Other outputs besides the major products or services of an organization include waste products from the transformation process, and money paid for the inputs of labor, supplies, equipment, and energy. The product or service provided by a business organization is exchanged for money inputs, which are used in turn to pay for other necessary inputs. Thus the cycle of inputs, transformations, and outputs is continually repeated. Organizations that do not sell their products or services, such as public schools, museums, and libraries, must rely on periodic infusions of income from other sources (e.g., government funding, donations, member contributions).

Just as with biological organisms, the survival and growth of an organization depends on a favorable ratio of inputs and outputs. In terms of funds, the organization must receive at least as much as it expends in the transformation process and the maintenance of itself. If there is an excess of monetary inputs, i.e., the organization "earns a profit," the excess can be used as a reserve against hard times, or for the expansion and growth of the organization. If it cannot operate efficiently, the organization can only survive by finding someone to "subsidize" it. In addition to monetary inputs, the organization must be able to obtain adequate inputs of other types, especially labor, energy, and supplies to maintain itself.

Organization Goals

The behavior of an organization, like that of advanced biological organisms, is goal-directed rather than purely reflexive or random. Organizations usually have one or more formal, explicit goals. There may also be informal, implicit goals that can be inferred from organizational decisions and actions. An organization's central goals and the strategy chosen to attain them are the result of a political decision process. Organization members with substantial influence, such as higher level executives and administrators, frequently disagree about goals and priorities. Such conflicts are resolved through a process of persuasion, bargaining, coalition formation, and power plays (Cyert and March, 1963).

One central goal of nearly all organizations, whether explicit or implicit, is survival. If an organization achieves the original objectives for which it was created, or if these become incompatible with survival, new objectives may be found to replace them. For example, an organization established to raise funds for research on a certain disease is unlikely to disband after the disease has been conquered. Instead, the organization will probably evolve new objectives, such as other diseases to fight. Similarly, a business organization with an obsolete product or service may try to branch into other products or services rather than passively accepting bankruptcy or dissolution.

The major objectives of an organization are related to its input-transformation-output cycle. For example, a manufacturing firm makes products to sell at a profit. The firm's goals are likely to include such things as increased profits, increased market penetration, higher sales, and development of new markets. A business organization may also have supplementary social goals that are not directly related to its primary transformation process, such as promoting the welfare of its employees, or contributing to the development and welfare of the local community. In some cases, specific functional or social goals are set as a result of external pressure from governmental agencies or political pressure groups. For example, business organizations have recently been required to establish an equal employment opportunity goal (see Chapter 12). Another example is provided by the automobile manufacturing companies, which have been forced to establish auto safety, pollution reduction, and gas mileage goals for the design of new cars.

Environmental Influences

Many economic, political, cultural, and scientific developments in the external environment can affect an organization's goals or disrupt the regular input-transformation-output cycle. Major environmental elements affecting a business organization are shown in Figure 2–1. Customers and competitors are key determinants of the market demand for the organization's products or services. Suppliers, and competitors for sources of supplies and labor, are principal determinants of whether the organization can obtain an adequate amount of these inputs. Government regulatory agencies, owners or stockholders, creditors, labor unions, and consumer groups exert conflicting pressures on the organization and influence its goals and activities. Finally, the values and behavior of organization members are shaped by their cultural environment.

FIGURE 2–1
Multiple Environmental Influences on an Organization

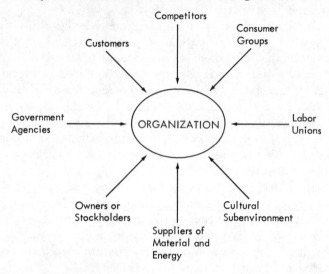

Adaptation to Environmental Change

Because an organization is dependent on the environment in so many ways, it must adapt to changes in the environment in order to survive and prosper. Thus, it is essential to monitor outside events and develop plans to cope with relevant changes. The more unstable and unpredictable a certain sector of the environment is, the more important it is to monitor that sector closely, especially when the consequences of events are momentous ones. For example, manufacturing firms with a dynamic and unpredictable market must frequently monitor customer reactions and the actions of competitors.

The survival of many types of organizations that are not subsidized depends in large part on the efficiency of their transformation process. These organizations seek to develop rational procedures for minimizing costs and using people, equipment, and other resources in the most efficient manner. Greater efficiency can be achieved in the transformation process when there is a stable supply of inputs and a fairly stable and predictable demand for the organization's products or services. Thus, organizations try to insulate their core transformation process from fluctuations in the input supply or output demand. Organizations attempt to gain some control over the relevant environmental events, to minimize their dependence on unpredictable suppliers and customers, and to "buffer" the effects of environmental events that cannot be controlled or avoided (Thompson, 1967). For example, a power generating company may attempt to insure a regular supply of coal by buying it from more than one coal company, by making long-term contracts for future supplies, by stockpiling supplies, or even by acquiring ownership of its own coal company.

ORGANIZATION STRUCTURE

The capacity of an organization to react quickly to environmental threats and maintain an efficient ratio of outputs to inputs depends in part on its "structure." The structure of an organization is the pattern of prescribed roles and role relationships, the allocation of activities to separate subunits, the distribution of authority among administrative positions, and the formal communication network. In effect, structure is the formal plan for achieving an efficient division of labor and effective coordination of member activities.

Since the structure of an organization consists of role relationships and prescribed interactions rather than physical things like buildings and equipment, it has been difficult to find ways to describe and classify different structures. Various organization theorists have proposed somewhat different sets of structural dimensions. We will examine several structural attributes that have been frequently discussed in the management and organizational behavior literature.

Vertical Differentiation and the Authority Hierarchy

In large organizations, the authority for making key policy decisions is usually assumed by a small group of persons who are appointed by the owners, elected by the members, or who emerge on top after repeated power struggles. Many kinds of organizations have a board of directors, or a board of trustees, or an elected legislative body to share ultimate authority with a designated chief executive officer (CEO). For example, in business corporations, there is usually a board of directors. The chief executive officer may be either the chairman of the board or the president.

The larger an organization grows, the more intermediate levels of managers are added to assist the top executives in coordinating and controlling the behavior of the nonsupervisory members of the organization. This process of "vertical differentiation" results in an "authority hierarchy" with two or more levels of authority.

Span of Control

The number of authority levels in an organization will depend in part on the "span of control" at each level. Span of control is the number of subordinates a manager is responsible for supervising. Depending on the amount of coordination and direction necessary to insure that subordinates perform their roles effectively, there is a limit to the number of subordinates a manager can handle. When the nature of the task and the subordinates is such that a large span of control is feasible, fewer "first-line managers" are necessary than when only a small span of control is feasible. For example, consider an organization with 64 nonsupervisory employees. The number of first-line managers needed is 4 when the span of control is 16, 8 when the span of control is 8, and 16 when the span of control is 4 subordinates (see Figure 2–2).

FIGURE 2–2
Span of Control for First-Line Managers

A. Span of Control is 16:

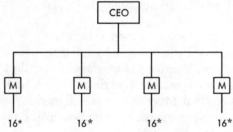

B. Span of Control is 8:

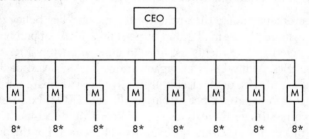

C. Span of Control is 4:

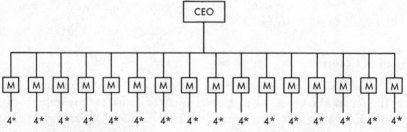

* Nonsupervisory employees.

Span of control considerations also apply to the coordination and control of the first-line managers by the next higher authority level. If there are more first-line managers than the chief executive can handle, it will be necessary to create another level of managers between the CEO and the first-line managers. For example, the executive with 16 first-line managers may find it advisable to add some "middle managers" to the authority hierarchy, as shown in Figure 2–3.

FIGURE 2–3
Authority Hierarchy with Three Authority Levels and a Uniform Span of Control of Four Subordinates

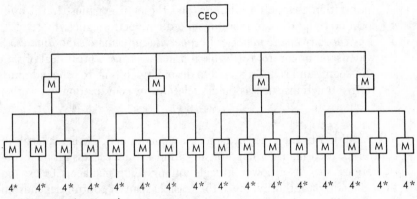

* Nonsupervisory employees.

As the examples demonstrate, for a given number of nonsupervisory employees, the smaller the average span of control, the more authority levels will be needed. The organization represented by Figure 2–2B has an average span of 8, which results in two authority levels and a 9:64 ratio of managers to nonsupervisory employees. The "taller" organization represented by Figure 2–3 has an average span of 4, which results in three authority levels and a 21:64 ratio of managers to nonsupervisory employees. Since administrative costs are greater for a tall organization with proportionally more managerial personnel, it is economical to make each manager's span of control as large as possible. On the other hand, the larger the span of control, the greater the risk of reduced control and coordination.

The feasible span of control for a manager will depend on several factors (Bell, 1967; Steiglitz, 1962; Udell, 1967):

1. *Complexity and repetitiveness of subordinate tasks.* The more simple and repetitive the tasks are, the easier it is to supervise subordinates, especially when standardized work procedures have been established.

2. *Similarity of subordinates' tasks.* The feasible span of control is smaller when subordinates have dissimilar tasks, because the manager cannot readily become an expert in the knowledge of each task.
3. *The skill and motivation of subordinates.* Less supervision is necessary when subordinates are competent and highly motivated, so it is feasible to have a larger span of control.
4. *Degree of interdependence among subordinate roles.* When subordinates have highly interdependent task roles, more coordination is necessary, and the manager cannot handle as many subordinates.
5. *The proximity of work locations.* It is more difficult to supervise subordinates who work in widely dispersed locations, especially if communication channels are limited and the manager must travel from location to location to monitor subordinate performance.
6. *The capacity of the manager to supervise immediate subordinates.* A wider span of control is feasible if a manager has a great deal of skill and energy and is not required to devote much time to other administrative functions such as public relations or coordination with other subunits.

In addition to the kinds of factors just mentioned, the actual span of control for each manager in an organization will reflect less rational considerations, such as a power struggle among some managers to expand their domain of authority. Since the feasible span of control depends on so many different factors, it is not surprising that the actual span of control in an organization varies for managers of different subunits and for managers at different levels in the authority hierarchy. Unlike our hypothetical examples, there is not likely to be a uniform span of control or a uniform number of authority levels for each major subunit of the organization. For example, in a manufacturing company, there may be a large number of production employees and several levels of middle managers under a production vice president. In the finance department, there may be a much smaller number of nonsupervisory employees and only one level of management between them and the finance vice president.

Centralization of Authority

When additional levels of management are created in an authority hierarchy, some of the authority possessed by the top executives is "delegated" to the intermediate managers so that they can carry out their responsibilities. Delegation can take different forms. In its most restricted form, the lower level manager can only deal with problems for which there are prescribed rules and procedures, and any exceptions must be referred to higher authority levels. In its least restricted form, the lower level manager is free to take actions within certain broad limitations and guidelines, although he must report periodically on the consequences of his decisions. Between these extremes are intermediate degrees of delegation, as for example, when the lower level manager can make a decision but must clear it with the boss before taking action.

The extent to which authority is centralized in an organization can be measured in terms of the number and importance of delegated decisions, and the level in the authority hierarchy to which they are delegated. All organizations can be placed along a centralization-decentralization continuum. In a highly centralized organization, most decisions are made at the top level, and lower level managers have little discretion to act on their own initiative. In a highly decentralized organization, certain types of decisions are still made at the top level (e.g., general policy, broad goals, global planning and strategy formation), but authority to make many other kinds of decisions is delegated to middle and lower level managers.

Centralization has certain potential advantages (Flippo and Munsinger, 1975; Melcher, 1976; Webber, 1975):

1. The top executives are more aware of the overall needs of the organization and are more likely to make decisions in the organization's best interests.
2. There is greater uniformity of policy and action when decisions are made by the executive office.
3. Decisions can be made with the aid of a central staff of specialized experts. There is less risk of mistakes and bad judgement by lower level managers who lack adequate decision skills and initiative.
4. It is easier to maintain the secrecy of strategic plans and proposals.

On the other hand, decentralization has certain potential advantages:

1. Operating decisions for geographically dispersed subunits are made by the managers most knowledgeable about "local" conditions.
2. Pressing problems faced by lower level managers can be dealt with more quickly when they have authority to make immediate decisions rather than having to refer the problems to higher levels.
3. The motivation and enthusiasm of lower level managers is greater when they are entrusted to make decisions rather than simply executing orders and implementing plans made at a higher level.
4. Making decisions provides excellent training for lower level managers in preparation for their advancement to higher positions.
5. Decentralization of operating decisions allows top executives more time for policy formation and long-range planning.

Formalization

Some organizations have detailed formal rules and procedures, with an extensive amount of required paperwork, such as memos, forms, and reports ("red tape"). Other organizations have few rules and procedures, and their communication is more often of the spoken variety. The amount of rule orientation and reliance on written, formal communications is referred to as the degree of "formalization" in an organization (Reimann, 1973).

Formalization is one way to regulate the behavior and limit the discretion of lower level employees. While not synonymous with centralization, formalization is often found in organizations with centralized authority. In organizations with a high degree of formalization, there is usually an elaborate control system. Not only is role behavior clearly specified in detail, it is also monitored closely to insure compliance with the rules and formal procedures. Managers are required to keep detailed records on the use of resources and expenditure of funds, and they must make frequent, lengthy reports on the activities and performance of their subunits. While formalization offers top management the advantage of tighter control, it also has certain undesirable consequences, which are discussed in the next chapter.

Departmentation

Departmentation is the grouping of individual positions and activities into separate subunits of the organization. At each authority level where there is more than one manager needed, some basis must be found to determine who will be responsible for which activities. Just as there is role specialization in the design of individual jobs, so too can the concept of specialization be applied to subunit formation at each authority level. The importance of departmentation is greatest at the upper level, immediately under the chief executive officer. Subunit formation at this level will be referred to as "primary departmentation." Even at lower levels, the type of subunits created will affect coordination, communication, employee attitudes, and goal orientation.

BASES FOR PRIMARY DEPARTMENTATION. There are several bases used for establishing separate departments at the upper level, including (1) function, (2) product or service, (3) client or type of customer, and (4) geographical location. Departmentation by function means that persons performing the same function are grouped together in a primary department. For example, in a manufacturing company the major functions usually include production, marketing, finance, and research. The functions in a retail chain store usually include merchandise, marketing, finance, distribution, real estate, and personnel. In an insurance company, major functions include such things as underwriting, claims, marketing, investments, and finance. An example of functional departmentation in a manufacturing company is shown in Figure 2–4A.

FIGURE 2–4
Examples of Primary Departmentation

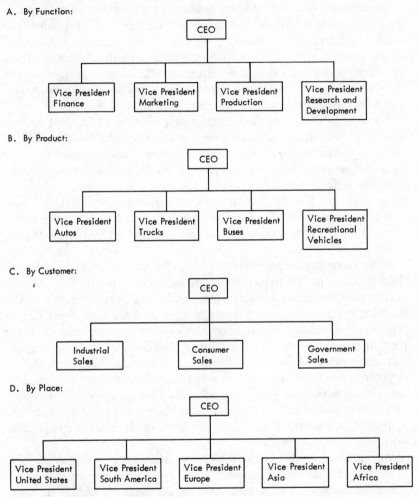

A. By Function:

B. By Product:

C. By Customer:

D. By Place:

Departmentation according to product or service is feasible if an organization offers a wide variety of different products and/or services and there are separate groups of functional specialists (e.g., production, sales) assigned to each product or service. An example of primary departmentation on the basis of product is shown in Figure 2–4B. In this example, the vice president of the automobile division is responsible for all activities necessary to design, produce, and market cars. The other vice presidents have similar responsibility for their respective products. With this form of departmentation, certain functions that are not directly involved in producing and selling the product may be retained as a separate functional department at the upper level (e.g., finance).

Departmentation according to customer or client is possible when an organization has several distinct clients or several mutually exclusive categories of customers. For example, an advertising company with several major clients may establish separate subunits containing all of the functional specialists needed to service a client. A manufacturing company with several distinct markets for its products may form primary departments on the basis of customer category, as in Figure 2–4C.

Departmentation according to geographical location ("place") is possible with organizations that have several, widely dispersed facilities that are essentially self-contained and independent in their operations. Some examples include a chain of retail stores, service outlets, or professional offices in different cities. Departmentation by place is also appropriate for large multinational organizations with operations in several countries. With this form of departmentation, each department is responsible for all organizational operations within its geographical territory (see Figure 2–4D).

SECONDARY DEPARTMENTATION. Just as at the upper level in the authority hierarchy, the basis for forming subunits at the next level down (i.e., within the primary departments) will depend on the nature of the organization and the scope of its activities. This "secondary departmentation" may be based on function, product or service, customer or client, or place, if any of these bases is appropriate. The basis for secondary departmentation need not be the same within each primary department. For example, a manufacturing company with functional primary departments may have functionally specialized subunits within its production department, and product subunits within its marketing department. A few examples of organizations with different forms of secondary departmentation are shown in Figure 2–5.

At the lowest levels of management, the basis for grouping activities is usually functional specialization. Subunits of nonsupervisory employees under the direction of a first-line supervisor are usually located in the same office or work area. The employees may have identical jobs or they may perform different roles as part of a team that is responsible for one step in the production of a product or the provision of a service. In organizations with departments that operate both day and night, there are usually parallel subunits for different time periods (e.g., day shift, evening shift, graveyard shift).

COMPARATIVE ADVANTAGES OF FUNCTIONAL DEPARTMENTS. Departmentation on the basis of function offers several advantages (Kover, 1963; Litterer, 1965; Walker and Lorsch, 1968). The interaction among similar specialists facilitates mutual assistance and sharing of ideas. There is likely to be greater professional development, more accurate evaluation of indi-

FIGURE 2–5
Examples of Secondary Departmentation

A. By Function:

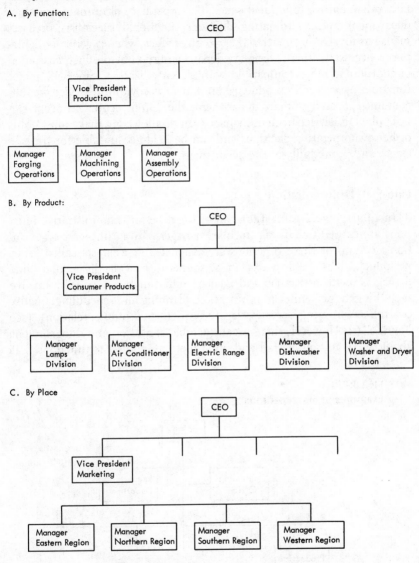

B. By Product:

C. By Place

vidual competence, and greater satisfaction with co-workers. A functionally specialized department provides more opportunity for advancement within a person's specialty area, without the necessity of becoming a general administrator of several specialty areas. Economies can result from greater use of specialized personnel and special-purpose equipment. Moreover, there is usually less duplication of effort than in organizations with product or customer departmentation.

On the other hand, departmentation by product, service, or customer also offers certain advantages. There is more concern with product goals rather than narrow functional issues. The experience of running a product department and coordinating different functional specialists prepares managers for advancement to the executive office, where a general orientation is necessary. Finally, primary departmentation by product, customer, or location is more compatible with decentralization. Since all major functions necessary for producing a product or providing a service are self-contained in each primary department, the "profit center" concept can be applied. Each department manager can be allowed to make most of his or her own operating decisions and can be held accountable for the efficiency and profitability of the department.

Line-Staff Differentiation

In a pure "line organization," all of the necessary administrative functions are carried out by the regular managers. In a "line-staff organization," certain of these functions are assigned to specialists called "staff personnel." It is the duty of staff personnel to provide the regular "line managers" with assistance and advice. Staff functions typically involve such things as personnel administration, planning and scheduling, quality control, engineering services, legal counsel, and public relations (see Figure 2–6). However, there is considerable confusion and disagreement about the definition of staff and line functions, and some functions that

FIGURE 2–6
Examples of Staff Positions

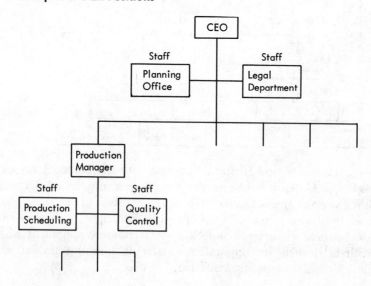

are regarded as staff functions in one kind of organization are line functions in other organizations. Actually, the principal distinction between line and staff is not in terms of functions performed, but rather in terms of authority (Woodward, 1965). Staff personnel have no direct authority over the subordinates of the line manager whom they advise. Officially, a staff person is not allowed to direct line personnel except when specifically authorized to do so by the appropriate line manager. In practice, however, staff personnel often exercise direct influence over line personnel by virtue of their expertise, professional status, control over information, or close connections with high-level line officers (Filley, House, and Kerr, 1976).

As an alternative to a line or a line-staff form, some organizations have special administrative subunits or offices with limited authority over lower level employees. That is, some administrative or support function is removed from the sphere of authority of a line manager and established as a separate office. The director of the new office is given direct authority over lower level employees, but only in certain narrowly defined matters ("functional authority"). For example, if production does not place enough emphasis on maintaining quality, a quality control office may be created and given functional authority over quality standards and inspection (see Figure 2–7). Similarly, an engineering methods office may be created and given authority to design jobs and develop work procedures. The director of an office with functional authority typically reports to the same boss as the line manager who originally possessed the director's authority. The director may or may not have subordinate specialists to give assistance. This kind of special administrative office can be created at the same level as the primary departments or at a lower level within the

FIGURE 2–7
Examples of Functional Authority in Special Administration Offices

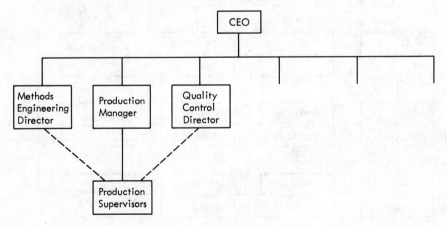

primary departments, depending on how important its function is and how much authority is needed to carry out this function.

Matrix Organization

A novel organization structure that was designed to obtain the advantages of functionally specialized departments while avoiding the disadvantages is called a "matrix organization." In a matrix organization, two bases for primary departmentation (usually function and one other basis, such as product), are used at the same time. An example of a matrix structure for a manufacturing company is shown in Figure 2–8. Each of the four product vice presidents is responsible for coordinating the three functions involved in attaining their respective product goals. Each of the

FIGURE 2–8
Example of a Matrix Organization

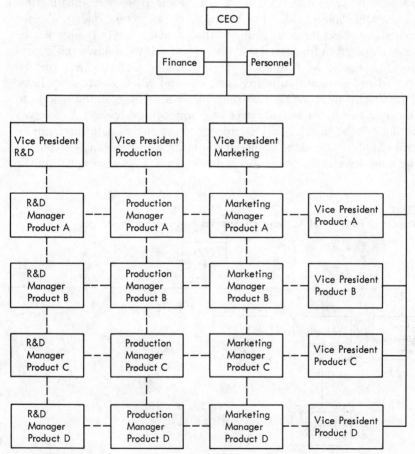

three functional vice presidents supervises and coordinates any lower level personnel who are performing their respective functions. In each cell of the matrix is a functional manager assigned to a specific product. These subunits are under the dual authority of the corresponding function vice president and product vice president. Thus, for example, the vice president for product A and the production vice president both have authority over the production manager for product A.

Teams and Committees

Although a matrix structure has certain advantages, new problems are created such as role conflict, confusion due to overlapping jurisdiction, and the expense of a dual set of upper level managers. Less complex and more flexible structural devices such as teams and committees are often able to accomplish the same objectives at less cost (Galbraith, 1973).

Organizations with functional departments can form temporary project teams or "task forces" to carry out special projects requiring close coordination and joint problem solving among functional specialists. Examples of projects suitable for a team approach include bringing a new product into production, and designing a unique product to meet customer specifications. A project team has members from relevant functional departments and is directed and coordinated by a project manager. There are likely to be some team members who are assigned full time, while other members only participate part-time and may belong to more than one team. The composition of the team may change somewhat over the course of the project if the importance of various functions changes at each stage. Figure 2–9 provides a simplified example of an aerospace organization with project teams for the design and development of missiles and aircraft. When a project is completed, the team is disbanded, and team members return to their regular duties in their respective functional departments or are assigned to new project teams.

A committee is a group of persons from the same subunit or from different subunits who meet periodically to coordinate subunit activities and solve joint problems. Committees are often formed when coordination and joint problem solving are too complex to be carried out effectively either through the regular authority hierarchy or through informal lateral communication. A committee may be formed at any level in the authority hierarchy, and it may contain organization members from different levels. As is the case of teams, committees are usually composed of those persons who have the knowledge, skill, and authority necessary to solve specific kinds of problems or make certain kinds of operating decisions (e.g., coordination and scheduling decisions). Committees may be either temporary or permanent additions to the regular structure of the organization.

FIGURE 2–9
Example of a Project Team Structure within an Engineering Department

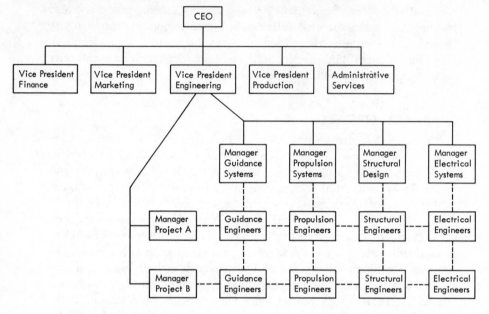

SUMMARY

An organization can be described as an open system that has transactions with its environment. In order to survive and prosper, an organization must maintain a favorable ratio of inputs to outputs. Necessary resource inputs must be obtained, and customers or clients must be found for the organization's products or services. If a stable input-transformation-output cycle can be maintained, more efficient transformation procedures can be developed. Thus, organizations attempt to gain control over undependable sources of supplies and to insulate the core transformation process from any uncontrollable variations in input supplies or output demand.

The structure of an organization is one determinant of its capacity to function efficiently and adapt to the environment. Major aspects of structure include span of control and vertical differentiation, centralization of authority, formalization, line-staff differentiation, and type of departmentation.

There are several bases for departmentation at the primary and secondary levels. Subunits can be formed on the basis of function, product or service, client or customer, or geographical location. Functional departments have certain advantages and certain disadvantages in comparison to product, customer and geographical departments. A matrix organization is a structural form designed to obtain the advantages of more than one type of departmentation. However a matrix structure has certain costs and limitations of its own. Other kinds of structural mechanisms designed to facilitate coordination and lateral communication include teams and committees.

REVIEW AND DISCUSSION QUESTIONS

1. Define or explain each of the following key terms: open system, input, output, transformation process, organization structure, authority hierarchy, span of control, centralization, formalization, departmentation, functional specialization, line-staff differentiation, line authority, functional authority, matrix organization, teams, committees.
2. What factors determine the feasible span of control for a manager?
3. What are the advantages and disadvantages of decentralization?
4. What are some different bases for departmentation?
5. What are the comparative advantages and disadvantages of departmentation based on function?
6. What are the reasons for establishing staff positions?
7. What is a matrix organization structure and how does it differ from functional departmentation?
8. What are some factors that determine whether an organization is able to adapt and survive in a changing or hostile environment?

REFERENCES

Bell, G. D. Determinants of span of control. *American Journal of Sociology,* 1967, 73, 90–101.

Cyert, R. M., & March, J. G. *A behavioral theory of the firm.* Englewood Cliffs, N.J.: Prentice-Hall, 1963.

Filley, A. C., House, R. J., & Kerr, S. *Managerial process and organizational behavior.* Glenview, Ill.: Scott, Foresman & Co., 1976.

Flippo, E. B., & Munsinger, G. M. *Management.* Boston: Allyn & Bacon, 1975.

Galbraith, J. *Designing complex organizations.* Menlo Park, Calif.: Addison-Wesley, 1973.

Katz, D., & Kahn, R. L. *The social psychology of organizations.* New York: Wiley, 1966.

Kover, A. J. Reorganizing in an advertising agency: A case study of a decrease in integration. *Human Organization,* 1963, 22 (Winter), 252–259.

Litterer, J. *Analysis of organizations.* New York: Wiley, 1965.

Melcher, A. J. *Structure and process of organizations: A systems approach.* Englewood Cliffs, N.J.: Prentice-Hall, 1976.

Reimann, B. C.   On the dimensions of bureaucratic structure: An empirical reappraisal. *Administrative Science Quarterly*, 1973, *18*, 462–467.

Steiglitz, H.   Optimizing the span of control. *Management Record*, 1962, *24* (Sept.), 25–29.

Thompson, J. D.   *Organizations in action*. New York: McGraw-Hill, 1967.

Udell, J. G.   An empirical test of hypotheses relating to span of control. *Administrative Science Quarterly*, 1967, *12*, 420–439.

Walker, A. H., & Lorsch, J.W.   Organizational choice: Product versus function. *Harvard Business Review*, 1968 (November–December), 129–138.

Webber, R. A.   *Management: Basic elements of managing organizations*. Homewood, Ill.: Irwin, 1975.

Woodward, J.   *Industrial organization: Theory and practice*. New York: Oxford University Press, 1965.

3

DESIGN OF EFFECTIVE ORGANIZATIONS

In the preceding chapter we described several important aspects of organization structure, including span of control and vertical differentiation, centralization of authority, formalization, departmentation, and staff-line differentiation. The structural features of an organization are, for the most part, a systematic and intentional design rather than a random pattern. Management usually attempts to organize in a way that will facilitate the attainment of organization goals. Since there are a vast number of structural variations possible, finding one that will be appropriate for a given organization is an exceptionally complex problem. Some of the questions that must be answered in organizing include the following:

1. What is the best basis for grouping activities at each level?
2. What is the maximum feasible span of control for each kind of subunit, and how many levels of authority should be created in each major department?
3. To what extent should related administrative functions be divided into separate staff and line roles, and what authority and status should be allocated to staff positions?
4. How much formalization should exist for positions at each level?
5. To what extent should authority be centralized or decentralized in the authority hierarchy?
6. What lateral communication channels and supplementary decision-making groups (e.g., teams, committees) should be established?

In order to answer such structural design questions, a number of prescriptive organization theories have been formulated, including (1) classical (or "traditional") organization theories, (2) humanistic organization theories, and (3) contingency theories of organization design. Each of these approaches is described in this chapter.

CLASSICAL ORGANIZATION THEORY

Several prescriptive organization theories and sets of organizing principles were proposed by individuals in different countries during the early half of this century, including "scientific management" (Taylor, 1911), "bureaucratic organization" (Weber, 1947), and "administrative management" (Fayol, 1929; Mooney and Reiley, 1939; Urwick, 1940). The organizing principles recommended by each of these "classical" organization theorists differed somewhat, but there was considerable convergence of viewpoints on most major issues. The basic approach favored by each theorist was to achieve internal organization efficiency by dividing tasks into specialized roles, devising detailed rules and procedures, and establishing an authority hierarchy with elaborate controls to insure that the rules and procedures were followed. A set of organizing principles that reflects the general viewpoint of the classical theorists includes the following:

DIVISION OF LABOR. Tasks should be subdivided into specialized functions, and these should be assigned to persons with the required skills.

CLEARLY DEFINED DUTIES, RULES, AND RESPONSIBILITIES. Each person in the organization should have a clearly defined set of duties and responsibilities. At the lower levels, work should be simplified and the one "best" procedure for performing each job should be determined and specified for the employee.

UNITY OF COMMAND. There should be a clear chain of command from the top to the bottom of the authority hierarchy. No person should receive orders from more than one boss, and there should be no overlapping of authority (or responsibility) at the same level.

UNITY OF DIRECTION. Jobs should be grouped so as to permit those with the same objective to be under the same plan and directed by one manager.

NARROW SPAN OF CONTROL. Each manager should be responsible for supervising only a small number of subordinates to insure effective control and coordination of subordinate activities.

AUTHORITY COMMENSURATE WITH RESPONSIBILITY. The authority delegated to each manager should be sufficient for him to carry out his responsibilities.

The "ideal" organization prescribed by the classical theorists was quite "bureaucratic," with a high degree of role specialization, work simplification, centralization of authority, and formalization. Since a small span of control was recommended, there must also be a "tall" authority hierarchy with a relatively large number of authority levels. Control was to be achieved through formal rules, role prescriptions, and work procedures, with compliance insured by close supervision and a system of incentives and sanctions. Any coordination problems not covered by predetermined rules and standard procedures would be referred upward in the authority hierarchy to a person with the authority to make a decision.

Although the classical theorists recognized the comparative merits of different bases for departmentation, their prescriptions are biased in favor of the efficiency provided by functionally specialized departments (Miles, 1975). Certain structural arrangements such as a matrix organization, project teams, or special administrative offices with functional authority would clearly violate the "unity of command" principle. Thus the ideal organization designed by classical theorists would probably be a line or line-staff organization with functionally specialized subunits at most levels.

HUMANISTIC ORGANIZATION THEORY

Humanistic organization theories and organizing principles were initially formulated during the 1950s and 1960s. These theories reflect the influence of a growing humanistic movement and its concern for the physical and mental health and welfare of all individuals. The humanistic organization theories also reflect the influence of early research by psychologists and sociologists on group dynamics and human motivation. The famous Hawthorne studies (Roethlisberger and Dickson, 1939) revealed the existence of an "informal organization" that had been largely ignored by the classical theorists. Subsequent research confirmed that employees have motives besides the obvious need for economic subsistence and job security, and that informal behavior is vital for understanding organizational processes. The primary focus of the humanistic organization theorists was on human relations and the interaction between organization structure and human characteristics. The best known humanistic theorists are Douglas McGregor (1960), Chris Argyris (1957, 1964), and Rensis Likert (1961, 1967).

McGregor's Theory X and Theory Y

McGregor (1960) pointed out that the kind of bureaucratic organization prescribed by classical theorists reflects a very negative view of human nature, which he labeled "Theory X." The emphasis on regulating the behavior of lower level employees presumes that they are lazy, dislike work, have little ambition, avoid responsibility, lack creativity, and are motivated only by a desire for economic gain and security. McGregor proposed a completely different view of human nature, which he called "Theory Y." It assumes that work is as natural as play or rest, people are motivated by other needs besides survival, and employees are capable of self-direction, initiative, and creativity. According to McGregor, organizations will be more effective if designed to be compatible with Theory Y assumptions about human nature. To achieve this objective, he proposed the use of participative management, job enrichment, and management by objectives. These practices will be described in subsequent chapters.

Argyris' Personality and Organization Theory

The incompatibility between human nature and a bureaucratic organization was also the major theme of Argyris (1957, 1964). He proposed a theory of personality and organization with the central postulate that effective organizations have a structure compatible with member characteristics. Argyris pointed out that there is a normal sequence of human development from infancy to mature adulthood. Specifically, a person becomes less passive, acquires the capacity for a greater variety of behavior, develops deeper and more lasting interests, moves from a short time perspective to a long time perspective, develops from a lack of self-awareness to a sense of self-identity, and moves from complete dependence toward self-reliance. A bureaucratic organization structure forces most employees to be passive, dependent, and subservient, thereby frustrating employees who desire meaningful work, self-reliance, and psychological growth. The reaction of frustrated employees, including lower and middle-level managers as well as nonsupervisory employees, will be one or more of the following:

1. Physical withdrawal (e.g., absenteeism or turnover).
2. Psychological withdrawal (e.g., apathy, daydreaming, drugs).
3. Aggressive acts and informal group resistance to controls.
4. Fixation on instrumental rewards such as pay and benefits, together with de-emphasis of unobtainable outcomes such as achievement, recognition, and accomplishment of meaningful tasks.

In effect, the structure of an organization designed according to the prescriptions of classical organization theory results in a "self-fulfilling prophecy." After being exposed to such an organization for a long period of time, employees become what Theory X assumes they already were. If top management reacts to employee resistance and aggression by a further tightening of controls (e.g., more rules and reports, closer supervision, additional standards and sanctions), the frustration of employees will merely be increased. The result of incompatibility between organization structure and member needs is lower organizational effectiveness. Less human energy will be applied to productive effort, and there will be a lack of initiative in solving problems.

In order to achieve a better fit between organization structure and member needs, Argyris recommended that an organization should have flexible roles, open communication, and reliance on self-direction. He also advocated the creation of supplementary structural forms such as project teams and even a council of representatives from each level and major subunit to make decisions that are not appropriate for the regular authority hierarchy. The kind of organization favored by Argyris would be achieved by the use of change programs such as sensitivity training, job enrichment, and organization development. These programs are described later in the book.

Likert's Systems 1–4 Theory

A third humanistic organization theorist who has had a major influence is Likert (1961, 1967). His theory is based largely on research conducted during the 1950s to discover differences between effective and ineffective managers. Likert concluded from this research that managers who acted in accordance with classical organization theory were less effective than managers who followed behavior patterns designed to develop cohesive groups with high performance goals. He noted characteristic differences between effective and ineffective subunits with respect to several organizational processes, including leadership, communication, decision making, goal setting, and control. Likert devised a typology with four categories to classify an organization in terms of these characteristic differences. For each process (e.g., communication), information is obtained from a questionnaire and used to classify the organization as a *System 1, System 2, System 3,* or *System 4* organization. Table 3–1 summarizes the attributes of the two extreme types (System 1 and System 4) for each organizational process. Application of the classical organizing principles results in a Systems 1 or 2 organization, while the subunits found most effective by Likert were usually System 4 organizations.

In order to achieve a System 4 organization, Likert (1967) suggested the application of three basic concepts: the principle of supportive relationships, group decision making, and high performance goals. The "principle of supportive relationships" is stated as follows (Likert, 1961, p. 103): "The leadership and other processes of the organization must be such as to ensure a maximum probability that in all interactions and in all relationships within the organization, each member, in the light of his background, values, desires, and expectations, will view the experience as supportive and one which builds and maintains his sense of personal worth and importance." Implementation of this principle calls for managers to be considerate and supportive, to keep subordinates informed, to provide recognition for effective performance, and to consult with subordinates before making decisions affecting them.

TABLE 3–1   Characteristics of Processes in Systems 1 and 4 Organizations

System 1 Organization	*System 4 Organization*
1. *Leadership process* includes no perceived confidence and trust. Subordinates do not feel free to discuss job problems with their superiors, who in turn do not solicit their ideas and opinions.	1. *Leadership process* includes perceived confidence and trust between superiors and subordinates in all matters. Subordinates feel free to discuss job problems with their superiors, who in turn solicit their ideas and opinions.
2. *Motivational process* taps only physical, security, and economic motives through the use of fear and sanctions. Unfavorable attitudes toward the organization prevail among employees.	2. *Motivational process* taps a full range of motives through participatory methods. Attitudes are favorable toward the organization and its goals.
3. *Communication process* is such that information flows downward and tends to be distorted, inaccurate, and viewed with suspicion by subordinates.	3. *Communication process* is such that information flows freely throughout the organization— upward, downward, and laterally. The information is accurate and undistorted.
4. *Interaction process* is closed and restricted; subordinates have little effect on departmental goals, methods, and activities.	4. *Interaction process* is open and extensive; both superiors and subordinates are able to affect departmental goals, methods, and activities.
5. *Decision process* occurs only at the top of the organization; it is relatively centralized.	5. *Decision process* occurs at all levels through group processes; it is relatively decentralized.
6. *Goal-setting process* located at the top of the organization, discourages group participation.	6. *Goal-setting process* encourages group participation in setting high, realistic objectives.
7. *Control process* is centralized and emphasizes fixing of blame for mistakes.	7. *Control process* is dispersed throughout the organization and emphasizes self-control and problem solving.
8. *Performance goals* are low and passively sought by managers who make no commitment to developing the human resources of the organization.	8. *Performance goals* are high and actively sought by superiors, who recognize the necessity for making a full commitment to developing, through training, the human resources of the organization.

Source: Adapted from J. L. Gibson, J. M. Ivancevich, and J. H. Donnelly, Jr., *Organizations: Structure, Processes, Behavior* (Dallas: Business Publications, Inc., 1976), p. 277.

The second fundamental concept is the use of group decision making instead of the one-to-one supervision and autocratic decisions characteristic of bureaucratic organizations. Likert proposed an overlapping group structure in which each manager serves as the "linking pin" between a group of subordinates and the authority level above (see Figure 3–1).

FIGURE 3–1
Overlapping Group Form of Organization

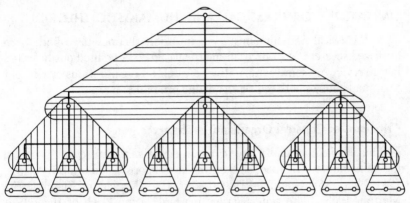

Source: R. Likert, *New Patterns of Management* (New York: McGraw-Hill, 1961), p. 105.

The purpose of this structure is to improve vertical and intragroup communication and to formally establish task groups composed of a manager and his or her subordinates. In addition to these vertical overlapping groups, Likert (1967) recommended use of overlapping horizontal groups with a common member to act as a liaison person or "horizontal linking pin" (see Figure 3–2). Overlapping groups together with committees and

FIGURE 3–2
Overlapping Groups and Horizontal "Linking Pins"

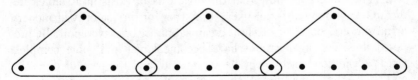

teams should be used as needed to insure coordination and effective lateral communication among departments with related operations.

According to Likert, overlapping vertical groups and participative management would insure the setting of high performance goals, which is the third prerequisite for a System 4 organization. Subordinates are expected to participate with their boss in making operating decisions and setting subunit goals. This process of group decision making is repeated at each level in the authority hierarchy. An individual manager remains accountable for the performance of the subunit, but specific responsibilities are shared with the group. Participation will supposedly increase subordinate commitment to achieve goals and to successfully implement decisions. Informal group pressure can be used to encourage compliance by any reluctant members of the group.

LIMITATIONS OF CLASSICAL AND HUMANISTIC THEORIES

The classical and humanistic organization theories have both been criticized severely. We will examine the weaknesses pointed out by critics before reviewing some comparative research on organizations carried out to evaluate one or both sets of organizing principles.

Criticisms of Classical Organization Theory

The classical principles have come under attack from several quarters, including humanistic theorists, contingency theorists, and others (Argyris, 1964; Bass, 1965; Gouldner, 1954; Likert, 1961, March and Simon, 1958; Merton, 1968). The general criticisms range from "lack of theoretical sophistication" and "lack of clarity and consistency" to "inaccurate premises" and "unanticipated dysfunctional consequences." A few of the specific criticisms are as follows:

1. The implicit premise that lower level employees are of a Theory X type is incorrect. There has been an increase in the education level and the standard of living since the early classical organization theories were formulated, and most employees are no longer uneducated peasants and immigrants who are willing to accept any kind of industrial job. When employees are of the Theory Y type, extreme formalization, centralization, and work simplification will result in frustration, withdrawal, and aggression.

2. The implicit premise that the organization exists in a stable, predictable environment is not likely to be true for the majority of modern organizations. Since the classical organization theories were initially proposed, business organizations have become larger and more complex. Great advances in technology have occurred, and the pace of discovery and change has quickened. New forces such as unions, consumer groups, and regulatory agencies have appeared in the environment of business organizations. The degree of interdependence among firms in the national and world economies has increased. It is not feasible to create a bureaucratic organization with rules and standard procedures for every contingency when an organization exists in a dynamic and uncertain environment.

3. An extreme amount of centralization has important disadvantages, as noted in the preceding chapter, including lack of quick adaptation to variation in local conditions, loss of potential ideas and innovations from lower level employees, and lack of lower level commitment to decisions made at the top.

4. Extreme amounts of formalization and specialization lead to several undesirable consequences not anticipated by the classical theorists. These "bureaucratic syndromes" include a focus on rules rather than on the goals that the rules were designed to attain, a neglect of functions that do not clearly fall within one's sphere of responsibility, and a tendency to respond to a novel problem in a standard but inappropriate way, rather than showing initiative in recognizing the problem and dealing with it.

Criticisms of Humanistic Organization Theory

In recent years, the humanistic theories have been subject to increasing attacks (Filley, House and Kerr, 1976; Hellriegel and Slocum, 1974; Lawrence and Lorsch, 1969; Leavitt, 1962; Morse and Lorsch, 1970; Perrow, 1972; Strauss, 1969). A few of the specific criticisms are as follows:

1. If the classical theorists' perception of human nature was too cynical, the humanistic assumptions are too idealistic. Most lower level employees in organizations probably fall somewhere between the two extremes of Theory X and Theory Y. Many of these people are likely to find that the informal structure and flexible roles advocated by humanistic theories present unacceptable levels of role ambiguity and role conflict. Moreover, many lower level employees may lack the personality and motivational traits that are essential for job enrichment, participative leadership, and group action to be successful (see Chapters 5 and 8).

2. Humanistic organization theorists have assumed that decentralization and participation would result in the integration of organization goals, subunit goals, and member needs. This assumption may be unrealistic for many kinds of organizations. There are some basically incompatible differences in objectives between workers and executives, between soldiers and military leaders, between professors and university administrators, and between leaders of local affiliates or subsidiaries and the executives in the headquarters office. Despite broad areas of mutual interest that provide the basis for some cooperation and accommodation, the underlying differences remain and are reflected in a continuing process of conflict and power politics. Therefore, any structural arrangement that greatly increases the power of lower level participants may threaten the capacity of the organization to achieve its fundamental purpose.

3. In their concern about the fit between organization structure and individual characteristics, the humanistic theorists have neglected the fit between organization structure and the environment. Even though organi-

zations are referred to as open systems in some of the humanistic organization literature, the implications of technology and environment for structural design are not seriously considered. Consequently, the humanistic theorists have not acknowledged the existence of situations where an organization, or some of its subunits, must be designed according to classical prescriptions rather than humanistic prescriptions in order to be efficient enough to survive.

4. Since the focus of humanistic theorists is on human relations, some broader questions about organization design have been neglected. Humanistic theory does not specify what basis should be used for departmentation, what degree of horizontal and vertical differentiation is required, what span of control is feasible for group decision making, or when and where teams, committees and overlapping groups are necessary.

ENVIRONMENT, TECHNOLOGY, AND ORGANIZATION DESIGN

The classical and humanistic organization theories are "universal theories" that specify the best design for an organization, regardless of its size, purpose, or environment. The classical prescriptions were based on logic and personal experience and the humanistic prescriptions were based primarily on research with individuals and organizational subunits. The kind of research necessary to adequately test an organization theory involves comparison of effective and ineffective organizations to identify the structural characteristics associated with organizational effectiveness. As evidence from this kind of comparative research on organizations began to accumulate during the 1960s, it became obvious that neither classical nor humanistic theory was universally applicable. The effectiveness of different structural arrangements was found to depend to a large extent on the organization's environment and the technology used in its transformation process. Among the most important comparative studies are those conducted by Burns and Stalker (1961), Morse and Lorsch (1970), and Woodward (1965). Each of these studies will be described in more detail below, and another important comparative study by Lawrence and Lorsch (1969) will be described later in this chapter.

Burns and Stalker Study

The earliest comparative study on the importance of the environment was carried out by Burns and Stalker (1961). These researchers interviewed managers in 20 industrial firms located in Scotland and England. The organizations were classified in terms of structure and management practices along a continuum ranging from "mechanistic" to "organic." Mechanistic organizations had a structure like that prescribed by the classical organization theories. The organic form of organization had flexible roles, open communication, coordination by committees, and other features consistent with humanistic organization theory. Burns and Stalker evaluated the effectiveness and environment of the organizations and concluded that the mechanistic form was appropriate for organizations with a relatively stable commercial and technical environment (e.g., a rayon mill). The organic form was appropriate for organizations with a dynamic, uncertain environment where there are frequent new scientific discoveries, technical inventions, and changes in market conditions (e.g., an electronics firm).

Woodward Study

In another British study, Woodward (1965) used interviews and records to investigate the relationship between structure and organization effectiveness for 100 manufacturing firms. Woodward classified the firms into three broad categories of production technology. *Job order production* firms developed and produced single "custom-made" articles or small batches of a product according to each customer's specifications (e.g., firms making prototypes of electronic or mechanical equipment). *Mass production firms* made large batches of standardized products on an assembly line (e.g., firms making automobiles, consumer appliances, television sets). *Process production* firms carried out highly automated, continuous flow production of liquids, gases, and crystaline substances (e.g., firms engaged in refining petroleum; firms producing chemicals or plastics).

The firms with a given type of production technology did not have identical structural characteristics, but they tended to be more similar to each other than to firms with another type of production technology. Some of these differences are summarized in Table 3–2. The most important discovery was that the successful firms in each category of production technology differed in structure from the less successful firms with the

TABLE 3–2
Relationship between Technology and Structural Characteristics

Structural Characteristic	Job-Order Production	Mass Production	Process Production
Chief executive's span of control*	4	7	10
First-line supervisor's span of control*	23	48	15
Number of authority levels*	3	4	6
Ratio of managers: nonsupervisory employees*	1:23	1:16	1:8
Percent of firms with management committees	12%	32%	80%
Degree of formalization	Low	High	Low

* Median value for firms with the same production technology.
Source: Joan Woodward, *Industrial Organization: Theory and Practice* (New York: Oxford University Press, 1965), pp. 51–67.

same production technology. The more successful firms tended to have the median structural characteristics for their kind of technology, as shown in Table 3–2. In general, successful mass production firms had a "mechanistic" structure consistent with the classical prescriptions, while successful job order and process production firms had more "organic" characteristics.

Most of these results from Woodward's research have been successfully replicated by Zwerman (1970) in a study of 55 manufacturing firms in the United States. However, some comparative research by Child and Mansfield (1972) and Hickson, Pugh, and Pheysey (1969) suggested that the association between technology and structure is less important for large organizations than for small ones. Organizations tend to become more mechanistic or bureaucratic as they grow large, regardless of their technology or purpose. Child and Mansfield found that in large organizations, production technology was more closely related to the structural features of the immediate subunit in which the production process is housed (e.g., production department) than to the structure of other subunits or to the overall structure of the organization.

Morse and Lorsch Study

The importance of an appropriate fit between a subunit's internal structure and its functionally-specialized task has been investigated in a study by Morse and Lorsch (1970). Four organizational units were compared: an effective research laboratory, a less effective research laboratory, an effective container manufacturing plant, and a less effective container plant. As predicted, there were essential differences between the effective research lab and the effective container plant, as well as between each effective unit and its ineffective counterpart. The effective container plant had a "mechanistic" structure, with centralized authority and precisely defined rules, procedures and performance standards. The effective research lab had a low degree of centralization and formalization, and was essentially an "organic" system. Each of the ineffective units had inappropriate structural characteristics for its basic task. The ineffective research lab was too mechanistic for its unpredictable, creative research task. The ineffective container plant was not mechanistic enough to efficiently perform its routine, predictable production task. The results from this study are consistent with results from other studies on the association between a subunit's structure and function (e.g., Hall, 1962; Lawrence and Lorsch, 1969).

CONTINGENCY THEORIES OF ORGANIZATION DESIGN

The findings from the early comparative studies led to the development of "contingency theories" of organization design. These theories consider the fit between organization structure and the environment (or technology) of the organization, as well as the fit between structure and employee characteristics. In the remainder of this chapter we will summarize two of the most promising of these contingency theories.

Galbraith's Information Processing Model

According to Galbraith (1973), an organization can be viewed as an information processing network. The amount of information needed to perform a task depends on three factors: (1) the diversity of outputs, (2) the number of different resource inputs used in the transformation process, and (3) the difficulty of the performance goal. "The greater the diversity of outputs, number of resources, and level of performance, the greater the number of factors that must be considered simultaneously when making decisions" (p. 5).

Uncertainty is the difference between the amount of information needed to perform a task and the amount already possessed by the organization. Uncertainty limits the possibility of planning resource allocations, schedules, and work procedures in advance. If the necessary information is not possessed in advance, either it must be obtained during the performance of the task, or the task must be redefined to reduce the amount of necessary information (e.g., by lowering performance standards). Thus, as uncertainty increases, an organization usually attempts to increase its capacity for processing information, or it attempts to reduce the need for information processing. Each of these strategies involves certain changes in organization structure.

In a bureaucratic-mechanistic organization with a stable, predictable task and environment, coordination can be achieved among interdependent activities by means of predetermined rules and standard procedures. These structural features minimize the need for communication among task specialists and avoid the necessity for them to decide individually or jointly how to deal with every event as it occurs. Any rare exceptions that are not covered by standard rules and procedures or that exceed the limits established for individual discretion must be referred to a higher level for a decision. The appropriate person to make coordination, scheduling, and resource allocation decisions that involve two or more subunits is the manager who has authority over all affected parties.

As the amount of uncertainty increases for an organization, a bureaucratic structure is unable to carry out the necessary information processing. Exceptions to rules and standard procedures occur frequently when there is uncertainty, because it is not possible to anticipate events and plan standardized responses with any precision. As more and more exceptions are referred upward in the hierarchy for a decision, the information processing required on the part of middle and upper-level managers exceeds their capacity; they become "overloaded." Delays occur in making decisions, some coordination problems are not resolved, and conflicts are aggravated. When this happens, there are four kinds of options available to an organization: (1) slack resources, (2) self-contained departments, (3) improved vertical information system, and (4) lateral relations.

SLACK RESOURCES. The amount of necessary information processing will be reduced if the organization commits more resources to the transformation process, or lowers its performance goals. For example, scheduling personnel and equipment to perform a given set of tasks in a limited amount of time will be easier if extra personnel and machines are available. Of course, it will cost the organization more to use these extra resources, and the organization will have to accept the fact that it is now operating less efficiently. A related approach is to set lower goals in terms of time to complete a task. For example, if sales quotes a longer delivery time to customers, it is easier to schedule available personnel and equipment to perform the task. The cost in this example is likely to be a lower ability to compete with other firms in providing fast delivery to customers.

Slack resources can take many other forms, including lower quality of output, rejection of potential projects, larger inventories of finished goods, larger stockpiles of supplies, and use of "buffer stocks" between sequential production operations. In each case the burden of processing information to make coordination and scheduling decisions is reduced, but organizational efficiency or effectiveness is also reduced.

SELF-CONTAINED DEPARTMENTS. The amount of necessary information processing can also be reduced by grouping activities into self-contained departments. As noted in the preceding chapter, it is sometimes possible to form primary subunits on the basis of product, customer, or geographical location. When the functional specialists and equipment is divided up and allocated to the separate subunits, the overall difficulty of achieving coordination among functions is reduced. Although some coordination and scheduling decisions are still necessary, less information must be processed to make the decisions, and they are decentralized to a lower level close to the source of the relevant information. The same approach can sometimes be used on a smaller scale to reduce the amount of decision making necessary to resolve conflicts over scarce resources or support personnel (e.g., word processing centers, duplicating services, equipment maintenance). In this case, the scarce resources would be divided up and allocated to the competing subunits, so that day-to-day allocation and scheduling decisions would no longer be necessary by higher level managers. The cost of using self-contained subunits is in terms of less efficient utilization of specialized personnel and equipment.

VERTICAL INFORMATION SYSTEM. A third option is to increase the amount of relevant information available to decision makers, reduce delays in collecting it, and increase the capacity of the decision makers to analyze it. This approach involves the application of computers, data processing technology, and perhaps even quantitative decision models.

With more timely information and faster analysis, plans and schedules can be revised more often to accommodate changing conditions. Scheduling and coordination decisions having implications for many subunits of the organization can be more readily centralized. The cost of this option is in terms of the extra expense of information processing equipment and the personnel needed to operate the system.

LATERAL RELATIONS.   The final option is to improve information processing capacity by decentralizing some operating decisions and creating lateral decision processes at lower levels. Some coordination and joint problem solving can be accomplished through direct lateral communication among affected parties. However, as uncertainty increases, direct lateral contact should be supplemented by special lateral decision mechanisms, such as (1) liaison personnel, (2) temporary task forces, teams, or committees, (3) permanent teams or committees, (4) integrators, integrating departments, or linking-managerial roles, and (5) a matrix structure. These lateral mechanisms are listed here in order of increasing cost to the organization. As the difficulty of achieving coordination increases due to more uncertainty or more complex interdependence among subunits, mechanisms such as liaison personnel and temporary decision-making groups are not sufficient to cope with the required information processing. When this happens, more complex lateral mechanisms like permanent committees, integrators, or a matrix structure are needed. However, the more complex lateral mechanisms are more costly in terms of managerial time and personnel, so they should not be used unless necessary. Finally, it should be noted that the various kinds of lateral mechanisms are not mutually exclusive. A variety of different combinations of lateral mechanisms can be used in the same organization depending on the amount of information processing necessary and the pattern of relationships among subunits.

CHOICE OF STRATEGY.   Galbraith reminds us that the four options just described are the only ones available to an organization. One or more of these options must be utilized when uncertainty increases. If an intentional choice is not made, the first option—slack resources and lower performance—will happen automatically as the organization's capacity to process information within the authority hierarchy is exceeded. Galbraith's theory provides guidelines for selecting the option or combination of options most appropriate for the degree of uncertainty and type of task interdependencies faced by an organization. The reader is referred to Galbraith's (1973) book for a more detailed discussion of the factors to consider in making a rational choice among options and suboptions.

Lawrence and Lorsch Theory

The more effective an organization is at gathering and utilizing information about relevant sectors of the environment, the more successful it will be in achieving its goals. The purpose and strategy of the organization (i.e., products, services, markets, activities) and the nature of the environment jointly determine what information is needed and how difficult it is to obtain. The structure of each major subunit of the organization and the cognitive-behavioral orientation of subunit members are important determinants of the organization's capacity to process information and achieve a unified effort by employees.

Organizations tend to have separate functional subunits corresponding to different sectors of the environment. For example, in a manufacturing company there is usually a marketing department to deal with the market sector or "subenvironment," and a research and development department to deal with the scientific subenvironment. In order to carry out its function effectively, a subunit's structure and the orientation of its members must be compatible with the characteristics of its tasks and subenvironment. One major characteristic of the task and subenvironment is uncertainty. There is more uncertainty when little information about changing conditions is available, little is known about causal relationships among environmental events, and there are long delays in obtaining feedback about the consequences of actions. It is appropriate for a subunit to have a high degree of formalization when there is little uncertainty in the task and subenvironment, but not when there is great uncertainty. It is appropriate for subunit members to have a long time orientation if feedback about consequences of actions is delayed, but it is appropriate to have a short time orientation when feedback is rapid. It is appropriate for subunit members to be "people oriented" if the function of the subunit is people oriented, like sales, public relations, and personnel administration. Finally, the goal orientation of subunit members should be consistent with the goals inherent in its function and subenvironment. For example, marketing personnel should be primarily concerned about sales, customer service, and meeting competition. Production personnel should be concerned about costs and quality. Research and development personnel should be concerned about discovering new knowledge and applying it to the organization's products. Since goals direct behavior and influence the level of motivation (see Chapter 5), the performance of a functionally-specialized subunit will be less than optimal if members are not oriented toward appropriate functional goals.

DIFFERENTIATION. Lawrence and Lorsch (1969) use the term "differentiation" to describe the differences among organization subunits with respect to (1) formalization, (2) time orientation, (3) goal orientation, and (4) interpersonal orientation. When the relevant subenvironments of an organization are very diverse with respect to task requirements and uncertainty, the organization should be highly differentiated. In other words, separate subunits should be created with a specialized function and member orientation that is appropriate for their respective subenvironments. When the relevant subenvironments of an organization are very similar in uncertainty and task requirements, much less differentiation is necessary. In general, organizations will be more effective when the amount and form of differentiation is appropriate for the environment.

INTEGRATION. The effectiveness of an organization depends on its "integration" as well as on its differentiation. Integration is defined as "the quality of the state of collaboration . . . among departments that are required to achieve unity of effort by the environment" (Lawrence and Lorsch, 1969, p. 11). In other words, integration is the degree of coordination and cooperation among subunits with interdependent tasks. The greater the degree of interdependence among tasks, the more integration is necessary. The difficulty in achieving integration depends on the amount of uncertainty and the amount of differentiation among subunits. When there is uncertainty, plans and schedules frequently need to be changed, and any adjustments made by one subunit will require adjustments by other closely related subunits. Thus the number of necessary coordination decisions is substantial. When there is also a high degree of differentiation, the problem is further complicated. Since each subunit has different goals and behavior patterns, conflicts are likely to result (see Chapter 9), and it is difficult to get the subunits to cooperate in solving scheduling, resource allocation, and coordination problems.

A variety of structural mechanisms are used by organizations to achieve integration. What mechanisms will be appropriate depends on the amount of integration needed and the difficulty of achieving this amount. When little integration is needed, the necessary amount can usually be achieved through the authority hierarchy. As the necessary amount of integration increases, additional mechanisms become appropriate, such as direct lateral contact, teams, and committees. Even these mechanisms will not be sufficient if there is a high degree of differentiation. In this case, the organization should utilize structural mechanisms with a greater capacity for resolving conflict and achieving coordination. Lawrence and Lorsch suggest the use of special integrators or integrating departments. An integrator is a person whose job is to help two or more departments solve problems of coordination and scheduling. When this job becomes too big for a single integrator, a separate department with several integrators may be justified. Integrators will be effective to the extent that they have the personal skills, attitudes and authority necessary to insure that conflicts among subunits will be confronted and resolved in a rational manner (see Chapter 9).

When joint decisions involving more than one subunit are made, it is important that the relative influence of each subunit reflect the relative importance of that subunit's specialized function. For example, in an organization where research and development is the most crucial function for organizational effectiveness, as in Woodward's (1965) job order firms, the R&D department should have more influence than other departments in making joint decisions. Effective integration also requires an appropriate degree of centralization. When the environment is uncertain, more decentralization is required for effective decision making, and decisions about coordination and scheduling should be made by lateral mechanisms at the level where the required knowledge about the task and environment is greatest.

ORIGINAL COMPARATIVE RESEARCH.   Lawrence and Lorsch (1969) tested their theory by comparing effective and ineffective manufacturing firms in three industries: plastics, packaged foods, and standardized containers. The container firms had a low and relatively uniform degree of uncertainty in their environment (see Figure 3–3). The major competitive

FIGURE 3–3
Relative Uncertainty of Environmental Sectors for Three Industries

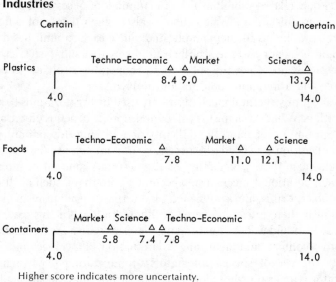

Higher score indicates more uncertainty.
Source: P. R. Lawrence and J. W. Lorsch, *Organization and Environment* (Homewood, Ill.: Richard D. Irwin, Inc., 1969), p. 91.

issues were fast delivery and high quality, and these objectives were shared by production, marketing, and R&D. Thus not much differentiation was needed in the container firms. A considerable amount of integration was needed because of certain interdependencies among departments. Close coordination was necessary between production and sales to meet tight delivery schedules, and cooperation was needed between development engineers and production personnel to improve product quality.

The plastics firms had a diverse and uncertain environment. There was a higher degree of uncertainty in the scientific subenvironment (R&D), than in the market (sales) and techno-economic (production technology) subenvironments (see Figure 3–3). The major competitive issue was product innovation. Joint effort by sales and R&D was needed to develop new varieties of plastic that would be acceptable to customers (who were manufacturing firms). Close cooperation was also needed between production and R&D to develop production techniques for the new plastics. These characteristics of the plastics firms required both a high degree of differentiation and a high degree of integration for effective performance.

The packaged food firms were between the container firms and the plastics firms in degree of environmental uncertainty and diversity, but were more like the plastics firms than the container firms (see Figure 3–3). The major competitive issue was product innovation, and close cooperation between marketing and R&D was needed to develop packaged foods that would appeal to the unpredictable taste of consumers. The characteristics of the packaged food firms required a fairly high degree of differentiation, and a high degree of integration.

After determining the appropriate degree of differentiation and integration according to the theory, Lawrence and Lorsch compared the effective firms in different industries. The results were as expected. There was high differentiation in the effective plastics firms, moderate differentiation in the effective packaged food firm, and low differentiation in the effective container firm. The degree of integration was high in all of the effective firms, but different structural mechanisms were used in each industry to achieve integration. The container firm relied on rules, procedures, direct lateral contact, and the authority hierarchy. This firm had a high degree of formalization. The effective packaged food firm used individual integrators and temporary cross-functional teams in addition to some rules, procedures, direct lateral contact, and the authority hierarchy. The effective plastics firms used an integrating department and permanent cross-functional teams at three levels of management, in addition to some rules, procedures, direct lateral contact and the authority hierarchy. In the effective container firm, operating decisions were highly centralized, whereas in the packaged food and plastics firms there was a considerable amount of decentralization. Finally, the relative influence of the primary departments in each kind of firm corresponded to the importance and uncertainty of their subenvironment.

Lawrence and Lorsch also compared the effective and ineffective firms within each kind of industry. The less effective firms in each case had structural characteristics that were inappropriate in many ways for their respective tasks and environments. In general, the results of the research provide strong support for the theory.

Evaluation of Contingency Theories

It is too soon to evaluate the accuracy of the two contingency theories presented in this chapter, because not enough comparative research has been conducted yet. The theories are consistent for the most part with each other and with previous comparative research. As more research slowly accumulates, a better assessment will become possible. Even though new research may require some modification and elaboration of the theories, it is unlikely that the major implications will change. All organizations face the dual problem of attaining an efficient degree of subunit specialization and achieving effective coordination between specialized subunits. The contingency theories provide a useful way to conceptualize these issues and provide guidelines for the organizational designer to aid him in finding a structure that is appropriate.

SUMMARY

Three types of theories have been formulated to specify the appropriate structural design for an organization. Classical organization theory sought to achieve internal efficiency in organizations by creating narrowly specialized positions, determining efficient work procedures, and establishing an elaborate control system to ensure compliance with rules and procedures. This rather "mechanistic" form of organization was based on the premise that lower-level employees are not capable of working effectively on their own without detailed rules and instructions, close supervision, and economic incentives.

Humanistic organization theory prescribed an organization with flexible roles, open communication, participative leadership, and decentralized decisions. This "organic" form of structure assumed that organization members are responsible, creative, and self-motivated. In such an organization, influence would be based primarily on expertise rather than on formal authority, and control would be achieved by reliance on self-motivation and group pressure. Major humanistic theories include McGregor, Argyris, and Likert.

Comparative research on total organizations revealed that the kind of structure that is necessary for an organization to be effective depends on the organization's environment and technology. An organic structure was found to be more appropriate in some situations, and a mechanistic structure was more appropriate in other situations. Contingency theories were formulated to provide a conceptual framework for analyzing the situation and determining what kind of structural design is appropriate. Galbraith and Lawrence and Lorsch have developed contingency theories that are consistent with most of the comparative research.

REVIEW AND DISCUSSION QUESTIONS

1. Define or explain each of the following key terms: Theory X and Theory Y, classical organization theory, humanistic organization theory, contingency theories, unity of command, System 1 and System 4 organizations, principle of supportive relationships, linking pin function, overlapping groups, mechanistic and organic systems, job-order production, mass production, process production, technology, uncertainty, lateral relations, slack resources, vertical information system, self-contained subunits, subenvironment, time orientation, goal orientation, differentiation, integration, integrator.

2. What kind of organization was favored by the classical organization theorists?

3. What kind of organization is advocated by the humanistic organization theorists?

4. What are some criticisms of classical organization theory?

5. What are some criticisms of humanistic organization theory?

6. What was found by behavioral scientists in their comparative research on organizations?

7. According to Galbraith, what are the available options for an organization that lacks the capacity to process information effectively for coordination and scheduling decisions?

8. According to Lawrence and Lorsch, how is differentiation and integration related to organization effectiveness? What determines how much differentiation and integration are necessary?

9. If you were trying to design an appropriate structure for an organization, what kind of information about the organization and its environment would be most helpful to you?

REFERENCES

Argyris, C. *Personality and organization.* New York: Harper, 1957.

Argyris, C. *Integrating the individual and the organization.* New York: Wiley, 1964.

Bass, B. M. *Organizational psychology.* Boston: Allyn and Bacon, 1965.

Burns, T., & Stalker, G.M. *The management of innovation.* London: Tavistock Publication, 1961.

Child, J., & Mansfield, R. Technology, size, and organizational structure. *Sociology,* 1972, 6, 369–393.

Fayol, H. *General and industrial management.* Trans. by J. A. Conbrough. Geneva: International Management Institute, 1929.

Filley, A. C., House, R. J., & Kerr, S. *Managerial process and organizational behavior.* Glenview, Ill.: Scott, Foresman & Co., 1976.

Galbraith, J.   *Designing complex organizations.* Menlo Park, Calif.: Addison-Wesley, 1973.

Gouldner, A. W.   *Patterns of industrial bureaucracy.* New York: Free Press, 1954.

Hall, R. H.   Intra-organizational structural variation. *Administrative Science Quarterly,* 1962, 7, 295–308.

Hellriegel, D., & Slocum, J. W., Jr.   *Management: A contingency approach.* Reading, Mass.: Addison-Wesley, 1974.

Hickson, D. J., Pugh, D. S., & Pheysey, D.   Operations technology and organization structure. *Administrative Science Quarterly,* 1969, 14, 378–397.

Lawrence, P. R., & Lorsch, J.W.   *Organization and environment: Managing differentiation and integration.* Homewood, Ill.: Irwin, 1969.

Leavitt, H. J.   Unhuman organization. *Harvard Business Review,* 1962, 40 (July–August), 90–98.

Likert, R.   *New patterns of management.* New York: McGraw-Hill, 1961.

Likert, R.   *The human organization.* New York: McGraw-Hill, 1967.

March, J. G., & Simon, H. A.   *Organizations.* New York: Wiley, 1958.

McGregor, D.   *The human side of enterprise.* New York: McGraw-Hill, 1960.

Merton, R. K.   *Social theory and social structure.* New York: Free Press, 1968.

Miles, R. E.   *Theories of management.* New York: McGraw-Hill, 1975.

Mooney, J. D., & Reiley, A. C.   *Onward industry.* New York: Harper, 1939.

Morse, J. J., & Lorsch, J. W.   Beyond theory Y. *Harvard Business Review,* 1970 (May–June), 61–68.

Perrow, C.   *Complex organizations: A critical essay.* Glenview, Ill.: Scott, Foresman & Co., 1972.

Roethlisberger, F. J., & Dickson, W. J.   *Management and the worker.* Cambridge: Harvard University Press, 1939.

Strauss, G.   Human relations, 1968 style. *Industrial Relations,* 1969, 7, 262–276.

Taylor, F.W.   *The principles of scientific management.* New York: Harper & Row, 1911.

Urwick, L.   *The elements of administration.* New York: Harper, 1940.

Weber, M.   *The theory of social and economic organization.* Trans. by A. M. Henderson & T. Parsons. New York: Oxford University Press, 1947.

Woodward, J.   *Industrial organization: Theory and practice.* New York: Oxford University Press, 1965.

Zwerman, W. L.   *New perspectives on organizational theory.* Westport, Conn.: Greenwood Publishing Co., 1970.

4

COMMUNICATION
PROCESSES

COMMUNICATION can be defined as the transmission of information between two or more persons. Communication may also involve information exchange between humans and machines. Communication is a vital process in organizations, because it is necessary for effective leadership, planning, control, coordination, training, conflict management, decision making, and other organizational processes. Studies of managerial behavior indicate that the major part of a manager's time at work is spent communicating with other people (Burns, 1954; Kelly, 1964).

While communication is obviously important, there is no comprehensive theory of human communication on which to base the diagnosis and solution of communication problems in organizations. In fact, there is no clearly distinct and unified field of communication. Instead, scientists and practitioners in a variety of disciplines have pursued their separate interests, often without being aware of each other's efforts (Thayer, 1968).

It is not feasible in the space of one chapter to present a comprehensive survey of the diverse and extensive literature on communication. Instead we will introduce the reader to some key concepts and research findings that provide a better understanding of the communication process in organizations. The chapter begins with a discussion of interpersonal communication. Then the focus shifts to organizational communication. The types of communication problems commonly found in organizations are identified, and some approaches for avoiding or coping with these problems are discussed.

NATURE OF INTERPERSONAL COMMUNICATION

Each time a communication episode occurs, we can identify several components of it. There is a "communicator" who wants to send a "mes-

53

sage." The message is expressed or "encoded" in terms of some kind of "language." The language may consist of words, mathematical symbols, diagrams, gestures, and so forth. The message is transmitted through some "medium." A variety of communication media are used in organizations, including face-to-face conversation, telephone conversation, written memos, a public-address system, bulletin boards, and many others. There are one or more intended "recipients" of the message. When a recipient receives the message, it is interpreted or "decoded."

Communication Objectives

Communication episodes usually have some purpose or objective. The objective of the communicator may be to inform the recipient about something, to influence the recipient's attitudes, to provide psychological support to the recipient, or to influence the recipient's behavior (e.g., request for information, for compliance with an order, or for psychological support). Many communication episodes involve some combination of these different objectives.

The effectiveness of a communicator can be evaluated in terms of how well that person's objectives are attained. The first requirement for successful communication is to get the *attention* of the recipient. If the message is transmitted but the recipient ignores it, the communication effort will fail. Successful communication also depends upon the recipient's *comprehension* of the message. If the recipient does not understand the message, it is unlikely to successfully inform or influence him or her. A final requirement is recipient *acceptance* of the message. Even if a message is understood, the recipient may not believe that the information is true, or that the communicator really means what is said. If the recipient's attention, comprehension, and acceptance of the message can be insured, the likelihood of achieving the communicator's objectives will be maximized.

One-Way and Two-Way Communication

Up to this point, we have described a communication episode in terms of "one-way communication" from the communicator to the recipient. Depending upon the relationship between the communicator and recipient, there may or may not be an opportunity for the recipient to respond to the communicator. When "two-way communication" is possible, a communicator can obtain "feedback" about the consequences of the message. Thus the communicator can evaluate whether the recipient paid attention to the message, comprehended it, and accepted it. Acceptance is the hardest to evaluate, because the recipient may choose not to reveal whether the message was really believed.

Perception and Communication

People respond to their perception of the world rather than to objective conditions as they actually exist. A person can only attend to a small portion of the available sensory stimuli at any moment, and this portion is interpreted in accordance with an individual's expectations, values, and beliefs. Thus human perceptual processes inevitably complicate interpersonal communication.

DETERMINANTS OF ATTENTION. Any message sent to a person must compete with other sensory stimuli for the person's attention. A primary determinant of attention is a person's needs and goals. A person will attend to stimuli that are assumed to be relevant for the fulfillment of important needs. Attention is also influenced by beliefs and values. People will often ignore information that is inconsistent with their images of the world or of themselves.

LANGUAGE AND COMPREHENSION. Whether a message is comprehended in the manner intended by the communicator will depend upon how the recipient interprets it. The language used in a message seldom has exactly the same meaning to the recipient as it does to the communicator, or to another recipient. Meanings are in people rather than in words or symbols. A word often means different things to the communicator than to the recipient. Or the communicator may use a word or symbol that has several different meanings without indicating which meaning is the intended one. This is illustrated by the case of a sales manager who told the shipping foreman to "rush" an order to an important customer. The sales manager wanted the order shipped by air freight, because the customer needed it immediately. The shipping foreman interpreted "rush" to mean sending a special truck, which cost more than air freight and took much longer.

In some cases, the message may contain words that are unfamiliar to the recipients and have no meaning to them (e.g., uncommon words or symbols, technical jargon). An example is provided by the anecdote about a plumber who discovered that hydrochloric acid opened clogged drains and wrote to a government bureau to ask if it was a good thing to use. The reply was as follows: "The efficacy of hydrochloric acid is indisputable, but the corrosive residue is incompatible with metallic permanence." The plumber was not very well educated and interpreted the message to mean that it was all right to use the acid. After he thanked the bureau for their assurance, the bureau sent another message with easier language: "Don't use hydrochloric acid, it eats the hell out of pipes!"

Sometimes a message contains words that unintentionally evoke memories and emotions in the recipient. These associations may bias the recipient's interpretation of the message. For example, in the early years of commercial aviation, a stewardess would tell the passengers: "We're flying through a *storm*. You had better fasten your *safety* belts; it will be less *dangerous*." These instructions caused some passengers to fear that the plane was likely to crash. So the language of the instructions was eventually changed to elicit more pleasant and secure associations. Today the stewardess says: "We're flying through some *turbulence* now; please fasten your *seat* belts; you will be more *comfortable*." (Haney, 1973, p. 443).

DISTORTION AND REJECTION. Even if the recipient is capable of understanding a message, he or she may distort its meaning if the information is not consistent with the individual's beliefs, values, and self-image. Distortion of a message is easiest when the message is ambiguous. If the recipient cannot distort a disagreeable message, he or she may simply reject it or forget it. For example, if a co-worker suggests a way to improve a person's job performance, and the person perceives the message to be a criticism of his competence, the suggestion may be dismissed as impractical rather than being seriously considered.

Acceptance or rejection of a message can also be influenced by a person's immediate emotional state. A person who is depressed or angry is less likely to accept reasonable requests or suggestions from others (Strauss and Sayles, 1972).

EVALUATION OF THE COMMUNICATOR. The interpretation and acceptance of a message is partially determined by the recipient's perception of the communicator's intentions. For example, a compliment from somebody who is perceived to desire a favor is less likely to be believed than the same compliment from somebody who has nothing tangible to gain.

Acceptance of a message also depends on how much *credibility* the communicator is perceived to have. A communicator's credibility depends on expertise in the subject of the message, and on the extent to which the communicator is trusted by the recipient. A person can create a "credibility gap" by making careless statements and exaggerated claims, by self-contradiction, by changing positions frequently, by a lack of consistency between words and actions, and by obvious attempts at deception. Finally, message acceptance is more likely when the recipient likes or identifies with the communicator than when the communicator is a stranger or an enemy.

Verbal and Nonverbal Communication

When two people interact, information about feelings is communicated as well as information about ideas. Information about a person's feelings is conveyed verbally by what the person says and how it is said. The meaning of the words is enhanced by the communicator's tone of voice, inflections, loudness, rate, and timing. A person's feelings are also expressed by a variety of nonverbal cues. In face-to-face conversation, a person communicates feelings and mood through gestures, facial expressions, body movements, posture, physical contact, and eye contact. For example, when students avoid eye contact with the teacher and appear to be busy arranging their notes, they are probably communicating that they do not want the teacher to call upon them. When we are concerned about whether a person likes us, we may become very sensitive to subtle nonverbal cues such as the person's duration of eye contact, how close the person stands while talking to us, the enthusiasm shown in a handshake, and the presence or absence of a smile.

Overt and Latent Meaning

We typically use our observations of a person's nonverbal actions and manner of speech to help interpret what the person is saying. These cues often enhance the message and provide a better understanding of its real meaning. However, the "latent meaning" conveyed by such cues is not necessarily consistent with the overt message. Occasionally a person says one thing, but the tone of voice, expression, or gestures contradict what is being said. For example, someone may say "That is a fine idea," while the tone of voice and expression indicate disapproval. This type of contradiction does not pose a communication problem as long as the speaker is aware of it and is careful to indicate which message is the correct one (Schein, 1969). However, sometimes a person is not aware of expressing a contradictory latent meaning. He may inadvertently reveal certain feelings that he is trying to conceal from the recipient. For example, a person who is trying to sound very confident may reveal in his stiff posture, nervous movements, and unsteady voice that he is actually quite anxious and insecure. A person who is trying to appear friendly may reveal that he actually feels indifferent or even hostile. Sometimes the latent meaning reflects feelings that the speaker has concealed from himself because he is ashamed of them or finds them to be inconsistent with his self-image.

Status and Communication

When two people interact in an organizational setting, their behavior reflects their relative status and power. The high-status person tends to dominate the conversation by asserting personal opinions and interrupting, whereas the low-status person is more inhibited about expressing opinions or interrupting. Furthermore, the low-status person usually tries to make a good impression on the high-status person by offering praise, showing respect, and agreeing with that person's views, or at least by avoiding overt disagreement (Cohen, 1958; Jones, Gergen and Jones, 1963; Kelley, 1951).

People with low status usually prefer to interact with a high-status person rather than with other persons of low status, even though it is necessary to show deference and be careful about what one says. Lawler, Porter, and Tennenbaum (1968) found that managers judged communication with their boss to be more satisfying and valuable than communication with subordinates. However, high-status persons would rather interact with each other than with low-status persons (Allen and Cohen, 1969; Hurwitz, Zander, and Hymovitch, 1953).

ORGANIZATIONAL COMMUNICATION NETWORKS

A communication network is a system of information-processing and decision-making centers connected by some configuration of communication channels. The system is designed to acquire, transport, and process information. Information processing includes such things as analysis, rearrangement, duplication, storage, and retrieval of information. The information received in the decision centers is used to regulate and coordinate the internal activities of the organization and to achieve adaptation to the external environment.

The formal communication network in an organization prescribes and limits the flow of information among organizational personnel. Without some restrictions and the specification of appropriate channels and types of messages, there would be complete chaos. The situation would be analogous to a meeting in a room where everybody is trying to talk at the same time.

It is easier to understand the function of an organization's communication network if we distinguish between upward, downward, and lateral communication. Each has a somewhat different function in organizations.

Downward Communication

Downward communication flows from top management to middle management, to lower level management, and finally to nonsupervisory personnel (see Figure 4–1). The functions of downward communication include: direction, instruction, indoctrination, inspiration, and evaluation. Orders and instructions usually become more detailed and specific as they are interpreted by each intermediate level in the authority hierarchy. The managers at each level act as a filter in determining how much of the information that they receive from upper levels will be passed on to subordinates. In addition to orders and instructions, downward communication may include information about organizational goals, policy, rules, restrictions, incentives, benefits, and privileges. Finally, subordinates may receive feedback about how well they are performing their jobs.

Face-to-face meetings, telephones, and written memos or directives are the media most often used for downward communication. However, many other communication media are available, including bulletin boards

FIGURE 4–1
An Example of Upward and Downward Communication through the Chain of Command

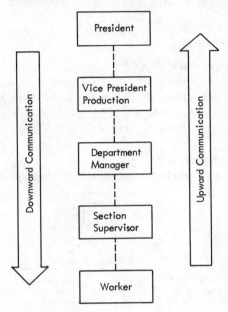

and posters, letters to employees' homes, inserts in pay envelopes, pamphlets, employee handbooks, procedural manuals, orientation and training films or videotapes, an organization magazine or newsletter, and published annual reports. Although used less often, these media may be important supplementary channels of downward communication.

Upward Communication

Upward communication flows from lower to higher levels of the authority hierarchy, usually along the chain of command. The primary function of upward communication is to obtain information about the activities, decisions, and performance of lower level personnel. Upward communication may include: performance reports, suggestions and recommendations, budget proposals, opinions, complaints, and requests for assistance or instructions. As in the case of downward communication, personnel at intermediate levels in the authority hierarchy act as filters of the information channeled through them. They integrate, condense, and summarize information about events and performance at lower levels.

The media used for most upward communication are face-to-face meetings, written reports and memos, and the telephone. Some organiza-

tions also use other media such as questionnaire surveys, spies and inform-
ers, special meetings with employees, meetings with labor union representatives, a grievance system, exit interviews with departing employees, and
special investigating committees.

Lateral Communication

Lateral communication occurs between persons who are at the same
level in the authority hierarchy ("horizontal communication") or between persons at different levels who have no direct authority over each
other ("diagonal communication"). Horizontal and diagonal communication are illustrated in Figures 4–2 and 4–3. Lateral communication

FIGURE 4–2
An Example of Horizontal Communication

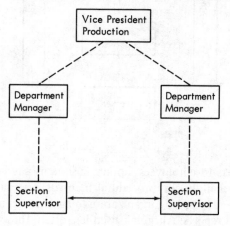

FIGURE 4–3
An Example of Diagonal Communication

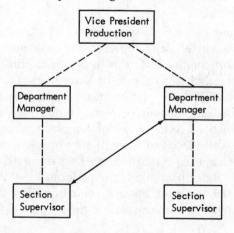

occurs regularly among employees who work together as a team, between members of different work groups with interdependent tasks, between members of separate functional departments, and between line and staff personnel. The pattern of lateral communication is closely related to the workflow in the organization (Landsberger, 1961; Sayles, 1958). The media used most often for lateral communication are face-to-face meetings, the telephone, and written memos, job orders, and requisition forms.

The primary function of lateral communication in the formal communication network is coordination and problem solving (Landsberger, 1961; Simpson, 1959). Lateral communication is faster and more direct than communication through a common superior in the chain of command. For example, if the two section supervisors in Figure 4–2 communicate through the chain of command, each message must be sent up to a department manager, then up to the vice president of production (the common superior), then down to the other department manager, and finally down to the other section supervisor. If the two supervisors have periodic problems that they are able to deal with effectively by themselves, direct lateral communication is likely to be used, especially when immediate solutions are needed. However, it is usually advisable to keep superiors informed so that they can monitor developments and retain effective control.

Informal Communication

The communication process in organizations includes informal communication as well as formal communication. Informal communication, which is sometimes referred to as the "grapevine," occurs outside of prescribed channels. It is carried out by means of face-to-face interaction and occasionally by telephone.

A major function of informal communication is the maintenance of social relationships (e.g., personal friendships, informal groups) and the distribution of personal information, gossip, and rumors. Informal communication may also be task related. Since the formal communication network seldom distributes sufficient task information, some informal channels usually emerge to fill the void. For example, informal lateral communication usually occurs where it is essential for coordination and formal lateral channels have not been provided (Wickesberg, 1968). In addition, the grapevine may be used by top management to "get the word around" quickly and to make unofficial announcements (e.g., intentional "leaks," "off-the-record" statements).

The grapevine has not been studied extensively, but a few studies provide some insight into how it operates (Davis, 1953; Jacobson and Seashore, 1951; Sutton and Porter, 1968). One salient characteristic of the grapevine is its speed. Messages typically travel much faster in the grapevine than through formal channels. The grapevine is also selective.

While some violations of confidentiality occur, information is usually not shared indiscriminately with inappropriate persons (Davis, 1953).

In the grapevine, information is usually passed along by only a few of the people who receive it. Thus the typical pattern of transmission is a "cluster chain" like those shown in Figure 4–4. Someone who passes on the information to several other people is called a "liaison individual." In the governmental agency studied by Sutton and Porter (1968), a small number of persons consistently acted as liaison individuals. In the manufacturing company studied by Davis (1953), different types of information were passed on by different liaison individuals. Liaison individuals are most likely to pass on information about a job function in which they are interested, or information about someone that they know personally. The more recent the information, the greater the likelihood that a person will pass it on.

Persons at higher levels in the authority hierarchy receive more information through the grapevine than persons at lower levels. In the company studied by Davis, the predominant flow of communication was downward and horizontal. If an event happened at a lower level, news of it usually flowed upward to a person at a high level, then it spread downward and horizontally. People who are geographically isolated and people with low status are less likely to receive grapevine information, and if they get it at all it will be late.

The grapevine can have both positive and negative consequences for the organization. It can transmit disruptive rumors and malicious gossip,

FIGURE 4–4
Examples of Cluster Chains in the Grapevine

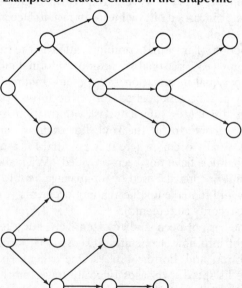

but it can also serve as an important supplement to the formal communication system. Moreover, it is essential for the development and maintenance of social relationships. Thus managers and administrators should recognize the existence of the grapevine in their organizations and attempt to utilize it constructively.

Criteria of Network Effectiveness

Communication networks reflect the communication requirements created by the organization's functions, technology, and authority structure (Galbraith, 1973; Hage, Aiken and Marrett, 1971; Simpson, 1959). However, the extent to which the communication network meets these requirements varies from organization to organization. Some organizations have very effective communication networks, while other organizations suffer with chronic communication problems.

The most obvious criterion of effectiveness is *network efficiency*. An efficient communication network is one that provides accurate and relevant information to persons who need it, when they need it. An additional criterion is *network economy*. An economical network is one in which information is acquired and distributed at a minimal cost. Still another criterion is the *satisfaction* of organization members. Research indicates that some types of networks are more satisfying to participants than other types (Shaw, 1964; Smith and Brown, 1964).

These three criteria are not necessarily compatible. Depending on the type of task, the network that is most efficient may not be most economical or most satisfying to participants. The most comprehensive criterion of network effectiveness is probably the long-term overall contribution to the attainment of organization goals. Needless to say, this general criterion is more difficult to measure than efficiency, economy, or participant satisfaction.

COMMUNICATION PROBLEMS AND REMEDIES

Inefficient communication may be caused by many different kinds of human and technical problems. In this section we will examine four kinds of human communication problems that frequently occur in organizations. The problems include: (1) incomplete comprehension, (2) overloading, (3) insufficient upward communication, and (4) insufficient downward communication. Some potential remedies and preventative measures will also be examined.

Incomplete Comprehension

We now have the technology to transmit a message quickly to almost anywhere on the earth, or even to the moon, but there is no way to insure that the person who receives the message will understand it. As we saw earlier in this chapter, there are many reasons why a person may fail to interpret a message correctly. There are no magic techniques to guarantee that none of these things will happen. Nevertheless, some guidelines can be observed to increase the probability of message comprehension.

DETERMINE OBJECTIVES AND ANALYZE SITUATION.   The first step for a communicator is to determine the objectives of the communication. Then the communicator should analyze the situation, taking into account both the nature of the intended recipients and the available media, channels of communication, time constraints, and so forth. The structure and language of the message and the medium used to transmit it should be suited to the objectives, recipients, and situation (Thayer, 1968). The communicator should try to anticipate what communication problems are likely to occur and take steps to avoid them.

USE SIMPLE LANGUAGE.   Messages with a few ideas are usually easier to understand than long messages with many different ideas. Simple, direct language is usually better than vague, difficult language. The reading ease of a written message can be measured by means of the "Flesch formula" (Flesch, 1948). Careful attention to language is especially important when management is preparing written communications to workers with little education. Davis (1968) measured the reading ease of employee handbooks used in several large corporations and found that most of the handbooks were too difficult for employees to comprehend.

USE REDUNDANCY.   Another characteristic of the message that is likely to affect recipient comprehension is the amount of redundancy it contains. Redundancy means repeating the message or restating it in a different way. Some redundancy will improve the likelihood of recipient comprehension, but as usual, the appropriate degree and form of redundancy will depend on the specific situation.

INSURE APPROPRIATE FEEDBACK.   In most cases it is advisable to provide for some form of feedback to determine whether the message was received and understood, especially if the message is complex. If feedback reveals incomplete comprehension or lack of acceptance, the communicator can then try again. There are several ways that a communicator can obtain feedback about recipient comprehension, and some approaches are better than others. The communicator can ask if the recipient understood the message, or invite questions if the message was not understood. Neither of these approaches will be useful unless the recipient realizes that he or she did not interpret the message correctly and is willing to admit failure to understand it. The communicator can ask the recipient to repeat the message, but this will only reveal whether it was received intact, not whether it was understood. If face-to-face communication is used, the communicator can observe the recipient in an attempt to detect subtle cues indicating comprehension and acceptance of the message.

The best approach·in most situations is to ask the recipient *what* was understood (Berlo, 1960). The recipient is invited to restate the message in his or her own words, and if the message is an order or request, the recipient can be invited to say what actions will be taken. A related approach that is sometimes appropriate is to ask the recipient specific questions about the message to test for comprehension.

When there is two-way communication with unrestricted opportunity for feedback, the result will usually be greater recipient satisfaction with the interaction, as well as better comprehension of the message (Leavitt and Mueller, 1951). With one-way communication, the recipient may be anxious about whether he understood the message, and may be frustrated about not being able to respond. A limitation of two-way communication is that it is usually more time consuming than one-way communication.

BUILD RECIPIENT SKILLS.   Improving the communication of information between two persons should not be regarded as simply a matter of increasing the communicator's skill. A person's skill as a recipient of information can also be increased. For example, training can be provided in "effective listening." A person can learn to pay attention, show interest, avoid premature evaluation of the communicator or the message, and avoid premature conclusions about what the speaker is going to say. Training can also be provided in the use of feedback techniques such as restating or summarizing what the communicator has said and asking questions that do not intimidate the communicator (Strauss and Sayles, 1972).

Overloading

Communication inefficiency in a network may be caused by distribution of too much information as well as by too little information. A person has a certain capacity for decoding incoming messages, and if this capacity is exceeded, the person becomes "overloaded." This problem is likely to occur with top administrators and executives in a growing organization as the quantity of upward communication increases. Overloading is also a problem for scientists and certain technical specialists who are trying to cope with the "knowledge explosion." There are several different ways of responding to overloading (Katz and Kahn, 1966; Miller, 1960). Short-term measures include filtering and queuing, while more drastic measures include special training or information reduction through structural changes.

FILTERING.   One response to overloading is to reject certain messages on the basis of their source, medium, or an estimate of likely relevance. For example, the recipient may discard junk mail and certain kinds of reports and correspondence, or refuse to accept calls from or make appointments with certain types of persons. Filtering may also include ignoring certain parts of a long message, such as parts that are difficult to comprehend, or parts that the communicator believes are redundant with information already received. The limitation of filtering is that, unless the recipient is able to make accurate judgments about relevance, some important information will be inadvertently rejected.

QUEUING. Another possible response to overloading is to postpone the processing of low priority messages until a slack period. For example, some written messages can be put in the person's "hold" box, and some calls, appointments, and meetings can be postponed or rescheduled for a later time. The effectiveness of queuing will depend on the accuracy of a person's judgments about message priority and on the availability of periodic slack periods in which to process deferred messages.

INCREASE INFORMATION PROCESSING CAPACITY. If an overloaded recipient tries to speed up processing of messages, the number of interpretation errors is likely to increase. However, with special training, some speedup is usually possible without loss of comprehension. The information processing capacity of a person can often be increased with training in speedreading, report analysis, memorizing, stenography, or effective interviewing. Another way to increase information processing capacity is through the use of computers. They can provide valuable assistance in analyzing quantitative data and presenting statistical summaries or even graphical displays.

INFORMATION REDUCTION. The amount of information sent to an overloaded person can be reduced by changes in communication procedures or by changes in the structure of the communication network. The quantity and length of reports and memos can be restricted, the number of meetings can be reduced, and appointments or telephone calls can be limited to certain time periods during the day. More intermediary personnel ("gatekeepers") can be added to summarize incoming information, filter out trivial messages, and make decisions about routine matters. Examples of gatekeepers include staff advisors, administrative assistants, and appointments secretaries. The amount of information received by an overloaded manager can also be reduced by delegating more decisions to individuals or groups at lower levels in the authority hierarchy. A more drastic structural change is the subdivision of an overloaded person's job into two separate jobs, each performed by a different person who would only receive information relevant to his or her specialized functions. In planning structural changes, it is important to remember that other issues besides information processing should be taken into account (see Chapters 2 and 3).

Insufficient Upward Communication

Research in industrial organizations reveals that insufficient upward communication is a common problem. In one study with a large sample of workers, foremen, and general foremen, each person was asked to indicate what they wanted from a job (Kahn, 1958). In addition, the foremen were asked to estimate how their subordinates would answer the question, and general foremen were asked to estimate how the foremen would answer it. The foremen overestimated the importance of pay and security to the workers and underestimated the importance workers attached to job content and relations with co-workers. The general foremen made the same mistake in estimating the attitudes of the foremen. Thus at each level of management, the boss did not understand his subordinates' attitudes and had an uncomplimentary stereotype of the subordinates.

In another study, upper-level managers in five companies and one subordinate of each manager were interviewed to determine their perception of the subordinate's job (Maier, Hoffman, Hoover, and Read, 1961). There was little agreement between boss and subordinate about what specific duties were performed by the subordinates or about the problems encountered by the subordinates (who were also managers) in their jobs. Apparently this information was not communicated to the managers by their subordinates.

Some reasons why subordinates don't speak up were revealed in a study of supervisors, engineers, white collar workers, and blue collar workers in eight companies (Vogel, 1967). A large majority of the sample believed that their boss was not interested in their problems and that they would get into "a lot of trouble" if they were completely open with their boss. Some other studies indicate that upward communication is least likely to be accurate when: (1) subordinates are ambitious for advancement, (2) subordinates perceive their boss to have substantial control over desired outcomes (e.g., retention, promotion, pay increase), (3) subordinates do not trust their boss, and (4) subordinates feel insecure (Athanassiades, 1973; Cohen, 1958; O'Reilly and Roberts, 1974; Read, 1962).

Upward communication is unlikely to be improved if management is unaware that there is a problem. Unfortunately, managers tend to overestimate their understanding of subordinate needs, attitudes, and job difficulties. In one study, 95 percent of the foremen said they understood the workers' problems well, but only 34 percent of the workers agreed that the foremen understood their problems well. Similarly, 90 percent of the general foremen said they understood the foremen's problems well, but only 51 percent of the foremen agreed (Hamann, 1956). Thus an effort should be made to periodically assess the effectiveness of upward communication rather than assuming that it is adequate.

Upward communication can be evaluated by conducting a survey of employee attitudes with questionnaires or with interviews by an outside consultant to see if these attitudes differ from management's assumptions about lower level employees. Organization development techniques also have as one of their objectives the detection of communication problems and the improvement of superior-subordinate communication (see Chapter 15).

When subordinates "cover up" mistakes and difficulties, their boss will not have accurate information on which to base his decisions, nor be able to help subordinates deal with their job problems. This is a serious communication failure, and there are two general approaches for dealing with it. One approach assumes that subordinates cannot be trusted to communicate accurate information and it must therefore be obtained from independent sources. Special personnel such as quality control inspectors, investigators, financial auditors, and informants are used to keep track of subordinate performance, detect mistakes, and uncover improper conduct. The existence of alternate sources of information should by itself reduce subordinate attempts to cover up problems and mistakes. The subordinates will discover that it is better to reveal unfavorable information to their boss than for the boss to hear about it from another source.

A quite different approach for improving upward communication is to try and develop a relationship of trust and openness between personnel at each level in the organization. If such a climate is to be created, a manager must be nonpunitive and problem oriented when a subordinate has difficulties or makes mistakes. Instead of criticizing the subordinate when a mistake is made, the manager helps the individual in solving the problem and planning how to avoid similar mistakes in the future. The subordinate is judged according to his or her progress in learning to cope with job responsibilities over a reasonably long period of time, rather than on short term performance. One way of applying these prescriptions is in a Management by Objectives program (see Chapter 15).

The two approaches mentioned for improving upward communication, namely independent sources of information and a trusting relationship, are probably not compatible with each other. Each manager should determine which one is most appropriate for his or her situation, subordinates, and objectives. Managers who desire to develop subordinates and to utilize them as a source of ideas and advice will find the human relations approach to be more appropriate. If subordinates do not trust their boss and are afraid of being punished for revealing their real opinions, they will say only what they think the boss wants to hear, or they will simply avoid offering any opinions and suggestions.

Insufficient Downward Communication

Downward communication is inadequate when a manager fails to transmit relevant information to subordinates. In some cases, the information originates at the top of the authority hierarchy and middle managers fail to pass it on to lower level personnel. An example of this kind of downward "filtering" is provided by a study conducted in one plant of a large manufacturing company (Davis, 1968). Top management held a meeting with the middle managers and told them about a change in the parking lot and tentative plans for layoffs of personnel. The middle managers were instructed to relay the information along to the foremen below them, who would then relay it to the assistant foremen. The layoff information was passed on to 94 percent of the foremen and to 70 percent of the assistant foremen. The parking information was passed on to 38 percent of the foremen and to 15 percent of the assistant foremen. Downward filtering was greater for the parking information, because it was less important and not directly relevant to production. Similar results have been found in a study conducted in a retail merchandising organization (Sanborn, 1961).

Managers tend to overestimate the effectiveness of their downward communication, just as they tend to overestimate the effectiveness of upward communication from subordinates. In a study conducted in a public utility, 92 percent of the foremen said that they always or nearly always told workers in advance about changes which would affect them or their work. However, only 47 percent of the workers said they were nearly always informed about changes in advance. Similarly, 100 percent of top managers said they always or nearly always informed the foremen about changes in advance, but only 63 percent of the foremen agreed (Likert, 1961, p. 52). As in the case of upward communication, there is not likely to be any improvement in downward communication unless management is aware that there is a problem. Thus it would be advantageous to conduct periodic surveys of personnel at each level to see if they perceive downward communication to be adequate.

Some filtering in downward communication can be avoided by using appropriate media. When information is communicated orally, the more links in the communication chain, the greater the chance that information will be lost or distorted. For messages that do not need to be translated and elaborated for lower level personnel, it is often advisable to use written media. For example, the parking information in the Davis (1968) study described earlier would have been more effectively disseminated by written notices to all of the supervisors. Written media are especially appropriate for lengthy and detailed messages and for messages of a very formal nature. However, for messages that need to be translated and explained to recipients with varying orientations and expertise, oral media are usually superior. Oral messages are also superior when immediate reactions and feedback are desired from recipients. One way to overcome the limitations of each type of media is to use a combination of oral and written messages. For example, a meeting can be held to announce major decisions and policy changes, and a detailed written statement for individual study and future reference can be distributed either before or after the meeting. Research suggests that use of multiple media increases the likelihood that a message will be received and comprehended (Dahle, 1954).

Lack of sufficient downward communication sometimes occurs because a manager is not aware that the information would help subordinates in the performance of their duties. Many managers do not realize the importance of clarifying subordinate role requirements, instructing subordinates in job procedures, and providing relevant performance feedback. Management training can be carried out to educate managers about the importance of providing more information to subordinates. An attempt can also be made to facilitate downward communication by formalizing performance feedback and joint problem solving, as for example in a Management by Objectives program (see Chapter 15).

Another reason why a manager may withhold information from subordinates is that he feels insecure and wants to maintain control. Such a manager will try to keep subordinates dependent on him for guidance and will try to prevent subordinates from obtaining enough information to criticize his decisions. Improvement in downward communication will be unlikely unless the attitudes of the insecure manager can be changed. Sensitivity training and some organization development techniques may be helpful in this respect. The alternative of bypassing the manager with direct communication of certain information to his subordinates can be used, but it will tend to undermine the manager's authority.

Achieving Effective Communication in Organizations

Communication can be improved in organizations by designing communication networks that acquire and distribute relevant information to decision centers efficiently and economically. Improvements can also be obtained by training personnel to use a communication network effectively. Network design and personnel training are complementary approaches that should be used together.

It is better to conduct a systematic and comprehensive assessment of an organization's communication effectiveness than to wait until communication breakdowns occur and try to deal with each one separately. Any specific communication breakdown may be part of a broader problem of inappropriate network design or inadequate training. Several types of communication problems may be interrelated, and efforts to solve one problem may create or aggravate other problems. For example, use of gatekeepers to reduce overloading may result in excessive filtering in upward communication. Or use of extensive redundancy to improve reliability of transmission and comprehension may increase any overloading problems that exist for recipients, as well as increasing communication costs.

Some "communication breakdowns" will turn out to be merely the symptoms of a different kind of problem, such as interpersonal or intergroup conflict. Here the solution lies not in steps to improve communication, but rather in steps to solve the underlying problem itself. Once this problem is solved, the communication difficulties are likely to disappear (Shutz, 1958).

SUMMARY

Communication is a vital process in organizations because it is essential for all other organizational processes. Communication networks in organizations acquire and distribute information to information-processing and decision-making centers. Upward communication provides top-level decision makers with information about the activities, performance, attitudes, and needs of lower level personnel. Downward communication conveys orders, instructions, performance feedback, and general information to lower level personnel. Lateral communication facilitates coordination and problem solving. Informal communication supplements the formal communication network, serving both task-related and social-maintenance functions.

Interpersonal communication is complicated by human perceptual processes. Messages must compete for a person's attention and may be ignored if perceived to be irrelevant or unfavorable. The language of the message will determine to a large extent whether it is comprehended. The recipient's acceptance of the message will be influenced by perception of the communicator's intentions and credibility, as well as by the message content.

Communication failure due to incomplete comprehension can be minimized if the message content and transmission media are compatible with the recipients, the situation, and the communicator's objectives. Comprehension is facilitated by simple, direct language, ample redundancy, and provision for feedback.

Insufficient upward communication is a widespread and serious problem in authority hierarchies. Two different approaches for improving upward communication include use of independent information sources and development of a climate of mutual trust and problem solving.

Insufficient downward communication is likely when managers are not sensitive to the information needs of subordinates or attempt to retain control by deliberate hoarding of information. The use of appropriate media can help to reduce downward filtering and distortion of messages. Managerial training and formalized information sharing procedures are additional remedies for insufficient downward communication.

Improvements in an organization's communication processes are more likely when a systems approach is used rather than dealing with individual problems separately. Communication problems are often related to each other and to other kinds of problems.

REVIEW AND DISCUSSION QUESTIONS

1. Define or explain each of the following key terms: communication, attention, message comprehension, message acceptance, media, one- and two-way communication, feedback, credibility, verbal and nonverbal communication, overt and latent meaning, upward communication, downward communication, lateral communication, horizontal communication, diagonal communication, informal communication, the grapevine, communication network, redundancy, overloading, filtering, queuing, gatekeepers.

2. Explain the statement: "People respond to their perceived world rather than to objective conditions." What is the significance of this for communication in organizations?

3. What are major functions of upward, downward, and lateral communication?

4. What are some positive and negative consequences of the grapevine in organizations? What position should management take regarding the grapevine?

5. What are the criteria by which a communication network can be evaluated?

6. What are some common communication problems in organizations? For each type of problem, describe some possible remedies.

7. What general strategy should an organization pursue to maintain effective communication?

REFERENCES

Allen, T. J., & Cohen, S. I.   Information flow in research and development laboratories. *Administrative Science Quarterly*, 1969, *14*, 12–20.

Athanassiades, J.   The distortion of upward communication in hierarchical organization. *Academy of Management Journal*, 1973, *16*, 207–226.

Berlo, D. K.   *The process of communication.* New York: Holt, Rinehart, and Winston, 1960.

Burns, T.   The direction of activity and communication in a departmental executive group: A quantitative study in a British engineering factory with a self-recording technique. *Human Relations*, 1954, *7*, 73–97.

Cohen, A. R.   Upward communication in experimentally created hierarchies. *Human Relations*, 1958, *11*, 41–53.

Dahle, T. L.   An objective and comparative study of five methods of transmitting information to business and industrial employees. *Speech Monographs*, 1954, *21*, 21–28.

Davis, K.   Management communication and the grapevine. *Harvard Business Review*, 1953, *31* (September–October), 43–49.

Davis, K.   Success of chain-of-command oral communication in a manufacturing management group. *Academy of Management Journal*, 1968, *11*, 379–387.

Davis, K.   Readability changes in employee handbooks of identical companies during a fifteen-year period. *Personnel Psychology*, 1968, *21*, 413–420.

Flesch, R.   A new readability yardstick. *Journal of Applied Psychology*, 1948, *32*, 221–223.

Galbraith, J.   *Designing complex organizations.* Menlo Park, Calif.: Addison-Wesley, 1973.

Hage, J., Aiken, M., & Marrett, C.   Organization structure and communication. *American Sociological Review*, 1971, *36*, 860–871.

Hamann, J. R.   Panel discussion. American Management Association. *General Management Service*, 1956, No. 182, 21–23.

Haney, W. V.   Communication and organizational behavior. Homewood, Ill.: Irwin, 1973.

Hurwitz, J. I., Zander, A. F., & Hymovitch, B.   Some effects of power on the relations among group members. In D. Cartwright and A. Zander (Eds.), *Group Dynamics.* Evanston, Ill.: Row Peterson, 1953.

Jacobson, E., & Seashore, S.   Communication practices in complex organizations. *Journal of Social Issues*, 1951, *7*, 28–40.

Jones, E. E., Gergen, K. J., & Jones, R. C.   Tactics of ingratiation among leaders and subordinates in a status hierarchy. *Psychological Monographs*, 1963, *77*, No. 566.

Kahn, R. L.   Human relations on the shop floor. In E. M. Hugh-Jones (Ed.), *Human relations and modern management.* Amsterdam: North Holland Publishing Co., 1958.

Katz, D., & Kahn, R. L.   *The social psychology of organizations.* New York: Wiley, 1966.

Kelley, H. H.   Communication in experimentally created hierarchies. *Human Relations*, 1951, *4*, 39–56.

Kelly, J.   The study of executive behavior by activity sampling. *Human Relations*, 1964, *17*, 277–287.

Landsberger, H.   The horizontal dimension in bureaucracy. *Administrative Science Quarterly*, 1961, *6*, 299–332.

Lawler, E. E., III, Porter, L. W., & Tennenbaum, A.   Manager's attitudes toward interaction episodes. *Journal of Applied Psychology*, 1968, *52*, 432–439.

Leavitt, H. J., & Mueller, R. A. H.   Some effects of feedback on communication. *Human Relations*, 1951, *4*, 401–410.

Likert, R.   *New patterns of management.* New York: McGraw-Hill, 1961.

Maier, N. R. F., Hoffman, L. R., Hoover, J. J., & Read, W. H.   *Superior-subordinate communication in management.* New York: American Management Association, Research Study 52, 1961.

Miller, J. G.   Information input, overload, and psychopathology. *American Journal of Psychiatry*, 1960, *116*, 695–704.

O'Reilly, C. A., & Roberts, K. H.   Information filtration in three organizations: Three experiments. *Organizational Behavior and Human Performance*, 1974, *11*, 253–265.

Read, W. H.   Upward communication in industrial hierarchies. *Human Relations*, 1962, *15*, 3–16.

Sanborn, G. A.   An analytical study of oral communication practices in a nationwide retail sales organization. Unpublished doctoral dissertation, Purdue University, 1961.

Sayles, L. R.   *Behavior of industrial work groups.* New York: Wiley, 1958.

Schein, E.   *Process consultation: Its role in management development.* Reading, Mass.: Addison-Wesley, 1969.

Shaw, M.   Communication networks. In L. Berkowitz (Ed.), *Advances in experimental social psychology,* vol. 1. New York: Academic Press, 1964.

Shutz, W. C.   Interpersonal underworld. *Harvard Business Review*, 1958, *36* (July–August), 123–135.

Simpson, R. L.   Vertical and horizontal communication in formal organizations. *Administrative Science Quarterly*, 1959, *4*, 188–196.

Smith, C. G., & Brown, M. E.   Communication structure and control structure in a voluntary association. *Sociometry*, 1964, *27*, 449–468.

Strauss, G., & Sayles, L. R.   *Personnel: The human problems of management.* (3d ed.), Englewood Cliffs, N.J.: Prentice-Hall, 1972.

Sutton, H., & Porter, L. W.   A study of the grapevine in a governmental organization. *Personnel Psychology*, 1968, *21*, 223–230.

Thayer, L.   *Communication and communication systems.* Homewood, Ill.: Irwin, 1968.

Vogel, A.   Why don't employees speak up? *Personnel Administration*, 1967, *30*, (May–June), 20–22.

Wickesberg, A. K.   Communication networks in the business organization structure. *Academy of Management Journal*, 1968, *11*, 253–262.

5

EMPLOYEE MOTIVATION TO WORK

MOTIVATION is usually defined as the process by which behavior is energized and directed. Despite its intuitive appeal, the concept of motivation has been a very troublesome one for psychology. One reason for this is that motivation is not directly observable. It is a hypothetical process that can only be inferred by observing people's behavior, measuring changes in their performance, or asking them to describe their needs and goals. Although there are a few physiological needs such as hunger and thirst that can be aroused through deprivation, most of the human needs that have been proposed cannot be readily manipulated in this fashion. Inferring motives from behavior is difficult, because behavior can serve more than a single motive, and the same motive can be manifest in different kinds of behavior. Inferring motivation from changes in performance is risky, because performance depends on a person's ability and perception of job requirements as well as on motivation. Use of self-reports also has limitations since it is questionable whether people can accurately identify the nature and strength of their own motives. Some motives appear to be unconscious, and even conscious motives may not be revealed if a person is embarrassed about them or suspicious of the researcher.

Despite the difficulty of measuring motivation, it has proven to be an extremely useful concept for the analysis of behavior in organizations. Hundreds of studies have been conducted to test various motivation theories and to evaluate different approaches for "motivating" employees. One objective of this chapter will be to review the major theories that have been developed to explain motivated behavior in organizations. We will also discuss the practical implications of these theories for increasing employee motivation. Finally, we will examine two kinds of programs for motivating employees, namely pay incentives and job enrichment.

MOTIVES RELEVANT TO BEHAVIOR IN ORGANIZATIONS

Because of the difficulty of measuring motives, psychologists are not sure about how many different kinds of human motives or "needs" exist. While some needs appear to be innate, other needs may be largely or entirely the result of learning and childhood experiences. Most psychologists agree that there are a variety of human motives, but many different lists of needs have been proposed over the years. Several of these proposed needs appear to be especially relevant to behavior in organizations.

EXISTENCE NEEDS. Some physical and physiological needs such as food and shelter can be satisfied directly by the organization or indirectly through income earned by organization members.

SECURITY NEEDS. Security or safety needs involve protection from threat of physical harm or loss of income. These needs can be satisfied by elimination of hazardous working conditions and by safeguards against the risk of personal economic disaster. Such safeguards include health insurance, disability insurance, unemployment insurance, job tenure or a long-term employment contract, and rules or appeals procedures which protect an employee against arbitrary suspension, layoff, or dismissal.

AFFILIATION NEEDS. Affiliation or social needs involve the common desire of humans for companionship and for interpersonal relationships in which affection and nurturance are received and given. This type of need may be satisfied in organizations to the extent that an employee is able to develop close friendships with other employees or with regular clients and customers. The desire to satisfy social needs is a major reason for the formation of informal groups in an organization (see Chapter 7). Of course, not everyone desires to satisfy their social needs in the organization where they are employed. Some employees satisfy their social needs outside of their job setting and are not interested in forming close friendships with co-workers.

ESTEEM NEEDS. People typically desire appreciation, respect, and status. Esteem needs may be satisfied in an organization to the extent that a person's co-workers, subordinates, and superiors treat the person as a valuable and important member of the organization. Esteem is expressed by others through praise, recognition of accomplishment (e.g., awards, honors), and provision of status symbols.

INDEPENDENCE NEEDS. Human infants are completely dependent upon adults for satisfaction of their existence needs. As a child grows older, it gradually becomes less dependent. An internal conflict develops between the comfort of dependence and the frustration of being controlled by the people upon whom one is dependent (Haire, 1964). The relative strength of the desire for dependence and the desire for independence is influenced by childhood experiences and will differ from person to person. The strength of an adult's need for independence will determine how the person responds to authority figures and to the opportunity for autonomy and responsibility in the job.

ACHIEVEMENT AND COMPETENCE NEEDS.   All infants appear to have an innate competence need which motivates them to learn how to cope effectively with their environment (White, 1959). Whether this competence need develops into a strong need for achievement in an adult depends largely on a person's childhood experiences (McClelland, 1961). Some people learn to seek out and enjoy challenging tasks that test their competence, while other people learn to fear and avoid such tasks. A person with a high need for achievement obtains satisfaction from experiencing personal success in accomplishing a difficult task or attaining a standard of excellence. Achievement motivation is distinct from esteem needs because gratification depends upon objective feedback about successful performance, not on recognition of one's success by other people. A person may have all the esteem he or she desires and still continue to be motivated by new challenges. Research by McClelland (1961, 1965) and other psychologists has shown that a person with a high need for achievement prefers a job with the following characteristics: (1) performance depends on the person's own effort and ability rather than on chance factors beyond the individual's control or on teamwork, (2) the tasks and assignments are moderately difficult rather than easy or impossible, (3) there is frequent concrete feedback about how well the person is performing.

NEED HIERARCHY THEORY

If humans have many different needs, how many of these needs are active at the same time? Are some needs more important than other needs? Maslow (1954) formulated a "need hierarchy theory" to answer questions such as these. According to Maslow, there are five different classes of needs: physiological needs, safety needs, social needs, esteem needs, and need for self-actualization. Maslow proposed that these needs are common to all humans and are arranged in a hierarchy of prepotency, as depicted in Figure 5–1. At any point in time, only the lowest unsatisfied need in the hierarchy controls a person's behavior. After this need is mostly satisfied, it declines in importance and the person's behavior is then controlled by the next unsatisfied need in the hierarchy. Thus, physiological needs must be mostly satisfied before safety needs will assume a potent influence over behavior. Safety needs must be mostly satisfied before social needs will become important, and so on. The last need to be activated is self-actualization, and Maslow suggests that few people ever reach this step in their need hierarchy. Self-actualization can be defined as the need to grow and develop psychologically, to find one's identity and realize one's potential. Self-actualization is a "growth need" that is never

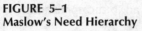

FIGURE 5–1
Maslow's Need Hierarchy

completely satisfied. If a person is successfully fulfilled in one way, that individual will then seek other avenues of self-development and self-expression.

Research on Need Priorities

Since Maslow's theory is so widely known, many people assume that it has been well validated. However, a recent review of relevant research concludes that there is actually very little support for the theory (Wahba and Bridwell, 1976). There is some evidence that physiological needs take precedence over other kinds of needs, but there is no good evidence that the other needs are activated in the order proposed by Maslow. Furthermore, the concept of "self-actualization" is poorly defined, and there is little reason to believe that self-actualization exists as a separate and distinct human need.

Research on human needs indicates that the relative importance of a person's needs fluctuates over time. As one need is temporarily satisfied, other needs become important. Nevertheless, there is no sound basis for the hypothesis that only a single need will be activated at a given time, as Maslow proposes. Rather, it is generally accepted that a person's behavior can be influenced by several needs simultaneously. Sometimes these needs are compatible and can be satisfied together, while at other times they are incompatible and a person must decide which to satisfy and which to ignore. An example of a conflict between needs is provided by the employee who wants to earn more money under an incentive program but would be socially rejected by co-workers if he or she became a "rate buster" (i.e., someone who produces more than the group norm).

Practical Implications

Even though need hierarchy theories, such as the one proposed by Maslow (1954), are not very well substantiated, the proposition that some needs take priority over other needs appears to be a valid one. This proposition has important practical implications. An organization cannot improve employee motivation to work or increase job satisfaction until it discovers what needs are currently important to each employee. For example, if an employee is primarily concerned about job security or with earning an adequate income on which to live, the employee is not likely to be motivated by recognition or job enrichment. Conversely, more health insurance or safer working conditions will not increase the motivation or satisfaction of an employee whose security needs are already fulfilled. The motivational programs in an organization should be flexible enough to accommodate individual differences in needs and possible changes in employee need priorities over time.

PROCESS THEORIES OF MOTIVATION

To postulate that a person has certain needs does not by itself explain why the person will try to perform at a superior level rather than at an average or substandard level. The amount of effort a worker exerts in a job depends on certain aspects of the job situation as well as on the person's needs. The manner in which needs and situational variables jointly determine a person's behavior is the subject of various "process theories" of motivation. Three of the most promising of these process theories are (1) drive-reinforcement theory, (2) expectancy theory, and (3) goal theory.

Drive-Reinforcement Theory

The ancient principle of "hedonism" states that people try to maximize pleasure and avoid pain. Thorndike (1911) proposed the "law of effect" to explain how the experience of pleasure and pain influences later behavior. The law of effect states that responses followed closely by pleasurable outcomes ("rewards") are strengthened and will be more likely to occur again in the same situation, while responses followed closely by unpleasant outcomes ("punishment") are weakened and will be less likely to occur again in the same situation. Hull (1943) further elaborated this explanation by differentiating between the directing of behavior and the energizing of behavior. Energizing was attributed to various physiological "drives" (like needs), while directing was attributed to the joint effects of drives and "habits." A habit is the association formed between a response and a specific stimulus as the result of "reinforcement" in the form of pleasant or unpleasant outcomes. According to drive theory, habits will be strongest when: (1) reinforcement occurs quickly after the response is made, (2) the experience of reinforcement is repeated many times, and (3) the magnitude of the reinforcer (i.e., the reward or punishment) is large.

REWARDS VERSUS PUNISHMENT. Research on "behavior modification" suggests that reinforcement of behavior with rewards is usually more effective than reinforcement with punishment. Use of punishment often has certain unfavorable side effects, such as disruptive anxiety, resentment, hostility, and withdrawal. Moreover, punishment can induce a person to stop making a particular response, but it usually does not increase the likelihood of making a correct response. In fact, unless an incorrect response is easily observed or detected, punishment may simply induce a person to make it in a manner designed to avoid the punishment. There are some occasions where the threat of punishment is appropriate, such as the suppression of behavior that recklessly endangers other people, but as a general rule, punishment should otherwise be avoided.

Skinner (1953, 1969) has proposed that behavior can be effectively modified by rewarding desired responses and ignoring undesired responses. If the person seldom or never makes the desired response, a process of "shaping" can be followed. Shaping means that a person is initially rewarded for any response that is similar to the desired response or is part of a desired response sequence. Then reinforcement is gradually limited to only the desired response or response sequence so that it will be learned.

SCHEDULES OF REINFORCEMENT. Skinner (1938, 1969) and his followers have discovered that the effects of reinforcement depend in part on the "schedule of reinforcement" experienced by an organism. In other words, behavior is influenced by the pattern of repeated reinforcements as well as by the magnitude and immediacy of reinforcement. With a "*continuous reinforcement schedule*" the reinforcement occurs every time the correct response is made. With a "*partial reinforcement schedule*" the reinforcement occurs only after a certain number of correct responses have been made or a certain interval of time has elasped since the previous reinforcement. The number of correct responses or the amount of time between reinforcements may be constant, or it may vary around some average value. One example of partial reinforcement is a variable interval schedule. With this schedule, a correct response (e.g., coming to work on time) is reinforced randomly a predetermined percentage of the times it is made. A person on a 25 percent variable interval schedule would be reinforced on one out of four of the days he comes to work on time, but he would not know in advance on which days the reinforcement would occur.

RESEARCH ON REINFORCEMENT. Hundreds of studies with animals have shown that both continuous and partial reinforcement schedules can be used to maintain a high rate of responding (Skinner, 1938, 1969). Research with humans yields similar results, although only a few systematic studies have been conducted with employees in formal organizations (see review by Schneier, 1974). Pay incentives for performance are a form of behavior modification, and studies of pay incentive programs have found that they often result in higher productivity (Lawler, 1971). Recent re-

search on the relative effectiveness of continuous and partial reinforcement schedules for administration of pay incentives has not yielded consistent results (Yukl and Latham, 1975; Yukl, Latham and Pursell, 1976;
Yukl, Wexley and Seymour, 1972).

Several studies have reported the successful application of reinforcement principles in the modification of other aspects of employee behavior
besides their work performance. Three studies found that money or prizes
contingent on perfect attendance during a specified time interval (e.g.,
a week or a month) resulted in lower absenteeism (Lawler and Hackman,
1969; Nord, 1970; Pedalino and Gamboa, 1974). Another study found
that a monetary reward for punctual attendance reduced the frequency
of tardiness for employees who previously had a record of chronic tardiness
(Hermann, DeMontes, Dominguez, Montes, and Hopkins, 1973).

At Emery Air Freight performance feedback and praise have been used
to shape and reinforce appropriate job behavior (Anacom, 1973). Supervisors were provided with training workbooks explaining how to administer feedback and positive reinforcement. The supervisors were urged to
reinforce desirable behavior at least twice a week in the beginning, then
gradually reduce the rate of reinforcement so that praise would be less
frequent and less predictable. In one example, employees who load freight
containers were given individual feedback about the percentage of times
containers were utilized to capacity, and improvement was praised. Container utilization increased from 45 percent to 95 percent, resulting in a
substantial cost savings.

PRACTICAL IMPLICATIONS. Drive theory and the results from reinforcement research have a number of practical implications for motivating employees in organizations (Jablonsky and DeVries, 1972; Nord, 1969).

1. Determine and specify what behavior is correct or desired.
2. Positively reinforce the correct behavior, using shaping if necessary to
   develop the desired responses.
3. Ignore undesired or incorrect behavior rather than punishing it, unless
   there are serious consequences.
4. Avoid excessive delay in reinforcement of correct behavior so that the
   behavior-reward contingency is evident.
5. Determine what schedule of reinforcement and type of reinforcer are
   appropriate for the individual and the situation to maintain the correct behavior after it is learned.

Expectancy Theory

Expectancy theory is a variation of early cognitive theories and decision
theories developed by scholars in a variety of disciplines (see Wahba and
House, 1974). According to expectancy theory, a person's behavior reflects

a conscious choice based on a comparative evaluation of different behavior alternatives. Although a number of versions of the theory have been proposed (Campbell, Dunnette, Lawler and Weick, 1970; Georgopolous, Mahoney and Jones, 1957; Graen, 1969; Porter and Lawler, 1968; Vroom, 1964), they share certain basic features. Each version proposes that a person will choose a behavior alternative that is likely to have favorable consequences. In this respect, expectancy theory is an extension of hedonism, as was drive theory. However, while drive theory explained behavior in terms of the mechanical triggering of learned habits by various external and internal stimuli, expectancy theory postulates a deliberate and rational choice process.

SIMPLIFIED MODEL.   A simplified version of expectancy theory will be presented before considering the more complex refinements. The key concepts in the theory are (1) outcome, (2) valence, and (3) expectancy. An outcome is any potential need-related consequence of behavior. Outcomes in a work context include such things as a pay increase, promotion, recognition, job retention or dismissal, intrinsic satisfaction from accomplishment, co-worker acceptance, fatigue, illness, and accidents. The valence of an outcome is the degree to which it is desirable or undesirable. The expectancy of an outcome is the perceived probability that it will in fact occur if a given behavior alternative is chosen. The attractiveness of a behavior alternative depends on the expectancies and valences of the outcomes associated with the alternative. A numerical score can be computed for the attractiveness of a behavior alternative by multiplying the expectancy of each outcome by the valence for that outcome ($E \times V$) and then summing the resulting products. According to the theory, a person will choose the behavior alternative with the highest attractiveness score.

An example is presented in Table 5–1. A worker is trying to decide whether to violate a safety rule in carrying out an assignment. If he violates the rule, he will be able to finish the job faster, which would allow him to earn more money. On the other hand, violating the rule may result in an accident, and if he is caught, he may be fired. On a valence scale ranging from $+100$ (most desirable) to -100 (least desirable), earning more money is quite desirable, while having an accident or getting fired

TABLE 5–1
Hypothetical Example of Expectancy Theory

Need-Related Outcomes	Outcome Valence	Observe Rule		Violate Rule	
		Expectancy	$E \times V$	Expectancy	$E \times V$
Have an accident	−50	.00	0	.20	−10
Get fired	−80	.05	−4	.10	− 8
Earn more money	+50	.10	+5	.80	+40
Attractiveness of Alternative (sum of $E \times V$):			+1		+22

are very undesirable. Will the worker observe the safety rule? According to expectancy theory, the more attractive alternative in this example is to violate the safety rule.

EXTENDED MODEL. The theory becomes more complicated if the behavior alternatives are not obviously discrete, as in the case of an employee trying to decide how much effort to exert or how high a performance goal to set. Since effort level and goal level are continuous variables, how many alternative levels will the employee consider when deciding how to behave? In this case it is usually assumed that a person will simplify the decision problem and consider only a few alternatives. For example, an employee may only consider making a maximum effort, a moderate effort, or a minimum effort.

When used to predict employee effort, most versions of expectancy theory differentiate between two types of outcomes. A "first-level outcome" is performance related. That is, a first-level outcome is some specific quantity of output or some specific level of performance quality. A first-level outcome may also be expressed as performance relative to the performance of other employees, as for example being the "best performer" in the group. A "second-level outcome" is need related, just as the outcomes in the simplified model described earlier. The distinction between two kinds of outcomes was made because many need-related outcomes are contingent upon a performance outcome rather than on effort itself. For example, a sales representative does not get a commission for trying hard to sell products, only for actual sales. In this case, two kinds of expectancies must be considered in determining the attractiveness of a behavior alternative. First, there is the perceived probability that a given effort level will result in the successful attainment of a certain performance outcome. This is referred to as an "$E \rightarrow P$ expectancy." Second, there is the perceived probability that the performance outcome will lead in turn to the attainment of a need-related outcome. This is referred to as a "$P \rightarrow O$ expectancy." The distinction between the two types of expectancies is defended on the grounds that they are determined by different conditions. The expectancy that effort will lead to a performance outcome depends in part on a person's ability, the difficulty of the task, and the person's self-confidence. The expectancy that a performance outcome will lead to the attainment of a need-related outcome depends on a person's perception of the reinforcement contingencies existing in the organization.

The attractiveness of a behavior alternative in the extended version of expectancy theory depends on both kinds of expectancies as well as on the valences of the need-related outcomes. A graphic description of the extended model is shown in Figure 5–2. In this example, only two behavior alternatives are being considered.

RESEARCH EVIDENCE. Research on expectancy theory provides some support for the theory. However, the results have not been entirely con-

FIGURE 5–2
A Graphic Illustration of Expectancy Theory

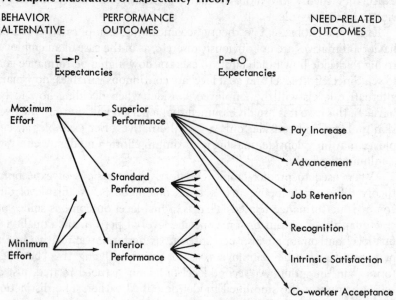

sistent from study to study, and the prediction of effort and performance has usually been quite weak (Heneman and Schwab, 1972; House, Shapiro and Wahba, 1974). Most of the studies have had methodological problems which prevent a completely adequate test of the theory. Moreover, the theory itself suffers from a number of logical and conceptual problems which need to be resolved before further progress can be made (Mitchell, 1974; Wahba and House, 1974).

PRACTICAL IMPLICATIONS.   Expectancy theory has several practical implications for motivating members of an organization.

1. The organization should develop appropriate procedures for evaluating employee performance.
2. An incentive program should be established with monetary and other kinds of rewards contingent upon superior performance by employees.
3. The organization should minimize any undesirable outcomes (e.g., layoffs, accidents) that employees may perceive to be a result of superior performance.
4. Employees should not be assumed to have an accurate perception of reward contingencies. The reward contingencies should be explained in a manner that will insure accurate $P \rightarrow O$ expectancies.
5. The organization should insure that each employee has a high $E \rightarrow P$ expectancy by providing adequate training, making job assignments appropriate to an employee's ability, and eliminating obstacles to effec-

tive performance (see the path-goal theory of leadership in Chapter 8).

6. The valence attached by an employee to potential need-related outcomes should be investigated by the organization, since this will differ from employee to employee. Only outcomes with a high valence for employees should be used as incentives for superior performance.

Goal Theory

Another motivation theory that explains employee behavior in terms of conscious mental processes is "goal theory." This theory, as formulated by Locke (1968), is an extension of Lewin's (1935) "level of aspiration" concept and Ryan's (1958) proposition that task characteristics influence goals and behavior. Locke's basic premise is that a person's behavior is regulated by the individual's goals and intentions. According to the theory, goals mediate the effects on behavior of task characteristics, incentives, supervision, and performance feedback. Goal difficulty and a person's commitment to attain a goal jointly determine the level of effort that will be expended. Specific goals such as a certain level of performance or a definite deadline for the completion of an assignment will have a greater effect on performance than generalized goals such as "do your best" or "finish as soon as possible." Hard goals will result in higher performance than easy goals, as long as the goal is actually accepted by the employee.

RESEARCH EVIDENCE. Locke (1968) and his associates have conducted a large number of laboratory studies to test the theory, and these studies provide strong support for it. Field studies conducted in actual organizations also provide evidence in support of the theory (see review by Latham and Yukl, 1975). Setting specific goals has resulted in higher productivity for a variety of different kinds of employees, including salesmen, truck drivers, office workers, logging crews, production workers, and managers. In studies where the effect of goal difficulty was investigated, hard goals usually resulted in better performance than easy goals. The field studies did not provide relevant evidence concerning the hypothesis that goal setting must occur for incentives or feedback to affect performance. As with the other motivation theories, more research is needed to further validate and refine goal theory.

PRACTICAL IMPLICATIONS. The findings in research on goal setting have the following practical implications for motivating members of an organization:

1. Employees should have specific performance goals to maintain motivation and guide their behavior.
2. The goals can be assigned by a supervisor, or they can be set jointly by an employee and a supervisor. Employee participation in goal setting is recommended when acceptance of an assigned goal is unlikely (see

the Vroom and Yetton leadership theory in Chapter 8 for further discussion of this subject).

3. The goal should be set at a level that is perceived by the employee to be challenging but not impossible to attain.

4. Accurate performance feedback should be provided so that progress can be determined and goals can be revised if necessary.

MOTIVATING EMPLOYEES

The practical implications of drive-reinforcement theory, expectancy theory, and goal theory are generally compatible. Together the three theories provide considerable insight into the way a person's behavior is jointly determined by needs and perception of the situation. These theories can be applied together in the development of programs to improve employee motivation to work. Three major types of motivational programs are (1) pay incentive plans, (2) job enrichment, and (3) management by objectives. The latter program will be discussed in Chapter 15 since it incorporates principles from the chapters on performance appraisal (Chapter 10) and leadership (Chapter 8) as well as motivational principles.

Pay Incentive Programs

Pay incentive programs make some portion of each employee's compensation contingent on the employee's performance.

TYPES OF INCENTIVE PLANS. The types of incentive plans that are most commonly used in organizations include: merit pay increase, individual performance bonus, individual piece rate or commission, group performance bonus, and profit sharing. A *merit pay increase* is simply an increase in the hourly rate or salary of an employee as a reward for superior performance. A *performance bonus* is a cash payment for superior performance during a specified time period. An incentive program that uses bonuses can establish a closer contingency between performance and pay than a program that uses merit pay increases (Lawler, 1971). Since merit increases are seldom revoked, an employee who has been given a merit pay increase will continue to receive this higher level of pay, even if his performance subsequently deteriorates. With a bonus plan, if performance declines the amount of the next bonus will also decline.

Individual *piece rates* are based on an employee's output. The employee receives a set amount of money for each unit of output above some standard or quota. An individual *commission* is similar to a piece rate, but it is used with sales personnel rather than production personnel. The employee receives a percentage of sales volume as a reward for successful sales. In some cases, the commission can only be earned on sales that exceed a specified quota.

With a *group performance incentive,* the reward is based on a measure of the group's performance rather than on the performance of each individual member. Members of the group share the reward equally or in proportion to their regular pay rates. A group incentive is more feasible than individual incentives when employees work together as a team on interdependent tasks. In this situation, it is difficult to measure an individual's performance, because each person is dependent on the other members of the group. Even in a situation where individual performance can be measured, a group incentive may be preferable if individual incentives would create harmful competition among employees. For example, in one department store, an individual incentive based on sales volume created conflict among the sales personnel. Each sales person tried to "tie up" customers or to steal customers from other employees. Important duties not covered by the incentive were neglected, including taking care of stock and displays. When the individual incentive was replaced by a group incentive, these problems were resolved and employees were more satisfied (Babchuk and Goode, 1951).

As a supplement to individual and group incentives, an organization may also use an incentive plan based on overall organizational performance. Two examples of this kind of plan are "cost reduction sharing" and "profit sharing." The "Scanlon Plan" is based on cost reduction sharing, and it is described in Chapter 15. A *profit sharing* plan distributes a part of the organization's profit to employees, usually in proportion to their salaries or according to their type of job. Profit sharing is not likely to have much influence on an employee's motivation, because the employee will not perceive any close connection between individual performance and the incentive (Lawler, 1971). For example, an employee whose performance is excellent would receive the same profit share as a similar employee whose performance is poor. Moreover, in a year when economic conditions are poor and the organization does not have any profits, an employee with excellent performance will not receive any profit share.

LIMITING CONDITIONS FOR PAY INCENTIVES. There are several requirements for a pay incentive program to be feasible as a means of improving employee performance or modifying employee behavior.

1. There is a behavior or performance problem that can be attributed in part to insufficient employee motivation.
2. Procedures can be developed to accurately measure this aspect of employee behavior or performance.
3. Employees are not prevented from attaining the desired performance level by extraneous factors beyond their control, such as insufficient knowledge, skill, equipment, supplies and quantity of work.
4. Pay incentives can be made contingent upon the desired behavior or performance in a manner that is understood by employees.

5. Employees perceive the magnitude of the pay incentive to be large enough to be highly desirable and equitable.
6. Employees perceive the incentive plan to be basically beneficial rather than detrimental to their welfare.
7. The incentive plan would be economical to the organization; that is, the direct and indirect expenses of administering the program would not exceed the benefits.

It is obvious from the preceding list that there are some situations where it is not feasible to utilize a pay incentive program. In those situations, the organization must rely on some other approach such as effective supervision and job design to motivate employees. Some of the limiting conditions for the use of pay incentives require further explanation and will be discussed in more detail.

EMPLOYEE ACCEPTANCE. If employees mistrust management and expect higher productivity to have adverse economic consequences, they will not respond favorably to an incentive program. Mistrust is more likely to be a problem with nonsupervisory employees than with managers. Workers will probably try to restrict their output if they perceive that increased productivity will result in an eventual increase in the standard or quota, a reduction in the incentive rate, elimination of overtime, or layoffs due to insufficient work. These fears are sometimes realistic, but even when inaccurate, they are likely to nullify the positive motivational effects of an incentive. In some cases, employees fail to accept a pay incentive plan because it is too mathematically complex for them to understand how they will benefit (Yukl and Latham, 1975).

One approach for increasing employee acceptance of a pay incentive plan is to allow employees to participate in designing it. Lawler and Hackman (1969) conducted a study in which they found that an incentive plan was very effective in modifying the behavior of employees who participated in developing the plan, but it did not affect the behavior of employees who had not participated.

IMPORTANCE OF PERFORMANCE APPRAISAL. The absence of an accurate and objective measure of performance for many kinds of jobs poses another obstacle to the introduction of an incentive plan. When it is necessary to rely on subjective ratings of performance because objective performance measures are not available, employees are more likely to suspect that the incentive is administered on the basis of favoritism or inaccurate judgments about performance. Studies have shown that most employees perceive themselves to be well above average in performance when their performance is not readily determined by an objective measure (Meyer, 1975). An incentive based on subjective ratings is likely to upset the majority of employees, because they will get a smaller pay increase or bonus than they feel is justified. For these employees, the perceived link between performance and the incentive will tend to be very weak, and the incentive may fail to motivate better performance.

Even when there is an objective performance measure, an incentive plan can be weakened if the measure is contaminated by extraneous factors. For example, executives often receive a bonus based on company or division profits. Since profits are partly dependent on economic conditions, an executive may earn a large bonus in a year when profits are high for the entire industry, even though the profits of the executive's division were less than they should have been and the division lost ground to competitors (Patton, 1972). Thus when pay incentives are based on objective performance measures, it is sometimes advisable to use a composite of different measures (e.g., profits, share of market, profit growth, etc.), or to make adjustments to eliminate the influence of extraneous factors.

The performance measure upon which incentives are based should be inclusive of all relevant aspects of an employee's job. Otherwise, the employee is likely to neglect aspects of the job not reflected in the performance measure. For example, if the incentive is based solely on quantity of performance, quality may suffer. Incentives for managers should reflect long-term aspects of performance as well as short-term performance. When an executive's bonus is based only on short-term profits, he or she will be encouraged to increase these at the expense of future division performance by cutting such things as research, advertising, inventories, maintenance, and training (Patton, 1972).

Job Enrichment

Job enrichment is an approach for redesigning jobs to increase intrinsic motivation and job satisfaction. "Intrinsic motivation" is a term used to describe effort that is expended in an employee's job to fulfill growth needs such as achievement, competence, and self-actualization. Jobs are enriched by allowing employees more responsibility, self-direction, and the opportunity to perform interesting, challenging, and meaningful work. The redesign of jobs usually includes such steps as:

1. Combine several jobs into a larger job involving a wider variety of skills.
2. Give each employee a natural unit of work ("work module") so he or she can complete a meaningful task.
3. Allow employees more responsibility for quality control and self-determination of work procedures.
4. Allow employees to deal directly with clients, support personnel, and persons performing related jobs.
5. Provide channels of performance feedback so that an employee can monitor and self-correct work behavior (Ford, 1973).

SCIENTIFIC MANAGEMENT. The job enrichment movement is a reaction to the excesses of "scientific management." In the early part of this century, scientific management was widely acclaimed as a method of designing jobs effectively. Frederick Taylor (1911), a major proponent of scientific management, argued that jobs should be simplified and specialized. Efficient work procedures for these jobs should be determined by industrial engineers, and employees should be given detailed instructions in the use of these procedures to perform their work. The best example of the application of scientific management is the mechanized assembly line. Each worker on the assembly line performs one or two simple operations, and these operations must be repeated hundreds of times each day. The work is machine paced, and each worker must keep up with the line. An employee has no control over how the work is done; he is not able to vary his speed, and is not allowed to rest except at specified times when someone is available to replace him.

The advantages promised by scientific management were appealing. Labor costs would be minimized because unskilled workers would be employed, and there would be little expense for selection and training. Furthermore, most workers could be easily moved around to other jobs as needed, since any job could be quickly learned. Control would be simplified because work procedures were standardized and supervisors could readily determine if workers were following these procedures. Specialization would increase each worker's efficiency, and simplification of work would practically eliminate the likelihood of errors and quality defects.

In actual practice, the benefits have not always been as great as anticipated. As workers have become better educated and their standard of living has gone up, it has become increasingly harder to find enough unskilled people who will accept these jobs, and even with higher wages, the turnover rate has often been excessive. Absenteeism and turnover for jobs in industries like automobile manufacturing have become an expensive problem, and quality of work has declined due to carelessness and deliberate sabotage.

CONSEQUENCES OF JOB ENRICHMENT. Advocates of job enrichment predict that if simple, specialized jobs are redesigned to intrinsically motivate employees, the quality of employee performance will improve and there will be less absenteeism and turnover. These predictions have been supported in most of the studies conducted to evaluate job enrichment programs (Davis, 1966; Ford, 1969, 1973; Lawler, 1969; Maher, 1971; Paul, Robertson and Herzberg, 1969).

The implications of job enrichment for employee productivity are less clear, and the results for studies in which productivity could be measured are mixed. Productivity depends on how rapidly employees work and how efficiently their effort is utilized. An increase in intrinsic motivation will not necessarily cause an employee to work faster. An employee who is trying to do high quality work may produce a smaller quantity of output rather than a larger quantity after job enrichment. Efficiency, the other determinant of productivity, depends on several aspects of work organization and job design, including specialization, simplification, sequencing, workload balancing, and mechanization. Efficiency will begin to decrease at some point as jobs become more complex, less specialized, and less mechanized. However, certain jobs are "over-specialized," with unnecessary duplication of effort and excess idle time due to coordination problems or workload fluctuation. For these jobs, some reduction in specialization may actually improve efficiency. Thus, the effect of job enrichment on productivity will depend on whether efficiency is increased or decreased, and on the extent to which any reduction in efficiency is compensated by an increase in how fast employees work.

Even when the individual productivity of employees is not increased by job enrichment, there is likely to be some reduction in direct and indirect labor costs as a result of improved quality and lower absenteeism and turnover. Labor costs per unit of output will be lower if improved quality permits a reduction in the number of quality control personnel (e.g., inspectors) and a reduction in the number of worker-hours needed to correct errors or redo defective production. Lower absenteeism will probably permit a reduction in the size of the workforce, and lower turnover will lead to a reduction in expense for recruitment and selection. The reduced labor costs reported in many of the job enrichment studies can probably be attributed more to these benefits than to higher individual productivity.

EXAMPLES OF JOB ENRICHMENT PROGRAMS. Job enrichment programs have been carried out in several major corporations in this country and in Europe, including AT&T, IBM, Texas Instruments, Philips N.V., Volvo, and Saab. Three representative examples of successful programs are described to demonstrate the kinds of changes that have been made to enrich jobs

Directory Clerks. A job enrichment program for directory clerks at Indiana Bell Telephone Company was described by Ford (1973). Before enrichment, the compilation of telephone directories was laid out in 21 steps, such as manuscript reception, manuscript verification, keypunch, keypunch verification, ad copy reception, ad copy verification, and so forth. The directory clerks were indifferent about their jobs, and turnover was a serious problem. The first step in job enrichment was to have clerks check their own work, thereby eliminating seven verification steps. Next, certain clerks were allowed to compile their "own" directories, carrying out each of the remaining 14 steps. This change gave a directory clerk a complete "work module" to perform. Directories that were too large for a single clerk were divided up according to blocks of letters, and each clerk was allowed to carry out all of the 14 steps for her block. In the process of compiling their directories, the clerks were permitted to deal directly with salesmen, the printer, service representatives, and with supervisors in other departments.

Sales Representatives. A job enrichment program for sales representatives in a British company was described by Paul, Robertson, and Herzberg (1969). The job was changed to give sales representatives more authority to make decisions and do business with the customer directly, without having to continually refer back to headquarters. Sales representatives were no longer required to write reports on each customer call, they were given responsibility for determining how often to call on customers, they were authorized to handle customer complaints about product performance (e.g., buy back items, make cash settlements up to a predetermined amount), and they were allowed to set the price of most products within a predetermined range of discretion. After these changes were made, sales improved and profits were greater than those for a control group without the changes.

Truck Assembly Workers. This case illustrates the concept of a "semiautonomous work group." At a truck assembly plant owned by Volvo in Sweden, some of the traditional assembly lines have been replaced by production teams. There are 5 to 12 employees in each group, and they elect their own coordinator. The team members decide among themselves how the work will be divided up and distributed, and they are responsible for their own quality control. They can vary their work pace and schedule work breaks, as long as they meet the production standards established by management. The group also performs some of the support, maintenance, and housekeeping activities formerly carried out by staff and service personnel. Group members can deal directly with other departments in solving joint problems and obtaining necessary supplies, a responsibility formerly carried out by a production supervisor.

Job Attributes and Intrinsic Motivation. Job enrichment programs typically include changes in several aspects of the job, and it has not been clear which changes are most essential. In order to gain a better understanding of the conditions necessary to insure intrinsic motivation, Hackman and Lawler (1971) conducted a study with 200 employees of a telephone company. A followup study was conducted by Hackman and Oldham (1975) with samples of employees from seven organizations. These studies found that several "core dimensions" of the job were related to the intrinsic motivation and job satisfaction of employees. Jobs that were high on the core dimensions were more intrinsically motivating than jobs that were low on them. The core dimensions found by Hackman and Oldham were labeled and defined as follows (pp. 161–162):

> *Skill Variety.* The degree to which a job requires a variety of different activities in carrying out the work, which involve the use of a number of different skills and talents of the employee.
>
> *Task Identity.* The degree to which the job requires completion of

a "whole" and identifiable piece of work—that is, doing a job from beginning to end with a visible outcome.

Task Significance. The degree to which the job has a substantial impact on the lives or work of other people—whether in the immediate organization or in the external environment.

Autonomy. The degree to which the job provides substantial freedom, independence, and discretion to the employee in scheduling the work and in determining the procedures to be used in carrying it out.

Feedback from the Job Itself. The degree to which carrying out the work activities required by the job results in the employee obtaining direct and clear information about the effectiveness of his or her performance.

The questionnaire developed to measure these dimensions is called the Job Diagnostic Survey (Hackman and Oldham, 1975). This questionnaire also contains scales to measure employee growth needs and intrinsic motivation. The questionnaire should prove useful for diagnosing jobs and planning how to enrich them. It can also be used to help evaluate the consequences of a job enrichment program.

EMPLOYEE DIFFERENCES. The effectiveness of job enrichment depends in part on the characteristics of the employees whose jobs are redesigned. Hackman and Lawler (1971) found that enriched jobs are only intrinsically motivating for employees who have strong higher order needs. Employees who do not have strong needs for achievement and independence are unlikely to be more satisfied and more intrinsically motivated by enriched jobs. Self-esteem and work-ethic values are also likely moderators of job enrichment effects. A job enrichment program is more likely to be successful if conducted with employees who are not afraid of the new responsibilities and who believe that it is important to work hard and attain personal success in one's occupation (Hulin and Blood, 1968; Robey, 1974; Turner and Lawrence, 1965; Wanous, 1974).

JOB ENRICHMENT CONCLUSIONS. Job enrichment is a promising approach for increasing motivation and improving employee performance, but there are some limiting conditions. It is not effective with all kinds of employees, and it is not appropriate for all kinds of jobs. The cost of redesigning or replacing equipment makes extensive job redesign uneconomical in certain situations. The feasibility of job enrichment is also doubtful where the loss in efficiency would greatly exceed any benefits from increased motivation and satisfaction. Finally, some jobs appear to defy attempts at enrichment (e.g., toll collector, garbage truck loader), although perhaps many of these jobs can eventually be automated.

SUMMARY

Motivation is the process by which behavior is energized and directed. Security, affiliation, esteem, independence, achievement, and existence needs are all potentially relevant influences on behavior in an organizational setting. Need hierarchy theory attempts to explain how certain needs dominate a person's behavior at some point in time. Process theories of motivation explain how a person's behavior is jointly determined by his needs and the job situation.

Drive-reinforcement theory explains behavior in terms of the mechanical triggering of learned habits by internal drives and external stimuli. Habits will be stronger when behavior is reinforced immediately and frequently. The extent to which behavior is modified by an incentive will depend on the type of incentive (reward versus punishment), the magnitude of the incentive, and the schedule of reinforcement.

Expectancy theory explains behavior in terms of conscious choices among alternative actions or levels of effort. According to this theory, a person will choose the behavior alternative that appears most attractive. The attractiveness of an alternative depends on the expectancy that it will lead to various outcomes, and on the valence of these outcomes.

Goal theory explains behavior in terms of the influence of conscious goals and intentions. According to this theory, task characteristics, incentives, supervision, and feedback will only affect a person's behavior if they cause the individual to change goals or set new ones. The effect of a goal on behavior depends on its specificity, difficulty, and acceptance by employees.

Pay incentive programs are one approach for motivating employees to work, but they are only feasible in certain situations. There must be an accurate performance measure that reflects all important aspects of the job, and employees must perceive the plan to be personally beneficial. While the magnitude of the incentive should be large enough to motivate employees, it must not be so large that it is uneconomical to the organization.

Job enrichment is an approach for increasing the intrinsic motivation of employees. Most job enrichment programs have resulted in better performance quality and lower absenteeism and turnover. The consequences of job enrichment for productivity and labor costs depend on a variety of complex factors. Although job enrichment has been successful in a majority of cases, it is not feasible for all kinds of employees or for every kind of situation.

REVIEW AND DISCUSSION QUESTIONS

1. Define or explain each of the following key terms: motivation, existence needs, security needs, affiliation needs, esteem needs; independence needs, achievement and competence needs, need hierarchy, process theories of motivation, law of effect, reinforcement, behavior modification, shaping, continuous reinforcement schedule, partial reinforcement schedule, expectancy, valence, first-level outcome, second-level outcome, goal, incen-

tive, bonus, job enrichment, intrinsic motivation, scientific management, core dimensions.

2. Explain Maslow's theory and evaluate its relevance for motivating employees.
3. What are the practical implications of drive-reinforcement theory for motivating employees?
4. Explain expectancy theory. What are its practical implications for motivating employees?
5. How is goal setting related to performance?
6. What are the major types of pay incentive plans?
7. What are the limiting conditions for the effectiveness and feasibility of incentive plans?
8. What kinds of job changes are usually made in a job enrichment program?
9. Under what conditions is job enrichment most likely to increase employee performance?

REFERENCES

ANACOM, American Management Association. At Emery Air Freight: Positive reinforcement boosts performance. *Organizational Dynamics*, 1973, *1* (Winter), 41–50.

Babchuk, N., & Goode, W. J. Work incentives in a self-determined group. *American Journal of Sociology*, 1951, *16*, 679–687.

Campbell, J. P., Dunnette, M. D., Lawler, E. E.,III, & Weick, K. E. *Managerial behavior, performance, and effectiveness.* New York: McGraw-Hill, 1970.

Davis, L. E. The design of jobs. *Industrial Relations*, 1966, *6*, 21–45.

Ford, R. N. *Motivation through the work itself.* New York: American Management Association, 1969.

Ford, R. N. Job enrichment lessons from AT&T. *Harvard Business Review*, 1973 (January–February), 96–106.

Georgopoulos, B. S., Mahoney, G. M., & Jones, N. W., Jr. A path-goal approach to productivity. *Journal of Applied Psychology*, 1957, *41*, 345–353.

Graen, G. Instrumentality theory of work motivation: Some experimental results and suggested modifications. *Journal of Applied Psychology*, 1969, *53*, 1–25 (Monograph).

Hackman, J. R., & Lawler, E. E.,III. Employee reactions to job characteristics. *Journal of Applied Psychology*, 1971, *55*, 259–286.

Hackman, J. R., & Oldham, G. R. Development of the job diagnostic survey. *Journal of Applied Psychology*, 1975, *60* 159–170.

Haire, M. *Psychology in management.* New York: McGraw-Hill, 1964.

Heneman, H. G., & Schwab, D. P. Evaluation of research on expectancy theory predictions of employee performance. *Psychological Bulletin*, 1972, *78*, 1–9.

Hermann, J. A., DeMontes, A. I., Dominguez, B., Montes, F., & Hopkins, B. L.

Effects of bonuses for punctuality on the tardiness of industrial workers. *Journal of Applied Behavior Analysis,* 1973, *6,* 563–570.

House, R. J., Shapiro, H. J., & Wahba, M. A.   Expectancy theory: Reevaluation of empirical evidence. *Decision Sciences,* 1974 (December/Special Issue), 54–77.

Hulin, C. L., & Blood, M. R.   Job enlargement, individual differences, and worker responses. *Psychological Bulletin,* 1968, *69,* 41–55.

Hull, C. L.   *Principles of behavior.* New Haven: Yale University Press, 1943.

Jablonsky, S. F., & DeVries, R.   Operant conditioning principles extrapolated to the theory of management. *Organizational Behavior and Human Performance,* 1972, *7,* 340–358.

Latham, G. P., & Yukl, G. A.   A review of research on the application of goal setting in organizations. *Academy of Management Journal,* 1975, *18,* 824–845.

Lawler, E. E.,III.   Job design and employee motivation. *Personnel Psychology,* 1969, *22,* 426–435.

Lawler, E. E.,III.   *Pay and organizational effectiveness.* New York: McGraw-Hill, 1971.

Lawler, E. E.,III, & Hackman, J. R.   Impact of employee participation in the development of pay incentive plans: A field experiment. *Journal of Applied Psychology,* 1969, *53,* 467–471.

Lewin, K.   *Dynamic theory of personality.* New York: McGraw-Hill, 1935.

Locke, E. A.   Toward a theory of task motivation and incentives. *Organizational Behavior and Human Performance,* 1968, *3,* 157–189.

Maher, J. R. (Ed.).   *New perspectives in job enrichment.* New York: Van Nostrand Reinhold, 1971.

Maslow, A. H.   *Motivation and personality.* New York: Harper, 1954.

McClelland, D. C.   *The achieving society.* Princeton: Van Nostrand Reinhold, 1961.

McClelland, D. C.   N-achievement and entrepreneurship: A longitudinal study. *Journal of Personality and Social Psychology,* 1965, *1,* 389–392.

Meyer, H.   The pay-for-performance dilemma. *Organizational Dynamics,* 1975, *3* (Winter), 39–50.

Mitchell, T. R.   Expectancy models of job satisfaction, occupational preference, and effort: A theoretical, methodological, and empirical appraisal. *Psychological Bulletin,* 1974, *81,* 1053–1077.

Nord, W.   Beyond the teaching machine: The neglected area of operant conditioning in the theory and practice of management. *Organizational Behavior and Human Performance,* 1969, *4,* 375–407.

Nord, W.   Improving attendance through rewards. *Personnel Administration,* 1970 (November–December), 37–41.

Patton, A.   Why incentive plans fail. *Harvard Business Review,* 1972 (May–June), 58–66.

Paul, W. J.,Jr., Robertson, K. B., & Herzberg, F.   Job enrichment pays off. *Harvard Business Review,* 1969, *47* (March–April), 61–78.

Pedalino, E., & Gamboa, V. U.   Behavior modification and absenteeism: Intervention in one industrial setting. *Journal of Applied Psychology*, 1974, *59*, 694–698.

Porter, L. W., & Lawler, E. E., III.   *Managerial attitudes and performance.* Homewood, Illinois: Irwin-Dorsey, 1968.

Robey, D.   Task design, work values, and worker response: An experimental test. *Organizational Behavior and Human Performance*, 1974, *12*, 264–273.

Ryan, T. A.   Drives, tasks, and the initiation of behavior. *American Psychologist*, 1958, *71*, 74–93.

Schneier, C. E.   Behavior modification in management. *Academy of Management Journal*, 1974, *17*, 528–548.

Skinner, B. F.   *The behavior of organisms.* New York: Appleton-Century, 1938.

Skinner, B. F.   *Science and human behavior.* New York: Macmillan, 1953.

Skinner, B. F.   *Contingencies of reinforcement.* New York: Appleton-Century-Crofts, 1969.

Taylor, F. W.   *The principles of scientific management.* New York: Harper & Row, 1911.

Thorndike, E. L.   *Animal intelligence: Experimental studies.* New York: Macmillan, 1911.

Turner, A. N., & Lawrence, P. R.   *Industrial jobs and the worker: An investigation of response to task attributes.* Boston: Division of Research, Harvard Business School, 1965.

Vroom, V. H.   *Work and motivation.* New York: Wiley, 1964.

Wahba, M. A., & Bridwell, L. G.   Maslow reconsidered: A review of research on the need hierarchy theory. *Organizational Behavior and Human Performance*, 1976, *15*, 212–240.

Wahba, M. A., & House, R. J.   Expectancy theory in work and motivation: Some logical and methodological issues. *Human Relations*, 1974, *27*, 121–147.

Wanous, J. P.   Individual differences and reactions to job characteristics. *Journal of Applied Psychology*, 1974, *59*, 616–622.

White, R. W.   Motivation reconsidered: The concept of competence. *Psychological Review*, 1959, *66*, 297–333.

Yukl, G. A., & Latham, G. P.   Consequences of reinforcement schedules and incentive magnitude for employee performance: Problems encountered in an industrial setting. *Journal of Applied Psychology*, 1975, *60*, 294–298.

Yukl, G. A., Latham, G. P., & Pursell, E. D.   The effectiveness of performance incentives under continuous and variable ratio schedules of reinforcement. *Personnel Psychology*, 1976, *29*, 221–231.

Yukl, G. A., Wexley, K. N., & Seymour, J. D.   The effectiveness of pay incentives under variable ratio and continuous reinforcement schedules. *Journal of Applied Psychology*, 1972, *56*, 19–23.

6

EMPLOYEE ATTITUDES
AND JOB SATISFACTION

JOB SATISFACTION is the way an employee feels about his or her job. It is a generalized attitude toward the job based on evaluation of different aspects of the job. While there are hundreds of job characteristics to be considered by an employee, certain clusters of job characteristics tend to be evaluated together in the same way. The clusters most often found in statistical analyses of attitude questionnaires include: pay, working conditions, supervision, co-workers, job content, job security, and promotion opportunity. In effect, an employee can be assumed to have a component attitude toward each of these aspects of the job as well as a composite attitude about the job as a whole.

A person's attitude toward his job reflects pleasant and unpleasant experiences in the job and his expectations about future experiences. However, despite several thousand studies on job attitudes during the last three decades, it is not possible to specify precisely how job satisfaction is determined. Most of the research has attempted to discover what things are related to job satisfaction, but the causal basis for the relationship has usually been ignored (Lawler, 1973). For example, many studies were conducted to determine how satisfied employees are, and to compare the job satisfaction of men versus women, old versus young employees, skilled versus unskilled workers, and so on. Other studies were conducted to determine what aspect of the job is perceived to be most important to employees (e.g., pay, supervision, etc.). The reasons why some employees are more satisfied than others or the reasons why employees consider some job features to be more important than others were seldom considered. A comprehensive theory of job attitudes has not yet been developed to integrate the diverse findings of the satisfaction research (Lawler, 1973). However, a few satisfaction theories of more limited scope have been proposed, including: (1) discrepancy theory, (2) equity theory, and (3) two-factor theory.

DISCREPANCY THEORY

According to Locke (1969), satisfaction or dissatisfaction with some aspect of the job depends on the discrepancy between what a person perceives he is getting and what he desires. The "desired" amount of a job characteristic is defined as the minimum amount necessary to fulfill the person's current needs. A person will be satisfied if there is no discrepancy between desired and actual conditions. A person will be dissatisfied if there is *less* than the desired amount of a job characteristic. The greater the deficiency and the more important the thing desired, the greater will be the dissatisfaction. If there is *more* than the minimally acceptable amount of some job factor and the excess is beneficial (e.g., extra pay), a person will be even more satisfied than when there is no discrepancy between the desired and actual amount. However, if the excess is perceived to be detrimental (e.g., extra workload, longer hours), the person will be just as dissatisfied as when there is less than the desired amount.

Other variations of the discrepancy model of job satisfaction have been proposed. For example, Porter (1961) defined satisfaction as the difference between how much of something there "should be" and how much there "is now." This conception is basically similar to Locke's model, but Porter's "should be" implies more emphasis on equity considerations and less on needs as the determinant of the preferred amount of a job factor. A study by Wanous and Lawler (1972) found that employees respond differently depending on how the discrepancy is defined. They conclude that people have more than one kind of feeling about their job, and no "one best way" exists to measure job satisfaction. The appropriate way of defining and measuring satisfaction will depend on the purpose of the measurement.

EQUITY THEORY

Equity theory specifies the conditions under which an employee will perceive the benefits and inducements in the job to be fair and reasonable. The theory was developed by Adams (1963), and it is a variation of earlier theories of social comparison processes. The principal components in equity theory are "inputs," "outcomes," "comparison person," and "equity-inequity." An *input* is anything of value that an employee perceives that he contributes to his job, such as education, experience, skills, amount of effort expended, number of hours worked, and personal tools, supplies, or equipment used on the job. An *outcome* is anything of value that the employee perceives he obtains from the job, such as pay, fringe benefits, status symbols, recognition, and opportunity for achievement or self-expression.

According to the theory, an employee judges the fairness of his outcomes by comparing his outcome:input ratio to the outcome:input ratio of one or more *comparison persons*. The comparison person may be someone in the same organization, someone in a different organization, or even the person himself in a previous job. The theory does not specify how an employee selects a comparison person or how many comparison persons will be used. If an employee's ratio of outcomes to inputs is equal to the ratio for the comparison person(s), a state of *equity* is perceived to exist by the employee. If the employee perceives the ratios to be unequal, a state of *inequity* will usually be perceived to exist.

Types and Magnitude of Inequity

Inequity can occur in many ways. For example, an employee will perceive his salary to be inequitable if other employees with similar qualifications are receiving a higher salary, or if employees who are less qualified are receiving the same salary. These are both examples of under-compensation inequity. According to the theory, an employee will also experience inequity if overcompensated relative to the comparison person. Table 6–1 lists the conditions in which there will be equity, overcompensation

TABLE 6–1
Equity and Inequity in Social Comparisons

	Own Self		Comparison Person
I.	*Equity Conditions:*		
1.	High outcomes/High inputs	=	High outcomes/High inputs
2.	Low outcomes/Low inputs	=	Low outcomes/Low inputs
3.	High outcomes/Low inputs	=	High outcomes/Low inputs
4.	Low outcomes/High inputs	=	Low outcomes/High inputs
5.	Low outcomes/Low inputs	=	High outcomes/High inputs
6.	High outcomes/High inputs	=	Low outcomes/Low inputs
II.	*Undercompensation Inequity:*		
7.	Low outcomes/Low inputs	≠	High outcomes/Low inputs
8.	High outcomes/High inputs	≠	High outcomes/Low inputs
9.	Low outcomes/High inputs	≠	Low outcomes/Low inputs
10.	Low outcomes/High inputs	≠	High outcomes/High inputs
11.	Low outcomes/High inputs	≠	High outcomes/Low inputs
III.	*Overcompensation Inequity:*		
12.	High outcomes/High inputs	≠	Low outcomes/High inputs
13.	High outcomes/Low inputs	≠	Low outcomes/Low inputs
14.	High incomes/Low inputs	≠	High outcomes/High inputs
15.	High outcomes/Low inputs	≠	Low outcomes/High inputs
16.	Low outcomes/Low inputs	≠	Low outcomes/High inputs

inequity, and undercompensation inequity, assuming that the total inputs and total outcomes are dichotomized as either "high" or "low" on some value scale. The amount of inequity will depend on the magnitude of the difference between outcome:input ratios. The larger the difference between an employee's outcome:input ratio and that of the comparison person(s), the greater the perceived inequity. For example, in Table 6–1, there will be greater perceived inequity for situation 11 than for situation 10.

Reactions to Inequity

Inequity is one source of job dissatisfaction, and it is accompanied by a state of dissonance that acts as a motive for the person to restore equity. The emotional reaction to overcompensation is likely to be a feeling of guilt, whereas with undercompensation, the feeling is likely to be anger and resentment at the organization or the boss. There are a variety of ways that an employee can attempt to restore equity:

1. Increase or decrease personal inputs, especially effort.
2. Persuade the comparison person to increase or decrease personal inputs.
3. Persuade the organization to alter the employee's personal outcomes or those of the comparison person.
4. Psychologically distort personal inputs or outcomes.
5. Psychologically distort the inputs or outcomes of the comparison person.
6. Select a different comparison person.
7. Leave the organization.

How an employee attempts to reduce inequity will depend on the nature of the outcome and input discrepancies and on the relative cost and feasibility of alternative reactions in the given situation. One weakness of the theory is that it does not specify in any detail how a person will choose among the available reactions to inequity.

Implications for Employee Performance

Equity theory has implications for employee performance as well as for job satisfaction. The theory predicts that an employee will alter his or her effort input when this is more feasible than other reactions to inequity. An employee who is undercompensated and is paid a salary or hourly rate will restore equity by reducing his effort input, thereby decreasing the quality or quantity of his performance. If an employee is undercompensated and a substantial portion of his pay is contingent on performance quantity (e.g., piece rate), the employee will try to increase his incentive earnings without increasing effort. Unless quality control is tight, an employee can usually increase the quantity of his output without extra effort by letting quality deteriorate.

For an employee who is overcompensated and is paid on an hourly or salary basis, equity can be restored by an increase in his effort input. This should result in an increase in the quantity or quality of performance. If an employee is overcompensated and a substantial portion of his pay is contingent on performance quantity, the employee will try to increase his effort input without a corresponding increase in incentive earnings. According to the theory, the employee will increase performance quality while reducing or holding constant performance quantity. These predictions about employee performance when there is undercompensation and overcompensation inequity are summarized in Table 6–2.

TABLE 6–2
Performance Implications on Inequity

	Undercompensation	Overcompensation
Hourly Rate or Salary	Lower quality and/or quantity of output	Higher quality and/or quantity of output
Piece Rate or Commission	Lower quality and greater quantity	Higher quality, lower or same quantity

Empirical Support

The prediction that an employee will restrict or reduce his incentive earnings if he perceives himself to be overcompensated is highly controversial. This prediction is contrary to expectancy theory and drive-reinforcement theory, which imply that larger incentives will result in an increase in the quantity of employee performance. Most of the research on equity theory has tested the performance implications of the theory, including the prediction just mentioned. Other important questions have been mostly neglected, including the basis for selecting a comparison person, the basis for choosing between different reactions to inequity, and the basis for determining what personal attributes and job characteristics will be regarded as inputs and outcomes in the social comparison process.

Recent reviews of the equity theory research by Goodman and Friedman (1971) and Lawler (1971) find that the empirical evidence is mixed. The occurrence of social comparison processes among employees and the phenomenon of perceived inequity are well validated. However, the implications of inequity for performance have not been conclusively demonstrated. Most of the studies have had methodological problems of one sort or another and have been too short in duration to evaluate anything but the immediate short-term effects of inequity on performance. Thus for the present, equity theory appears to be less useful for predicting effort and performance than for predicting whether an employee will be dissatisfied with certain aspects of the job for which social comparisons are likely to occur, such as pay, advancement, recognition, and status symbols.

TWO-FACTOR THEORY

The two-factor theory of job attitudes states that job satisfaction is qualitatively different from job dissatisfaction (Herzberg, 1966; Herzberg, Mausner and Snyderman, 1959). According to the theory, job characteristics can be grouped into two categories, one called "dissatisfiers" or "hygiene factors" and the other called "satisfiers" or "motivators." The hygiene factors include such things as pay, supervision, interpersonal relations, working conditions, job security, and status. A certain amount of the hygiene factors is necessary to fulfill a person's biological drives and basic needs such as safety and affiliation. When these needs are not fulfilled, the person will be dissatisfied. Once there is a sufficient amount of the hygiene factors to fulfill these needs, a person will no longer be dissatisfied, but neither will he be satisfied. A person will only be satisfied if there is an adequate amount of the job factors called satisfiers. Satisfiers are job characteristics that are relevant to a person's higher order needs and psychological growth, including work that is interesting and challenging, responsibility, and opportunity for achievement, recognition, and advancement. An insufficient amount of the satisfiers will prevent an employee from experiencing the positive satisfaction that accompanies psychological growth, but will not result in job dissatisfaction.

Two-factor theory is quite different from conventional theories of job attitudes that portray satisfaction and dissatisfaction as opposite poles of a single bipolar continuum with a neutral point (neither satisfied nor dissatisfied) in the center. In two-factor theory, there are two distinct continua, one for satisfaction and the other for dissatisfaction. The two incompatible conceptions of job attitudes are illustrated graphically in Figure 6–1. When two-factor theory was proposed, it generated a great deal of controversy and was vigorously attacked by proponents of the conventional attitude theory. The controversy was fueled by Herzberg's (1968) claim that the only way to motivate employees was to increase the satisfiers, an approach referred to as "job enrichment." In other words, according to Herzberg, both satisfaction and motivation are dependent on the job factors called satisfiers. Pay incentives, better supervision, and other programs were viewed as ineffective approaches for improving satisfaction and motivation.

Many studies were conducted to test two-factor theory. The results have been mixed. Studies that have employed the methods used in the original research by Herzberg, Mausner and Snyderman (1959) generally provide support for the theory, while studies using other research methods have usually failed to support the theory. In reviewing this research, King

FIGURE 6–1
Two Views of Job Attitudes

Conventional Bipolar Continuum:

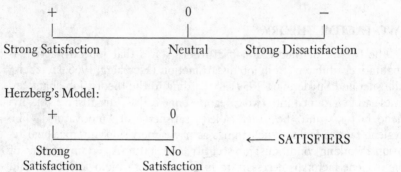

Herzberg's Model:

(1970) concluded that there have actually been several different versions of two-factor theory tested in previous studies, and none of the versions have been adequately validated. It is now generally accepted that, contrary to the extreme version of the theory, some job factors can cause either satisfaction or dissatisfaction. Moreover, it has been clearly demonstrated that employees can be motivated by approaches other than job enrichment. However, it is not yet possible either to accept or reject the hypothesis that satisfaction is qualitatively different from dissatisfaction (Lawler, 1973).

MEASUREMENT OF JOB ATTITUDES

Job attitudes can be measured in a variety of ways. Information about employee attitudes can be obtained by individual interviews, by a questionnaire survey, or during regular or special group meetings. The type of questions used to discover employee attitudes also varies. With an "open-ended question," employees are asked to describe in their own words their feelings about various aspects of the job. With a "fixed response question" the employees are asked to select one of several predetermined answers to a specific question. There are several different kinds of fixed-response questions and most of them have been developed for use in a questionnaire rather than in an interview. Nevertheless, it is possible to use fixed-response questions in an interview, and this is occasionally done in opinion surveys.

One kind of fixed-response question is based on the assumption that satisfaction and dissatisfaction are part of the same bipolar attitude continuum. This type of item is used in the *Minnesota Satisfaction Questionnaire* (Weiss, Dawis, England, and Lofquist, 1967). The short form of the MSQ is shown in Figure 6–2. General job satisfaction can be measured

FIGURE 6–2
Short Form of the Minnesota Satisfaction Questionnaire

Ask yourself: How **satisfied** am I with this aspect of my job?

Very Sat. means I am very satisfied with this aspect of my job.

Sat. means I am satisfied with this aspect of my job.

N means I can't decide whether I am satisfied or not with this aspect of my job.

Dissat. means I am dissatisfied with this aspect of my job.

Very Dissat. means I am very dissatisfied with this aspect of my job.

On my present job, this is how I feel about . . .	Very Dissat.	Dissat.	N	Sat.	Very Sat.
1. Being able to keep busy all the time	□	□	□	□	□
2. The chance to work alone on the job	□	□	□	□	□
3. The chance to do different things from time to time	□	□	□	□	□
4. The chance to be "somebody" in the community	□	□	□	□	□
5. The way my boss handles his men	□	□	□	□	□
6. The competence of my supervisor in making decisions	□	□	□	□	□
7. Being able to do things that don't go against my conscience	□	□	□	□	□
8. The way my job provides for steady employment	□	□	□	□	□
9. The chance to do things for other people	□	□	□	□	□
10. The chance to tell people what to do	□	□	□	□	□
11. The chance to do something that makes use of my abilities	□	□	□	□	□
12. The way company policies are put into practice	□	□	□	□	□
13. My pay and the amount of work I do	□	□	□	□	□
14. The chances for advancement on this job	□	□	□	□	□
15. The freedom to use my own judgment	□	□	□	□	□
16. The chance to try my own methods of doing the job	□	□	□	□	□
17. The working conditions	□	□	□	□	□
18. The way my co-workers get along with each other	□	□	□	□	□
19. The praise I get for doing a good job	□	□	□	□	□
20. The feeling of accomplishment I get from the job	□	□	□	□	□
	Very Dissat.	Dissat.	N	Sat.	Very Sat.

Source: D. J. Weiss, R. V. Dawis, G. W. England, & L. H. Lofquist, *Minnesota Studies in Vocational Rehabilitation: 22, Manual for the Minnesota Satisfaction Questionnaire.* Vocational Psychology Research, University of Minnesota, 1967 (© 1963).

by summing the scores for all 20 items. Certain subsets of item scores can be summed to obtain a measure of extrinsic satisfaction and a measure of intrinsic satisfaction. The long form of the MSQ has 100 items, and has been administered to a large variety of occupational groups. The scores obtained by each occupational group provide a set of norms against which the scores obtained by a similar group of employees can be compared.

Another job satisfaction scale using fixed-response items is the *Job Descriptive Index* (Smith, Kendall, and Hulin, 1969). The JDI has separate scales for satisfaction with pay, promotion, supervision, work, and people. Some examples of the items in these scales are shown in Figure 6–3.

Scale scores are obtained by summing the scores for the items in a given scale, and the overall satisfaction of an employee can also be computed. Like the MSQ, the JDI has been used with a large variety of employee samples, and norms are provided for employees according to their age, sex, education, income, and type of community.

A third type of fixed-response scale for job attitudes is based on the discrepancy theory of satisfaction. Each item has two questions, one for "should be" and one for "is now." Some items from Porter's (1961) Need Satisfaction Questionnaire are shown in Figure 6–4. An item in this scale is scored by subtracting the numerical value of the respondent's choice on the "is now" part from the numerical value of his choice on the "should be" part. The greater this difference, the more dissatisfied the respondent is with this aspect of the job. Overall job dissatisfaction can be measured by summing the scores on all of the items. Although not shown in Figure 6–4, the NSQ also contains questions regarding the importance of each aspect of the job to the respondent. These questions provide an opportunity to measure the strength of a need as opposed to need satisfaction.

As with fixed-response questions, a respondent's answers to open-ended questions can be coded to yield a measure of attitude strength. However, with open-ended questions the process of assigning a numerical score to represent the job satisfaction of a respondent is more difficult, subjective, and time consuming. On the other hand, open-ended questions provide more insight into the reasons why an employee likes or dislikes the job. Moreover, it is easier to detect misinterpretation of the question by the respondent should this occur. Open-ended questions can be used either in a questionnaire or in an interview. They are especially effective in an interview where the interviewer can probe the respondent to obtain more information about the respondent's attitudes. In a questionnaire, the advantages of both kinds of questions can be obtained by using a combination of fixed-response and open-ended items.

FIGURE 6–3
Sample Items from the Job Descriptive Index (each scale is presented on a separate page)

Think of your present work. What is it like most of the time? In the blank beside each word given below, write

Think of the pay you get now. How well does each of the following words describe your present pay? In the blank beside each word, put

Think of the opportunities for promotion that you have now. How well does each of the following words describe these? In the blank beside each word put

__Y__ for "Yes" if it describes your work
__N__ for "No" if it does NOT describe it
__?__ if you cannot decide

__Y__ if it describes your pay
__N__ if it does NOT describe it
__?__ if you cannot decide

__Y__ for "Yes" if it describes your opportunities for promotion
__N__ for "No" if it does NOT describe them
__?__ if you cannot decide

Work on Present Job

_____Routine
_____Satisfying
_____Good
_____On your feet

Present Pay

_____Income adequate for normal expenses
_____Insecure
_____Less than I deserve
_____Highly paid

Opportunities for Promotion

_____Promotion on ability
_____Dead-end job
_____Unfair promotion policy
_____Regular promotions

Think of the kind of supervision that you get on your job. How well does each of the following words describe this supervision? In the blank beside each word below, put

Think of the majority of the people that you work with now or the people you meet in connection with your work. How well does each of the following words describe these people? In the blank beside each word below, put

__Y__ if it describes the supervision you get on your job
__N__ if it does NOT describe it
__?__ if you cannot decide

__Y__ if it describes the people you work with
__N__ if it does NOT describe them
__?__ if you cannot decide

Supervision on Present Job

_____Impolite
_____Praises good work
_____Influential
_____Doesn't supervise enough

People on Your Present Job

_____Boring
_____Responsible
_____Intelligent
_____Talk too much

Note: The Job Descriptive Index is copyrighted by Bowling Green State University. The complete forms, scoring key, instructions, and norms can be obtained from Dr. Patricia C. Smith, Department of Psychology, Bowling Green State University, Bowling Green, Ohio 43403.

FIGURE 6–4
Examples of Items from the Need Satisfaction Questionnaire

INSTRUCTIONS: Circle the number on the scale that represents the amount of the characteristic being rated. Low numbers represent low or minimum amounts, and high numbers represent high or maximum amounts.

1. The opportunity for personal growth and development in my management position.

    a. HOW MUCH IS THERE NOW?
       (Minimum)   1   2   3   4   5   6   7   (Maximum)

    b. HOW MUCH SHOULD THERE BE?
       (Minimum)   1   2   3   4   5   6   7   (Maximum)

2. The feeling of security in my management position.

    a. HOW MUCH IS THERE NOW?
       (Minimum)   1   2   3   4   5   6   7   (Maximum)

    b. HOW MUCH SHOULD THERE BE?
       (Minimum)   1   2   3   4   5   6   7   (Maximum)

Source: L. W. Porter, "A Study of Perceived Need Satisfaction in Bottom and Middle Management Jobs, *Journal of Applied Psychology*, 45 (1961), p. 3.

DETERMINANTS OF JOB ATTITUDES

The research evidence suggests that the best way to explain how job attitudes are determined is by means of an "interaction model." That is, a person's job satisfaction depends jointly on the characteristics of the job situation and the characteristics of the person. Of the three satisfaction theories described earlier, the one most compatible with an interaction model is probably discrepancy theory. A person's perception of what "should be" in a job will be determined by employee characteristics and situational variables, while perception of what "is now" in a job will be determined mostly by actual job conditions. An example of how discrepancy theory can be extended to include these satisfaction determinants is shown in Figure 6–5.

Three kinds of employee characteristics that affect "should be" perceptions are needs, values, and personality traits. Needs are important because an employee will desire more of any job factor that is instrumental in fulfilling currently activated needs. Once enough of a job factor (e.g., recognition) is present in the job to fill needs to which it is relevant (e.g., esteem), additional amounts of the job factor will not be desired by the employee and will not increase job satisfaction. Values are the relatively stable beliefs of a person about what is "right" and "wrong" be-

FIGURE 6–5
A Hypothetical Model of Job Satisfaction Determinants

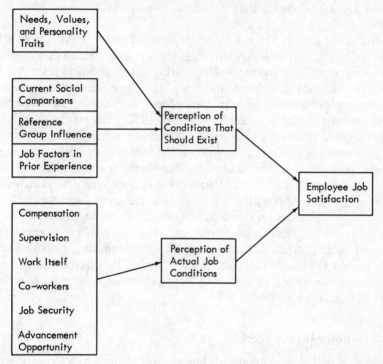

havior and what are desirable and undesirable life goals. Values influence an employee's preferences for certain kinds of occupations and job content. Finally, personality traits such as self-esteem modify a person's job aspirations and preferences. Self-esteem is the extent to which a person likes and values himself and perceives himself to be a competent, adequate human being. An employee with high self-esteem will prefer a job that is important, or one that provides the opportunity for advancement and personal success. An employee with low self-esteem will prefer a low prestige job that is consistent with his unfavorable self-image and is not very demanding (Korman, 1970).

Three aspects of the job situation that affect "should be" perceptions are social comparisons with other employees, previous job characteristics, and reference groups. The social comparison process was described earlier in the section on equity theory. An employee will compare the beneficial outcomes received from his job to the outcomes received by other employees with similar jobs, after taking into account any differences between his "inputs" and those of the comparison persons. An employee's perception of what "should be" in the job is also influenced by his perception of "what was" in the past. Previous conditions are important in that they set a minimum expectation for the present. Nobody wants to receive lower pay or less benefits than were received earlier in the same job or in a previous job.

Reference groups are a third situational influence on an employee's "should be" perceptions. A reference group is one to which a person looks for guidance in interpreting and evaluating personal experiences. A person's expectations and aspirations for a job will be influenced by the reference group's conception of what kind of job and working conditions are appropriate for that individual (Korman, 1971). An employee will be more satisfied if his job is endorsed by the reference group than if it is not. A good example of a reference group is the influence of a labor union on worker perceptions of a fair and reasonable increase in pay and benefits.

In the remainder of this section we will examine the determinants of employee satisfaction with job content, compensation, and supervision. A majority of studies on the determinants of job attitudes have focused on either the influence of job characteristics or the influence of employee characteristics, rather than examining the joint influence of both kinds of variables. We will emphasize the few studies that have included employee characteristics as well as job characteristics to explain how job satisfaction is determined.

Satisfaction with the Work

Studies on the importance of different job characteristics consistently find that the nature of the work itself is a major determinant of job satisfaction. Several recent studies have attempted to identify the major dimensions of job content and to see how employee satisfaction is jointly determined by job content and individual traits (Hackman and Lawler, 1971; Hackman and Oldham, 1975; Hulin and Blood, 1968; Turner and Lawrence, 1965; Wanous, 1974). The most elaborate study of this type was conducted by Hackman and Oldham (1975). They administered a questionnaire called the Job Diagnostic Survey to several hundred employees working in 62 different jobs. The following five "core dimensions" were identified (pp. 161–62):

> *Skill Variety.* The degree to which a job requires a variety of different activities in carrying out the work, which involve the use of a number of different skills and talents of the employee.
>
> *Task Identity.* The degree to which the job requires completion of a "whole" and identifiable piece of work—that is, doing a job from beginning to end with a visible outcome.
>
> *Task Significance.* The degree to which the job has a substantial impact on the lives or work of other people—whether in the immediate organization or in the external environment.

Autonomy. The degree to which the job provides substantial freedom, independence, and discretion to the employee in scheduling the work and in determining the procedures to be used in carrying it out.

Feedback from the Job Itself. The degree to which carrying out the work activities required by the job results in the employee obtaining direct and clear information about the effectiveness of his or her performance.

Each of these core dimensions involves some aspects of the job content that can affect an employee's work satisfaction (Hackman and Oldham, 1975). The greater the variety of activities performed by an employee, the less boring the job will be. The most boring jobs are those in which the same simple actions must be repeated every few minutes, hundreds of times each day. The more a job involves the use of skills and talents relevant to the employee's self-identity, the more the employee can feel that he is performing meaningful work rather than simply "putting in time."

Task identity and task significance also affect the experienced meaningfulness of the work. An employee who solders three connections on an electrical panel as it passes by on the assembly line is not likely to find the work very meaningful. The employee is not really "making" a television set, or even a significant component of a television set. On the other hand, an employee who assembles the entire finished product, or who makes an important component of the finished product, will experience a sense of completion and will probably perceive the work to be meaningful.

The amount of autonomy an employee has in the job and the degree to which the work provides objective performance feedback will determine how much opportunity there is for satisfaction of higher order needs such as achievement and independence. When an employee has no control over work procedures or work pace, as on most mechanically-paced assembly lines, there is little opportunity to experience the intrinsic satisfaction of successfully accomplishing a challenging task. On the other hand, in a job where the employee has substantial autonomy, the task is challenging, and performance feedback is available, there is a good opportunity for fulfillment of achievement needs. A job in which an employee can set his own work pace, can vary the pace and rest when he wants, and can do the job in the way he thinks it should be done, within the limits imposed by work schedules and performance standards, will also allow fulfillment of independence needs.

How an employee reacts to the job content will depend on the employee's needs as well as the nature of the work. Research indicates that the relationship between the core dimensions and job satisfaction is strongest for employees who desire responsibility, meaningful work, self-direction, performance feedback, and the opportunity for achievement (Hackman and Lawler, 1971; Hackman and Oldham, 1975; Wanous, 1974). In other words, employees with strong, higher order needs will be more satisfied if they have jobs that are high on the core dimensions. Employees with weak, high order needs will not be very concerned whether their job is high or low on the core dimensions. Their job satisfaction is more dependent on other job characteristics such as pay, security, and co-worker relations.

The effect of job content on employees' attitudes will depend on their values as well as their needs. Of course, values and needs are related to each other, since peoples' values tend to reflect their needs. One kind of value that has been found to affect job satisfaction is called the "work-ethic" value. Someone with a strong work-ethic value typically believes that work makes you a better person, that a person's worth is indicated by how well the job is performed, and that success in a respectable occu-pation is an important objective in life (Hulin and Blood, 1968). The influence of work-ethic values and job content on employee satisfaction has been investigated in a study by Wanous (1974). He found that em-ployees with strong work-ethic values responded more favorably to jobs high in task identity, variety, and autonomy than to jobs that were low on these three core dimensions. For employees with weak work-ethic values, job satisfaction was not significantly affected by the core dimensions.

Satisfaction with Compensation

Several studies have found that pay is the job characteristic most likely to be a source of employee dissatisfaction (see Lawler, 1971, p. 218). For example, in a study by Porter (1961), 80 percent of a sample of man-agers were dissatisfied with their pay. A major cause of pay dissatisfaction is perceived inequity. As noted earlier in the section on equity theory, employees judge their pay by making social comparisons. The "going rate" for employees in the same occupation is one influence on a person's belief about what salary he should be paid. The higher the level of educa-tion and professionalism, the more likely it is that an employee will make social comparisons with persons outside the immediate organization but in the same profession (Goodman, 1974). If an organization pays less than the "going rate" in the community for a given type of job, employees will probably be dissatisfied with their pay.

An employee will also compare his salary to that of co-workers in the same organization. In the case of managers, social comparisons will prob-ably be made with subordinates as well as with peers. Managers will expect their pay to reflect the difference in responsibility, experience, and ability that they perceive to exist between themselves and subordinates. The higher a person is in the authority hierarchy and the more responsibility, education, skill, and seniority a person has, the more pay he or she will expect to receive.

Managers and certain categories of nonsupervisory employees such as sales personnel usually prefer their pay to reflect how well they perform on the job (Lawler, 1971). If pay is not based on performance, high performing employees will be dissatisfied that they are earning the same or less than low performers. Nevertheless, an incentive program to reward superior performance will not necessarily result in higher pay satisfaction. As was noted in Chapter 5, where there is no objective measure of performance, most employees tend to overestimate their performance. In this situation, which is quite common, employees are likely to feel that they are not paid as much as their performance justifies (Meyer, 1975).

In addition to equity considerations, pay satisfaction will be affected by an employee's needs and values. If an employee's pay is sufficient to provide for his own and his family's existence needs, he will be more satisfied than if his pay is less than necessary to insure an adequate standard of living (Goodman, 1974). Of course, as an employee's income gradually increases, his standard of living rises, and past "luxuries" become present "necessities." Thus higher wages are likely to result in only a temporary improvement in satisfaction. Even if the standard of living to which an employee aspires does not increase, inflation is likely to erode his or her satisfaction with any given level of pay. The more dependent employees are on their pay to satisfy existence needs, the more their pay satisfaction will be affected by the cost of living. Hulin (1966) found that workers in communities with a high cost of living were not as satisfied as workers who earned the same salary but lived in communities where the cost of living was lower.   *objectively (vs relatively)*

Pay is also a means of fulfilling certain security needs. A person who worries about economic disaster will be less satisfied with a given level of pay than a person who does not feel insecure, and much more pay will be needed to satisfy him. Finally, an employee's attitude toward his pay will reflect his underlying values regarding money and materialism. Pay will be a more important determinant of job satisfaction for people who value money and material possessions than for people who do not.

Satisfaction with Supervision

The behavior of the immediate supervisor is another important determinant of an employee's job satisfaction. However, the reaction of employees to their supervisor will usually depend on characteristics of the employees as well as on characteristics of the supervisor. As is pointed out in Chapter 8, there is seldom any simple and consistent relationship between leader characteristics and subordinate satisfaction. The only leader behavior that has a predictable effect on subordinate satisfaction with the leader is *consideration*. The results from most studies indicate that employees are more satisfied with leaders who are considerate and supportive than with leaders who are either indifferent or hostile toward subordinates (see review by Yukl, 1971). This finding is not particularly surprising; people who are warm and considerate are usually better liked, whether they are leaders or not. Even so, it should be noted that individuals differ somewhat in their preference for leader consideration (Hunt and Liebscher, 1973; Kavanagh, 1975). Having a leader who is considerate and supportive is likely to be more important for employees with low self-esteem or very unpleasant and frustrating jobs (House, 1971; House and Mitchell, 1974).

The effects of a supervisor's task-oriented behavior on subordinate satisfaction is less predictable. In some studies, employees have been more satisfied with leaders who engage in a great deal of task-oriented behavior, while other studies indicate greater satisfaction with leaders who are not very task-oriented (see reviews by Kerr et al., 1974; Yukl, 1971). These inconsistent results probably reflect differences among studies with regard to employee preferences for task-oriented leadership. In a job situation where subordinate work roles are quite ambiguous, the subordinates will prefer a leader who clarifies their role requirements. That is, if subordinates are not capable of figuring out how to perform the work by themselves, they will prefer a leader who provides adequate guidance and instruction. On the other hand, where work roles are clearly defined and the subordinates are highly competent to perform without frequent guidance and instruction, a leader who does not supervise closely will be preferred (House, 1971; House and Mitchell, 1974). Finally, if subordinates are not very motivated and they find the work to be unpleasant, they will prefer a leader who does not pressure them to maintain a high level of performance.

The amount of participation allowed employees also affects their satisfaction with the supervisor, although once again the relationship is complex. Subordinate preferences for participation in decision making will vary, depending on the type of decision, the personality and needs of the subordinates, and the extent to which they trust their leader (Heller, 1971; Kavanagh, 1975; Yukl, 1971). In a study by Morse (1953), workers were most satisfied when the amount of participation was equal to the desired amount, regardless of how much was desired. However, researchers have only begun to identify what specific individual traits and situational variables shape an employee's preferences for participative supervision.

CONSEQUENCES OF JOB SATISFACTION AND DISSATISFACTION

Some behavioral scientists have studied job satisfaction because they believe that the quality of work experience has important implications for a person's mental health and psychological adjustment (e.g., Kornhauser, 1965). A second reason for studying job satisfaction is that it may have direct or indirect consequences for organizational effectiveness. Most of the research on job attitudes has reflected a greater concern for organizational effectiveness than for employee welfare. Numerous studies have been conducted to determine whether job attitudes affect productivity, absenteeism, turnover, and other aspects of employee behavior relevant to organizational effectiveness.

Satisfaction and Performance

In the early research on job attitudes, it was commonly assumed that employees who were satisfied would be more motivated and thus more productive than dissatisfied employees. If true, this assumption would imply that an organization could improve productivity by providing employees with pleasant working conditions, a fair salary, considerate supervisors, and sufficient amounts of other kinds of rewarding outcomes. The early conception of the causal relationship between satisfaction and performance is illustrated in Figure 6–6.

FIGURE 6–6
Early Conception of the Relationship between Satisfaction and Performance

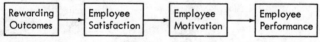

Reviews of the research literature by Brayfield and Crockett (1955) and by Vroom (1964) found that satisfaction and performance were not closely related to each other in any simple fashion. In a majority of studies, there was a positive correlation, but the size of the correlation was usually quite small. Thus the assumption that job satisfaction leads to superior performance was discredited. Building on the analyses and recommendations made by Brayfield and Crockett, more complex and sophisticated models have been developed to explain how satisfaction and performance are related.

The best example of the newer models is the one proposed by Lawler and Porter (1967). According to their model, performance causes satisfaction rather than the other way around. However, the causal connection only occurs when employees perceive that intrinsic and extrinsic rewards are associated with superior performance. Intrinsic rewards result from superior performance in those situations where an employee can assume credit for successfully accomplishing a challenging task that requires the use of important skills. Extrinsic rewards are administered by the organization and include such things as pay, promotion, status symbols, and formal recognition. When the organization makes extrinsic rewards contingent on performance, employees with superior performance will receive more rewards than employees with average or inferior performance. As long as these extrinsic rewards are perceived to be equitable, the superior performers will also tend to be more satisfied. In other words, when performance leads to intrinsic and extrinsic rewards, and these lead in turn to higher job satisfaction, performance and satisfaction will be positively correlated with each other. However, when performance does not lead to intrinsic and extrinsic rewards, performance and satisfaction will not be correlated positively with each other. Extrinsic rewards are usually less closely related to performance than intrinsic rewards, because extrinsic rewards are administered by the organization and intrinsic rewards are "self-administered."

The causal relationships in the Lawler and Porter model are illustrated in Figure 6–7. The results of research conducted to test the Lawler-Porter model have not been consistent. Several studies have supported the model (Cherrington et al., 1971; Greene, 1973; Koppelman, 1975; Lawler and

FIGURE 6–7
Lawler-Porter Model of the Relation between Satisfaction and Performance

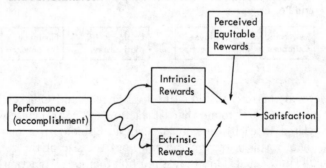

Source: E. E. Lawler and L. W. Porter, "The Effect of Performance on Satisfaction," *Industrial Relations*, 7 (1967), p. 23.

Porter, 1967; Siegel and Bowen, 1971), but other studies have failed to find supporting evidence or have yielded mixed results (Kesselman et al., 1974; Pritchard, 1973; Sheridan and Slocum, 1975; Wanous, 1974; Wood, 1974). The findings in some of these studies suggest that the model may need to be further refined and elaborated.

Dissatisfaction and Withdrawal

The literature reviews mentioned earlier (Brayfield and Crockett, 1955; Vroom, 1964) found a consistent relationship between dissatisfaction and withdrawal in the form of turnover and absenteeism. Employees who are dissatisfied with their jobs are more likely than satisfied employees to stay away from work or resign. Other forms of withdrawal behavior such as drinking and taking drugs have received less attention in the research literature, but it is likely that they are also associated to some extent with job dissatisfaction.

Withdrawal behavior by employees usually has adverse consequences for the organization. Absenteeism disrupts normal operations, causes delays, increases expenses for "sick pay," and necessitates the employment of extra personnel to substitute for employees who don't show up for work. Turnover also disrupts normal operations, and the expense of selecting and training replacements is often very substantial.

Dissatisfaction and Aggression

The frustration that accompanies job dissatisfaction can lead to aggressive behavior rather than withdrawal. Aggression may take the form of sabotage, deliberate errors, and militant union activities such as wildcat strikes, slowdowns, and excessive grievances. Aggression may also be displaced to other parties, such as co-workers or an employee's family. Thus, there may be a lot of bickering and fighting among employees when they are very frustrated. When aggressive acts interfere with operations, reduce the quality of production, and inhibit cooperation and teamwork, they can prove costly to the organization. Dissatisfaction with inadequate compensation or boring work can also contribute to the incidence of employee theft. Stealing of money, merchandise, and supplies by employees has been a serious problem in some organizations.

IMPROVING EMPLOYEE SATISFACTION

When an employee or a group of employees are dissatisfied, the first step for improving satisfaction should be to determine the reasons for the dissatisfaction. There may be a variety of causes, such as poor supervision, poor working conditions, lack of job security, inequitable compensation, lack of opportunity for advancement, interpersonal conflict among co-workers, or lack of opportunity to fulfill higher order needs. For employees who desire to perform their jobs well, dissatisfaction may be due to unnecessary restrictions and delays ("red tape"), inadequate supplies, or faulty equipment. In the case of managers, dissatisfaction may result from insufficient authority to deal with their problems and carry out their responsibilities.

It is not always easy to discover the cause of employee dissatisfaction. Employees may complain or file grievances about one aspect of their job, when in fact it is really something else that bothers them. For example, employees may complain about working conditions or the food in the cafeteria when the problem is actually inconsiderate supervision. Employees may be reluctant to reveal their real complaints if they fear retaliation for being critical. When dissatisfaction is fairly widespread among employees, anonymous questionnaires are a good approach for discovering the reasons, although even this approach may not be successful if employees are very suspicious.

An approach called "nondirective counseling" is sometimes effective for handling an individual employee who is upset about something. Here it is important to find out whether the employee is dissatisfied with some aspect of the job or has a personal problem not directly related to the job. The supervisor should initially try to get the employee to talk about what is bothering him or her. The supervisor should be careful to avoid making a diagnosis or suggesting solutions at this time, since the employee may perceive these as a criticism. Instead, the supervisor should encourage the employee to diagnose the problem and suggest some solutions. This nondirective approach avoids making the employee defensive, allows him to reduce tension by talking about his problems, and enhances his self-esteem by allowing him to develop his own remedies (Maier, 1973). However, if the problem involves other employees or the solution requires significant job changes, the supervisor may need to take a more active role in planning how to deal with the problem after the employee has had a chance to make the initial diagnosis. Finally, it is important to remember that there are certain kinds of psychological problems that supervisors are not trained to handle. When this is the case, the employee should be referred to a professional counselor.

Remedies for Dissatisfaction

Once the source of dissatisfaction has been determined, a variety of approaches can be used to deal with the problem. One approach is to make changes in working conditions, supervision, compensation, or job design, depending on the job factor responsible for employee dissatisfaction. A second approach is to transfer employees to other jobs to achieve a better match between employee characteristics and job characteristics. Personnel may also be reassigned to form more compatible work groups. Obviously, transferring employees is only feasible in certain limited cases.

A third approach involves an attempt to change the perception or expectations of dissatisfied employees. This approach is appropriate when employees have misconceptions based on inadequate or incorrect information. For example, if employees are worried due to false rumors about layoffs, they can be assured that there is no danger. Of course, employees are not likely to believe these assurances unless they trust top management.

Precautionary Actions

Whenever possible, precautions should be taken to avoid unnecessary job dissatisfaction rather than waiting until it occurs to take action. A well-run salary administration program will help to avoid the worst types of inequity problems. Systematic selection and training programs will help to ensure a close match between job requirements and employee characteristics (see Chapters 11–14). Proper socialization and orientation are especially important when new employees are recruited and hired. Research has shown that providing accurate information about the job and the organization to applicants will greatly reduce subsequent dissatisfaction and turnover (Ilgen and Seely, 1974; Wanous, 1973; Weitz, 1956). Applicants who are incompatible with the organization are less likely to join it when they are given accurate information, and new members will have more realistic expectations. Unfortunately, many organizations take the opposite approach during recruiting. Exaggerated promises are made, and disadvantages are ignored, leading to eventual employee disappointment and dissatisfaction when the truth is discovered.

SUMMARY

Job satisfaction is the way an employee feels about his/her job. Employee satisfaction is affected by several aspects of the job, including pay, working conditions, supervision, co-workers, job content, job security, and opportunity for advancement. Job attitudes are determined jointly by job characteristics and employee characteristics. What an employee wants in a job will depend on the individual's needs, values, and personality traits. Whether an employee will perceive current job conditions to be satisfactory will also depend on social comparisons, previous job conditions, and reference group influences.

Major theories of job satisfaction include discrepancy theory, equity theory, and two-factor theory. Each of these theories is narrowly focused, and none of them have been conclusively supported in research studies.

Job attitudes can be measured in a variety of ways. The most commonly used methods are questionnaires and interviews. Respondents can be asked either open-ended or fixed-response questions. Each type of method and question format has certain advantages and disadvantages.

The relationship between satisfaction and performance is complex and indirect. Early conceptions that satisfied employees will be more productive have been replaced by more sophisticated models which postulate that performance leads to satisfaction under certain conditions but not under other conditions. Employee dissatisfaction has been found in most studies to result in aggression or withdrawal behavior.

The first step in dealing with employee dissatisfaction is to discover the reasons for it. Remedial steps include changing job conditions, transferring employees to more compatible jobs, and altering expectations and perceptions. A number of precautionary actions are recommended to avoid unnecessary employee dissatisfaction.

REVIEW AND DISCUSSION QUESTIONS

1. Define or explain each of the following key terms: job satisfaction, composite attitude, equity, input, outcome, comparison person, social comparison process, hygiene factor, satisfier, open-ended question, fixed-response question, reference group, core dimensions, work-ethic value, intrinsic rewards, extrinsic rewards, nondirective counseling.
2. Explain discrepancy theory.
3. Under what conditions is an employee likely to perceive pay or some other aspect of the job to be inequitable?
4. What are the different ways an employee can react to inequity?
5. What are the implications of equity theory for employee performance?
6. Explain Herzberg's two-factor theory. How does it differ from traditional views of job attitudes?
7. In what different ways can employee attitudes be measured? What three job satisfaction questionnaires were described in this chapter?
8. What are some determinants of employee satisfaction with compensation? With the supervisor? With the work itself?
9. How are satisfaction and performance related according to Lawler and Porter?
10. What are some typical consequences of employee dissatisfaction?
11. How can an organization improve employee job satisfaction?

REFERENCES

Adams, J. S. Toward an understanding of inequity. *Journal of Abnormal and Social Psychology*, 1963, 67, 422–436.

Brayfield, A. H., & Crockett, W. H. Employee attitudes and employee performance. *Psychological Bulletin*, 1955, 52, 396–424.

Cherrington, D. L., Reitz, H. J., & Scott, W. E., Jr. Effects of reward and contingent reinforcement on satisfaction and task performance. *Journal of Applied Psychology*, 1971, 55, 531–536.

Goodman, P. S. An examination of referents used in the evaluation of pay. *Organizational Behavior and Human Performance*, 1974, 12, 170–195.

Goodman, P. S., & Friedman, A. An examination of Adam's theory of inequity. *Administrative Science Quarterly*, 1971, 16, 271–288.

Greene, C. N. Causal connections among manager's merit pay, job satisfaction, and performance. *Journal of Applied Psychology*, 1973, 58, 95–100.

Hackman, J. R., & Lawler, E. E., III Employee reactions to job characteristics. *Journal of Applied Psychology*, 1971, 55, 259–286.

Hackman, J. R., & Oldham, G. R. Development of the job diagnostic survey. *Journal of Applied Psychology*, 1975, 60, 159–170.

Heller, F. *Managerial decision-making.* London: Tavistock, 1971.

Herzberg, F. *Work and the nature of man.* Cleveland: World Press, 1966.

Herzberg, F. One more time: How do you motivate employees? *Harvard Business Review,* 1968, *46* (January–February), 53–62.

Herzberg, F., Mausner, B., & Snyderman, B. B. *The motivation to work.* New York: Wiley, 1959.

House, R. J. A path-goal theory of leader effectiveness. *Administrative Science Quarterly,* 1971, *16*, 321–339.

House, R. J., & Mitchell, T. R. Path-goal theory of leadership. *Contemporary Business,* 1974, *3* (Fall), 81–98.

Hulin, C. L. The effects of community characteristics on measures of job satisfaction. *Journal of Applied Psychology,* 1966, *50*, 185–192.

Hulin, C. L., & Blood, M. R. Job enlargement, individual differences, and worker responses. *Psychological Bulletin,* 1968, *69*, 41–55.

Hunt, J. G., & Liebscher, V. K. Leadership preference, leadership behavior, and employee satisfaction. *Organizational Behavior and Human Performance,* 1973, *9*, 59–77.

Ilgen, D. R., & Seely, W. Realistic expectations as an aid in reducing voluntary resignations. *Journal of Applied Psychology,* 1974, *59*, 452–455.

Kavanagh, M. J. Expected supervisory behavior, interpersonal trust, and environmental preferences: Some relationships based on a dyadic model of leadership. *Organizational Behavior and Human Performance,* 1975, *13*, 17–30.

Kerr, S., Schriesheim, C. A., Murphy, C. J., & Stogdill, R. M. Toward a contingency theory of leadership based on the consideration and initiating structure literature. *Organizational Behavior and Human Performance,* 1974, *12*, 62–82.

Kesselman, G. A., Wood, M. T., & Hagen, E. L. Relationship between performance and satisfaction under contingent and non-contingent reward systems. *Journal of Applied Psychology,* 1974, *59*, 374–376.

King, N. A clarification and evaluation of the two-factor theory of job satisfaction. *Psychological Bulletin,* 1970, *74*, 18–31.

Koppelman, R. E. Organizational control system responsiveness and work motivation. *Proceedings of the Academy of Management National Meetings,* 1975, 125–127.

Korman, A. K. Toward a hypothesis of work behavior. *Journal of Applied Psychology,* 1970, *54*, 31–41.

Korman, A. K. *Industrial and organizational psychology.* Englewood Cliffs, N.J.: Prentice-Hall, 1971.

Kornhauser, A. *Mental health of the industrial worker.* New York: Wiley, 1965.

Lawler, E. E., III. *Pay and oragnizational effectiveness.* New York: McGraw-Hill, 1971.

Lawler, E. E., III. *Motivation in work organizations.* Monterey, Calif.: Brooks/Cole, 1973.

Lawler, E. E., III, & Porter, L. W.   The effect of performance on job satisfaction. *Industrial Relations,* 1967, 7, 20–28.

Locke, E. A.   What is job satisfaction? *Organizational Behavior and Human Performance,* 1969, 4, 309–336.

Maier, N. R. F.   *Psychology in industrial organizations.* Boston: Houghton-Mifflin, 1973.

Meyer, H.   The pay-for-performance dilemma. *Organizational Dynamics,* 1975, 3 (Winter), 39–50.

Morse, N.   *Satisfaction in the white collar job.* Ann Arbor: University of Michigan, Institute for Social Research, 1953.

Porter, L. W.   A study of perceived need satisfaction in bottom and middle management jobs. *Journal of Applied Psychology,* 1961, 45, 1–10.

Pritchard, R. D.   Effects of varying performance-pay instrumentalities on the relationship between performance and satisfaction. *Journal of Applied Psychology,* 1973, 58, 122–125.

Sheridan, J. E., & Slocum, J. W., Jr.   The direction of the causal relationship between job satisfaction and work performance. *Organizational Behavior and Human Performance,* 1975, 14, 159–172.

Siegel, J. P., & Bowen, D.   Satisfaction and performance: Causal relationships and moderating effects. *Journals of Vocational Behavior,* 1971, 1, 263–269.

Smith, P. C., Kendall, L. M., & Hulin, C. L.   *The measurement of satisfaction in work and retirement.* Chicago: Rand-McNally, 1969.

Turner, A. N., & Lawrence, P. R.   *Industrial jobs and the worker: An investigation of response to task attributes.* Boston: Division of Research, Harvard Business School, 1965.

Vroom, V. H.   *Work and motivation.* New York: Wiley, 1964.

Wanous, J. P.   Effects of a realistic job preview on job acceptance, job attitudes, and job survival. *Journal of Applied Psychology,* 1973, 58, 327–332.

Wanous, J. P.   Individual differences and reactions to job characteristics. *Journal of Applied Psychology,* 1974, 59, 616–622.

Wanous, J. P.   A causal-correlational analysis of the job satisfaction and performance relationship. *Journal of Applied Psychology,* 1974, 59, 139–144.

Wanous, J. P., & Lawler, E. E., III.   Measurement and meaning of job satisfaction. *Journal of Applied Psychology,* 1972, 56, 95–105.

Weiss, D. J., Dawis, R. V., England, G. W., & Lofquist, L. H.   *Manual for the Minnesota satisfaction questionnaire; Minnesota studies in vocational rehabilitation.* Vocational Psychology Research, University of Minnesota, 1967.

Weitz, J.   Job expectancy and survival. *Journal of Applied Psychology,* 1956, 40, 245–247.

Wood, D. A.   Effects of worker orientation differences on job attitude correlates. *Journal of Applied Psychology,* 1974, 59, 54–60.

Yukl, G. A.   Toward a behavioral theory of leadership. *Organizational Behavior and Human Performance,* 1971, 6, 414–440.

7

GROUP PROCESSES IN ORGANIZATIONS

INDIVIDUAL behavior in organizations is profoundly influenced by groups. In this chapter we will attempt to provide a general understanding of group processes. The reasons why informal groups emerge and coexist with formal groups will be examined. The ways that groups can influence their members and the consequences for group performance will be described. We will also examine the processes of decision making and role differentiation in groups. Finally, we will review some practical implications for improving the effectiveness of groups.

THE NATURE OF GROUPS IN ORGANIZATIONS

A group is a collection of people who interact with each other regularly over a period of time and perceive themselves to be mutually dependent with respect to the attainment of one or more common goals. A collection of strangers on a bus or in an elevator is not a group. However, if a collection of strangers were stranded for several days in a situation where they must cooperate in order to survive and be rescued, the properties of a group would rapidly develop. Once the existence of a common goal was recognized, procedures for attaining the goal would be formulated, specialized task roles for each person would be determined, norms would develop to regulate behavior, and one or more leaders would emerge.

Formal and Informal Groups

"Formal groups" exist in all organizations. A formal group is a legitimate subunit of the organization that has been established by the organization's charter or by managerial decree. Work crews, committees, small departments, and project teams are all examples of a formal group. In formal groups, the goals, rules, membership, and selection of a leader are usually specified by the parent organization. Although a formal group must operate within these organizational constraints, the "formal leader" is usually allowed considerable discretion over task procedures, job assignments, and the allocation of organizational rewards.

"Informal groups" can also be found in all organizations. These groups develop apart from the officially prescribed plan of the organization, and they exist as relatively autonomous subcultures within the organization. There are informal groups composed of managers as well as informal groups composed of nonsupervisory employees (Burns, 1955). An informal group usually forms when people work in close proximity to each other or interact frequently in their jobs. Consequently, the membership of an informal group often coincides with the membership of a formal work group. However, informal groups tend to be quite small, and in a large formal group, there are likely to be several small informal "cliques." These cliques are usually composed of persons who have the same type of job or have similar interests and backgrounds. Informal groups may also develop among employees who are not members of the same formal group if they work in the same location or interact frequently during lunch or after work.

The Importance of Informal Groups

Informal groups satisfy a variety of employee needs. Membership in an informal group provides an opportunity to satisfy social needs such as friendship, affection, and nurturance. Security needs are served when informal groups restrain harmful competition among employees and help them to join together in resisting unpopular changes or pressure for increased performance. Informal groups also facilitate cooperation among employees in dealing with problems in their jobs. For example, employees may agree to provide help to anyone in their group who gets behind in his work or needs to leave early.

One especially important function of informal groups is the regulation of social and task behavior. Although some norms for social conduct are provided by the formal organization and by the external culture, there is a need for elaboration of these norms within the job situation. Informal groups provide guidelines about what behavior is acceptable, such as the "right" way to dress, the "in" slang words and expressions. Informal groups also provide elaboration of formal task rules and procedures when these are too general or ambiguous to provide adequate guidance for employees. The informal procedures and norms that develop are not necessarily compatible with the rules and goals of the formal organization.

The importance of informal groups as a source of influence over employee behavior and performance was demonstrated in the 1930s by the Hawthorne studies (Roethlisberger and Dickson, 1939). In one of these studies ("Bank wiring room"), a group of men who were wiring and soldering telephone panels was observed over a period of several months. These employees had informal norms about the acceptable production rate and other aspects of behavior on the job. The proper rate of production according to the informal norm was two panels per day, and the employees paced themselves to finish the second panel just as the work period ended. Anyone who tried to deviate from group norms received ridicule or minor physical punishment from other group members. The consequences of the informal group for the organization were falsified reports and a serious restriction of production, despite the existence of a pay incentive plan.

Social Influence in Groups

It is obvious from the preceding example that groups can have a substantial influence over their members. In order to gain a better understanding of this influence, it is useful to distinguish between influence over a person's public behavior and influence over a person's private attitudes and beliefs.

Groups can influence member behavior directly by means of social pressure. Behavior that conforms to group norms is referred to as "compliance," and it may or may not be discrepant with the person's private attitudes. It is difficult to tell if a group has changed a person's private attitudes as well as his behavior. A study by Coch and French (1948) provides a good example of compliance without private acceptance of the group norm. A new girl began working with a group of clothes pressers who were each working at approximately the same rate. As she learned the job, her production increased and she soon exceeded the production norm set by the group. The other workers began to exert social pressure, and her performance dropped back to the group norm. After a couple of weeks, the group was broken up, and the workers were sent to separate locations. At this time the girl's production abruptly doubled, and it stayed at this higher level during the remainder of the study.

The reason for compliance with group norms is usually fear of punishment or rejection by the group. As we saw in the Bank Wiring Room study, groups have a variety of tactics for insuring compliance. These tactics include: teasing, sarcasm, ridicule, threats, violence, destruction of personal property, and the "silent treatment." It is an unusual person who is able to resist complying in the face of this social pressure. Studies of employees who produce more than the group norm (rate busters) reveal that the few people who do not conform are unconcerned about acceptance by the group. Instead, they are strongly motivated by their internal values or by the desire to earn more incentive pay.

Groups can also influence a person's attitudes and beliefs. When members of a group are together frequently and they depend upon each other to help interpret their common experiences, they tend to develop the same attitudes and beliefs. Moreover, when a person belongs to a group and strongly identifies with it, the individual tends to accept the norms and values of this "reference group." A good example of the way a person's attitudes are influenced by the job role and reference group can be found in a study by Lieberman (1956). He found that the attitudes of workers who were promoted to foreman gradually became more promanagement, whereas the attitudes of workers who became union stewards gradually became more prounion. When a recession caused some of the foremen to become regular workers again, there was a parallel reversal in attitudes (i.e., they became less promanagement). An attitude reversal was also found among union stewards who were not reelected to another term.

By influencing member attitudes and beliefs, groups indirectly influence member behavior, since a person's behavior tends to be consistent with his attitudes unless there is considerable social pressure to act differently. Thus groups have two potential sources of influence over member behavior: direct influence from social pressure and indirect influence from attitude induction.

Group Cohesiveness and Performance

A major determinant of the amount of influence a group has over its members is group "cohesiveness." The term cohesiveness refers to the solidarity among group members and their attraction toward membership in the group. In a very cohesive group there is a high degree of mutual friendship and esteem, and the group provides satisfaction of its members' social needs. Since the members are very concerned about group acceptance, cohesive groups are able to exert greater social pressure for member compliance than noncohesive groups. Moreover, a cohesive group is more likely to serve as a reference group for its members.

Even though cohesive groups are more likely to develop performance norms and enforce compliance with them, the level of these norms depends to a large extent on the relationship between the group and the parent organization. In a study of 228 industrial work groups, Seashore (1954) found that the performance of noncohesive groups was *lower* than the performance of those cohesive groups that perceived management to be supportive and dependable. Conversely, the performance of noncohesive groups was *higher* than the performance to those cohesive groups whose members felt insecure in their relation to the company.

Therefore it is obvious that cohesiveness determines the amount but not the direction of group influence. Cohesive groups can be equally effective in either encouraging or restricting member performance.

Cohesiveness affects group performance in other ways besides increasing compliance with performance norms. When the task roles in a group are highly interdependent, close cooperation and coordination are necessary for effective performance. Cooperation and teamwork are more likely to occur in cohesive groups than in noncohesive groups. Furthermore, there is likely to be less absenteeism and turnover in cohesive groups.

Status Consensus in Groups

A group is not likely to be highly cohesive if there is a lack of "status consensus." A person's "status" is the amount of respect and prestige he is accorded by other group members. Status can be based on a variety of things such as seniority, age, sex, skill, education, and prior accomplishments. There is status consensus when group members agree on the relative status of each person in the group. When members disagree about the status hierarchy, they will be frustrated and resentful (see review by Heslin and Dunphy, 1964). There is likely to be a status struggle where each person strives to protect or improve his position in the "pecking order."

The status consensus will be disrupted whenever status symbols are allocated in a manner that is highly discrepant with the existing status hierarchy. For example, if the most important task, the largest office, or the highest pay grade is given to a person who has low status, there is bound to be resentment by some other group members. Status discrepancies are also caused by characteristics of the work flow that result in a low status person directing or initiating action for a higher status person. A case study by Whyte (1948) nicely illustrates this kind of status problem. In the restaurant studied by Whyte, order runners communicated customer orders from the waitresses to the cooks and carried the completed food to the waitresses. The high status cooks resented being "told" what dishes to prepare and which orders to rush by the low status order runners. Frequent arguments resulted, disrupting performance.

BEHAVIOR IN GROUPS

We have seen that the behavior of group members is strongly influenced by group norms and social pressure. Now it is time to take a closer look at behavior patterns in groups. The classification and analysis of behavior has been a major subject of small group research in laboratory settings since interest in group dynamics blossomed in the early 1950s. Several category systems have been developed for use by observers in classifying the verbal and nonverbal behavior of group members (see review by Weick, 1968). For example, in the best known category system, called "Interaction Process Analysis" (Bales, 1950), each gesture, comment, or other action is classified in sequence into one of twelve categories, and the identity of the actor and other parties to the interaction is recorded.

Task-Oriented Behavior

Research on behavior in groups has identified two categories of behavior that are essential for the success and continuity of any group. The first category, called "task-oriented behavior," includes behavior that aids the group in selecting goals and making progress in attaining them. The specific types of task-oriented behavior that occur in a group depend largely on the nature of the task (Carter et al., 1951; Morris, 1966). In a group that is working on a routine production task, most of the task-oriented behavior will consist of production activities such as sorting, assembly, testing, repair, packaging, transporting, labeling, fabricating, and the operation of machines. In a group working on a decision-making task, most of the task-oriented behavior will consist of the exchange, analysis, and evaluation of information and ideas. For example, in a typical decision-making session, some members will provide information about the problem that the group must solve. Other members will interpret this information, offer opinions about the source of the problem, and suggest possible solutions. Someone may ask for clarification or elaboration of another person's comment. Periodically, someone may summarize what has been said up to that time, or point out that the discussion has wandered away from the original problem. Eventually someone will test progress toward agreement on one solution and press for a decision.

Group Maintenance Behavior

The other category of behavior that is essential for group effectiveness and continuity is known as "group maintenance behavior" or "maintenance-oriented behavior." This broad category includes any behavior that aids in improving interpersonal relationships, maintaining cohesiveness, and managing conflict among group members. When there is excessive hostility and conflict in a group, performance will suffer, and the continued existence of the group may be threatened. For this reason, maintenance-oriented behavior is just as important as task-oriented behavior. Many specific types of maintenance-oriented behavior are possible. For example, if one member feels anxious and insecure, other members can provide encouragement and support. Members can help to create a climate of acceptance by expressing their esteem and affection for each other. If an interpersonal conflict develops, someone may act as a mediator or peacemaker. If a person is about to withdraw from the group because of feeling ignored or rejected, someone can encourage the person to remain in the group. If the group faces a difficult challenge or an outside threat, someone can point out the need for members to pull together as a team and to present a united front.

Self-Oriented Behavior

In addition to task-oriented and maintenance-oriented behavior, there is usually some self-oriented behavior in groups. This behavior category includes actions by persons that serve their individual needs but do not facilitate the attainment of group goals or cohesiveness. Self-oriented behavior often distracts the group from its task activities and interferes with problem solving. For example, a person may seek attention with provocative comments, excessive joking, bragging and horseplay. A person may seek sympathy by talking about personal problems and physical ailments. Self-oriented behavior also includes attempts to dominate group discussion by continually interrupting and "shouting down" other speakers. Other attempts to dominate include threats to leave the group or to withhold assistance if a person does not get his own way. Excessive self-oriented behavior can adversely affect cohesiveness as well as task performance. Cohesiveness is damaged when disagreement, competition, or jealousy lead to personal insults, sarcasm, threats, and aggressive acts.

ROLE DIFFERENTIATION IN GROUPS

A person's behavior is jointly determined by forces in the situation (e.g., social pressure, job requirements) and forces in the person (e.g., values, attitudes, and needs). The concept of "role" is used to describe how a person perceives the various situational forces on her or him. The concept of "role differentiation" is used to describe how a group establishes distinct roles for each member. These concepts and related ones are helpful for understanding group processes.

Roles

A role is the set of behaviors expected of a person who occupies a particular position in a group or organization. Specific "role expectations" are communicated to a person by other members ("role senders") with whom the person has important relationships. Role expectations are also derived from the obvious requirements of the task itself and from written job descriptions, rules, and standards. If the total set of role expectations does not clearly designate what duties a person is supposed to perform and how the individual should behave, there will be "role ambiguity."

Role ambiguity may be due either to insufficient role expectations or to inconsistent role expectations.

Role Conflict

Inconsistent role expectations create a "role conflict" for a person. There are at least three kinds of role conflict. The first kind occurs when two or more role senders communicate incompatible role expectations. First-line supervisors often experience this kind of role conflict. Management expects a supervisor to represent the interests of the company, while subordinates of the supervisor expect him to go to bat for them and protect their interests.

A second kind of role conflict occurs if a single role sender communicates inconsistent role expectations. For example, a subordinate may be encouraged by the boss to show initiative on some occasions but reprimanded for not following established procedures on other occasions. The same kind of conflict occurs when an employee is expected to attain two goals that are not compatible (e.g., increase production and reduce errors when speed affects error rate).

The third kind of role conflict involves multiple roles. A person often belongs to more than one group, or holds more than one position in the organization. The designated behavior for one role may be inconsistent with the designated behavior for another role. For example, if a person is responsible for performing a function and for auditing his own performance, he will experience a role conflict and will probably not perform the second role adequately. This kind of conflict may also involve a second role outside of the organization. For example, a contract officer may be a partner in one of the companies bidding for the contract that he is expected to assign objectively.

When a person experiences a serious role conflict, he is likely to become frustrated and upset. The person has a tough time trying to decide which role expectations to accept and which to ignore. Some people try to resolve role conflict by discussing the discrepancies with the role senders, while other people vacillate in their behavior, or become paralyzed by indecision. Filley and House (1969, pp. 311–314) reviewed research on the consequences of role conflict and concluded that job satisfaction was lower and individual performance was adversely affected. Thus while some role conflict is probably inevitable, it should be prevented from becoming excessive.

Task-Role Organization

The differentiation of specialized roles is one of the most important processes in groups. In order to achieve its optimal level of performance, a group must develop an efficient "task-role organization." That is, the group's tasks must be subdivided into differentiated task roles in such a way as to obtain the advantages of specialization without creating unmanageable problems of coordination. Then group members must be assigned to these roles in such a way as to achieve a close match between their individual skills and the skill requirements for performance of each role. The optimal task-role organization for a group depends on its task and on the extent to which members are similar or dissimilar with respect to their task skills. More role specialization is required for some kinds of tasks than for others. If a group handles a variety of tasks from time to time, corresponding changes in task-role organization will probably be necessary to handle each task in the most efficient manner. As yet there has not been much research on task-role organization in groups, but the few studies that have been conducted suggest that the consequences for group performance are very substantial (Hewett and O'Brien, 1971; Lanzetta and Roby, 1956; O'Brien and Ilgen, 1968).

DECISION MAKING BY GROUPS

Many of the important decisions in organizations are made by groups rather than by individuals. Some groups are established exclusively to make organizational decisions. These decision-making groups may be permanent management teams or temporary committees formed to deal with a particular problem. Some planning decisions are necessary even in lower level groups that have a production task as their primary mission, and these decisions are sometimes made by the group as a whole rather than by the leader alone.

Is a decision made by a group superior in quality to a decision made by one individual such as the leader? Groups sometimes make better decisions, but there are many instances where they do not. Whether a group decision is of superior quality depends on the type of decision, the composition of the group, and the decision-making procedures used by the group. When the decision involves a complex problem and the group has more relevant information and ideas than any individual person, a group decision is potentially superior. However, there are many things that can prevent the group from effectively utilizing its resources and achieving its potential.

The most extensive research on decision making in groups has been conducted by Maier and his colleagues at the University of Michigan (Maier, 1970). Maier distinguishes between problem solving and solution selection, and he points out that a poor decision may be the result either of failure to generate good solutions or of failure to select the best solution when one or more good alternatives have been generated. Maier has attempted to identify the conditions necessary for effective decision making by groups, and much of the following discussion is based on the findings of his research (Maier, 1970, 1973).

Problem Diagnosis

The first step in efficient decision making is diagnosis of the problem. Since the problem is usually defined in terms of a set of obstacles to be overcome in attaining a goal, it is important for group members to agree about the goal. When the members of a group initially disagree about the goal, this disagreement should be resolved before the group begins to identify the obstacles to goal attainment. Consider, for example, a department that had to cut its budget because of an economic recession. Members with substantial seniority defined the problem in terms of the goal of protecting their own jobs and expenditures. They favored laying off newer workers and reducing service. The newer workers defined the problem in terms of the goal of keeping everybody employed and maintaining service. Thus they favored reducing overtime, increasing productivity, and eliminating some special fringe benefits. If a group is unable to agree about goals, the decision will be made by bargaining, coalition formation, and power plays rather than by rational problem solving.

How well a group diagnoses the problem greatly influences the quality of the eventual decision. Problem diagnosis is a difficult process, even if the group has agreed on its goal. Some common mistakes made during diagnosis of a problem include: confusing facts with opinions, confusing symptoms with causes, looking for scapegoats to blame, proposing solutions before the problem is clearly understood, and biasing the problem diagnosis to favor a preferred solution. It is important at this stage of problem solving for the leader to focus the group's attention on diagnosis and to discourage premature consideration of solutions. The group should be encouraged to explore any differences in member perception of the problem and to propose alternative diagnoses before reaching any conclusion about what is "really" the problem. Analysis of factual data from organizational records, surveys, and other sources should be used whenever feasible to supplement subjective opinions about the causes of the problem.

Solution Generation

After the problem diagnosis has been completed, the next step is the generation of potential solutions to the problem. Some common mistakes that are made by groups during solution generation include: suggesting solutions that are irrelevant to the problem, discussing what should have been done in the past instead of what can be done in the present, discussing the advantages and disadvantages of a solution before everyone has had a chance to suggest solutions, and focussing on solutions that have been used in the past without any attempt to create novel solutions. The role of the leader should be to encourage members who are shy or inhibited to contribute their ideas, and to help the group avoid the common mistakes made at this stage of problem solving. The leader should avoid showing favoritism to any particular member's solution, and should not propose any solutions of his own until group members have finished suggesting their solutions. Otherwise, the leader will unduly influence and limit the range of solutions considered.

One procedure that was developed to avoid inhibition of creative ideas is called "brainstorming." Each group member suggests any solution that comes to mind, regardless of how silly it may appear. Any criticism of ideas is avoided, including nonverbal rejection (e.g., scowls), so that member fears of being embarrassed will be minimized. Unfortunately, even when brainstorming is used, considerable inhibition still occurs. Research suggests that the quantity and quality of solutions can be improved by having group members generate written solutions by themselves (perhaps anonymously) rather than proposing solutions out loud (Van de Ven and Delbecq, 1971). After the solutions are generated, they can then be discussed by the group, and other solutions can be added to the initial list.

Solution Evaluation

The next step is to evaluate each of the proposed solutions in terms of how successful it is likely to be. The evaluation includes the prediction of major consequences and side effects. Often a particular solution will create new problems, and these may be more difficult to solve than the original problem. It is helpful to arrive at some estimate of the probability of success for each proposed solution and to compare its benefits with its costs. The leader should encourage the use of quantitative methods of forecasting and benefit analysis when these appear to be preferable to subjective judgments.

The mistakes commonly made by groups during the solution evaluation process include: failure to devote adequate attention to forecasting the multiple consequences of a solution, biasing estimates of consequences and estimates of probability to support a "favorite" solution, making verbal attacks on other members instead of limiting discussion to the solutions themselves, and making a hasty choice before the solutions are properly evaluated. Again, the leader can play an important role in helping the group to avoid these kinds of mistakes.

Solution Choice

After the proposed solutions are evaluated separately, the group should compare them and attempt to select the best one. Sometimes the choice will be predetermined during the evaluation stage when it becomes obvious that one solution is superior in every respect. However, it is more often the case that there will be several reasonably good solutions, each with its good features and bad features. The group must then weigh all of the tangible and intangible factors and try to come to an agreement.

The best known choice procedures for groups are "consensus" and "majority rule." We will define consensus as a decision where each member of the group is willing to support a particular solution, even though it is not necessarily a person's first choice. Decision by consensus has certain advantages over majority rule. When decisions are made by majority rule, the greatest danger is that a majority faction or coalition will force a decision before there is adequate time for discussion. When a group is required to reach consensus, it is less likely to make a rash choice or to select an alternative strongly opposed by a sizeable minority of members. On the other hand, achieving consensus may require an excessive amount of time. Moreover, consensus decisions encourage compromise solutions designed to accommodate each member, and this kind of solution is sometimes not in the best long-term interests of the group.

A common mistake made at the choice stage is "false consensus." When some members loudly advocate one solution and the other members remain silent, the silent ones are usually assumed to be in agreement. In fact, silence may indicate dissent rather than agreement. To avoid a false consensus, each member should be encouraged to express a preference and to participate in making the group choice. A secret ballot may be necessary in some cases when group members are very reluctant to openly state their preferences. It is especially difficult to get members to disagree with the majority opinion when the group is very cohesive.

It is usually the responsibility of the group leader to insure that everybody participates and to determine what choice procedure is appropriate. For example, the leader may initially try to obtain a consensus, and if this is impossible, the leader may then try for a majority decision or suggest that the group try to generate additional solutions.

Action Planning

The final step in decision making is planning how the decision will be implemented. Detailed action steps and methods for monitoring and evaluating progress should be developed. Some good decisions are unsuccessful simply because nobody bothers to see that this last step is carried out.

When the decision is going to be implemented by persons not involved in making it, these persons may not understand why a particular solution was chosen. Consequently, they may reject the decision, or they may implement it without any real enthusiasm. The best way to avoid this kind of failure is to allow some or all of the implementation personnel to participate in making the decision. If this is not possible, the persons responsible for implementation should at least be informed about what was discussed at each step of the decision-making process and the reasons for the final choice (Schein, 1969).

IMPROVING GROUP EFFECTIVENESS

Now that several major group processes have been examined, we will consider the practical implications for improving group effectiveness. The performance of groups that are responsible for production tasks depends mostly on how well the group is organized and the degree of member motivation and cohesiveness. We will consider how these variables can be affected by the organization, and we will also discuss some approaches for improving decision making in groups.

Improving Task-Role Organization

We have seen earlier in this chapter that a group will not be able to attain its maximum potential performance unless there is an effective differentiation of roles, and these roles are assigned to members in a way that matches role requirements with individual skills. Organizations can use staff experts or outside consultants in industrial engineering, operations research, and personnel placement to design jobs, develop specialized roles, and determine role assignments for work groups with a production task that is relatively structured and repetitive. For groups with a very unstructured production task, work organization and role assignments are usually the responsibility of the leader. The subordinates in these groups may or may not participate in planning how the group will be organized. How the leader should handle this responsibility will be discussed in Chapter 8.

Increasing Member Motivation

In the last chapter we described how an individual's motivation and performance could be improved by the use of incentives and job enrichment. These techniques are applicable to people who work together in groups as well as to people who work alone. However, we have seen in this chapter that the influence of group norms on individual motivation and performance is often greater than the influence of the formal reward system established by the parent organization. The level of performance in a cohesive group depends primarily on the group's performance norms, which depend in turn on the kind of relationship that exists between the group and the parent organization. The formal leader is a vital link in this relationship, and one way of improving group performance is to improve the leadership. The leader's role in shaping member motivation is explored in Chapter 8.

Building Cohesive Groups

There are several approaches that can be used to increase group cohesiveness. One approach is to allow employees to select their own teammates. Forming groups on the basis of mutual choices greatly reduces the possibility that members will be incompatible with each other. A study by Van Zelst (1952) demonstrated that this approach can improve the performance of groups in which cohesiveness and cooperation are important. Two-man and four-man construction crews were reassembled on the basis of the employees' mutual choices. Productivity during the preceding 9 months was compared to productivity during the first 11 months after the change. There was a substantial increase in productivity and a decrease in turnover. One of the workers made the following comment about the change: "Seems as though everything flows a lot smoother. It makes you feel more comfortable working, and I don't waste any time bickering about who's going to do what and how. We just seem to go ahead and do it. The work's a lot more interesting when you've got your buddy working with you. You certainly like it a lot better, anyway." (Van Zelst, 1952, p. 183.)

A variation of this approach is to form groups composed of persons who appear to have the same attitudes and cultural background. A considerable amount of research has shown that there is greater mutual attraction and compatibility among persons who have similar attitudes, interests, and values (see review by Lott and Lott, 1965). Once the groups are formed, cohesiveness can be nurtured by maintaining stability of membership. Of course, it is often infeasible to make assignments to groups on the basis of compatibility alone. In fact, in some cases, forming homogeneous groups would require racial or ethnic considerations in making job assignments, and these assignments would be in violation of antidiscrimination laws (see Chapter 12).

In forming task groups, it is important to consider the impact of group size as well as member composition. Studies have consistently shown that large groups are less cohesive than small groups (Thomas and Fink, 1963). As the number of persons in a group increases beyond a certain range (five to eight), the possibility of maintaining close, informal relationships rapidly diminishes, and there is a tendency toward centralization of control and formalization of procedures, accompanied by the emergence of separate informal cliques. Therefore, when it is feasible, cohesiveness can be improved by restricting the size of work groups and breaking up large work groups into small ones.

One major obstacle to development of cohesiveness in a work group is the lack of opportunity for pleasant interaction among group members. In some jobs communication among employees is inhibited by physical separation or noisy equipment. Walker and Guest (1952) found that this was often the case on automobile assembly lines. The development of friendships among workers can be facilitated by eliminating such barriers to communication when feasible. Conversation among employees should not be discouraged unless it clearly interferes with performance. If it is not feasible for employees to interact regularly as they work, other interaction opportunities such as periodic meetings and social events can usually be arranged.

It is important to remember that increased opportunity for interaction will not necessarily increase cohesiveness. There must be a basic compatibility of group members and the absence of conditions creating serious conflicts of interest within the group, such as a reward system based on competition, or the allocation of status symbols in a manner that upsets the status consensus. The more sources of conflict that exist, the more maintenance-oriented behavior will be necessary to preserve cohesiveness. Specific approaches for managing conflict will be discussed in Chapter 9.

Improving Group Decision Making

There are two major approaches for improving the effectiveness of group decision making, and both approaches can be used together. One approach is to insure that the group includes persons with essential information and ideas about the problem. Research has demonstrated that better solutions to problems are produced by heterogeneous groups than by homogeneous groups (Hoffman and Maier, 1961). Therefore, it is advisable to include in the group persons who have a variety of opinions, backgrounds, and technical specialties. The group should be large enough to provide this diversity, but not so large that open discussion becomes unwieldly and participation is inhibited.

A second approach for improving group decision making is to insure that the group follows efficient decision procedures and avoids the common mistakes discussed earlier in this chapter. It is important for the group to have a leader who is skilled in decision-making procedures and can guide the group in using them. A leader lacking these skills should be provided with special training. Although there has not been much research on training leaders to use effective decision procedures, the available evidence indicates that such training will improve decision making in groups (Maier and Hoffman, 1960; Maier and McRay, 1972). Even if the group has a capable leader, the likelihood that efficient procedures will be followed can be increased, and the leader's burden reduced, by providing special training to all members of the group. As an alternative to off-the-job training for group members, a process consultant can be brought in to help the group learn to analyze and improve its decision-making processes as they occur (see Chapter 15).

Making Teams and Committees Effective

As we saw in Chapters 2 and 3, some organizations use teams or committees with representatives from different subunits to make various kinds of operating decisions (e.g., coordination, scheduling). Galbraith (1973) has reviewed the aspects of group composition and procedure that are necessary for a team or committee of this type to be effective:

1. *Members should perceive their participation to be important and personally beneficial.* Serious participation is more likely if formal rewards (e.g., pay increase, promotion) are based in part on committee performance. Committee duties are more likely to be considered important if high-status persons are assigned to the committee on a long-term basis, rather than rotating membership frequently or selecting low-status employees as members.

2. *The group should include some of the persons who will be responsible for implementing its decisions.* As noted earlier, when there is a complete separation between decision makers and the persons responsible for implementing decisions, communication problems and lack of commitment are likely.

3. *Members should have knowledge and information relevant to the decision.* All departments that would be significantly affected by the decisions should be represented, and members should be selected from the appropriate level in the authority hierarchy. A common mistake is to select persons from too high a level who lack sufficient knowledge of technical processes to represent their functional specialty.

4. *Members should have sufficient authority to commit their respective departments.* A team or committee that is responsible for making decisions will not be able to carry out its responsibility unless members have some authority to commit their respective departments in matters relating to the decisions.

5. *Committee decisions should be integrated with regular subunit decisions.* When certain decisions are delegated to a committee, it is essential to keep the subunits that are represented by committee members fully informed, so that committee decisions will be compatible with subunit actions and decisions. It is often advisable to schedule meetings in each subunit following committee meetings to insure adequate communication of relevant information.

6. *The influence of members on decisions should be based on expertise.* If the team or committee must have members from more than one level of authority in order to include persons with relevant knowledge, care must

be taken to avoid the situation where the discussion is dominated by the members with higher authority. The group should explicitly establish the norm that influence will be based on relative knowledge rather than authority.

7. *Conflicts should be confronted and resolved with a problem-solving approach.* The group cannot make high quality decisions if conflicts relevant to the decisions are avoided or smoothed over rather than being confronted and resolved through a problem-solving process (see Chapter 9).

8. *Members should have appropriate interpersonal skills.* In order to deal successfully with role conflicts, overlapping responsibility, status ambiguity, and interdepartmental conflicts that intrude into the committee processes, members should have appropriate traits and interpersonal skills.

SUMMARY

Formal and informal groups can be found in any organization. The informal groups help to satisfy a variety of employee needs, including security and social needs. Consequently, it is not surprising that informal groups exert considerable influence over members' attitudes and behavior. Organizational management should learn to understand and work through informal groups rather than trying to ignore or destroy them.

A group that is cohesive may have either a high or low level of performance, depending on whether its relationship with the parent organization is one of trust and cooperation, or one of suspicion and hostility. Absenteeism and turnover are usually lower in cohesive groups, and cohesiveness facilitates cooperation on interdependent tasks. The amount of cohesiveness in a group depends on a variety of group and member characteristics, and some of these can be altered as a means of increasing cohesiveness and teamwork.

Task-oriented behavior and maintenance-oriented behavior are both necessary for the effectiveness and continuity of groups. A person's behavior is determined jointly by his individual predispositions and by the role expectations associated with his position. If there is role ambiguity or role conflict, the result will be dissatisfaction and suboptimal performance. All groups establish specialized roles for performance of essential functions. A group's effectiveness in performing its task will depend on how well it is organized in terms of differentiated task roles and member role assignments.

For a group with a decision-making task, effectiveness depends on the composition of the group, the amount of relevant information possessed by its members, and the decision procedures they use. A poor decision can be caused by mistakes made during the problem diagnosis, solution generation, solution evaluation, solution choice, or action planning steps of the decision-making process. Decision making by groups can be improved by altering the composition of the group, and by training the leader and other members to avoid the common mistakes.

REVIEW AND DISCUSSION QUESTIONS

1. Define or explain each of the following key terms: group, informal group, group norms, compliance, conformity, social pressure, cohesiveness, reference group, status, status consensus, interaction process analysis, task-oriented behavior, group maintenance behavior, self-oriented behavior, roles, role differentiation, role ambiguity, role conflict, task-role organization, problem solving, brainstorming, consensus, false consensus, action planning.

2. What functions are performed by informal groups and why are these groups important?

3. In what ways can groups influence member behavior?

4. How is cohesiveness related to group performance?

5. What kinds of member behavior are essential for the continuity and success of a group?

6. Under what conditions is role conflict likely to occur?

7. When and why is a decision made by a group superior to a decision made by one individual?

8. What are the recommended steps in problem solving and decision making?

9. How can the effectiveness of work groups be increased?

10. How can the effectiveness of committees and management teams be increased?

REFERENCES

Bales, R. F. A set of categories for the analysis of small group interaction. *American Sociological Review*, 1950, *15*, 257–263.

Burns, T. The reference of conduct in small groups: Cliques and cabals in occupational milieux. *Human Relations*, 1955, *8*, 467–486.

Carter, L., Haythorn, W., Meirowitz, B., & Lanzetta, J. The relation of categorizations and ratings in the observation of group behavior. *Human Relations*, 1951, *4*, 239–254.

Coch, L., & French, J. R. P. Overcoming resistance to change. *Human Relations*, 1948, *1*, 512–532.

Filley, A. C., & House, R. J. *Managerial process and organizational behavior*. Glenview, Ill.: Scott, Foresman, 1969.

Galbraith, J. *Designing complex organizations*. Menlo Park, Calif.: Addison-Wesley, 1973.

Heslin, R., & Dunphy, D.   Three dimensions of member satisfaction in small groups. *Human Relations*, 1964, *17*, 99–102.

Hewett, T. T., & O'Brien, G. E.   The effects of work organization, leadership style, and member compatibility upon small group productivity. Technical Report 71–22, Department of Psychology, University of Washington, 1971.

Hoffman, L. R., & Maier, N. R. F.   Quality and acceptance of problem solutions by members of homogeneous and heterogeneous groups. *Journal of Abnormal and Social Psychology*, 1961, *62*, 401–407.

Lanzetta, J. T., & Roby, T. B.   Effects of work group structure and certain task variables on group performance. *Journal of Abnormal and Social Psychology*, 1956, *53*, 307–314.

Lieberman, S.   The effects of changes in roles on the attitudes of role occupants. *Human Relations*, 1956, *9*, 385–402.

Lott, A. J., & Lott, B. E.   Group cohesiveness and interpersonal attraction: A review of relationships with antecedent and consequent variables. *Psychological Bulletin*, 1965, *14*, 259–309.

Maier, N. R. F.   *Problem solving and creativity in individuals and groups.* Belmont, Calif.: Brooks/Cole, 1970.

Maier, N. R. F.   *Psychology in industrial organizations.* Boston: Houghton-Mifflin, 1973.

Maier, N. R. F., & Hoffman, L. R.   Using trained "developmental" discussion leaders to improve further the quality of group decisions. *Journal of Applied Psychology*, 1960, *44*, 247–251.

Maier, N. R. F., & McRay, E. P.   Increasing innovation in change situations through leadership skills. *Psychological Reports*, 1972, *31*, 343–354.

Morris, C. G.   Task effects on group interaction. *Journal of Personality and Social Psychology*, 1966, *4*, 545–554.

O'Brien, G. E., & Ilgen, D.   Effects of organizational structure, leadership style, and member compatibility on small group creativity. *Proceedings of the American Psychological Association*, 1968, *3*, 555–556.

Roethlisberger, F. J., & Dickson, W. J.   *Management and the worker.* Cambridge: Harvard University Press, 1939.

Schein, E.   *Process consultation: Its role in organization development.* Reading, Mass.: Addison-Wesley, 1969.

Seashore, S. E.   *Group cohesiveness in the industrial work group.* Ann Arbor: University of Michigan, Institute for Social Research, 1954.

Thomas, E. J., & Fink, C. F.   Effects of group size. *Psychological Bulletin*, 1963, *60*, 371–384.

Van de Ven, A. H., & Delbecq, A. L.   Nominal versus interacting group processes for committee decision-making effectiveness. *Academy of Management Journal*, 1971, *14*, 203–212.

Van Zelst, R. H.   Sociometrically selected work teams increase production. *Personnel Psychology*, 1952, *5*, 175–185.

Walker, C. R., & Guest, R. H.   *The man on the assembly line*. Cambridge: Harvard University Press, 1952.

Weick, K. E.   Systematic observational methods. In G. Lindzey and E. Aronson (Eds.), *Handbook of social psychology*, Revised edition. Reading, Mass.: Addison-Wesley, 1968.

Whyte, W. F.   *Human relations in the restaurant industry*. New York: McGraw-Hill, 1948.

8

LEADERSHIP IN ORGANIZATIONS

EFFECTIVE LEADERSHIP is vital for the survival and success of an organization. There is no general agreement on the best way to define leadership, but most definitions imply that it is, at least in part, a process of exerting positive influence over other persons. Leadership involves influencing people to exert more effort in some task or to change their behavior. It is important to make a distinction between "leadership" and "effective leadership." Whether a leader is effective depends on the eventual outcomes of his leadership. The usual criterion of leadership effectiveness in an organization is the long-term performance of the leader's group or subunit. An effective leader or manager not only influences subordinates, he is also able to insure that they achieve their highest potential performance.

Interest in the subject of leadership has been evident during a considerable period of human history, however scientific research on leadership is a fairly recent phenomenon. While some progress has been made in probing the mysteries surrounding the process of leadership, many questions remain unanswered. The objective of this chapter is to examine several aspects of leadership in order to provide the reader with a better understanding of this vital and complex process. The question of greatest concern is the nature of effective leadership in organizations. Leadership research and some major leadership theories will be examined in an attempt to identify valid prescriptions for effective leadership. In addition, we will discuss the practical implications of selected leadership research and theory for improving the leadership in an organization.

MULTIPLE CONCEPTIONS OF LEADERSHIP

Leadership has been studied from a variety of viewpoints in an attempt to discover why some leaders are more effective than others. Three aspects

143

of leadership that have been dealt with most often in the literature on leadership in organizations are (1) leader traits, (2) leadership behavior, and (3) leader power and influence. Since most current leadership theory represents a mixture of these different conceptions of leadership, the current theories can better be understood if we review the results of research on leader traits, behavior, and power.

LEADER TRAITS

One of the earliest approaches used for research on leadership was the trait approach. It was probably an outgrowth of the attention devoted to the role of "great men" in history. Underlying this approach was the assumption that some persons are "natural leaders." Such persons were assumed to be endowed with certain traits that would enable them to be successful leaders in any situation. By comparing the traits of clearly successful leaders with the traits of unsuccessful leaders and nonleaders, it was hoped that the essential traits of natural leaders could be identified.

Research on leadership traits was facilitated by the rapid development of psychological testing during the 1930s and 1940s. Well over a hundred studies were conducted during this period with a large variety of leader traits, including physical characteristics (e.g., height, appearance, energy level), ability (e.g., general intelligence, verbal fluency, originality), and personality (e.g., self-esteem, dominance, initiative). Reviews of this research revealed a disappointing lack of consistent results (Mann, 1959; Stogdill, 1948). Leader effectiveness could not be accurately and reliably predicted from leader traits.

Attempts to identify critical leader traits for a narrower class of leaders, namely managers in business organizations, have been only slightly more successful. There is some evidence that effective managers tend to have a higher than average amount of intelligence, verbal fluency, self-assurance, initiative, achievement motivation, and ambition for power (Campbell et al., 1970; Ghiselli, 1963; Korman, 1968). However, the relationship between these traits and managerial effectiveness is a weak one, and a high score on the traits has not been shown to be either necessary or sufficient for a manager to be an effective leader. Even when relationships have been found, the traits used in this research have usually been so abstract that they fail to provide much insight into the dynamics of the leadership process or the reasons why some managers are more effective than others.

The most likely reason why the trait approach failed is that the leadership situation, including the nature of the subordinates and the task, determine what leader traits are essential for effective leadership. These essential traits are likely to differ somewhat from situation to situation. For example, Mann (1965) found that the relative importance of administrative skills, technical skills, and human relations skills was different for lower, middle, and upper level managers. Technical skills (e.g., knowledge about task procedures and equipment) and human relations skills (e.g., understanding of subordinate needs, ability to relate to subordinates) were most important for lower level managers, whereas administrative skills (e.g., planning, organizing, complex problem solving) were most important for upper level managers. The importance of various leader skills and personality traits depends also on many other aspects of the leadership situation, including the amount of organizational stability or change (Mann, 1965), the technology used by the organization (Woodward, 1965), and the purpose of the organization (e.g., business, political, religious, voluntary, military, and so forth).

LEADERSHIP BEHAVIOR

After the failure of the trait approach was realized in the early part of the 1950s, many leadership researchers began to study leader behavior (what leaders do) instead of leader traits (what leaders are). Leader behavior can be related more directly to the process of leadership and the requirements of a managerial position than can abstract traits. Also, a behavioral approach is more consistent with the discovery that leadership can be shared by several members of a group and does not necessarily have to be concentrated in a single person.

Consideration and Initiating Structure

Since the number of potential leadership functions and activities is nearly endless, one early objective of research on leadership behavior was the identification of relatively distinct and meaningful behavior categories. The most extensive program of research on leader behavior categories was conducted at the Ohio State University during the 1950s. The psychologists involved in these leadership studies developed questionnaires for subordinates, peers, or superiors to use in describing the behavior of a leader. The leadership questionnaires were composed of many items, and each item dealt with a specific aspect of a leader's behavior. Persons in different kinds of organizations were given the questionnaires and asked to use them to describe their leaders. The responses were analyzed to determine which behavior items tended to be answered in the same way. Two major behavior categories were found and they were labeled "consideration" and "initiating structure" (Fleishman, 1957; Halpin and Winer, 1957; Hemphill and Coons, 1957). Most of the other research on leadership behavior categories has also revealed the existence of categories or dimensions that are roughly equivalent to consideration and initiating structure.

Consideration is the degree to which a leader acts in a warm and supportive manner and shows concern for subordinates. Some examples of consideration include: being friendly and approachable, doing personal favors for subordinates, backing up or "going to bat" for subordinates, consulting with subordinates on important matters before going ahead, finding time to listen to subordinates' problems, being willing to accept subordinate suggestions, looking out for the welfare of individual subordinates, and treating a subordinate like an equal.

Initiating Structure is the degree to which a leader defines and structures his/her own role and the roles of subordinates toward attainment of the group's formal goals. Some examples of initiating structure include: criticizing poor work, emphasizing the necessity of meeting deadlines, assigning subordinates to tasks, letting subordinates know what is expected of them, coordinating the activities of subordinates, offering new approaches to problems, maintaining definite standards of performance, asking subordinates to follow standard operating procedures, and seeing that subordinates are working up to capacity.

Consideration and initiating structure were found to be relatively independent behavior categories. Some leaders are high on consideration and low on initiating structure, some leaders are low on consideration and high on initiating structure, some leaders are high on both behavior categories, and some leaders are low on both behavior categories.

Leader Decision Making

Subsequent studies have identified other important categories of leadership behavior (see for example Bowers and Seashore, 1966; Stogdill and Coons, 1963). The most important of these other leadership dimensions is probably the leader's style of decision making. There are a variety of procedures that a leader can use to make task and personnel decisions, and these procedures can be ordered along a continuum representing the degree of subordinate participation and influence over the decisions. Many different versions of this participation-influence continuum have been proposed, and one of these is illustrated in Figure 8–1. Autocratic decision making is where the leader makes a decision without asking his subordinates for their opinions and suggestions. With this decision procedure, the subordinates do not have any direct influence over the decision. With consultation, the leader does ask subordinates for their opin-

FIGURE 8–1
An Influence-Participation Continuum for Decision Procedures

	Autocratic Decisions	Consultation	Joint Decision Making	Delegation	
No Subordinate Influence					High Subordinate Influence

ions and suggestions before he makes the decision, so there is a limited amount of subordinate participation and influence. With joint decision making, the leader and his subordinates make the decision together, and there is substantial subordinate participation and influence. Finally, with delegation, the leader assigns the authority and responsibility for making certain decisions to one or more subordinates. Even though the leader may delimit the range of alternatives that a subordinate is allowed to select and may occasionally veto the subordinate's choice, delegation allows more subordinate influence than any other decision procedure (Heller and Yukl, 1969).

A leader's decision behavior can be regarded as relatively independent from other categories of leadership behavior. It is often incorrectly assumed that allowing subordinate participation is equivalent to being considerate. In fact, a leader who allows his subordinates to participate in making decisions is only being considerate if the subordinates desire such participation. The amount of participation desired by subordinates will be greater for some kinds of decisions (e.g., major changes in their job duties and work schedule) than for other kinds of decisions. Moreover, subordinates differ greatly in their willingness to assume the extra responsibility and effort required by any substantial degree of participation. Thus while some autocratic leaders are clearly inconsiderate (tyrants), other leaders are able to be both autocratic and considerate (benevolent autocrats) because their subordinates have no desire for participation in decision making. Likewise, a highly participative leader may be either considerate or inconsiderate, depending upon the subordinates' desire for participation. Finally, it should be remembered that consideration involves many other aspects of leader behavior besides consulting with subordinates. It is possible for a highly participative leader to be otherwise indifferent or hostile toward his subordinates (malevolent democrat).

A leader's decision behavior is also somewhat distinct from initiating structure. A leader who is high on initiating structure acts to insure that necessary task decisions are made and implemented. However, he or she does not need to make all of these decisions autocratically. A leader who is high on initiating structure may use a variety of decision procedures, and subordinates may be allowed substantial participation. For example, a leader who makes extensive use of joint decision making with subordinates will be high on initiating structure if he or she acts to insure that the group functions efficiently. Scheduling meetings, setting up an effective problem-solving procedure, keeping the discussion from wandering to irrelevant topics, encouraging participation by all subordinates, reviewing progress, and pressing for a decision are some of the structuring acts that the leader may perform. A leader who is highly participative but does not act to insure that subordinates make and implement task decisions (laissez faire leader) would be low on initiating structure. Likewise, there are autocratic leaders who are high on initiating structure and there are autocratic leaders who are low on initiating structure. An example of the latter is a leader who avoids making important task decisions, does not set hard goals or high standards, and fails to check on the implementation of his decisions by subordinates.

Interaction Facilitation and Group Integration

Another category of leadership behavior that appears to be important is referred to by Stogdill and Coons (1963) as "work group integration" and by Bowers and Seashore (1966) as "interaction facilitation." This category includes leadership behavior intended to increase group cohesiveness, promote cooperation and teamwork, and manage conflict. Interaction facilitation is different from consideration, even though both types of behavior facilitate group maintenance. While consideration builds good relations between the leader and his subordinates, interaction facilitation builds good relations among the subordinates themselves. Interaction facilitation has received much less attention in the leadership literature than consideration, initiating structure, or decision behavior, but it is evident from the research on groups discussed in the previous chapter (Chapter 7) that interaction facilitation can have important consequences for group performance.

Consequences of Leadership Behavior

A large number of studies has been carried out to determine how leader behavior is related to subordinate performance, satisfaction, absences, turnover, and other criteria of leader effectiveness. The procedure followed in most of these studies was to compare effective leaders to ineffective leaders or to assess the relationship between leader effectiveness and a measure of leader behavior. A few field experiments were also conducted in which leader behavior was manipulated to determine its consequences. Detailed reviews of this leadership research can be found in a number of publications, including Korman (1966), Likert (1961), Lowin (1968), Sales (1966), and Yukl (1971).

The relationship found between the behavior and effectiveness of a leader was stronger in most cases than the relationship between leader traits and effectiveness. However, as in the trait studies, there was a disturbing lack of consistency in results. For example, initiating structure was positively related to subordinate performance for some samples of leaders but not for others. Consideration was positively related to subordinate performance for some samples of leaders and was unrelated or negatively related to subordinate performance for other samples. It had been widely assumed that the subordinates of highly participative leaders would perform better than the subordinates of highly autocratic leaders, and while this was indeed the case in many studies, some notable exceptions were found.

Confusion about the meaning of the inconsistent results from leader behavior studies was increased when researchers found that the direction of causality can be the reverse of what is usually assumed. That is, leader behavior can be caused by subordinate performance rather than subordinate performance being caused by leader behavior (Farris and Lim, 1969; Lowin and Craig, 1968). For example, leaders may be more considerate to subordinates who perform well than to subordinates who perform poorly. This research pointed out that the direction of causality cannot be clearly interpreted for the large majority of leadership studies that did not actually manipulate leader behavior.

Importance of the Situation

Failure to find consistent consequences of leader behavior was partially due to problems with research design and measurement of the variables. However, the major reason was probably the same as in the trait studies. That is, the effect of leader behavior on subordinate performance and other criteria depends on the situation and is not constant across situations. Even though Stogdill pointed out the importance of the situation back in 1948, most research on leadership behavior during the following decade did not systematically measure and analyze the moderating effects of situational variables.

The importance of the situation was recognized by many leadership researchers only when they were confronted by the inconsistent results of the studies on leadership behavior. It became apparent that the amount of a given type of leadership behavior that is necessary for effective group performance is greater in some situations than other situations. For example, more initiating structure is needed when subordinates have a complex, unstructured task than when they have a simple, repetitive task. Furthermore, the relative importance of different aspects of a behavior category depends on the situation. Coordination of subordinates is more important if they have interdependent tasks than if they work at unrelated tasks. Finally, an effective leader must adapt his behavior to differences among his subordinates and to changing conditions. In the case of decision behavior, a leader's effectiveness depends less on the overall level of subordinate participation than on the use of decision procedures that are appropriate for the subordinates and for the types of decisions to be made.

LEADERSHIP INFLUENCE AND POWER

Analysis of a leader's power and influence is a third approach that has been used to study leadership. Power can be defined as the capacity to influence another person's behavior. A person has power as long as the potential for influence continues, regardless of whether any attempt is made to actually exert influence. There are a variety of power sources for leaders in organizations.

Bases of Power

French and Raven (1960) have distinguished five different sources of power: legitimate power, coercive power, reward power, referent power, and expert power. Legitimate power is derived from authority. It involves subordinate compliance with rules, orders, and instructions by the leader when these are perceived by subordinates to be legitimate in terms of the leader's scope of authority. The scope of authority is specified by the organization and by the terms of the subordinates' membership in the organization. The latter may be set forth in a formal contract of membership (e.g., an employment contract), or may simply involve an informal agreement. The legitimacy of managerial authority is likely to be high for such things as work procedures and work schedules, but low for such things as where the subordinates live, what kind of cars they drive, or what political party they join (Davis, 1968). Even the manager's scope of authority over work-related matters may be very narrow if these are predetermined by elaborate organizational policy or the terms of a union contract. The amount of influence a leader derives from authority is quite limited in most kinds of organizations, except when subordinates have an internalized value that obedience to authority is necessary and proper. Consequently, a manager's legitimate power is usually bolstered by some coercive and reward power.

Coercive power is based on fear that failure to comply with rules or instructions will result in some form of punishment. The source of a leader's coercive power is his control over negative outcomes for subordinates, such as fines, suspension, and dismissal. Reward power is derived from a leader's control over positive outcomes, such as a pay increase, promotion, favorable assignment, increased status, formal recognition, more responsibility, and a larger budget. If a leader can accurately measure subordinate performance or can maintain surveillance over the behavior of subordinates, he can use the rewards and punishments that he controls to influence their behavior and performance.

Referent power is based on identification and attraction. Some religious and political leaders have tremendous charisma or personal magnetism, and their followers are very loyal and dedicated. Although other kinds of leaders are seldom able to possess such magnitudes of referent power, it is nevertheless an important source of influence for them also. Referent power depends in part on a leader's personality and his capacity for inspiring followers and enunciating their hopes and values. It is also dependent upon how the leader treats his subordinates. The most feasible way for a manager to develop referent power is probably to be high on consideration.

The fifth source of influence is expert power. A leader can influence the opinions of subordinates when they perceive him to have greater knowledge and expertise. By directly influencing their opinions, a leader with expert power can indirectly influence subordinate behavior. For example, if there are several methods for performing the group task and the leader is perceived to have more relevant information and expertise than other group members, he can usually persuade them that his method is the best one. A leader's influence will be greater if he has exclusive access to important information and if he is a very persuasive person. However, a leader's expert power will usually not extend to subjects about which he obviously has little information and expertise. Furthermore, a leader's expert power is dependent upon his credibility. A leader who is not perceived to be a reliable and trustworthy source of information and advice will not have much expert power. Credibility will quickly vanish if the leader makes careless and inconsistent statements, if his judgments prove to be faulty, or if subordinates discover that he has been lying to them.

Position Power and Personal Power

Legitimate authority, reward power, and coercive power are largely determined by the organization for each formal leadership position. Consequently, they are often referred to as "position power." Expert and referent power depend largely on the traits and behavior of the person who occupies a leadership position, so they are referred to as "personal power." The less position power a leader has, the more he must rely on personal power as a source of influence over subordinates.

The relationship between the various types of power is not completely clear. They are often assumed to be additive, with the leader's potential influence equal to the sum of the separate types of power. However, it is also possible that some forms of power are incompatible with the use of other forms of power. For example, a leader's use of coercive power is likely to reduce his referent power if subordinates strongly resent the coercion. Likewise, use of reward power may be acceptable to subordinates if the leader has considerable personal power, but may be perceived as excessively manipulative if he does not.

Bilateral Power and Situational Constraints

Power is usually bilateral (two-way) rather than unilateral (one-way), and subordinates often possess substantial counterpower. The leader may control subordinate opportunities for a pay increase or promotion, but subordinates indirectly determine the same outcomes for the leader. If subordinates perform well, they can help their boss to gain a reputation as an effective manager. However, if subordinates restrict performance, sabotage production, initiate grievances, and complain to higher management, they can damage their leader's reputation as a manager. When there is a high degree of bilateral power, there is great potential for cooperation and mutual influence between the leader and the subordinates. However, if they cannot agree on a satisfactory exchange of influence and benefits, there is also great potential for a disruptive conflict in which each side uses its power to punish the other side.

Another limitation on a leader's influence over subordinates is their opportunity for moving to attractive positions in other organizations. The less dependent subordinates are on their present position, the less potential a leader has to force subordinates to comply with unpopular rules, orders, or policy. The leader's position power is further restricted if a subordinate is especially valuable to the organization and could not be easily replaced.

Subordinate counterpower, uniqueness, and mobility are obvious constraints on the leader's use of position power. The amount of usable position power possessed by a leader depends on the extent of these and other situational constraints as well as on his control over rewards and punishments.

Power and Leader Effectiveness

Only a small number of studies have been conducted to determine the consequences of leader power for group performance. No consistent results were found for the consequences of a leader's possession and use of position power. On the other hand, leaders who possessed and relied upon personal power were found to have subordinates with higher performance and lower absenteeism (Bachman et al., 1966; Ivancevich and Donnelly, 1970; Student, 1968). However, the magnitude of this relationship was modest.

There are several explanations for the tenuous relationship between leader power and leader effectiveness. First, the importance of power depends upon the situation. Leader power is not important when subordinates are strongly motivated to attain organization goals, and they agree with the leader on the best way to attain these goals. However, power is important if subordinates are not highly motivated, or if they are motivated but disagree with the leader on the best path to the goals. In these situations, power will be useful to the leader as a means of motivating subordinates or directing their behavior.

Second, even when leader power is important, possession of position power will not guarantee leader effectiveness. The leader's position power may be nullified by subordinate counterpower, or the leader may lack the skill to wield position power effectively. Even if the leader has substantial personal and position power, he may not choose to use his influence to motivate subordinates toward organizational goals, or he may lack the knowledge of a good way to attain these goals. Thus, once again, leader effectiveness is seen to depend on a complex interaction between characteristics of the leader and characteristics of the situation.

LEADER-SITUATION INTERACTION MODELS

As the importance of situational factors was recognized, leadership research became more sophisticated, and contingency models of leader effectiveness were formulated to explain the interaction between leader characteristics and the situation. These contingency models have attempted to identify what leader traits or behavior patterns are appropriate for each of a series of clearly specified leadership situations. The leader's influence over subordinates is usually included as an important explanatory mechanism in these contingency models. We will examine three of the models: (1) Fiedler's "contingency model of leadership," (2) the Vroom and Yetton "normative model of leadership," and (3) the "path-goal theory of leadership."

Fielder's Contingency Model of Leadership

One of the earliest leader-situation models was developed by Fiedler (1964, 1967) in an attempt to reconcile the inconsistent results of his previous research. This research was concerned with the relationship between leadership effectiveness and a leader trait referred to as an LPC ("least-preferred co-worker") score.

MEASUREMENT AND INTERPRETATION OF LPC. To determine a leader's LPC score, he is asked to think of all his past and present co-workers, to select the one with whom he could work least well, and to rate this person on a series of bipolar adjective scales. An LPC Scale is shown in Figure 8–2. The rating given by a leader on each bipolar adjective scale is coded in terms of a number ranging from 1 to 8. The LPC score for a leader is simply the sum of the numerical ratings of the "least-preferred co-worker" on all of the bipolar adjective scales. A leader who is generally critical in rating his least-preferred co-worker will obtain a low LPC score, whereas a leader who is generally uncritical in rating his least-preferred coworker will obtain a high LPC score.

The interpretation of LPC has changed several times over the years since the measure was first used by Fiedler, and there still remains a great deal of mystery about its meaning. To date, researchers have not been able to find any strong and consistent relationship between LPC scores and

FIGURE 8–2
Example of an LPC Scale

Instructions:
   People differ in the ways they think about those with whom they work. On the scale below are pairs of words which are opposite in meaning. You are asked to describe someone with whom you have worked by placing an "X" in one of the eight spaces on the line between the two words. Each space represents how well the adjective fits the person you are describing, as in the following example:

Very neat:_____:_____:_____:_____:_____:_____:_____:_____:Not neat
        8   7   6   5   4   3   2   1

        Very   Quite Some- Slight- Slight- Some- Quite Very
        neat   neat   what   ly   ly   what   untidy untidy
                      neat   neat   untidy   untidy

Now, think of the person with whom you can work least well. He may be someone you work with now, or he may be someone you knew in the past. He does not have to be the person you like least well, but should be the person with whom you had the most difficulty in getting a job done. Describe this person as he appears to you.

Pleasant	:___:___:___:___|___:___:___:___	: Unpleasant
Friendly	:___:___:___:___|___:___:___:___	: Unfriendly
Rejecting	:___:___:___:___|___:___:___:___	: Accepting
Helpful	:___:___:___:___|___:___:___:___	: Frustrating
Unenthusiastic	:___:___:___:___|___:___:___:___	: Enthusiastic
Tense	:___:___:___:___|___:___:___:___	: Relaxed
Distant	:___:___:___:___|___:___:___:___	: Close
Cold	:___:___:___:___|___:___:___:___	: Warm
Cooperative	:___:___:___:___|___:___:___:___	: Uncooperative
Supportive	:___:___:___:___|___:___:___:___	: Hostile
Boring	:___:___:___:___|___:___:___:___	: Interesting
Quarrelsome	:___:___:___:___|___:___:___:___	: Harmonious
Self-assured	:___:___:___:___|___:___:___:___	: Hesitant
Efficient	:___:___:___:___|___:___:___:___	: Inefficient
Gloomy	:___:___:___:___|___:___:___:___	: Cheerful
Open	:___:___:___:___|___:___:___:___	: Guarded

other leader traits or behavior. The most recent interpretation of LPC is in terms of a leader's motive hierarchy (Fiedler, 1971). The major motive of a high LPC leader is close interpersonal relations with others, including subordinates. The leader will be task oriented only if relations with subordinates are already good. The major motive of a low LPC leader involves doing a good job, and he or she will tend to be very task oriented. The secondary motive of establishing good relations with subordinates will be pursued only if the group is performing well and there are no serious task problems. It is too early yet to determine whether the current interpretation of LPC will provide a satisfactory explanation of the complex relationships in the Contingency Model.

SITUATION FAVORABILITY. According to the contingency model, the relationship between leader LPC and subordinate performance depends upon the favorability of the leadership situation. The favorability of the situation is determined by: (1) the degree of task structure, (2) the leader's position power, and (3) leader-member relations. How easily the leader can influence subordinates depends on each of these three aspects of the situation. When the task is highly structured, it is possible to specify exactly what subordinate behavior is required to perform the task effectively, and it is easy to monitor and evaluate subordinate performance. When the leader has a substantial amount of position power, he has control over important rewards and punishments that can be used to insure subordinate compliance with his instructions. Finally, when relations between the leader and his subordinates are good, he will have some referent power to supplement his position power.

LEADER EFFECTIVENESS. When the situation is either very favorable (e.g., structured task, high position power, good leader-member relations) or very unfavorable (e.g., unstructured task, low position power, poor leader-member relations), leaders with low LPC scores will be more effective than leaders with high LPC scores. Some examples of leaders in highly favorable situations include the well-liked commander of an artillery crew and the foreman of an open-hearth steel shop who is liked by his subordinates. Some examples of leaders in an unfavorable situation include the disliked chairman of a volunteer committee with a vague problem-solving task, and the unpopular chairman of the board of directors in a small, cooperatively-owned corporation.

When the situation is intermediate in favorability, leaders with high LPC scores will be more effective than leaders with low LPC scores. Some examples of leaders in this situation include the well-liked leader of a research team who has limited position power and an unstructured task, and the unpopular new supervisor of a crew of assembly-line workers with a highly structured task.

EMPIRICAL EVIDENCE FOR THE MODEL. Fiedler's leadership model was based on the results of over 50 studies of a large variety of leaders and situations (Fiedler, 1967). A number of subsequent studies have also provided support for the model (see Fiedler, 1971). However, there have also been criticisms of the model, and the validity of the supporting data has been questioned (Ashour, 1973; Graen et al., 1970; Graen et al., 1971; Korman, 1973). The controversy over Fiedler's model has not yet been resolved, and researchers are conducting additional studies to test the model.

The Vroom and Yetton Model of Leadership

The importance of using decision procedures that are appropriate for the leader and the situation has been recognized for some time. In an article published in 1958, Tannenbaum and Schmidt noted that a leader's choice of decision procedures reflects forces in the leader, forces in the subordinates, and forces in the situation. Maier (1963) pointed out that leaders should consider both the quality requirements of a decision and the likelihood of subordinate acceptance and commitment before choosing a procedure to make the decision. Vroom and Yetton (1973) have formulated a model of leadership that builds upon these earlier approaches but goes further in specifying which decision procedures will be most effective in each of several specific decision situations.

DECISION ACCEPTANCE AND QUALITY.   The Vroom and Yetton model is based on an analysis of how a leader's decision behavior affects decision quality and subordinate acceptance of the decision, which in turn jointly affect subordinate performance. Decision acceptance is the degree of subordinate commitment to implement a decision effectively. In some cases, subordinates will be highly motivated to implement a decision regardless of whether they have any influence in making it. This is likely to be true when the leader has substantial personal and position power. However, there are many situations where subordinates will not accept an autocratic decision unless it is consistent with their preferences among the possible alternatives. In such situations, a decision consistent with subordinate preferences is more likely to be made if the leader allows subordinates to participate in the decision making. In addition, if subordinates perceive that they have substantially influenced a decision, they will tend to identify with it. When subordinates perceive a decision to be "their decision," they will be more motivated to implement it successfully.

Decision quality refers to the objective aspects of a decision that affect group performance aside from any effect on subordinate motivation. Some kinds of decisions have important consequences for group performance, while other kinds of decisions do not. Examples of task decisions that usually have important consequences for group performance include the determination of performance goals and priorities, the determination of work procedures, and the assignment of tasks to subordinates, especially when subordinates differ in their qualifications for handling the various tasks. Some examples of decisions where decision quality is not likely to be important include choosing one of several capable subordinates to work overtime, determining which subordinate will get to use a newly acquired truck, assigning individual parking spaces to subordinates, and selecting a color to use in painting the coffee room. When decision quality is important and subordinates possess relevant information that the leader does not possess, the leader should use a decision procedure that provides for subordinate input into the decision.

LEADERSHIP DECISION PROCEDURES. The Vroom and Yetton model distinguishes five decision procedures that are appropriate for decisions involving some or all of the leader's immediate subordinates. These procedures include two varieties of autocratic decision (AI and AII), two varieties of Consultation (CI and CII), and joint decision making by the leader and subordinates as a group (GII). Five decision procedures that are appropriate for decisions involving a single subordinate are also distinguished. They include two varieties of autocratic decision making (AI and AII), consultation (CI), joint decision making (GI), and delegation (DI). Each of these decision procedures is defined in Table 8–1.

RULES FOR DETERMINING OPTIMAL DECISION PROCEDURES. According to the Vroom and Yetton model, the effectiveness of a decision procedure depends upon a number of aspects of the situation. These include the importance of decision quality and acceptance, the amount of relevant information possessed by the leader and by subordinates, the likelihood that subordinates will accept an autocratic decision, the likelihood that subordinates will cooperate in trying to make a good decision if allowed to participate, and the amount of disagreement among subordinates with respect to their preferred alternatives. The model provides the following set of rules for determining what decision procedure or procedures should not be used by the leader in a given situation because decision quality or acceptance would be risked (Vroom and Yetton, 1973, p. 218–220):

1. *The leader information rule.* If the quality of the decision is important, and the leader does not possess enough information or expertise to solve the problem alone, then AI is eliminated from the feasible set.

2. *The subordinate information rule* (applicable to individual problems only). If the quality of the decision is important, and the subordinate does not possess enough information to solve the problem alone, then DI is eliminated from the feasible set.

3. *The goal congruence rule.* If the quality of the decision is important, and the subordinate(s) is (are) not likely to pursue organizational goals in his (their) efforts to solve this problem, then GII, DI, and GI are eliminated from the feasible set.

4a. *The unstructured problem rule* (group problem). When the quality of the decision is important, if the leader lacks the necessary information or expertise to solve the problem alone and if the problem is unstructured, the method of solving the problem should provide for interaction among subordinates likely to possess relevant information. Accordingly, AI, AII, and CI are eliminated from the feasible set.

4b. *The unstructured problem rule* (individual problem). In deci-

TABLE 8–1. Decision Procedures for Group and Individual Problems

	Group Problems		*Individual Problems*
AI.	You solve the problem or make the decision yourself, using information available to you at the time.	AI.	You solve the problem or make the decision by yourself, using information available to you at the time.
AII.	You obtain the necessary information from your subordinates, then decide the solution to the problem yourself. You may or may not tell your subordinates what the problem is in getting the information from them. The role played by your subordinates in making the decision is clearly one of providing the necessary information to you, rather than generating or evaluating alternative solutions.	AII.	You obtain the necessary information from your subordinate, then decide on the solution to the problem yourself. You may or may not tell the subordinate what the problem is in getting the information from him. His role in making the decision is clearly one of providing the necessary information to you, rather than generating or evaluating alternative solutions.
CI.	You share the problem with the relevant subordinates individually, getting their ideas and suggestions without bringing them together as a group. Then *you* make the decision, which may or may not reflect your subordinates' influence.	CI.	You share the problem with your subordinate, getting his ideas and suggestions. Then you make a decision, which may or may not reflect his influence.
CII.	You share the problem with your subordinates as a group, obtaining their collective ideas and suggestions. Then you make the decision, which may or may not reflect your subordinates' influence.	GI.	You share the problem with your subordinate, and together you analyze the problem and arrive at a mutually agreeable solution.
GII.	You share the problem with your subordinates as a group. Together you generate and evaluate alternatives and attempt to reach agreement (consensus) on a solution. Your role is much like that of chairman. You do not try to influence the group to adopt "your" solution, and you are willing to accept and implement any solution which has the support of the entire group.	DI.	You delegate the problem to your subordinate, providing him with any relevant information that you possess, but giving him responsibility for solving the problem by himself. You may or may not request him to tell you what solution he has reached.

Source: Reprinted from *Leadership and Decision-Making*, p. 13, by Victor H. Vroom and Philip W. Yetton, by permission of the University of Pittsburgh Press. © 1973 by the University of Pittsburgh Press.

sions in which quality is important, if the leader lacks the necessary information to solve the problem alone and if the problem is unstructured, the method of solving the problem should permit the subordinate to generate solutions and in so doing provide information concerning all aspects of the problem. Accordingly, AI and AII are eliminated from the feasible set.

5. *The acceptance rule.* If the acceptance of the decision by the subordinate(s) is critical to effective implementation and if it is not certain that an autocratic decision will be accepted, AI and AII are eliminated from the feasible set.

6. *The conflict rule* (applicable to group problems only). If the acceptance of the decision is critical, an autocratic decision is not certain to be accepted, and disagreement among subordinates in methods of attaining the organizational goal is likely, the methods used in solving the problem should enable those in disagreement to resolve their differences with full knowledge of the problem. Accordingly, under these conditions AI, AII, and CI, which permit no interaction among subordinates and therefore provide no opportunity for those in conflict to resolve their differences, are eliminated from the feasible set. Their use runs the risk of leaving some of the subordinates with less than the needed commitment to the final decision.

7. *The fairness rule.* If the quality of the decision is unimportant, but acceptance of the decision is critical and not certain to result from an autocratic decision, it is important that the decision process used generates the needed acceptance. In group problems, the decision process used should permit the subordinates to interact with one another and negotiate over the fair method of resolving any differences with full responsibility on them for determining what is fair and equitable. In individual problems, the decision-making process should provide for the affected subordinate to be at least a full and equal partner. Accordingly, under these circumstances AI, AII, CI, and CII are eliminated from the feasible set.

8. *The acceptance priority rule.* If acceptance is critical, not certain to result from an autocratic decision, and if (the) subordinate(s) is (are) motivated to pursue the organizational goals represented in the problem, then methods which provide equal partnership in the decision-making process can provide greater acceptance without risking decision quality. Accordingly, AI, AII, CI, and CII are eliminated from the feasible set.

Vroom and Yetton have developed some decision process flow charts to simplify the application of the rules. One of these charts is shown in Figure 8–3. The rules are represented pictorially in the form of a decision tree. To use the chart, you start at the left side and ask yourself question A. If the answer is no, you then ask yourself question D, but if the answer to A was yes, you then ask yourself question B. In other words, you procede through the decision tree according to your answers until a terminal point is reached. The number at the terminal point indicates which of the feasi-

FIGURE 8–3
Decision-Process Flow Chart for Both Individual and Group Problems

A.   Is there a quality requirement such that one solution is likely to be more rational than another?

B.   Do I have sufficient information to make a high quality decision?

C.   Is the problem structured?

D.   Is acceptance of decision by subordinates critical to effective implementation?

E.   If I were to make the decision by myself, is it reasonably certain that it would be accepted by my subordinates?

F.   Do subordinates share the organizational goals to be attained in solving this problem?

G.   Is conflict among subordinates likely in preferred solutions? (This question is irrelevant to individual problems.)

H.   Do subordinates have sufficient information to make a high quality decision?

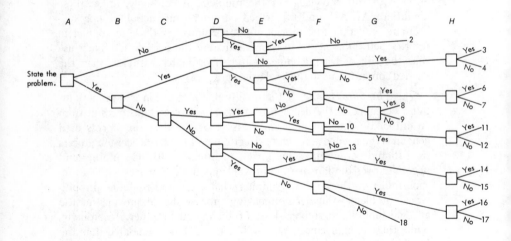

The feasible set is shown for each problem type for Group (G) and Individual (I) problems.

1   G: AI, AII, CI, CII, GII
    I: AI, DI, AII, CI, GI

2   G: GII
    I: DI, GI

3   G: AI, AII, CI, CII, GII
    I: AI, DI, AII, CI, GI

4   G: AI, AII, CI, CII, GII
    I: AI, AII, CI, GI

5   G: AI, AII, CI, CII
    I: AI, AII, CI

6   G: GII
    I: DI, GI

7   G: GII
    I: GI

8   G: GII
    I: CI

9   G: CI, CII
    I: CI

10 G: AII, CI, CII
    I: AII, CI

11 G: AII, CI, CII, GII
    I: AII, CI, GI

12 G: AII, CI, CII, GII
    I: DI, AII, CI, GI

13 G: GII
    I: CI

14 G: CII, GII
    I: DI, CI, GI

15 G: CII, GII
    I: CI, GI

16 G: GII
    I: DI, GI

17 G: GII
    I: GI

18 G: CII
    I: CI

Source: Reprinted from *Leadership and Decision-Making*, p. 194, by Victor H. Vroom and Philip W. Yetton by permission of the University of Pittsburgh Press. © 1973 by the University of Pittsburgh Press.

ble sets of decision procedures (below the decision tree) applies to the decision situation described by your answers to the questions.

For some types of decision situations, the model prescribes more than one feasible decision procedure. In this case, the choice among procedures should be based on other considerations such as time pressure, development of subordinates, and the leader's preferences. Vroom and Yetton have proposed that for decisions involving several subordinates the amount of time needed to make the decision can be minimized by using the least participative procedure in the feasible set. This additional guideline is based on the finding that less time is usually needed to make an autocratic decision than to make a decision by consultation, and consultation is usually faster than a group decision. Figure 8–4 shows how the model can be used in a specific case to select a decision procedure.

FIGURE 8–4
Application of the Vroom and Yetton Model to a Specific Case

Decision Situation

You are supervising the work of 12 engineers. Their formal training and work experience are very similar, permitting you to use them interchangeably on projects. Yesterday, your manager informed you that a request had been received from an overseas affiliate for four engineers to go abroad on extended loan for a period of six to eight months. For a number of reasons, he argued, and you agreed, that this request should be met from your group. All of your engineers are capable of handling this assignment, and from the standpoint of present and future projects, there is no particular reason why any one should be retained over any other. The problem is somewhat complicated by the fact that the overseas assignment is in what is generally regarded in the company as an undesirable location.

Analysis (based on Figure 8–3)

Question A (Quality requirement?):   NO

Question D (Subordinate acceptance critical?):   YES

Question E (Is acceptance likely without participation?):   NO

Feasible set of decision procedures: GII
Minimum manhour solution: GII

Rule violations:
  1. AI and AII violates the acceptance rule, the conflict rule, and the fairness rule.
  2. CI violates the conflict rule and the fairness rule.
  3. CII violates the fairness rule.

Source: Adapted from *Leadership and Decision-Making*, pp. 41–42, by Victor H. Vroom and Philip W. Yetton by permission of the University of Pittsburgh Press. © 1973 by the University of Pittsburgh Press.

EMPIRICAL EVIDENCE FOR THE MODEL.   The Vroom and Yetton model appears to be a promising development in leadership theory. It should be noted, however, that the rules and prescriptions of the model are based primarily on the results of previous research. Little new research has been conducted to test the model in its entirety. In our opinion, it is unlikely that subsequent research will disconfirm the logic of the model, although some refinements or modifications may prove to be necessary.

Path-Goal Theory of Leadership

The path-goal theory of leadership (Evans, 1970; House, 1971) explains how leader behavior affects subordinate motivation and performance in different work situations. The theory was derived from the "expectancy theory" of motivation that was discussed in Chapter 2. According to expectancy theory, an employee's motivation depends upon his expectancy that an effort to attain a superior level of performance would be successful, and his expectancy that superior performance would be instrumental for attaining positive outcomes and avoiding negative outcomes. Path-goal theory describes how leader behavior affects these expectancies, which in turn affect subordinate performance.

The major propositions of the theory are that a leader's behavior will increase subordinate motivation to the extent that (1) the leader makes satisfaction of subordinate needs contingent on effective performance, and (2) the leader provides necessary coaching, guidance, and support that would otherwise be lacking (House and Mitchell, 1974). The effects of leader behavior are moderated by two major types of situational variables: subordinate characteristics (e.g., ability, personality), and environmental factors (e.g., task characteristics, position power).

Somewhat different versions of Path-Goal Theory have been developed by Evans (1970), by House (1971), and by House and Dessler (1974). Despite the differences, there are certain leadership prescriptions that appear to be consistent with all three versions. These prescriptions will be expressed in terms of four specific categories of leader behavior: role clarification, structuring reward contingencies, work facilitation, and supportive leadership. The use of the first three behavior categories instead of a more inclusive task-oriented behavior dimension like initiating structure is a modification of the theory made by us to further clarify its practical implications.

ROLE CLARIFICATION.   Many members of organizations lack a clear understanding of their role requirements and are unsure about what behavior is expected by their bosses. When there is substantial role ambiguity, subordinates may be frustrated and upset. Since they do not know what they are supposed to do, the expectancy that effort will lead to positive outcomes is likely to be low.

Role ambiguity is most likely in a situation where there is an unstructured task requiring problem solving and innovative behavior by subordinates. As was noted in Chapter 3, when the task and environment are uncertain, it is inappropriate to have detailed rules and work procedures. Nevertheless, it is essential for subordinates to understand the objectives toward which they are supposed to be working. In order to clarify subordinate roles in this situation, the leader should inform subordinates about general objectives, priorities, and the constraints within which they must operate. The leader should also meet periodically with each subordinate to set specific goals for the next time interval. Finally, the basis for evaluating subordinate performance and progress toward goal attainment should be explained.

Role ambiguity is less likely in a situation where there is a routine, certain task; and detailed rules, procedures and standards have been specified by the organization. Nevertheless, the leader should insure that subordinates understand the rules and work procedures which are essential for effective performance of their jobs. The leader should also inform subordinates about the standards to be used for evaluating their performance, and individual performance goals should be set when appropriate.

In a situation where there is a routine, certain task, but rules and standard procedures have not been provided by the organization, the clarification of subordinate roles is likely to require some structuring behavior by the leader. Here the leader can improve subordinate performance by organizing the group's activities, assigning tasks, and developing effective work procedures. In making such task decisions, it may be appropriate for the leader to allow subordinate participation, as noted earlier in the Vroom and Yetton model.

In each of the above situations, the amount of role clarification and direction by the leader will depend on the characteristics of the subordinates as well as on the task. If subordinates are highly competent and independent, less structuring and direction are needed than if they are inexperienced and dependent. In a situation where there is little role ambiguity and subordinates know how to perform their jobs, they are likely to resent a leader who continually tries to structure activities and direct their behavior. Such behavior by the leader will be perceived as redundant and an unnecessary imposition of control.

ESTABLISHMENT OF FAVORABLE REWARD CONTINGENCIES. As we saw in Chapter 5, the reward contingencies in an organization affect subordinate motivation and behavior. The potential for improving subordinate performance by altering reward contingencies will be greatest when the present level of subordinate motivation is quite low and the leader has substantial authority and power. In this situation, the leader should make pay and other positive outcomes contingent upon performance to the greatest possible extent. In other words, the leader should insure that superior performance by subordinates is consistently recognized and rewarded. In addition, a leader with high position power should make punishments such as suspension or dismissal consistently contingent upon certain highly undesirable behavior by subordinates such as theft, violence, safety rule violations, and chronic tardiness or absenteeism. Subordinate motivation will be improved to the extent that they perceive the new outcome contingencies accurately. In order to avoid the problem of subordinates who have inaccurate expectancies and who have misconceptions about the consequences of their behavior, the leader should carefully explain incentive programs, disciplinary procedures, and other aspects of the formal reward system.

To supplement the formal organization rewards and punishments, a leader should try to discover other things that are valued by subordinates and can be used to increase subordinate motivation. Praise is usually effective, and special prizes, favors, or privileges may also be used to reward superior performance. It may also be possible for the leader to enrich subordinate jobs and delegate more responsibility so that subordinates will be more intrinsically motivated and satisfied. Finally, any negative outcomes (e.g., fatigue, safety risks, layoffs due to insufficient work) should be minimized and subordinate fears about these negative outcomes should be dispelled.

WORK (PATH-GOAL) FACILITATION. Once the path (i.e., required behavior) leading to superior performance has been clarified and reward contingencies improved so that the subordinate perceives that this path leads also to personal need fulfillment, then the leader should try to make the path easier for subordinates to follow. There are a number of ways that the leader can facilitate the work of the group and at the same time increase the subordinates' expectancy that their efforts to achieve superior performance will be successful.

In most jobs there are many extraneous factors that influence the performance of subordinates but are beyond their immediate control. These extraneous factors include such things as the availability of adequate supplies, equipment, and information, the existence of adequate working conditions (e.g., illumination, temperature, noise), and possession of adequate skills to carry out work assignments. The leader seldom, if ever, has complete control over extraneous factors, but can usually remove some of the obstacles to efficient subordinate performance. For example, the leader should try to insure that work supplies are adequate and necessary equipment repairs are made to avoid costly delays and quality problems. When there are serious deficiencies in subordinate skills, the leader should provide additional instruction or help the subordinate enroll in a training course. In addition, the leader should try to assign each subordinate to tasks that are appropriate in difficulty for the subordinate's skill level and self-assurance.

The importance of extraneous factors and the leader's control over them will vary across leadership situations. The greater the obstacles to subordinate efficiency and motivation, and the greater the leader's capacity to remove these obstacles, the stronger will be the relationship between a leader's work facilitation behavior and subordinate performance.

SUPPORTIVE LEADERSHIP. The leader should also try to make the path to superior performance easier to travel by providing psychological support for subordinates who have unpleasant, stressful, or frustrating tasks. The extent to which the task will be dissatisfying to subordinates depends on the situation. Supportive and considerate leadership are most important in situations where there is excessive job pressure, substantial role conflict, bitter interpersonal conflict, an emotionally exhausting task, or a very boring and fatiguing task. Of course, reactions to any job situation are likely to vary a great deal from employee to employee, and supervisory supportiveness will be more important to some subordinates than to others. For example, encouragement and psychological support will have a more positive effect on the motivation of a subordinate who lacks self-confidence than on a confident subordinate who has little anxiety about performance.

EMPIRICAL EVIDENCE. The research conducted to test path-goal leadership theory has been reviewed by House and Mitchell (1974). For the most part, this research has been an examination of the interaction between situational variables and measures of leader consideration and initiating structure within a correlational research design. The results from some of these studies and from other research on the contingent effectiveness of leader consideration and initiating structure (see review by Kerr et al., 1974) provide support for the theory. On the other hand, quite a few studies have failed to provide positive evidence, and certain methodological weaknesses in the type of research used to test the theory have been pointed out by Korman (1973). Thus, while the leadership prescriptions that we have summarized appear reasonable in light of the empirical evidence, they should not be regarded as infallible until much more evidence is obtained.

IMPROVING LEADERSHIP IN ORGANIZATIONS

There are three general approaches for improving leadership in organizations. One approach is selection, and the techniques used with this approach are described in Chapter 11. This approach assumes that it is possible to identify potentially effective leaders either among lower level employees who can be promoted or among external applicants who can be hired to fill leadership positions. The second approach for improving organizational leadership is training and management development, and the procedures used to carry out this approach are described in Chapter 14. This approach assumes that it is possible to identify and teach necessary leadership skills and behavior. The final approach for improving leadership is to alter the leadership situation directly. This approach involves changing such things as the organization climate, the leader's position power and scope of authority, the number of subordinates, and the type of tasks performed by the subordinates. The three approaches for improving leadership are not mutually exclusive, and it is possible for an organization to use a combination of approaches.

The Vroom and Yetton model and path-goal theory appear to be most applicable through leadership training. Both theories prescribe certain behavior for leader effectiveness in different situations, and these prescriptions can be incorporated into a training program for leaders. Vroom and Yetton (1973) have already developed such a training program based on their model. Managers who are being trained receive instruction about the rationale for the model and its prescriptions. The typical decision behavior of each manager is determined with a series of cases like the one shown earlier in Figure 8–4 (but omitting the analysis and recommendations based on the model). A manager is asked to read each case and indicate which decision procedure he would use in that situation. His answers are compared to the answers of other managers and to the answers prescribed by the model. This kind of feedback can be used as the basis for a group discussion. Trainees can practice applying the model by reading other cases and determining the appropriate decision procedures.

In order to use the Vroom and Yetton prescriptions successfully, a leader must be able to make reasonably accurate judgments about the decision situation. That is, the leader must be able to determine the quality requirements, the acceptance requirements, the distribution of relevant information, and so on. These judgments require a certain amount of skill on the part of the leader. The leader also has to know how to use the prescribed decision procedures in an effective manner. Procedures such as joint decision making with subordinates as a group, delegation, and consultation with subordinates must be used in a suitable manner or they will not produce the desired improvements in decision quality and subordinate acceptance. The same kind of statement can be made about application of prescriptions from path-goal theory. The leader must be able to accurately analyze the situation, and he must have the technical, administrative, and human relations skills necessary to carry out the prescribed behavior. Therefore, leadership training should include the teaching of relevant skills in addition to the teaching of principles and prescriptions. Case analysis, role-playing, and behavior modeling appear to be appropriate methods for providing this kind of leadership training (see

Chapter 14). In the training program developed by Vroom and Yetton (1973), role playing, case analysis, and observation of films demonstrating different decision styles have been used to facilitate development of essential skills.

Fiedler (1965) has argued that the best way to improve leader effectiveness is to directly change the leadership situation. He proposed that position power can be increased or decreased, relations with the subordinates can be altered, and the structure of the task can be changed to make the situation compatible with the leader, in accordance with the model. Recently, Fiedler and Chemers (1975) have developed a leadership training program based on the model. Training is carried out with a programmed textbook entitled *Leader Match*. The programmed textbook explains Fiedler's theory and shows a leader how to analyze his situation. The leader also fills out and scores an LPC scale. If the situation is not compatible with his LPC score, the leader is shown how to modify the situation to increase compatibility.

Another promising application of Fiedler's contingency model is the use of LPC scores in the selection and placement of leaders. Low LPC persons could be placed either in very favorable or very unfavorable leadership situations, and high LPC persons could be placed in situations of intermediate favorability. This approach would appear to be more feasible in some cases than major changes in the leadership situation. All that would be necessary is to administer an LPC scale to applicants for a leadership position, determine situation favorability for that position, and from among the applicants who are otherwise qualified, select one whose LPC score is appropriate for the situation. Unfortunately, no research has been conducted yet to evaluate this potential application of Fiedler's theory.

SUMMARY

Leadership in organizations is a vital but mysterious process. A great deal of research has been conducted to gain some insight into the reasons why some leaders are effective and others are not. One early approach for studying leadership was a search for traits that are essential for leadership effectiveness. A second approach focused on leader behavior rather than leader traits. Researchers investigated whether leadership effectiveness depended on a leader's consideration, initiating structure, interaction facilitation, or decision-making behavior. In yet another approach for studying leadership, researchers examined the sources and consequences of leader power and influence.

Research on leader traits, behavior, and power failed to yield consistent results, and the reason appeared to be the moderating effects of the leadership situation. Contingency models were developed to describe how characteristics of the leader interact with characteristics of the situation to determine whether a leader will be effective. Three of the leader-situation interaction models include: Fiedler's contingency model of leadership, the Vroom and Yetton model of leader decision making, and the path goal theory of leadership.

There are three general approaches for improving leadership in an organization: selection, training, and situational change. Fiedler's model has potential applications to all three approaches. The other two models appear to be primarily applicable to the improvement of leadership training and management development. The procedures used for the selection and training of managers and administrators are examined in subsequent chapters.

REVIEW AND DISCUSSION QUESTIONS

1. Define or explain each of the following key terms: leadership, leader traits, leadership behavior, consideration, initiating structure, interaction facilitation, participation, consultation, delegation, autocratic decision making, joint decision making, reward power, coercive power, legitimate power, expert power, referent power, position power, personal power, bilateral power, contingency or interaction models, LPC score, task structure, situation favorability, decision quality and acceptance.

2. What was found in the research on the effects of leader traits and behavior on subordinate performance?

3. Explain how consideration, initiating structure, and style of decision making are different aspects of leader behavior.

4. What are the five different sources or bases of power proposed by French and Raven?

5. How is power related to leader effectiveness?

6. What is the relationship between a leader's LPC score and his effectiveness according to Fiedler?

7. What rules were proposed by Vroom and Yetton to guide leaders in selecting an appropriate decision procedure?

8. What are some propositions of path-goal theory regarding what leadership behavior is appropriate in what situation?

9. How can the Fiedler, Vroom and Yetton, and path-goal (House and Evans) theories be applied to improve leadership in organizations?

REFERENCES

Ashour, A. A. The contingency model of leadership effectiveness: An evaluation. *Organizational Behavior and Human Performance*, 1973, 9, 339–355.

Bachman, J. G., Smith, C. G., & Slesinger, J. A. Control, performance, and satisfaction: An analysis of structural and individual effects. *Journal of Personality and Social Psychology*, 1966, 4, 127–136.

Bowers, D. G., & Seashore, S. E.   Predicting organizational effectiveness with a four-factor theory of leadership. *Administrative Science Quarterly*, 1966, 11, 238–263.

Campbell, J. P., Dunnette, M. D., Lawler, E. E., III, & Weick, K. E.   *Managerial behavior, performance, and effectiveness*. New York: McGraw-Hill, 1970.

Davis, K.   Attitudes toward the legitimacy of management efforts to influence employees. *Academy of Management Journal*, 1968, 11, 153–162.

Evans, M. G.   The effects of supervisory behavior on the path-goal relationship. *Organizational Behavior and Human Performance*, 1970, 5, 277–298.

Farris, G. F., & Lim, F. G., Jr.   Effects of performance on leadership, cohesiveness, satisfaction, and subsequent performance. *Journal of Applied Psychology*, 1969, 53, 102–110.

Fiedler, F. E.   A contingency model of leadership effectiveness. In L. Berkowitz (Ed.), *Advances in experimental social psychology*, vol. 1. New York: Academic Press, 1964.

Fiedler, F. E.   Engineer the job to fit the manager. *Harvard Business Review*, 1965, 43 (September-October), 115–122.

Fiedler, F. E.   *A theory of leadership effectiveness*. New York: McGraw-Hill, 1967.

Fiedler, F. E.   Validation and extension of the contingency model of leadership effectiveness: A review of empirical findings. *Psychological Bulletin*, 1971, 76, 128–148.

Fiedler, F. E., & Chemers, M. M.   *Leader match: A contingency model training program*. Seattle: University of Washington, Department of Psychology, 1975.

Fleishman, E. A.   A leader behavior description for industry. In R. M. Stogdill and A. E. Coons (Eds.), *Leader behavior: Its description and measurement*. Columbus: Ohio State University, Bureau of Business Research, 1957.

French, J. R. P., & Raven, B.   The bases of social power. In D. Cartwright and A. F. Zander (Eds.), *Group dynamics*. Evanston, Ill.: Row, Peterson, 1960.

Ghiselli, E. E.   Managerial talent. *American Psychologist*, 1963, 18, 631–642.

Graen, G., Alvares, K. M., Orris, J. B., & Martella, J. A.   Contingency model of leadership effectiveness: Antecedents and evidential results. *Psychological Bulletin*, 1970, 74, 285–296.

Graen, G., Orris, J. B., & Alvares, K. M.   Contingency model of leadership effectiveness: Some methodological issues. *Journal of Applied Psychology*, 1971, 55, 205–210.

Halpin, A. W., & Winer, B. J.   A factorial study of the leader behavior descriptions. In R. M. Stogdill and A. E. Coons (Eds.), *Leader behavior:*

Its description and measurement. Columbus: Ohio State University, Bureau of Business Research, 1957.

Heller, F. A., & Yukl, G. A.   Participation, managerial decision-making, and situational variables. *Organizational Behavior and Human Performance*, 1969, *4*, 227–241.

Hemphill, J. K., & Coons, A. E.   Development of the leader behavior description questionnaire. In R. M. Stogdill and A. E. Coons (Eds.), *Leader behavior: Its description and measurement.* Columbus: Ohio State University, Bureau of Business Research, 1957.

House, R. J.   A path-goal theory of leader effectiveness. *Administrative Science Quarterly*, 1971, *16*, 321–339.

House, R. J., & Dessler, G.   The path-goal theory of leadership: Some post hoc and a priori tests. In J. G. Hunt (Ed.), *Contingency approaches to leadership.* Carbondale, Ill.: Southern Illinois University Press, 1974.

House, R. J., & Mitchell, T. R.   Path-goal theory of leadership. *Contemporary Business*, 1974, *3* (Fall), 81–98.

Ivancevich, J. M., & Donnelly, J. H.   Leader influence and performance. *Personnel Psychology*, 1970, *23*, 539–549.

Kerr, S., Schriesheim, C. A., Murphy, C. J., & Stogdill, R. M.   Toward a contingency theory of leadership based upon the Consideration and Initiating Structure literature. *Organizational Behavior and Human Performance*, 1974, *12*, 62–82.

Korman, A. K.   Consideration, initiating structure, and organizational criteria —a review. *Personnel Psychology*, 1966, *19*, 349–362.

Korman, A. K.   The prediction of managerial performance: A review. *Personnel Psychology*, 1968, *21*, 295–322.

Korman, A. K.   On the development of contingency theories of leadership: Some methodological considerations and a possible alternative. *Journal of Applied Psychology*, 1973, *58*, 384–387.

Likert, R.   *New patterns of management.* New York: McGraw-Hill, 1961.

Lowin, A.   Participative decision-making: A model, literature critique, and prescriptions for research. *Organizational Behavior and Human Performance*, 1968, *3*, 68–106.

Lowin, A., & Craig, J. R.   The influence of level of performance on managerial style: An experimental object lesson in the ambiguity of correlational data. *Organizational Behavior and Human Performance*, 1968, *3*, 440–458.

Maier, N. R. F.   *Problem solving discussions and conferences: Leadership methods and skills.* New York: McGraw-Hill, 1963.

Mann, F. C.   Toward an understanding of the leadership role in formal organization. In R. Dubin, G. C. Homans, F. C. Mann, & D. C. Miller (Eds.), *Leadership and productivity.* San Francisco: Chandler, 1965.

Mann, R. D.   A review of the relationships between personality and performance in small groups. *Psychological Bulletin*, 1959, *56*, 241–270.

Sales, S. M. Supervisory style and productivity: Review and theory. *Personnel Psychology*, 1966, *19*, 275–286.

Stogdill, R. A. Personal factors associated with leadership: a survey of the literature. *Journal of Psychology*, 1948, *25*, 35–71.

Stogdill, R. M., & Coons, A. E. *Manual for the leader behavior description questionnaire—Form XII.* Columbus: Ohio State University, Bureau of Business Research, 1963.

Student, K. R. Supervisory influence and work group performance. *Journal of Applied Psychology*, 1968, *52*, 188–194.

Tannenbaum, R., & Schmidt, W. H. How to choose a leadership pattern. *Harvard Business Review*, 1958, *36* (March–April), 95–101.

Vroom, V. H., & Yetton, P. W. *Leadership and decision-making.* Pittsburgh: University of Pittsburg Press, 1973.

Woodward, J. *Industrial organization: Theory and practice.* New York: Oxford University Press, 1965.

Yukl, G. A. Toward a behavioral theory of leadership. *Organizational Behavior and Human Performance*, 1971, *6*, 414–440.

9

CONFLICT MANAGEMENT IN ORGANIZATIONS

A CONFLICT is a dispute or struggle between two parties that is characterized by overt expression of hostility and/or intentional interference in the goal attainment of the opposing party. Interference can involve either active attempts to block someone's goal attainment or passive resistance such as withholding necessary supplies and information from the other party (Schmidt and Kochan, 1972). Conflicts can occur regardless of whether two parties have goals that are incompatible. That is, conflict can occur even when the goals of two parties are compatible and the consequences will only be detrimental to everybody involved. This kind of conflict has been labeled a "pseudo-conflict" to distinguish it from conflicts where real differences exist between the goals or values of the parties (Rhenman, Stromberg and Westerlund, 1970).

Interpersonal and intergroup conflict occur to some extent in all organizations and are a natural part of social relationships. Conflict can occur between individuals in the same group, between a person and the boss, between two or more departments in an organization, between line and staff personnel, and between a labor union and management. In this chapter we will examine the consequences of conflict for organizations, the antecedent conditions leading to conflict, typical reactions to conflict by the parties directly involved, types of intervention by third parties, and the implications for effective management of conflict.

CONSEQUENCES OF CONFLICT

Until recently, behavioral scientists have assumed that conflict is an abnormal phenomenon with only negative consequences. Thus it is not surprising that conflict has usually been regarded as an evil to be eliminated whenever possible. In fact, conflict can have both good and bad consequences, and the objective should be to manage it in such a way that the benefits are retained and the adverse effects minimized.

The negative effects of conflict are primarily due to its disruption of communication, cohesiveness, and cooperation. When members of an organization have interdependent activities, performance of these activities will suffer if there is a lack of cooperation and refusal to share information due to chronic conflict. The productive activity of each party will be further reduced by diversion of time and energy to "winning" conflicts. Individuals engaged in conflicts typically experience stress, frustration, and anxiety; these, in turn, reduce job satisfaction, impair concentration on the task, create apathy, and encourage withdrawal in the form of absenteeism or turnover. When conflict is excessive, the organization may be torn apart, or it may be immobilized, unable to take unified action in a hostile environment.

On the other hand, without some conflict an organization would be unlikely to maintain its vigor and successfully adapt to a changing environment. Adaptation requires changes in procedures and priorities, and perhaps even in organization goals. Such changes create inconvenience and involve a redistribution of power and status. Consequently, major changes are usually avoided or resisted by many members of an organization. Unless there is overt conflict, changes are not likely to occur rapidly enough to insure successful adaptation. In addition, decisions are less likely to reflect "stagnant thinking" or biased perception if they are forged from disagreement, and conflict can be a major source of motivation to develop innovative methods.

ANTECEDENT CAUSES OF CONFLICT

Conflicts are created by a variety of antecedent conditions (Robbins, 1974; Walton and Dutton, 1969). Six major categories of antecedent conditions include: (1) competition for resources, (2) task interdependence, (3) jurisdictional ambiguity, (4) status problems, (5) communication barriers, and (6) individual traits. Many conflicts involve more than one of these antecedent conditions, and the categories are not always mutually exclusive.

Competition for Resources

One major source of conflict in organizations is competition for scarce resources such as budget funds, space, supplies, personnel, and supporting services (e.g., typing, duplicating, data processing, maintenance). The scarcer the supply of resources relative to the amount needed by the rival parties, and the more important the resources are to them, the greater the likelihood that conflict will develop and the more intense it will be. Cases of conflict resulting from competition over scarce resources can be found in most organizations. One example is a conflict between two sales departments over who could get priority in the scheduling of their product for production. "Top sales officials wasted hours personally exerting their authority in production offices to get schedule deviations" (Seiler, 1963, p. 126). Each time one sales department was able to get the schedule changed, problems were created for production personnel as well as for the other sales department.

Task Interdependence

When two individuals or two groups are dependent upon each other in some way for the successful performance of their tasks, conflict is likely to occur if the two parties have different goals or priorities. Task interdependence may be either one way or mutual, and the dependency may involve provision of supplies, information, assistance, or direction, as well as the necessity of coordinating the activities of the two parties. The greater the difference in goal orientation for the parties, the more likely it is that conflict will develop. This kind of conflict is commonly found between interdependent departments that are highly specialized, such as research and production, or sales and production. Strauss (1962, p. 164) provides an example from a study of purchasing agents:

> Engineers write up the specifications for the products that the agents buy. If the specifications are too tight, or what is worse, if they call for one brand only, agents have little or no freedom to choose among suppliers, thus reducing their social status internally and their economic bargaining power externally. Yet engineers find it much easier to write down a well-known brand name than to draw up a lengthy functional specification which lists all the characteristics of the desired item. Disagreements also arise because, by training, engineers look first for quality and reliability and thus, agents charge, are indifferent to low cost and quick delivery, qualities of primary interest to purchasing.

Jurisdictional Ambiguity

Conflict is likely when jurisdictional boundaries are unclear due to overlapping responsibility or gaps in responsibility, and one party attempts to assume more control over desirable activities or to relinquish its part in the performance of undesirable activities. Conflicts also develop when one party tries to take the full credit for success or to avoid the blame for failure in joint activities. Dutton and Walton (1965) describe a conflict between sales and production departments that was due in part to a jurisdictional disagreement. Each department tried to remain free of obligations and to establish jurisdictional limitations on the activities of the other department. When sales wanted new product designs, production resisted and found lots of reasons for not trying them. When production attempted to avoid producing an order by claiming that they did not have the necessary materials, sales took the initiative in locating and ordering the materials. Production reacted by accusing sales of violating established procedures and overstepping its jurisdiction. As a result of the conflicts that repeatedly occurred, few new designs were developed, profitable orders were lost, crews were dismissed for lack of work, orders were not filled on time, and defective orders were shipped to customers.

Status Problems

In Chapter 7 we saw how inconsistency between work-flow patterns and the status hierarchy created conflict between order runners and cooks in a restaurant. The same kind of conflict can also occur between two departments in an organization. Seiler (1963) describes what happened in one company where a low-status production engineering department initiated design and schedule changes for a production department that had equal or higher status. The production personnel resented being told what to do and how to do it by production engineers whose skills were no greater than their own. A great deal of time was wasted by the production managers searching for errors in engineering's drawings and preparing elaborate criticisms of these errors to embarrass the production engineers.

Conflict is also likely when one department tries to improve its status and other departments perceive this to be a threat to their position in the status hierarchy. In research on line-staff conflict, Dalton (1950) observed that staff personnel attempted to prove their worth by developing new production techniques. The line managers resisted applying these new techniques because they regarded their authority over production as a sacred right, and they resented the implication that they needed any help from the younger, less experienced staff personnel. The combination of status and jurisdictional issues created serious frictions, and the potential savings from some superior new techniques were never attained.

A final type of status conflict is caused by perceived inequities in rewards, job assignments, working conditions, and status symbols. If an individual or department believes that they are receiving fewer benefits or opportunities than they deserve, frustration and resentment can develop into conflict with the administrator responsible for the allocation of benefits, or with the persons who are receiving superior benefits.

Communication Barriers

In Chapter 4 we saw that there are many barriers to accurate communication between persons. Insufficient communication can contribute to the development of pseudo-conflict by preventing agreement between two parties whose positions are essentially compatible. The absence of adequate channels of communication can impede attempts to achieve coordination between parties with interdependent tasks. Semantic difficulties and selective interpretation of information can perpetuate misconceptions and encourage mutual distrust. For example, the animosity between a county welfare department and several other county agencies was found to be directly attributable to their ignorance about the welfare department's duties and contributions (Robbins, 1974, p. 37).

On the other hand, there are situations where too much open communication creates conflict that would not otherwise have occurred. Perfect knowledge can reveal inequities or value differences between parties, thereby stirring up resentment and hostility. Walton, Dutton and Cafferty (1969) found that conflict between departments in an organization was greater when the departments possessed substantial knowledge about each other's activities than when they did not.

Individual Traits

The likelihood of conflict is partially determined by the personality traits of the parties. In a review of bargaining research, Walton and McKersie (1965) concluded that conflict behavior was more likely when the parties were high in dogmatism and authoritarianism and low in self-esteem. Consider for example two dogmatic individuals who disagree. Each person is inflexible and unable to recognize any intermediate position upon which agreement might be possible.

Needs and values can also contribute to the development of conflict. For example, employees with a strong need for independence are likely to have a conflict with their boss if he is a very authoritarian individual who supervises closely and allows little autonomy. When there is competition among organization members, conflict is more likely to develop if the competitors are highly ambitious and have strong needs that will be satisfied by "winning." Finally, there is more likely to be a conflict between persons with different social, political, moral, or religious values than between persons with the same values.

DYNAMICS OF WIN-LOSE CONFLICT BETWEEN GROUPS

The most severe conflicts between groups occur when there is a "win-lose" orientation. That is, each group believes that only one group can "win" and they are determined to be the victor. Most conflicts are not inherently of the win-lose type, but they may become so if the parties regard any substantial concession as equivalent to defeat. The dynamics of win-lose conflicts have been studied extensively in a laboratory setting by behavioral scientists. Much of this research was conducted by Blake and

Mouton (1961, 1962, 1964). Their usual approach was to form groups composed of managers who were participating in a management training workshop. After 10 to 18 hours of group activities that developed group identification and cohesiveness, each group was asked to prepare a written proposal for the solution of a hypothetical problem. The proposals were circulated for examination by competing groups. Then a representative was chosen in each group, and the representatives were instructed to decide which proposal was the best one.

Many studies of this type have been conducted, and they reveal a predictable pattern of events. Group members nearly always regard their proposal to be superior to the proposals made by competing groups. This bias occurs even for members who do not participate in developing their group's proposal (Ferguson and Kelly, 1964). Even though competing proposals are examined, group members have more knowledge about their own proposal than about the other proposals. Similarities between own and other proposals are overlooked, and differences are exaggerated. Each group tends to claim as its own some points that are actually contained in competing proposals (Blake and Mouton, 1961).

When the representatives meet, each supports his own proposal and attacks the competing proposals. As members observe the debate between representatives, they listen closely to their own representative, but they tend to ignore or criticize speakers from other groups. If a representative shows signs of giving in, he or she is pressured by constituents to remain firm in support of their proposal. Thus invariably the representatives fail to reach an agreement about which proposal is the best one (Blake and Mouton, 1961).

Other studies have identified a typical pattern of events for a prolonged win-lose conflict between two groups (Sherif, 1966). After a number of competitive encounters, each group begins to see the other group as an "enemy." Members of the opposing group are perceived in terms of a negative stereotype. For example, in a labor-management conflict, union leaders believed that management was underhanded and deceitful, was concerned only with production, was desirous of gaining control over all aspects of the workers' lives, and was trying to destroy the union. Management perceived the union leaders as a legalistic and rigid minority clique that did not represent the workers, that wanted to interfere in management decisions, but was not really interested in management's problems (Blake, Mouton and Sloma, 1965). Such stereotypes are usually gross exaggerations that do not provide an accurate description of the majority of members in the opposing group.

When negative stereotypes develop, the actions of the other group are interpreted in accordance with whatever evil intentions are attributed to it. For example, if management subcontracts more work to other firms, union leaders may perceive this action as a plan to weaken the union. If there is considerable hostility and distrust, even conciliatory actions by the other side may be rejected as a "trick to put us off guard."

These findings from studies in the laboratory and with natural groups point out some of the reasons why win-lose conflicts are often so severe. There is little incentive to seek a compromise when each party believes it is completely right and the other party is wrong as well as untrustworthy. Win-lose conflicts are usually resolved on the basis of the relative power of the two parties or by a third party who arbitrates a settlement.

REACTIONS TO CONFLICT

There are a variety of ways that the parties involved in a conflict may react to it. We will examine each of the major types of conflict reactions that have been described by various behavioral scientists (Blake and Mouton, 1964; Pruitt, 1972; Walton and McKersie, 1965). Some reactions, such as withdrawal and smoothing, are attempts to avoid a confrontation over conflicting interests or values. Other reactions, such as persuasion, forcing, bargaining, and integrative problem-solving, are forms of confrontation with different consequences for resolution of a conflict.

Withdrawal

One reaction to conflict is for either or both parties to withdraw from the relationship. For example, if two individuals are having a conflict, one party may leave the organization, or they may simply avoid interacting with each other. Mutual avoidance can be an effective means of coping with conflict if the two parties have no need to interact in performing their organizational roles. However, if they have interdependent task roles that require coordination, mutual avoidance will seriously impair their performance.

Smoothing and Conciliation Tactics

Another reaction to conflict is for the parties to ignore their differences and attempt to "smooth over" the conflict. There are a number of conciliatory actions that a party can take to improve relations with the other side without actually confronting substantive issues. Some of the major conciliation tactics include the following:

1. Express a desire for cooperation and harmonious relations with the other party.
2. Offer compliments and statements of respect for the accomplishments of the other party.
3. Avoid making accusations, threats, or disparaging comments to the other party.

4. Reinforce conciliatory acts and statements by the other party by praising and reciprocating them.
5. Emphasize the common characteristics and mutual interests of both parties.
6. Make specific offers of assistance to the other party.
7. Agree not to bring up differences in values or beliefs.

Smoothing may be an effective approach for avoiding an escalation of open hostility and the disruption of work relationships, as long as the source of the conflict is not directly related to task performance. For example, if two persons have different political beliefs, religious convictions, or moral values and they get into frequent arguments about these differences, they can simply agree not to discuss them. However, like withdrawal, smoothing will not be effective if used to continually avoid confronting disagreements involving problems of coordination and joint performance. Such problems are likely to grow worse rather than disappear if they are ignored.

Persuasion

One approach for confronting conflict is an attempt to persuade the other party to change their position. Some common types of persuasive tactics include the following:

1. Provide factual evidence that supports your position.
2. Discredit information supporting the opponent's position and point out errors in his logic.
3. Point out possible costs and disadvantages of the other party's proposals that may have been overlooked (e.g., "It may come back to haunt you").
4. Point out how your proposals will benefit the other party.
5. Show how your proposals are consistent with prior precedent, prevailing norms, or accepted standards of justice and equity.

The success of persuasion depends on the credibility of the person making the persuasive appeal and the willingness of the other party to consider factual information relevant to the disagreement. If both parties are firmly committed to incompatible goals, persuasive appeals are likely to be either ignored or discounted. A persuasive appeal has a greater chance of success if the parties have compatible goals but simply disagree about the best way to attain them. The most effective persuasive tactics are probably those that do not threaten the ego or status of the other party. A direct attack on the other party's position is less likely to succeed than an indirect approach such as presenting facts that will lead the other party to draw the desired conclusions.

Forcing and Pressure Tactics

Another reaction to conflict is the use of pressure tactics to force the other party to give in. When one party has formal authority over the other's activities in the organization, as in the case of a boss and his subordinates, forcing is often employed by the boss to resolve a disagreement. Attempts to force the other party to make concessions can also be used in conflicts where no authority differential is present, such as in conflicts between two departments or between a union and management. The major types of pressure tactics include: (1) threats, (2) punishment sequences, and (3) positional commitments.

A threat is the explicit or implicit warning that an action detrimental to the other party will be carried out unless they comply with certain demands. For example, the union may threaten a strike or slowdown if management does not make significant wage increases. Threats will be ignored unless the other party perceives them to be credible. Credibility is dependent upon both the capacity and the willingness of the party making the threat to carry it out. Thus the parties may try to demonstrate their capacity and determination to take aggressive actions. For example, a union may publicize the fact that it has an adequate strike fund to support workers in the event of a strike, and members may be asked to authorize a strike even before negotiations begin in order to convince management that a strike will occur if a settlement cannot be reached.

A punishment sequence is one method for demonstrating to the other party that aggressive actions can be taken to punish them if necessary. A small amount of a party's coercive power is applied to give the other party "a taste of what will happen" if they do not meet certain demands. Another variation of this approach is to apply the full measure of punishment with the condition that it will be ended as soon as certain conditions are met by the other party. For example, an organization may suspend rebellious members until they agree to perform their duties as expected.

Threats and punishment sequences will not necessarily have the desired effect. While some persons can be influenced by them, other persons refuse to be intimidated. When both parties have threat capacity, use of threats by one party is likely to be met with counter threats by the other party. The same is true of punishment sequences. Such exchanges can easily lead to an escalating spiral of aggressive acts.

A positional commitment is a statement by one party that they will not concede further and the other party must give in or face the consequences of a deadlock. Examples of this approach are "nonnegotiable demands" and "take it or leave it" final offers. A positional commitment is most likely to succeed if a party can show that it is impossible to make any further concessions without losing more than would be gained from a settlement. However, a positional commitment will not succeed if the settlement that is demanded cannot satisfy the other party's minimal aspirations. Thus use of positional commitments requires estimating how far the other party is willing to concede and then demanding just that much and no more.

Since one party's capacity to force a settlement or pressure a favorable compromise depends on their power relative to that of the other party, one common tactic in organizational conflicts is "coalition formation." That is, a party will seek an ally that has enough power or influence to insure a decisive advantage over the opposing party. An illustration of this tactic is provided by a statement from one of the purchasing agents in a study by Strauss (1962, p. 177): "Engineering says we can't use these parts. But I've asked manufacturing to test a sample under actual operating conditions—they are easy to use. Even if engineering won't accept manufacturing's data, I can go to the boss with manufacturing backing me. On something like this, manufacturing is tremendously powerful."

Forcing is seldom the best way to resolve a conflict (Burke, 1970), although it is more effective than avoiding a conflict that involves interdependent activities of the parties (Lawrence and Lorsch, 1967, 1969). Forcing often creates considerable resentment in the weaker party, and they are likely to respond to forcing with passive resistance rather than enthusiastic compliance. The weaker party is often able to sabotage a plan by doing only what is specifically required and showing no initiative in dealing with unanticipated problems. Forcing can also lead to withdrawal by the weaker party in the form of increased absenteeism or turnover.

Bargaining and Exchange-Oriented Tactics

Bargaining can be defined as the process of exchanging concessions until a compromise is reached. Bargaining can be used to resolve conflicts in which there exists at least one mutually acceptable settlement. In other words, there has to be a potential settlement that provides each party with enough benefits to satisfy their minimal aspirations. Otherwise, bargaining will end in a deadlock without a settlement.

The goal of each party in bargaining is usually to obtain the maximum benefits possible under the circumstances, without concern for the benefits received by the other party. Experienced bargainers usually begin the bargaining by demanding more than they really expect to get. Both sides realize that some concessions will be necessary in order to avoid a deadlock. However, the necessity of making concessions presents a dilemma when each party is trying to avoid any sign of weakness. If a party concedes too easily, it is likely to appear weak, and the other party will be encouraged to demand more and offer less (Yukl, 1974). Pruitt (1972) provides some examples of exchange-oriented tactics that can be used in an attempt to cope with this dilemma:

1. Make a small unilateral concession and state that no further concessions will be made unless the other party concedes.
2. Suggest a specific exchange of concessions that would be acceptable.
3. Informally signal a willingness to make a concession later if the other party makes one now.
4. Propose that a mediator be obtained to help find an acceptable compromise.

Exchange-oriented tactics often involve "tacit communication" (Pruitt, 1971). Tacit communication occurs when one party signals a willingness to be flexible in exchanging concessions without actually making an explicit offer or promise. Tacit communication of this type encourages the other party to make a concession by implicitly promising that it will be reciprocated. There is little danger of appearing weak, because a tacit proposal can later be denied if it fails to elicit a positive response from the other party. Tacit proposals provide an additional advantage when bargaining is carried out by representatives of groups, because it is easier for representatives to avoid appearing weak to their constituents. However, since tacit communication is usually intentionally ambiguous, it can easily be overlooked or misunderstood by the other party.

Bargaining can be an effective method for resolving certain kinds of conflicts. However, as we have seen, there is no certainty that bargaining will result in an agreement. Bargaining is not likely to be used for resolving a win-lose conflict where the two parties do not believe that a mutually acceptable compromise is possible. Nor is bargaining likely to be used if the parties have no way to insure that an agreement will be observed and they do not trust each other to do so. Even when bargaining is feasible, it sometimes results in a compromise agreement that fails to deal with the underlying problem in a rational manner and is not in the best long-term interest of the parties. For example, two departments in an organization were competing for control over a new production process. The conflict was resolved by an agreement to divide up the new machines and personnel equally between the two departments. The cost of running duplicate operations eventually became excessive, and the departments had to continually compete for the available work. The arrangement turned out to be unsatisfactory for both parties and unprofitable for the company.

Integrative Problem Solving

Integrative problem solving is an attempt to find a settlement that reconciles or "integrates" the needs of both parties. The conflict is defined as a mutual problem, and the parties cooperate in searching for a solution that is satisfactory to both of them. During integrative problem solving, there is an open and honest exchange of information about facts, needs and feelings. Each party tries to understand the conflict from the other party's point of view and to discover what needs of the other party must be satisfied by any settlement. An open exchange of this sort is not possible unless the two parties trust each other. A party is unlikely to reveal its true preferences and minimal needs if it expects the other party to take advantage of this information and to provide inaccurate information in return. Thus a precondition for integrative problem solving is a minimal level of trust. Some of the conciliatory tactics discussed earlier are helpful for creating a climate of trust favorable to integrative problem solving.

A number of integrative tactics and procedures have been proposed (Blake and Mouton, 1962, 1964; Walton and McKersie, 1965):

1. Definition of the problem should be a joint effort so that is is based on "shared fact finding" rather than on the biased perception of each party. Ample time should be provided so that the problem can be explored in the absence of excessive pressure for a quick settlement (Yukl et al., 1976).
2. Problems should be stated in terms of specifics rather than abstract principles, and points of initial agreement in the goals and beliefs of the parties should be identified along with differences.
3. The parties should work together in developing alternative solutions. If this is not feasible, each party should present a range of acceptable solutions rather than promoting the solution that is best for them while ignoring or concealing other possibilities.
4. When there is a solution that maximizes joint benefits but favors one party, some way should be found to provide special benefits to the other party to make the solution equitable.
5. All agreements on separate issues should be considered tentative until every issue is dealt with, since some issues are probably interrelated and cannot be settled independently in an optimal manner.

It should be emphasized that the success of integrative problem solving is not insured by the use of any particular procedures. Integrative problem solving is a certain orientation rather than a set of tactics, and its success depends on the mutual cooperation and creativity of the parties (Walton and McKersie, 1965).

Most of the procedures used for integrative problem solving are incompatible with the kinds of tactics employed in forcing or bargaining (Walton and McKersie, 1965). Positional commitments and specific hard demands are inconsistent with the flexible, exploratory approach needed for integrative problem solving. Threats and punitive actions are inconsistent with creation of an atmosphere of trust and cooperation.

The kind of deception and bluffing commonly employed in bargaining is inconsistent with an open disclosure of needs and preferences and the sharing of factual information. Since it is usually not feasible to use forcing and bargaining tactics at the same time as integrative problem solving, the parties should determine what general approach is appropriate for the given situation, rather than attempting to use a mix of inconsistent tactics.

The effectiveness of integrative problem solving for resolving a conflict depends ultimately upon the nature of the conflict. This approach will be most successful when there exists a solution that would be optimally beneficial to both parties. An example of successful integrative bargaining is provided by Walton and McKersie (1965, p. 130):

> In the closing down of the McCormick Works of International Harvester, the following issue arose: As soon as the company announced the shutdown of the plant, the union wanted employees released so that they could apply for work at other International Harvester plants. For its part, the company desired to keep many of these employees since they were necessary in the phasing-out operation. The solution reached established a "pegged" seniority date at other plants, if at any point after the company announced its plans to shut down the plant a job opened at other plants which the given employee could fill. Thus, the employee continued on in the plant being terminated, all the time acquiring seniority at the plant to which he would be eventually transferred.

Another example of integrative problem solving is the practice called "productivity bargaining." In return for a large wage increase, the union cooperates with management in revising work rules and procedures to reduce costs and improve productivity.

THIRD PARTY INTERVENTIONS

When the parties involved in a conflict are unwilling to negotiate or have reached a deadlock in negotiations, a third party may become involved to help them resolve the conflict. The third party may be invited to intervene by the opposing parties or may act on its own initiative. The major types of third party intervention are (1) arbitration, (2) mediation, and (3) interparty process consultation. Each type of intervention has certain distinctive features and is more appropriately used for some kinds of conflict situations than for others.

Arbitration

Arbitration is a procedure whereby a third party hears both sides of a conflict and acts as a judge in determining a binding settlement. Even though the party who is not favored by an arbitration ruling may be dissatisfied, arbitration is an orderly way of settling disputes, and it is usually preferable to mutual aggression and disruptive practices such as unauthorized strikes by employees (Stagner and Rosen, 1965). An arbitrator will be most effective in finding a just settlement if he is well informed about the issues and practices over which the dispute has arisen, and is therefore not solely dependent on the biased arguments presented by the two opposing parties.

Arbitration is commonly used to settle disputes between two individuals or two departments in an organization. The arbitrator in this case is usually the common superior of the opposing parties, since the arbitrator has the authority to make a ruling and require its observance. Arbitration by a neutral third party may be used to settle union-management conflicts over grievances or interpretation of contract terms. Large corporations often have a full-time arbitrator whose salary and expenses are shared jointly by management and the union (Stagner and Rosen, 1965). The arbitrator will only be acceptable to both management and the union as long as they perceive him or her to be impartial and objective.

Mediation

Another common form of third party intervention is "mediation." A mediator from the federal or state mediation service is often invited to intervene by management and the union when they are not able to reach an agreement on a new contract. Unlike an arbitrator, a mediator has no direct authority over the opposing parties and the recommendations are not binding. Thus the mediator's success will depend on persuasiveness, prestige, and understanding of the two opposing positions (Stagner and Rosen, 1965).

One potential contribution of a mediator to the resolution of conflict is to reestablish communication that has broken down. For example, if the two parties refuse to negotiate directly with each other, the mediator can act as a "go between" who transmits offers and messages. Or if prior negotiations have been broken off, a mediator can attempt to persuade the parties to resume talks. Mediators also facilitate the exchange of specific concessions. A mediator usually tries to find out what one party expects in return for a certain concession, and can then propose this concession exchange to the other party. Since the concession exchange is suggested by the mediator rather than by one of the parties, potential compromises can be tested without either party appearing to have weakened. If a deadlock has resulted from an unsuccessful positional commitment by one party, the mediator can help the party "retreat" from this commitment without losing face by suggesting the necessity for mutual concessions.

A mediator can also facilitate integrative problem solving. One contribution to problem solving consists of helping to collect and clarify factual information when the facts are ambiguous and the parties disagree about them. Another contribution consists of helping each party to better understand its own preferences with regard to a settlement. Research suggests that conflict resolution can be inhibited by normal errors and limitations in human judgmental processes when the conflict involves many issues with qualitatively different payoffs. Balke, Hammond, and Meyer (1973) conducted a study with union and management negotiators who had settled a new contract only five months earlier. The negotiators were asked to individually judge the acceptability of sample contracts representing various package settlements for four of the original issues (i.e., duration of contract, percentage wage increase, number and use of machine operators, number of strikers to be recalled).

Analysis of the judgments revealed that each negotiator had a poor understanding of his own preferences for alternative settlements and his weighting of the relative importance of the issues. Moreover, there was some lack of agreement among members of each negotiating team. By helping individuals to discover their preferences, and by helping teams of negotiators to clarify their joint position, a mediator can increase the likelihood that a mutually acceptable settlement will be discovered during bargaining or integrative problem solving. Balke, Hammond and Meyer (1973) have developed a procedure to improve a party's understanding of their own position and to facilitate the accurate communication of this position to the other party.

Finally, a mediator who is able to obtain accurate information about each party's preferences and needs may be able to discover an integrative solution that was not obvious to the opposing parties. The problem-solving efforts of a mediator can be especially valuable in situations where the two parties will give the mediator information that they are unwilling to openly disclose to each other. Pruitt (1975) has described how the mayor of a city successfully mediated a strike by bus drivers. The drivers were asking for higher wages and a two-year contract instead of the normal one-year contract. The mediator learned that the bus drivers were primarily concerned about getting a two-year contract, whereas the bus company was primarily concerned about the money, especially in the first year. The mediator proposed a two-year contract with a small wage increase in the first year and a larger increase in the second year, and both parties accepted this settlement.

Although the intervention of a mediator improves the prospects of a settlement, there are many instances where mediation fails. The effectiveness of mediation depends in part on the talents and traits of the individual mediator. Some mediators are clearly more successful than others. As yet, however, there has been little research to determine the characteristics of effective mediators (Rehmus, 1965).

Inter-Party Process Consultation

Inter-party process consultation is a relatively new form of third party intervention, and it differs from arbitration and mediation in several respects (Fisher, 1972). The objective of the "process consultant" is to improve the relationship between the two parties and to develop their capacity to effectively resolve conflicts by themselves in the future. The process consultant has no power to arbitrate a settlement, and usually does not attempt to mediate any substantive issues that exist. Instead, the process consultant uses various techniques designed to increase each party's awareness of distorted perceptions and dysfunctional behavior that interferes with conflict resolution. In addition, the process consultant guides the parties toward use of mutual fact finding and problem solving, and he may provide special training to develop their problem-solving skills.

Blake, Mouton and Sloma (1965) provide a good example of the kind of procedure used by a process consultant to reduce intergroup hostility and distorted perception. After the consultants obtained the approval of the two groups (union leaders and top management) to conduct the intervention, a short meeting was held to inform the groups about the objectives of the intervention procedures. Then each group met separately to prepare two written descriptions: (1) how they perceived themselves, and (2) how they perceived the other group. These descriptions included goals, intentions, attitudes and behavior relevant to the relationship between the groups. The groups then exchanged descriptions and met separately to study the substantial discrepancy between their self-image and the image of them provided by the other group, and between their image of the other group and its own self-image. After a brief joint meeting to clarify the images, each group met separately to discuss the misperceptions that were revealed and to diagnose the underlying reasons for hostility in the relationship. Then the groups met together to exchange and discuss their diagnoses. Both groups were quite open about their feelings and attitudes at this point, and each group was willing to listen carefully to what the other group had to say. The groups identified issues that needed to be resolved to improve their relationship and planned what future actions should be taken to deal with these issues.

Blake and Mouton (1962) provide an example of one kind of procedure used by a process consultant to guide the parties in the use of problem solving. Management and union negotiators were first asked to seperately prepare a written analysis of the similarities in their positions as well as the differences. Next, each party presented a detailed explanation of their position in terms of underlying problems they face and their needs. Then separate committees composed of three management negotiators and three union negotiators were established for each major problem area. The job of each committee was to collect facts and propose a series of preferred solutions. Although win-lose conflict between management and union representatives quickly emerged in each committee as they assumed polarized positions, with the aid of the process consultants the committees were gradually able to become fact-oriented and to avoid the win-lose "trap." By the time three weeks had elapsed, the members of each committee were able to agree on a set of recommendations. These recommendations broke what had been a hopeless deadlock between management and the union and paved the way for an eventual settlement.

The techniques used by a process consultant for intervening in a conflict between two individuals are not very different from the procedures used for conflict between groups. Some examples include the following:

1. Regulate the location, timing, and duration of confrontations to insure that there is mutual positive motivation to resolve the conflict and that the confrontation occurs in an atmosphere of informality and impartiality.
2. Encourage both parties to diagnose the reasons for the conflict, and suggest behavioral science concepts and theories that may explain why the parties have been acting in a certain manner.
3. Encourage use of problem-solving procedures, and discourage nonproductive reactions such as threats, blaming, and derogatory comments.
4. Facilitate communication accuracy by summarizing each party's position or asking each party to repeat the other party's last statement before responding to it. Understanding of the other party's position can also be improved by having a debate in which each party presents the opposing position rather than his own (role reversal).

The reader can find a more extensive discussion of interpersonal peacemaking techniques in Walton (1969).

Process consultation interventions are most likely to be effective in facilitating resolution of conflicts where there is considerable hostility and distrust due to inaccurate perception of the other party's objectives and intentions. Several successful interventions by process consultants in union-management conflicts are described by Blake and Mouton (1962) and Blake, Shepard and Mouton (1964). Walton (1969) describes several cases where a process consultant was successful in reducing conflict between individual managers in organizations. Such interventions are not always successful, but the approach is quite new and it is still being developed and improved.

MANAGING CONFLICT IN ORGANIZATIONS

Successful management of conflict means maintaining a level of conflict that is optimal for organization survival and effectiveness. The level of conflict can be raised or lowered by altering the antecedent conditions leading to conflict. Conflict management also involves regulating the way conflicts are handled by the involved parties and by third parties.

General Approaches for Conflict Management

There are several general approaches that can be used to manage conflict in organizations.

1. Establish rules and standard procedures to regulate aggressive behavior, assure fair treatment of personnel, and resolve predictable disputes.
2. Modify work-flow arrangements, job design, jurisdictional boundaries, and other aspects of interpersonal and intergroup work relationships, thereby increasing or decreasing the likelihood of conflict.
3. Modify the reward system to encourage competition or cooperation.
4. Allow factions with a different goal orientation to be represented in policy-making groups (e.g., labor representatives on board of directors, student representatives in faculty senate) in order to encourage constructive confrontation and reduce the need for these factions to rely on coercive, distructive tactics.
5. Establish special positions responsible for mediation, arbitration, or third party peacemaking in order to facilitate resolution of predictable kinds of disputes.
6. Train key personnel in the appropriate use of tactics for coping with conflict. For example, train line managers how to deal with staff personnel and with the local union officials.

Each type of organizational conflict requires a somewhat different combination of approaches. It is beyond the scope of this book to examine in detail the management of all the many varieties of organizational conflict. We will limit our discussion to one type of conflict that is prevalent in all kinds of organizations, namely "lateral conflict" between peers and among departments.

Authoritative Intervention in Lateral Conflicts

Lateral conflict is typically settled by the parties themselves. When the parties are unable to resolve conflicts in a constructive manner, the manager who is the "common superior" of both parties usually intervenes. If the conflict is primarily interpersonal rather than work related, the common superior can counsel both parties to be more tolerant and attempt to smooth over their dispute. If the conflict is primarily work related rather than interpersonal, the manager can arbitrate it. However, there are limits to this approach, since the common superior will become overloaded if subordinates are continually asking to have their disputes settled. If the common superior is someone two or more levels higher in the authority hierarchy, too many other responsibilities may take priority over arbitrating low-level conflicts.

If the conflict involves a reoccurring issue, such as competition over use of equipment and support services, the common superior can establish rules and guidelines to avoid future conflicts or to settle them on an objective basis. For example, support services may be provided on a "first come first served" basis, or on the basis of a system of established priorities, rather than being determined by an influence struggle among users. However, rigid rules and decision criteria are not appropriate for some situations, such as when many day-to-day decisions of a nonroutine nature must be made to coordinate the activities of interdependent parties.

Structural Reorganization

In some cases, excessive conflict can be avoided by altering some aspect of the formal organization. One approach is to modify the reward system to increase the benefits from cooperation and to discourage competition. For example, bonuses can be based in part on the joint performance of the parties rather than on individual performance. Another approach is to reduce friction between interdependent parties by creating "buffers." For example, the pressure on production to fill rush orders for sales can be reduced by increasing inventory stocks of completed products, as long as inventory costs would not be substantially increased.

In some cases it is feasible to take more drastic steps and redesign jobs or reorganize departments in order to reduce task interdependence, eliminate competition, or clarify jurisdictional boundaries. Chapple and Sayles (1961) provide an example of conflict reduction by means of structural reorganization. The mechanics in a plant belonged to a separate maintenance department with their own supervisor. Hostility developed between the mechanics and production foremen, and among the production foremen themselves, because of competition over whose machines should be repaired first by the mechanics. The common superior, a vice president of manufacturing, frequently had to settle violent arguments. Attempts to establish standard decision criteria were unsuccessful. Finally the vice president modified the organization of departments and assigned mechanics to the general foremen of production, and in some cases, to individual production foremen. No additional mechanics were needed for this reorganization, and the result was an end to the conflict and reduction in work-flow delays.

Changing the organization structure to create self-contained departments is not always appropriate or "politically" feasible. As is pointed out in Chapter 2, it is often more efficient to have interdependent specialized departments than to create independent departments. There are also times when it is advantageous to have departments with over-lapping responsibility and joint responsibility, or to have other structural forms that tend to create conflict.

Integrators

When an organization has interdependent specialized departments, the use of "integrators" is one approach for achieving continuous coordination and managing conflicts due to different goal orientations (Lawrence and Lorsch, 1967). An integrator is a person who is assigned the express function of facilitating communication and coordination between the members of certain interdependent departments. The integrator typically participates in joint problem solving with the respective departments and uses a combination of mediation and arbitration to help resolve disputes.

Based on research with companies in various industries, Lawrence and Lorsch (1967) have reached certain conclusions about the necessary conditions for integrator effectiveness:

1. In the kinds of situations where special integrators are needed, their role should be formalized and backed up by position power. This will insure that the integrator is not ignored or rebuffed by the parties, and is given some capacity to arbitrate issues that cannot be otherwise resolved.

2. The integrator should be someone who has considerable technical knowledge about the functions to be coordinated. This knowledge will provide the integrator with expert power, which is an important source of influence for integrators. In addition, an integrator who can "speak the language" of different specialist groups is better able to facilitate accurate communication between them.

3. The integrator should have a balanced orientation that will allow an understanding and appreciation of the goals and concerns of each of the departments to be coordinated. The integrator must also have a balanced orientation, to be able to serve as a "neutral" third party in helping to settle conflicts.

4. The basis for evaluating and rewarding integrators should be the success of the products or projects that the integrator is responsible for coordinating. This will help to insure that the integrator is primarily concerned about organizational effectiveness rather than short-run harmony or pleasing strong departments at the expense of weaker ones.

5. The integrator should have traits and skills that contribute to effective leadership in structuring intergroup relations and guiding confrontation along productive channels. Lawrence and Lorsch (1967) found that successful integrators tended to possess self-confidence, verbal fluency, ambition, enthusiasm, flexibility, social poise, and persuasiveness.

SUMMARY

Conflict occurs in all organizations in varying degrees. The major antecedent conditions that contribute to the development of conflict include: competition for scarce resources, task interdependence, jurisdictional ambiguity, status problems, communication barriers, and certain individual traits. Conflicts are likely to be severe and difficult to resolve if there is a win-lose contest where each party believes it is right and the other party is wrong.

The parties involved in a conflict can react in a number of ways, including: withdrawal, smoothing, persuasion, forcing, bargaining, and integrative problem solving. The appropriateness of each approach and the consequences for conflict resolution depend on the nature of the conflict. If the parties are unable to settle a disruptive conflict by themselves, they may be assisted by a third party. Forms of third party intervention include: arbitration, mediation, and process consultation.

Conflict can have both positive and negative consequences for an organization. Effective conflict management requires the maintenance of an optimal level of conflict and the minimization of its undesirable consequences. The usual approaches for regulating conflict in organizations include: establishing rules and standard decision procedures, modifying work-flow arrangements and task interdependence, modifying the reward system, broadening representation in policy formation processes, providing for intervention by third parties, and training personnel how to handle conflict.

In the case of lateral conflict, several of these approaches can be used, depending on the specific situation. Use of "integrators" is an effective approach for managing conflict between departments in some situations. Successful integrators are likely to have formalized roles with position power, relevant expertise, a balanced orientation, and personality traits that aid them in structuring interunit relations and promoting cooperation.

REVIEW AND DISCUSSION QUESTIONS

1. Define or explain each of the following key terms: conflict, pseudoconflict, antecedent condition, win-lose conflict, stereotype, withdrawal, smoothing, conciliation, forcing, bargaining, integrative problem solving, third-party intervention, arbitration, mediation, interparty process consultation, lateral conflict, integrator.
2. What are the likely consequences of conflict in organizations?
3. What are the major antecedent conditions for the development of conflict?

4. What typically occurs when there is prolonged and intense competition between two groups?
5. What are some conciliation tactics?
6. What are some persuasion tactics?
7. What are some exchange-oriented tactics?
8. What are some pressure tactics?
9. What are some tactics used with integrative problem solving?
10. What general approaches are available for managing conflict in organizations?
11. What are the necessary conditions for integrator effectiveness?

REFERENCES

Balke, W. M., Hammond, K. R., & Meyer, G. D.   An alternate approach to labor management relations. *Administrative Science Quarterly*, 1973, *18*, 311–327.

Blake, R. R., & Mouton, J. S.   Reactions to intergroup competition under win-lose conditions. *Management Science*, 1961, 7, 420–425.

Blake, R. R., & Mouton, J. S.   The intergroup dynamics of win-lose conflict and problem solving collaboration in union-management relations. In M. Sheriff (Ed.), *Intergroup relations and leadership*. New York: Wiley, 1962.

Blake, R. R., & Mouton, J. S.   *The managerial grid*. Houston: Gulf Publishing Co., 1964.

Blake, R. R., Mouton, J. S., & Sloma, R. L.   The union-management intergroup laboratory: Strategy for resolving intergroup conflict. *Journal of Applied Behavioral Science*, 1965, *1*, 25–57.

Blake, R. R., Shepard, H. A., & Mouton, J. S.   *Managing intergroup conflict in industry*. Houston: Gulf Publishing Co., 1964.

Burke, R. J.   Methods of resolving superior-subordinate conflict: The constructive use of subordinate differences and disagreements. *Organizational Behavior and Human Performance*, 1970, *5*, 393–411.

Chapple, E., & Sayles, L. R.   *The measure of management*. New York: Macmillan, 1961.

Dalton, M.   Conflicts between staff and line managerial officers. *American Sociological Review*, 1950, *15*, 342–351.

Dutton, J. M., & Walton, R. E.   Interdepartmental conflict and cooperation: Two contrasting studies. *Human Organization*, 1965, *25*, 207–220.

Ferguson, C. K., & Kelly, H. H.   Significant factors in overevaluation of own group's product. *Journal of Abnormal and Social Psychology*, 1964, *69*, 223–228.

Fisher, R. J.   Third-party consultation: A method for the study and resolution of conflict. *Journal of Conflict Resolution*, 1972, *16*, 67–94.

Lawrence, P. R., & Lorsch, J. W. New management job: The integrator. *Harvard Business Review*, 1967, *45* (November–December), 142–151.

Lawrence, P. R., & Lorsch, J. W. *Organization and environment: Managing differentiation and integration*. Homewood, Ill.: Irwin, 1969.

Pruitt, D. G. Indirect communication and the search for agreement in negotiations. *Journal of Applied Social Psychology*, 1971, *1*, 205–239.

Pruitt, D. G. Methods for resolving differences of interest: A theoretical analysis. *Journal of Social Issues*, 1972, *28*, 133–154.

Pruitt, D. G. Power and bargaining. In B. Seidenberg and A. Snadowsky (Eds.), *Social Psychology*. New York: Free Press, 1975.

Rehmus, C. M. The mediation of industrial conflict: A note on the literature. *Journal of Conflict Resolution*, 1965, *9*, 118–126.

Rhenman, E., Stromberg, L., & Westerlund, G. *Conflict and cooperation in a business organization*. London: Wiley-Interscience, 1970.

Robbins, S. P. *Managing organizational conflict: A nontraditional approach*. Englewood Cliffs, N.J.: Prentice-Hall, 1974.

Schmidt, S. M., & Kochan, T. A. Conflict: Toward conceptual clarity. *Administrative Science Quarterly*, 1972, *17*, 359–370.

Seiler, J. A. Diagnosing interdepartmental conflict. *Harvard Business Review*, 1963, *41* (September–October), 121–132.

Sherif, M. *In common predicament*. New York: Houghton-Mifflin, 1966.

Stagner, R., & Rosen, H. *Psychology of union-management relations*. Belmont, Calif.: Wadsworth, 1965.

Strauss, G. Tactics of lateral relationship: The purchasing agent. *Administrative Science Quarterly*, 1962, *7*, 161–186.

Walton, R. E. *Interpersonal peacemaking: Confrontation and third party consultation*. Reading, Mass.: Addison-Wesley, 1969.

Walton, R. E., & Dutton, J. M. The management of interdepartmental conflict: A model and review. *Administrative Science Quarterly*, 1969, *14*, 73–84.

Walton, R. E., Dutton, J. M., & Cafferty, T. P. Organizational context and interdepartmental conflict. *Administrative Science Quarterly*, 1969, *14*, 522–542.

Walton, R. E., & McKersie, R. B. *A behavioral theory of labor negotiations*. New York: McGraw-Hill, 1965.

Yukl, G. A. Effects of the opponent's initial offer, concession magnitude, and concession frequency on bargaining behavior. *Journal of Personality and Social Psychology*, 1974, *30*, 323–335.

Yukl, G. A., Malone, M. P., Hayslip, B., & Pamin, T. A. The effects of time pressure and issue settlement order on integrative bargaining. *Sociometry*, 1976 (in press).

part two
PERSONNEL PSYCHOLOGY

10

MEASURING EMPLOYEE PROFICIENCY

ALTHOUGH much research has been done in recent years on the measurement of employee proficiency, behavioral scientists continue to speak of the so-called criterion problem—the difficulties involved in developing adequate measures of an individual's job performance. Most academicians and practitioners agree that there is much to learn before completely solving this problem.

The purpose of this chapter is to provide the reader with clear and applicable answers to the following questions about employee evaluation in organizations:

1. What are measures of employee proficiency typically used for in organizations?
2. What are the characteristics of dependable measures of employee proficiency?
3. What are some of the appraisal methods currently being used?
4. What are some of the errors and biases that enter into performance evaluations?
5. What are the advantages and disadvantages of the various performance appraisal methods?
6. What are some of the issues involved in implementing performance appraisal programs?

ORGANIZATIONAL USES OF MEASURES OF EMPLOYEE PROFICIENCY

Measures of employee proficiency serve many different purposes within an organization. Basically, the uses of these measures fall into two main categories: administrative and individual employee development. Some of the major uses of performance measures in each category are given below.

Administrative

As a basis for making decisions regarding promotions, layoffs, separations, and transfers (where seniority is not the all-important factor due to unionization).

As a means of determining training needs for various organizational units.

As criteria when validating selection and placement devices.

As a basis for evaluating the worth of training programs and the effectiveness of work schedules, work methods, organizational structure, supervisory styles, working conditions, and equipment.

As a basis for evaluating the productive efficiency of the organization as a whole as well as units within it.

As a method of administering wages and salaries so that they are contingent on performance.

Individual Employee Development

As a means of identifying employee weaknesses that might be alleviated through additional formal training.

As a means of improving the proficiency of employees by providing each of them with feedback regarding their performance during periodic appraisal interviews with their superiors.

As a means of increasing employee motivation by establishing behavioral and performance goals.

As a means of encouraging managers to observe the behavior of each of their subordinates and to take an interest in each individual's training and development needs.

As a means of pointing out past deficiencies and reinforcing employee strengths.

STANDARDS FOR EVALUATING THE ADEQUACY OF A MEASURE OF EMPLOYEE PROFICIENCY

Before any measure of employee proficiency is used for administrative or employee development purposes, it must meet three important requirements: validity, reliability, and practicality.

Validity

Validity (sometimes referred to as "relevancy") refers to the degree to which an obtainable measure of proficiency overlaps or is related to an ultimate or true measure of success (see Figure 10–1). Ultimate measures

FIGURE 10–1
Validity, Deficiency, and Contamination

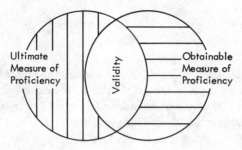

represent the ideal and it is not feasible to try to obtain them. For instance, an ultimate measure of success for a production worker might be
defined as total long-term productive contribution (i.e., quantity of output; quality of output; training costs; time lost by sickness, strikes, accidents; grievances; promotability) to the organization. Since we usually
cannot secure ultimate measures of success, we are forced to rely on
measures of employee proficiency which are immediately available and
are presumed to overlap as closely as possible with the ultimate measure.
We can never statistically measure validity since the ultimate measure
is unavailable. Therefore, validity must be determined by the judgments
of managers and personnel specialists familiar with the objectives of the
organization. The object is to come as close as possible to having complete
overlap between the ultimate and obtainable measures. This overlap
is usually less than perfect for two general reasons: measurement deficiency and measurement contamination (Cummings and Schwab, 1973).
Measurement deficiency is shown by the area with vertical lines in Figure
10–1. It refers to the fact that the obtained measure may not take into
consideration all of the elements found in the ultimate measure. For example, a measure of sales success that accounted for volume of sales, but
not customer relations, would probably be considered to be deficient.
Similarly, a measure of success in a production department that consisted
of quantity of units but not quality would also be thought of as deficient.
Measurement contamination is shown by the area with horizontal lines in
Figure 10–1. It is caused by the fact that the obtained measure is impure,
that is, it is influenced by factors that are unrelated to the ultimate measure. Variations in the condition of workers' machinery may contaminate
a measurement of their individual proficiency. Among a group of press
operators, for example, some may appear more productive than others.
However, this seemingly productive group may be using newer or more
efficient machinery, which accounts for the apparent differences in their
productivity. Many of the human errors discussed later in this chapter
can also seriously contaminate proficiency measures.

Validity is by far the most important requirement of any proficiency measure. Without it, the measure is worthless since it is not measuring what it is supposed to measure.

Reliability

A second important standard for any measure of proficiency is reliability. A measure of proficiency is reliable to the extent that it gives consistent numerical descriptions of individuals from one time to another or from one evaluator to another. This is assuming, of course, that the characteristic being measured remains constant. One way of assessing reliability is to measure the same group of employees on two separate occasions separated by some period of time. The time interval used (e.g., one year or three months) will depend upon the particular job and proficiency measure used. The degree of consistency between the two sets of measurements is estimated by a statistic known as a correlation coefficient. Coefficients of correlation vary between $+1.00$ and -1.00, with 0.00 representing the absence of any consistency or reproducibility. In general, one desires reliabilities to be positive ($+$) and as close to 1.00 as possible. High positive correlations such as $+.70$ and higher indicate that the order of employee proficiency tends to remain fairly constant from one time period to the next. Negative and near-zero correlations are clearly unacceptable since they indicate that the order of employee proficiency has changed over time. Thus, if one is interested in sales volume, this measure is said to be reliable if each individual's volume of sales does not vary greatly, for example, from month to month. Similarly, assessments from a rater can be considered reliable if they remain stable over time.

A second approach for estimating reliability is to determine the amount of correlation (i.e., consistency) between the appraisals given a group of employees at one point in time by two or more independent raters. A high positive correlation obtained in this case indicates that employees receiving high ratings from one rater tend to receive high ratings from the others. The converse is also true, that is, individuals obtaining low evaluations from one rater obtain low evaluations from the others.

Practicality

Practicality is a final requirement that should not be underestimated. Proficiency measures should be acceptable to management and to the employees being evaluated. In those blue-collar and white-collar jobs where workers are unionized, it is essential that the proficiency measures be supported by the union. This is especially true since unions have traditionally favored seniority in the determination of wages and promotions rather than formal evaluation programs. To insure this widespread acceptance of the proficiency measures employed, it is advisable to have a planning committee consisting of representatives from each management level and from the union. In this way, the viewpoints of all these groups can be taken into consideration in deciding upon the proficiency measures to be used. Whichever measures are chosen, they should be readily accessible and easily administered so as to save time and money and to minimize disruption of the organization's normal operations. An evaluation system which takes a considerable amount of a manager's time, interferes with productivity, entails an excessive amount of paperwork, or requires a large personnel staff to administer will interfere with organizational effectiveness.

THREE APPROACHES TO MEASURING EMPLOYEE PROFICIENCY

We have already discussed the purposes of performance appraisal and the concepts of validity, reliability, and practicality. With this in mind, we turn our attention now to a discussion of the many different methods of appraising employee proficiency. These methods can be classified into three general categories: (1) subjective procedures, (2) direct measures, and (3) proficiency testing. We shall begin our presentation with the subjective procedures. These procedures involve ratings or judgments of employees' job proficiency made by their superiors, subordinates, peers, outside observers, or self. Since all subjective procedures depend upon judgment and opinion, they are susceptible to certain kinds of human error likely to be found in the evaluation process.

HUMAN ERRORS IN SUBJECTIVE PROCEDURES

Undesirable distortions in subjective measures stem from certain errors in human judgment. What makes these errors so insidious is that in most instances the evaluators are not aware that they are making them; and in those instances in which they are aware, frequently they are unable to correct the judgment. The end result may be an employee who is erroneously promoted, transferred, terminated, or given an undeserved salary increase.

Leniency, Strictness, and Central Tendency

Some people, when asked to evaluate others, are reluctant to give extremely high or low scores. Instead, they tend to continuously use the center or average point on a rating scale (referred to as central tendency error) even though large differences in proficiency may exist among their subordinates. Others tend to concentrate their ratings toward the upper (leniency error) or lower end of the scale (strictness error). Every student is familiar with a similar problem involving the assignment of course grades. A grade of "C" from one instructor might be comparable to an "A" from another. Such differences in standards among managers cause problems whenever the evaluations are to be compared between employees in different departments. When such differences in standards exist, the ratings can only be compared by first converting them all to some common numerical scale (McCormick and Tiffin, 1974).

The Halo Effect

Halo effect refers to the tendency to rate an employee either high or low on many factors because the rater feels the employee is high or low on some single factor. For example, the supervisor who values self-reliance may tend to rate self-reliant subordinates high on characteristics other than self-reliance. While self-reliance may be an important personal quality needed on the job, it should be evaluated independently of other factors such as learning ability, emotional stability, leadership ability, and sociability. Unfortunately, there are many supervisors who tend to give a subordinate approximately the same rating on several different factors. One way of reducing halo error is to ask the supervisor to rate all subordinates on the first dimension (e.g., self-reliance), then rate all of the subordinates on the second dimension (e.g., emotional stability), and so on until the subordinates are rated on all the dimensions. At no time should the supervisor refer back to the ratings on previous dimensions. Halo error can also be reduced by making the rating scale benchmarks more behavioral and by expressing the factors to be rated in precise terms so that the raters are quite clear about each characteristic they are rating.

Rater Characteristics

There are certain factors inherent in the raters themselves which can influence the accuracy of ratings. For instance, it has been shown that supervisors who are effective in their own jobs are more capable of discriminating between good and poor employees and are less likely to commit leniency error (Kirchner and Reisberg, 1962). There is also evidence which suggests that better raters have higher intelligence, higher cognitive complexity, and better analytical thinking ability (Korman, 1971). The accuracy of a rater is also a function of the organizational distance between the rater and ratee—the more organizational distance, the less relevant the ratings. That is, one could expect an immediate supervisor to give more accurate evaluations than a supervisor two or three levels above the ratee. A closely related factor is the rater's firsthand knowledge of the behaviors involved in the job. Generally, the more the rater knows about the critical job behaviors, the more accurate are the ratings. Too often the authors have witnessed ratings based upon inadequate information about the job and/or the ratee. One obvious approach for reducing errors due to rater characteristics is to insure that all raters are well acquainted with the jobs and employees involved. This will involve providing the rater with the time and opportunity to observe employees' job behavior. *+ job* *know* *analysis*

Personal Bias

Certain factors such as an employee's physical attractiveness, race, ethnic background, seniority in the organization, level of education, social standing in the community, job experience, age, personality, and organizational unit can distort a manager's rating. Even the most conscientious rater may have a tendency to rate higher those subordinates who he perceives as being similar to self ("similar-to-me" effect) in terms of biographical background, attitudes, and behavior patterns (Rand and Wexley, 1975; Wexley and Nemeroff, 1974). For instance, you may meet all the requirements of the job, but if you like bowling and I like playing golf, if you are a Republican and I am a Democrat, if your father is a janitor and my father is a company president, and if you are the subordinate and I am the manager, your chances of obtaining a high rating might be substantially reduced.

The operation of sex-role stereotypes (Schein, 1975) may also distort performance ratings. Two examples of this might be: "Ruth is definitely corporate high potential, but I just can't see her as a senior vice president" or "Robert may have all the abilities, but I certainly cannot tolerate having a male secretary."

SUBJECTIVE PROCEDURES

The personnel specialist has a large number of subjective procedures available for appraising the job performance of employees. Among the procedures that can be used are the following:

1. Rating scales:
   a. Graphic.
   b. Multiple-step.
   c. Behaviorally anchored.
2. Checklist:
   a. Weighted.
   b. Forced-choice.
3. Employee comparison:
   a. Alternation ranking.
   b. Paired comparison.
   c. Forced distribution.

4. Critical incident.
5. Group appraisal.
6. Field review.
7. Essay evaluation.

Rating Scales

There are several different formats which rating scales can take (see Figure 10–2). With "graphic" or continuous rating scales (examples *a* and *b*) the rater is asked to place a checkmark anywhere along the line. This type of scale is scored by using a ruler to measure the distance checked along the line. "Multiple-step" or discrete scales provide the rater with several alternative categories from which to choose. The points on the scale may be defined through adjectives (example *c*), numbers (example *d*), or short phrases (example *e*).

Despite their widespread popularity with raters, it is clear that these simple rating formats are extremely susceptible to the human errors discussed previously. Think for a moment how easy it would be for an evaluator to bias ratings for or against a particular subordinate if desired using any of these formats. Imagine too how vulnerable these scales are to leniency, strictness, central tendency, and halo errors. For these reasons, the usefulness of these conventional rating scales is limited.

Is there any way to develop a rating scale that is acceptable to raters and, at the same time, reduces human errors? The procedure originally suggested by Smith and Kendall (1963) for the development of behaviorally anchored rating scales attempts to satisfy both of these requirements. To illustrate this rating approach, we will go through the steps necessary to construct these rating scales by providing a hypothetical example.

Step 1: Generation of Job Dimensions. Meetings are held with a group of supervisors who are familiar with the job in question. The purpose of these meetings is to identify and define independent dimensions of employee proficiency on the job. The following is an example of four dimensions identified and defined for a production job as a result of these meetings:

Job knowledge: the worker's knowledge of the procedures and materials involved in all phases of the job.

Motivation: the worker's desire and willingness to do a hard day's work.

Interpersonal relations with others: the worker's ability to get along with co-workers and supervision.

Supervision required: the worker's ability to solve problems with a minimum of supervision.

a. Ability to get along with others

Poor	Below average	Average	Above average	Excellent

b. Quality of work

Poor	Below average	Average	Above average	Exceptionally good
☐ Poor	☐ Below average	☐ Average	☐ Above average	☐ Excellent

c. Motivation and enthusiasm

d. How would you rate this employee's overall job proficiency?

☐ In the bottom 10 percent of workers	☐ In the next 20 percent of workers	☐ In the middle 40 percent of workers	☐ In the next 20 percent of workers	☐ In the top 10 percent of workers

e. Attitude toward work and employer (check only one)

☐ Does as little as can get by with	☐ Only mildly interested in work	☐ Occasionally has to be urged or warned	☐ Attitude more satisfactory than of most workers	☐ Attitude toward work and employer as desirable as could be wished	☐ Eager to do all that is called for

Step 2: Generation of Behaviors. Each supervisor is asked to provide several behavioral examples for each dimension, reflecting good, average, or poor employee performance. Listed below is an example of the behavioral items that might be submitted by a particular supervisor for the interpersonal relations dimension:

Good.   Other workers feel free to discuss personal as well as work-related problems because this worker tries to help.

Average.   This worker, when helping co-workers, is friendly, but since sometimes has a "know-it-all" manner, others feel hesitant about talking with worker.

Poor.   This worker puts blame on co-workers and supervision for own mistakes, which irritates others.

Step 3: Reallocation of Behaviors. Another group of supervisors is given the list of behavioral examples together with a list of the dimensions and definitions generated in Steps 1 and 2. These supervisors are asked to individually allocate each item to the dimension that the example is thought to illustrate. For instance, a supervisor might have read the item, "This worker is able to find sensible ways out of most difficulties alone," and assign it to the "supervision required" dimension. Those items which are not assigned to a dimension by more than a certain percentage (e.g., 60–90 percent) of the supervisors are eliminated. By doing this, all ambiguous items are discarded and independent dimensions of employee proficiency are determined.

Step 4: Assignment of Values. Each supervisor is given a booklet containing the established dimensions. For each dimension, there is a list of 20 or more items that met the standard established in Step 3. The supervisors are asked to read the definition of each dimension and then rate each of the items on a 5- to 9-point rating scale. If a 7-point scale is chosen, a value of 1 indicates that the item describes *very poor* performance on a dimension, while a 7 indicates *very good* and a 4 indicates *average* performance. Supervisors are told that each of the items can have a value of either 1, 2, 3, 4, 5, 6, or 7 depending upon what they themselves think is appropriate. They are told to assign only one value per item and not to leave any items blank. Listed below is an example of the values assigned by one supervisor to a few of the motivation dimension items:

Motivation—the worker's desire and willingness to do a hard day's work.

1.   This worker rarely wastes a minute by talking to buddies during work hours.   6

2.   This worker encourages others to restrict their output.   1

3.   This worker slows down whenever the supervisor isn't there to watch.   3

Only those items with small variations in the scores assigned are retained. That is, the retained items are those on which there is good agreement among supervisors as to the goodness of performance described by it. The final value for each item is determined by averaging all the supervisors' assigned values.

Step 5: Formation of the Rating Scales. The items used as anchors in the final rating scales are reworded from actual behaviors (e.g., "This worker encourages others to restrict output") to expected behaviors (e.g., "This worker could be expected to encourage others to restrict output"). Each item is then assigned to its proper dimension and given its correct position on the scale according to its determined scale value. This results in the type of behaviorally anchored rating scales shown in Figure 10–3. Essentially, raters must decide if a given behavior they have seen could lead them to *expect* any of the behaviors shown along the scale. The evaluators are required to support their checkmarks by describing the actual behaviors which they have observed.

There are several important advantages of constructing behaviorally anchored rating scales. First, the anchors are behavioral in nature and are expressed in the rater's own terminology. This eliminates much of the ambiguity found in those rating scales shown in Figure 10–2 which use phrases such as "exceptionally good," which have different meanings to different raters. Second, by actively participating in the development of the scales, the raters are more inclined to complete the ratings carefully and honestly. Third, the procedure has been used in a wide variety of settings for rating the performance of department store managers, nurses, grocery store clerks, university professors, and the motivation of engineers. Recent evidence suggests that these scales need not be job-specific. That is, it appears that a common set of scales can be developed for a number of jobs at one time (Goodale and Burke, 1975). Fourth, these scales have potential value for employee development. The rating process lends itself to providing employees with fairly specific behavioral feedback. In addition, the behavioral items collected during Step 2 can be used as a basis for developing training programs (Blood, 1974). The skills to be learned can be specified in terms of actual job behaviors. In this way, trainees can learn the exact behaviors expected of them on their jobs as well as how their performance will be evaluated.

In the last few years, several studies have been done to compare the relative merits of these scales with other more conventional rating formats. These comparisons have typically involved the following variables: leniency error, interrater reliability, differentiation between persons being rated, and halo error. In general, these studies have produced equivocal results (Borman and Dunnette, 1975). This current research suggests that the extra time and effort required to build behavior-based rating

FIGURE 10–3
Two Examples of Behaviorally Anchored Rating Scales

Instructions:

First read the name of the dimension and its definition. Then notice the examples which illustrate various points on the rating scale. These examples are included to give you clear anchor points to help you make more accurate evaluations. Don't worry about whether or not your subordinate has actually exhibited the behavior described in the example. By knowing your subordinate, you should be able to judge whether he or she *could be expected* to display the type of behavior described in the example. After reading all the examples on a dimension, decide where on the rating scale the worker belongs by making a checkmark anywhere along the scale. The value you assign can range anywhere from 1 which represents very poor performance to 7 which represents very good performance. This procedure should be followed for each dimension.

Motivation—the worker's desire and willingness to do a hard day's work.

7 –
–This worker could be expected to stimulate enthusiasm about the company and jobs from peers.

–This worker could be expected to be counted on in a crisis.

6 –
–This worker could be expected to do the job without much supervisory follow-up.

5 –

–This worker could be expected to meet the basic requirements of the job.

4 –

3 –
–This worker could be expected to take sick leave whenever the work load becomes high.

–This worker could be expected not to report hazardous working
2 – conditions or defective machinery because doesn't care.

–This worker could be expected to deliberately slow down on the job.

1 –

FIGURE 10–3 *(continued)*

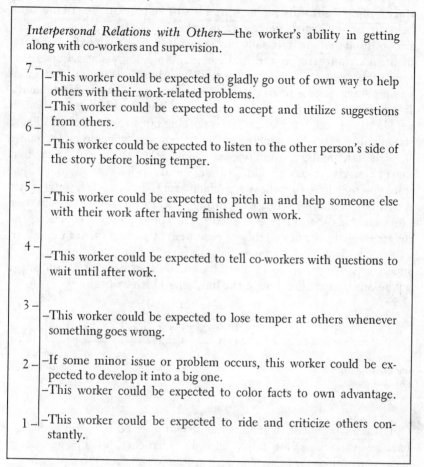

Interpersonal Relations with Others—the worker's ability in getting along with co-workers and supervision.

7 –
—This worker could be expected to gladly go out of own way to help others with their work-related problems.
—This worker could be expected to accept and utilize suggestions from others.
6 –
—This worker could be expected to listen to the other person's side of the story before losing temper.
5 –
—This worker could be expected to pitch in and help someone else with their work after having finished own work.
4 –
—This worker could be expected to tell co-workers with questions to wait until after work.
3 –
—This worker could be expected to lose temper at others whenever something goes wrong.
2 –
—If some minor issue or problem occurs, this worker could be expected to develop it into a big one.
—This worker could be expected to color facts to own advantage.
1 –
—This worker could be expected to ride and criticize others constantly.

scales may not be warranted if used solely for performance ratings. We feel it best to reserve any final evaluation of this approach until more research evidence has been accumulated.

Checklists

Another subjective approach to performance evaluation involves the use of checklists. Unlike rating scales, the rater is typically given a list of behavioral statements and asked to simply report on *having or not having observed* rather than *judging the goodness of* the ratee's job-related behavior. The two major types of checklists in use are "weighted checklists" and "forced-choice checklists."

WEIGHTED CHECKLISTS. Developing a weighted checklist involves three simple steps. First, a large number of statements describing work behavior are collected, ranging from behaviors that are unusually effective to those that are unusually ineffective. The best source of such statements are from written and oral comments made by supervisors about their subordinates' job performance. The authors have found that interviewing supervisors is an excellent way of obtaining behavioral statements. It is important that the interviewer *not* be satisfied with statements such as "He has a good attitude" or "She's nothing but a troublemaker." These statements are nonbehavioral and are therefore ambiguous. In response to such statements, the interviewer should ask, "What did he do that makes you say he has a good attitude?" and "What has she done that leads you to believe that she is a troublemaker?" Second, each statement is scaled by about 10–15 independent judges as to the degree of employee proficiency a subordinate described by it would possess. Typically, the judges estimate the desirability of each item by sorting them into 7, 9, or 11 piles with respect to favorable-unfavorable estimates. For instance, supervisors may be asked to place the item, "Can be counted on to get a job done on time," in one of the following 11 categories:

| 1 | 2 | 3 | 4 | 5 | 6 | 7 | 8 | 9 | 10 | 11 |

Extremely
undesirable (or
unfavorable)
behavior

Extremely
desirable (or
favorable)
behavior

Only those statements which are consistently scaled by the judges (i.e., have low variability) are employed in the final checklist. For instance, a statement would not be used if perhaps ten judges failed to agree among themselves on its desirability-undesirability (e.g., judgments of 2, 7, 11, 4, 5, 6, 7, 10, 1, and 8). On the other hand, an acceptable statement would have little or no variability in judgments (e.g., 4, 5, 5, 5, 4, 4, 4, 4, 4, and 4). Third, the scale value or weight of each statement is determined by averaging the judges' separate estimates. The weight of the above statement would be: $4 + 5 + 5 + 5 + 4 + 4 + 4 + 4 + 4 + 4 = 43/10 =$ 4.3. Table 10–1 shows some items taken from a weighted checklist used to measure the human relations competence of first-line supervisors by their superiors. The superior who uses the checklist simply places a checkmark next to any behaviors which he or she has seen the individual exhibit in the past. Notice that there are no weights shown on the checklist itself; the rater sees only the statements. The ratee's final score on the checklist is obtained by averaging the weights of all the items checked.

EVALUATION OF THE WEIGHTED CHECKLIST. A considerable amount

TABLE 10–1
An Example of a Weighted Checklist (used to assess human relations competence of first-line supervisors)

Instructions:

The following form is designed to evaluate the human relations competence of (name) _____. Included in this checklist are examples of behavior which you may have observed on the part of this supervisor in the past.

Would you please read each statement and carefully consider whether or not you have observed the behavior described, then do one of the following:

a. If you can recall having observed the described behavior, please place a checkmark (✔) in the place at the left of the statement.

b. If the behavior described has not been observed, or if you do not immediately recall having observed the behavior, leave the space blank.

1. _____ When making a job assignment, discussed significant details of the job with subordinates.

2. _____ Unable to settle personal differences between subordinates.

3. _____ Solicited subordinates' opinions and ideas and tried them whenever possible.

4. _____ Delegated responsibility for an important job, but refused to let subordinate perform it without interfering.

5. _____ Went out of way to give credit to subordinates and compliment them for a job well done.

6. _____ Failed to keep promises to subordinates.

7. _____ Demonstrated tact and patience when listening to a subordinate's gripes.

8. _____ Refused to consider seriously the opinion of others before making an important decision.

9. _____ Gained respect of subordinate by letting him/her "save face" in an embarrassing situation.

10. _____ Failed to apologize to subordinates when wrong.

---

of time and effort is required in obtaining statements having low variability and the full range of scale values. This is especially so since separate checklists must be developed for each job or family of similar jobs. On the positive side, this method provides an excellent vehicle for employee development since the manager can feed back actual observations of behavior rather than vague impressions.

Forced-Choice Checklists. The forced-choice checklist is one of the more statistically sophisticated, yet least popular, performance appraisal methods. The procedure was developed by a group of industrial psychologists during World War II in order to reduce leniency error in the rating of army officers. The rating form, which must also be constructed specially for each job or job family, consists of 10–20 tetrads or groups of four statements. In each tetrad, the evaluator is asked to check the one statement that is most descriptive of the employee being rated and the one statement that is least descriptive. The tetrads are constructed by a trained personnel specialist who makes sure that each tetrad contains two statements that appear favorable and two statements that appear unfavorable to the rater. In addition, of the two favorable-appearing statements, one of them discriminates between effective and ineffective personnel, while the other does not. Similarly, of the unfavorable-appearing statements, only one of the set actually discriminates. Essentially, the rater has no idea of whether he or she is evaluating a subordinate favorably or not since the actual discrimination and favorability values of the statements are kept confidential from the rater. All scoring is done in the personnel department. Two examples of forced-choice tetrads appear in Figure 10–4.

FIGURE 10–4
Two Forced-Choice Items (used to evaluate the proficiency of first-line supervisors)

In each group of four statements, select the one statement that you believe most characterizes the employee under consideration. Put an X in the box beside that statement in the column headed M (for *most*). Then consider the remaining three statements in the group. Decide which one of these three is least like the employee and put an X in the box beside that statement in the column headed L (for *least*).

	M	L
Compliments co-workers when they do a good job.	□	□
Displays indifference or hasty opposition to the ideas of subordinates.	□	□
Remains cool and calm under pressure.	□	□
Fails to keep promises to subordinates.	□	□
Fails to keep subordinates informed on matters which affect them.	□	□
Comes to work before starting time several times a week.	□	□
Fails to apologize to subordinates when wrong.	□	□
Demonstrates ability to settle personal differences between subordinates.	□	□

The major advantage of this method is that it reduces raters from intentionally giving favorable evaluations to those employees they happen to favor. Since the statements in each tetrad are equated for favorability and unfavorability, the rater has no idea which statements to check to "fake it." Moreover, the procedure can result in reduced personal bias and leniency error on the part of the rater. Unfortunately, this technique has its drawbacks too. It is costly and time consuming to construct. It also does not lend itself to feedback of results to employees for development purposes. After all, it is difficult and sometimes embarrassing for a supervisor to discuss ratings of a subordinate during an appraisal interview when the supervisor does not know how the tetrads were scored. Consequently, supervisors typically dislike the method. These negative attitudes may lower the reliability and validity of their evaluations, especially if they intentionally sabotage the entire rating system. Because of this, few organizations currently use this procedure.

Employee Comparisons

ALTERNATION RANKING.   Alternation ranking requires the rater to order individuals from lowest to highest. The usual procedure is to rank employees on the basis of their overall job proficiency. Another approach sometimes used is to first identify the separate dimensions of job proficiency and then rank the employees separately for each dimension. These separate rankings can then be converted into an overall ranking for each worker by averaging the rankings for the separate dimensions.

The ranking procedure is quite simple. Suppose Supervisor A has nine subordinates named Atkins, Rose, White, Dobson, Smith, Childs, Levine, Murphy, and Bear. Supervisor A would be asked to write down the name of the best worker (e.g. White), then the poorest worker (e.g., Childs), then the second-best worker (e.g., Bear), then the second-poorest worker (e.g., Dodson), as so on, until all nine subordinates are ordered. This "peeling off" process might result in the listing shown below:

1.	White	6.	Smith
2.	Bear	7.	Levine
3.	Rose	8.	Dodson
4.	Murphy	9.	Childs
5.	Atkins		

Supervisor A would have little difficulty distinguishing between the best and poorest workers. The task may be a problem for the supervisor when attempting to differentiate between subordinates (e.g., Murphy, Atkins, and Smith) in the middle range of ability. Although the supervisor may resist making such difficult distinctions, he or she is typically not permitted to assign the same rank to two or more individuals.

Each employee's performance appraisal score is the rank he/she receives from Supervisor A. If two or more raters can be secured who have had equally good opportunities to observe the employees, each employee can be assigned an average rank:

Employee	Supervisor A	Supervisor B	Supervisor C	Average Rank
Atkins	5	6	4	5.00
Bear	2	3	2	2.33
Childs	9	7	7	7.67
Dodson	8	9	8	8.33
Levine	7	8	9	8.00
Murphy	4	4	5	4.33
Rose	3	2	3	2.67
Smith	6	5	6	5.67
White	1	1	1	1.00

(handwritten margin note: what are dynamics of feeding back such info?)

PAIRED COMPARISONS. The method of paired comparisons simplifies and structures the decision-making processes of the rater. With this method, the rater is forced to systematically compare each subordinate with every other. For each possible pair of subordinates, the rater simply decides which of the two workers is superior.

In order to compare each subordinate with all others, the rater must make $N(N-1)/2$ comparisons, where N is the number of employees to be ranked. Imagine a situation where a manager has five subordinates: Hopkins, Miller, Tyson, Haber, and Bingham. In this instance, there will be $5(4)/2 = 10$ possible comparisons:

1. Hopkins versus Miller
2. Hopkins versus Tyson
3. Hopkins versus Haber
4. Hopkins versus Bingham
5. Miller versus Tyson
6. Miller versus Haber
7. Miller versus Bingham
8. Tyson versus Haber
9. Tyson versus Bingham
10. Haber versus Bingham

The first step for the personnel specialist in this particular situation is to prepare ten cards with each card containing one of the ten possible pairs of subordinate names. The cards should be shuffled and the position of the names on each card should be interchanged so that Hopkins' name, for example, is not always on the left-hand side. The cards should then be presented to the rater who is asked to check the name of the person preferred on each card. Suppose the manager gave the following judgments concerning the overall proficiency of the five subordinates:

Card #1	___ Hopkins Miller ✔	Card # 6 ✔ Miller Bingham ___
Card #2	___ Hopkins Haber ✔	Card # 7 ✔ Haber Tyson ___
Card #3	✔ Bingham Hopkins ___	Card # 8 ___ Tyson Bingham ✔
Card #4	✔ Miller Tyson ___	Card # 9 ___ Bingham Haber ✔
Card #5	___ Tyson Hopkins ✔	Card #10 ___ Haber Miller ✔

The next step for the personnel specialist is to record these judgments in some systematic manner. The most efficient procedure is to summarize the judgments in a matrix by using the following rule: Whenever a rater prefers a column to a row, place a checkmark in that matrix cell (Blum and Naylor, 1968). Shown below is a completed matrix summarizing the above judgments:

	Hopkins	Bingham	Miller	Tyson	Haber
Hopkins	✕	✔	✔		✔
Bingham		✕	✔		✔
Miller			✕		
Tyson	✔	✔	✔	✕	✔
Haber			✔		✕
Total number of times preferred over others	1	2	4	0	3

Notice from the "total number of times preferred over others" that this manager rates Miller as best, followed by Haber, Bingham, Hopkins, and Tyson.

The paired comparison method can also be used when a number of managers or supervisors evaluate the same subordinates. For example, the matrix below includes the hypothetical judgments of three independent managers:

	Hopkins	Bingham	Miller	Tyson	Haber
Hopkins	✕	✔✔✔	✔✔✔	✔	✔✔✔
Bingham		✕	✔✔✔	✔	✔✔
Miller			✕		✔
Tyson	✔✔	✔✔	✔✔✔	✕	✔✔✔
Haber		✔	✔✔		✕
Total number of times preferred over others	2	6	11	2	9

Generally, the more raters there are, the more accurate the estimate of a subordinate's true standing will be.

It is important to remember that the paired comparison procedure gives a simple ordering of employee proficiency. One cannot use the scores above to speak of the amount of difference between workers. There are, however, ways in which the paired comparison technique can be modified to allow us to determine how much two employees actually differ in proficiency. These more sophisticated procedures are discussed by Blum and Naylor (1968).

A problem with the paired comparison method is the large number of judgments a supervisor must make as the number of subordinates increases. If 40 subordinates are involved, for example, the supervisor must make 40(40–1)/2 or 780 comparisons. Fortunately, methods have been developed which reduce the number of comparisons required. Those readers interested in knowing more about reducing the number of pairs are referred to such sources as Lawshe, Kephart, and McCormick (1949) and McCormick and Bachus (1952).

FORCED DISTRIBUTION. A final version of the employee comparison approach is the forced distribution method. This method may be useful only when: (a) a large number of subordinates (e.g., 20 or more) are to be evaluated by a single rater; (b) rough discriminations among subordinates will suffice; and (c) it can be assumed that the job proficiency of subordinates conforms to a normal or bell-shaped curve. Typically, a supervisor or manager is asked to distribute the names of subordinates into five categories, with a predetermined percentage of employees in each category. The usual percentages employed conform to a bell-shaped frequency distribution and are as follows:

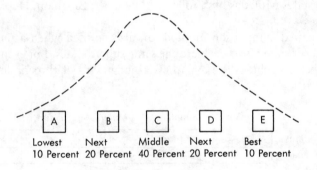

For instance, a supervisor with 60 subordinates would be forced to place the names of 6, 12, 24, 12, and 6 employees in categories A, B, C, D, and E, respectively. It is best to avoid category names such as "poorest" and "worst" since supervisors sometimes resent being forced to place employees in these slots. In one company, one of the authors used the following category names with no resistance from raters: below average, average, above average, excellent, and outstanding. Category names are relatively unimportant compared to acceptance of the method by raters and discriminability among ratees.

There are several problems encountered with this method that should be noted. First, quite often the assumption of normality (i.e., bell-shaped curve) is erroneous. This is true in those situations where employees have previously been screened by valid selection devices and/or given effective job training. In these cases, the distribution of employee proficiency would be "skewed" rather than bell-shaped (see Figure 10–5). Second, experience has shown that some supervisors resent being "forced" to pigeonhole their employees into a fixed distribution preset by someone else. As one supervisor said: "Most of my people belong in categories C, D, and E. I only have one or two who I think should be put in categories A and B. I'll do what you want, but I'm telling you honestly that it's not the way I really see them." Third, the rough classification of employees into only five or so categories can interfere with important administrative uses of performance evaluation. How can we give Smith a higher salary increase next year than Jones when they both received the same performance appraisal rating (e.g., "D")? We all know Smith is slightly better than Jones!

ADVANTAGES AND DISADVANTAGES OF EMPLOYEE COMPARISON. All employee comparison methods have one characteristic in common—they require the rater to evaluate workers relative to one another. These methods are thought of as having two principal advantages over other performance appraisal methods. First, employee comparisons seem to be natural to and easily understood by raters and therefore are often readily accepted by them. Second, unlike ratings and checklists, raters are forced to distinguish among subordinates. Thus, if there are 16 employees working in a department at different proficiency levels, only half of them can receive above-average evaluations. The constraints which employee comparisons place on raters is believed to be important in overcoming various rater tendencies such as leniency and central tendency errors. After all, it is impossible for someone to be "lenient" or "middle-of-the-road" when using these methods.

One disadvantage of these techniques is that they typically provide only information about serial arrangement. One cannot say that John is as much superior in proficiency than Bill as Bill is superior to Jim, even

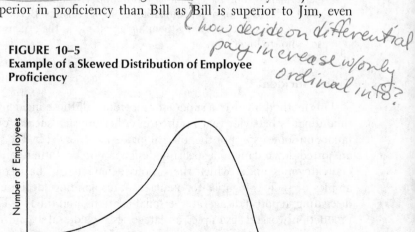

FIGURE 10–5
Example of a Skewed Distribution of Employee Proficiency

Number of Employees

Low   High

Employee Proficiency

though the three ranks assigned to them (e.g., 5, 6, and 7, respectively) are equally spaced. Without information about the magnitude of differences between individuals, it is virtually impossible for management to compare individuals across groups. This is particularly disturbing when attempting to make salary and promotion decisions. Of course, the conversion to a common numerical scale mentioned earlier is a possible solution.

Evaluating employees relative to one another often brings about some unanticipated and troublesome problems. One first-line supervisor in a large-sized manufacturing company described one problem this way:

> This performance appraisal technique forces me to give about half my people below-average evaluations. It's tough to sit down with 50 percent of your people and tell them they're doing substandard work when you know darn well that they're better than people on other crews. It's terribly discouraging for them. Their pride is hurt and they often won't give a good day's work for weeks.

Another supervisor told one of the authors this:

> I recently told one of my subordinates that I felt she was improving. When it came to rating her, however, I gave her the same evaluation I did six months before. When she asked me why, I explained that while her performance had improved, the performance of everyone else in our department improved about as much. It made me feel pretty foolish!

Here is what a middle level manager of a large-sized drug company told us:

> We have sales representatives whose salary increases are tied to their performance appraisals. Some of our minority group people have threatened to leave us for other companies at higher salaries. Between you and me, we find ourselves giving them higher ratings at the expense of others so as not to lose them.

[handwritten margin note: dysfunctional effects of system tie betw perf & compensation / compar &]

Critical Incident

This method involves a supervisor recording all those incidents in each subordinate's behavior that resulted in either unusual success or unusual failure on some aspect of the job. All incidents observed by the supervisor are jotted down daily in a specially designed notebook that contains general categories under which the various behaviors can be recorded. Examples of such categories for managers are planning, decision making, delegating, report writing, interpersonal relations, and the like. For hourly production workers, examples of categories include safety, initiative, cooperation with co-workers, accuracy of work, and alertness to problems. Space is provided in the notebook under each category heading for recording both positive and negative incidents.

This method provides concrete information that can be discussed with the employee during periodic appraisal interviews. The manager no longer has to speak in terms of vague generalities ("Joe, you've been having trouble getting along with your work group"), but can concentrate on discussing observable facts. The major problem with this procedure is that the manager's recordkeeping can lead to overly close supervision, causing subordinates to feel that "big brother is watching." It may also give subordinates the impression that everything they do will be jotted down in their superior's "little black book." Since the method is not quantifiable, it makes promotion and salary decisions difficult.

Group Appraisal

The group-appraisal procedure involves the immediate supervisor together with three or four other supervisors in the evaluation process. The additional supervisors are carefully chosen because they have some knowledge of the employee's work proficiency and can presumably contribute something to the evaluative discussions. The appraisal group has a coordinator whose main responsibility is keeping the evaluation as objective as possible. This is usually the manager who is directly superior to the group of supervisors. Sometimes it's a trained conference leader from the personnel department. In either case, the immediate supervisor has the major responsibility for rating the employee. The appraisal group aids the immediate supervisor by discussing the standards of performance for the job, the employee's current performance, possible reasons for this level of proficiency, and recommendations for improvement (Beach, 1975). One advantage of this method is the use of multiple judges who can cancel out any personal bias, leniency, strictness, central tendency, or halo error on the part of the immediate supervisor. Employee development is an important aspect of the procedure since the group arrives at a comprehensive action plan for each appraisee. The biggest problem with this method is its cost and the fact that it is often difficult to find others beside the immediate supervisor who are familiar enough with an employee's performance to serve as group members.

Field Review

This method derives its name from the fact that a representative of the personnel department goes into the "field" to question a supervisor or manager orally about the proficiency of individual employees. After asking a series of detailed questions about each employee's performance and occasionally interviewing employees themselves, the personnel administrator returns to the office to write the evaluation reports. These are sent to the manager who modifies them, if need be, and then signs them to indicate approval. This method provides managers with the professional assistance they sometimes need with their evaluations, cuts down on the amount of time they spend on form completion and report writing, and makes for greater standardization of the evaluation process throughout the organization. On the other hand, if not supported by high level management, the field review procedure can be used as an excuse by the supervisor to avoid responsibility for evaluating subordinates.

Essay Evaluation

This procedure asks the evaluator to write an essay describing each subordinate's strengths and weaknesses. In some organizations, the evaluator is required to group comments under specific headings such as job performance, reasons for this performance, employee characteristics, and developmental needs (Beach, 1975). Other organizations provide no guidelines with regard to topics to be covered; each manager is free to write anything he desires. The approach is time consuming for the manager. It makes promotional and wage and salary decisions extremely difficult since it is impossible to compare employees quantitatively. Frequently, in practice, managers write glowing reports about all their subordinates regardless of their proficiency for fear of putting negative comments down in writing. As one middle manager told us recently, "For all I know, he could end up being my boss in a couple of years." With this procedure, an employee's evaluation is highly dependent on the manager's skill and willingness to express himself or herself well in writing. The method is obviously vulnerable to personal biases, leniency error, halo, and so on. In short, it should be avoided wherever possible.

DIRECT MEASURES

All of the procedures discussed thus far require some sort of judgment on the part of the evaluator. Fortunately, there are certain types of jobs where subjective judgments are not necessary. Consider, for example, the assembly-line or press operator job. On these kinds of jobs an employee's proficiency can be obtained more directly by simply recording the number of units produced in a given time period, the number of unacceptable items produced, the number of accidents incurred during a certain span of time, and so on. The work performed on these jobs differs considerably from that of managers, personnel administrators, secretaries, engineers, and chemists. On such nonproduction jobs, there is no quantitative measure of output available and we must use quantitative assessments of employee proficiency.

There are two main types of direct measures: those dealing with production (e.g., scrappage, units produced, dollars earned, quality of work, amount of rejects) and those involving personal information (e.g., absenteeism, training time needed to reach some acceptable level of performance, grievances, tardiness, tenure, injuries, dispensary visits). Productivity measures can usually be obtained easily from the accounting or quality control departments. It will ordinarily be necessary to obtain several different kinds of measures of productivity (i.e., quality and quantity of output) since any single measure will be deficient. These measures should be taken over long enough periods of time (e.g., 12 months) to insure that random fluctuations are controlled. The correct time period for insuring reliable measurement will, of course, depend on the particular job and measure used.

How does one compare the output of employees on two or more different production jobs? Worker A produces six passenger tires per seven-hour day while Worker B produces 2½ industrial truck tires in the same span of time. It is difficult to determine who is the more proficient worker since the units of measurement on the two jobs are unequal. After all, it requires less time to build a small passenger tire than a massive truck tire. This problem can be dealt with by comparing each worker's output with some kind of standard or quota for his/her job. Suppose, for example, the standard for passenger tires is eight per day while standard for truck tires is two. Worker A has a performance index of 75 (6/8 times 100) while worker B is superior with an index of 125 (2.5/2 times 100). The most difficult problem encountered with this solution is the determination of an equitable standard for each job. No one solution is problem-free. The interested reader is referred to Ghiselli and Brown (1955) for a discussion of the various ways to set production standards.

Personal measures are considered primarily with production jobs, but they pertain to other jobs as well. Although these personal items are not as job related as productivity measures, they can tell us important things about an individual employee's proficiency. Consider for a moment the costs for an organization in lost productivity when an employee is excessively tardy and absent, takes considerable time to learn the job, quits soon after training, and files frequent grievances.

PROFICIENCY TESTING

Another approach to measuring the performance of job incumbents is to use various types of proficiency tests. One variant of this approach consists of using work samples or simulations. Here, using either the actual work environment or a simulation of it, the employee is asked to perform exactly the same work behaviors as involved in the job. Examples of this would include typing tests, simulated telephone calls to operators, repairing malfunctioning gear reducers, and tuning automobile engines. The Assessment Center (discussed in Chapter 11) illustrates the use of simulation devices for evaluating the proficiency of managerial personnel. A second variant of this approach involves constructing written tests to assess an employee's current level of job knowledge and comprehension. When such measures are used, it must be assumed that the knowledge being tested is a necessary condition for actual job performance. As an example, knowledge of electrical theory may have no relationship to the job proficiency of maintenance electricians whose major responsibility is wiring machinery and equipment. On the other hand, assessing the electrician's knowledge and understanding of AC and DC electrical currents would be quite important.

It is essential that the proficiency tests used be representative of the everyday work activities of the employee. If not, the measurement will be deficient. In addition, one must always remember that some individuals become nervous when tested and, consequently, do poorly. For these particular employees, proficiency tests will not provide an accurate evaluation.

IMPLEMENTING APPRAISAL PROGRAMS

Now that we have looked at a number of appraisal methods, let us discuss several important issues involved in implementing performance appraisal programs. Specifically, we will consider the following five questions:

1. Who should do the appraising?
2. What should be evaluated?
3. When should appraisals take place?
4. Why is there union resistance to appraisals?
5. Should evaluators be trained?

Who Should Appraise?

The prevailing practice in most organizations is for an employee to be appraised by an immediate supervisor or manager. It is assumed that the superior is in the best position to observe the subordinate's behavior and to evaluate this behavior in light of organizational goals (Glueck, 1974). In recent years, some organizations have come to realize that other parties besides an employee's immediate superior can provide appraisals. These parties include: (1) organizational peers of the employee, (2) subordinates of the employee, (3) the employee himself, and (4) persons outside the employee's work unit.

What can be said about each of these approaches? Peer evaluations have received significant support from research conducted in the military and in industry (Hollander, 1954; Roadman, 1964). It appears that appraisals by an employee's work associates yield valuable information about proficiency provided that the following conditions are met: (1) there is a high level of interpersonal trust among peers, (2) a noncompetitive reward system exists, (3) there is high organizational committment, and (4) information about an employee's proficiency is directly available to peers (Cummings and Schwab, 1973). It is unfortunate that peer ratings are not used widely today in business and industry. This is probably due to the fact that few personnel administrators are aware of its potential.

Appraisals by a manager's subordinates is an excellent development approach. It provides managers with an understanding of how their people see them and the behaviors they must change to improve. On the other hand, subordinate appraisals should rarely be used for promotional, salary, and other administrative decisions. Many managers consider subordinate appraisals to be inappropriate and an undermining of their legitimate position power.

Self-appraisals are typically inflated compared with those of superiors. Consequently, there is every reason to believe that they are subject to self-interests which seriously lower their validity. On the positive side, they are effective tools for stimulating self-development. Employees are encouraged to think about their own strengths and weaknesses and to establish goals for future improvement.

Evaluations by outsiders (i.e., external consultants or specialists from the personnel department) are especially useful when promotional decisions need to be made. Often, those in the work unit have vested interests in the evaluation and find it impossible to be totally objective. The approach is also useful when managers need outside help in making their appraisals.

What Should Be Evaluated?

The proficiency of any employee can be looked at in three different ways. It can be expressed in terms of the behaviors that the employee exhibits in performing the job. It can be looked at in terms of the tangible results or outcomes that the employee achieves. It can also involve ratings on such factors as drive, loyalty, initiative, leadership potential, and moral courage.

It has been shown that there is little utility in making trait ratings. They are of no value in helping an employee to do a better job. For instance, how does one improve "moral courage"? Moreover, these traits are usually defined poorly, which seriously reduces interrater reliability and encourages personal biases in evaluations.

The research evidence suggests that evaluating *both* behavior and results simultaneously is an organization's best course of action (Porter, Lawler, and Hackman, 1975). This motivates the employee to not only engage in effective behaviors, but to also achieve desired outcomes. For example, salespeople should be evaluated in terms of both their sales volume as well as their persistance on tough accounts, their use of new sales techniques, and their aid to customers with equipment and displays.

When Should Appraisals Take Place?

Most organizations schedule the appraisal of their employees at fixed intervals. For example, many companies designate one month each year during which time evaluations of all their employees are to take place. Other companies appraise each employee on the yearly anniversary of the month that the individual began work. This type of fixed-interval schedule is difficult to defend from a performance-improvement or psychological point of view (Cummings and Schwab, 1973). It is unlikely that the employee will perceive any link between the ups and downs of job performance and the annual (or even semi-annual) performance review. A more defensible approach is one that employs a variable-interval schedule. Here, appraisals occur whenever there are significant variations in an employee's behavior or performance. In this way, the feedback the employee receives is usually more frequent and more closely linked with performance variations.

Why Is There Union Resistance?

As you might have gathered by now, unions have generally been opposed to the implementation of formal performance appraisal programs in industry. The reason for this is their understandable desire to safeguard the job security of their union members (Schultz, 1973). For this reason, unions have traditionally favored the use of seniority as the prime factor in determining promotions, transfers, layoffs, pay increases, and so on. This, of course, is opposed to the underlying assumption of all appraisal systems—that an employee should be rewarded contingent on his or her merit.

It should be noted that union resistance to performance appraisal affects only those blue-collar and few white-collar jobs covered by union contracts. It has no bearing on the majority of American jobs (especially managerial positions) which are nonunionized.

Should Evaluators Be Trained?

Performance appraisals are almost inevitably contaminated by such well-known judgmental errors as halo and leniency. It would seem logical that to solve the problem of human errors, the evaluator must be trained. In a recent study, it was shown that a short five- to six-minute training session could be successful in reducing halo error (Borman, 1975). During the training, raters were warned not to provide an overall evaluation of a ratee and not to justify this evaluation by rating the individual at the same level on all dimensions. In another study, it was shown that managers in a large corporation could be successfully trained to eliminate several rating errors that occur in performance appraisal and selection interviews, namely, halo error, similarity effect (the tendency on the part of a rater to judge more favorably those perceived as similar to self), first impressions (the tendency to evaluate someone on the basis of a judgment made primarily after an initial meeting), and contrast effect (the tendency to evaluate subordinates in comparison to other subordinates rather than against a predetermined anchor or standard). The training involved a 9½ hour workshop in which participants saw videotapes of hypothetical job candidates being appraised by a manager. The trainees gave a rating as to how they thought the manager in the videotape evaluated the candidate, and how they themselves would rate the candidate. In this way, the trainees had an opportunity to observe videotaped managers making human errors, to actively participate in discovering the degree to which they themselves were prone to making such errors, to receive feedback as to their own ratings, and to practice job-related tasks to reduce any errors they were committing (Latham, Wexley, and Pursell, 1975). Research results suggest the tenacity of judgmental errors despite attempts to reduce them by means of warning or lecturing raters about them. It appears that these errors can only be reduced by a fairly intensive training program which takes into account some of the basic principles of learning (see Chapter 13) (Wexley, Sanders, and Yukl, 1973).

SUMMARY

Measurement of employee proficiency is an essential part of the control process in organizations. Performance data are used in making administrative decisions and for providing developmental feedback to employees. The usefulness of a performance measure is dependent on its validity, reliability, and practicality.

Performance measures can be classified into one of three general categories: subjective procedures, direct measures, and proficiency testing. Subjective procedures include rating scales, checklists, employee comparisons, critical incidents technique, group appraisal, field review, and essay evaluation. These procedures are susceptible to various kinds of human errors, including leniency, central tendency, halo effect, and personal biases. Some of the subjective procedures are more prone to these human errors than are other subjective procedures. The reliability and validity of subjective procedures also depend on the evaluator's skill and specific knowledge about the employees being judged.

Direct measures of employee performance include quantitative records of productivity and output quality, and personal measures such as absenteeism, tardiness, injuries, and so forth. These measures can be used as a basis for establishing performance standards or for setting performance goals.

The third category of performance measure is proficiency testing. Employee proficiency is evaluated by means of work samples or simulations involving the same behavior and skills required on the job. While not a direct measure of performance, proficiency tests can be used to determine if an employee is capable of performing at an acceptable level.

Employee performance can be judged by the immediate supervisor, by subordinates, by peers, by the employee himself (herself), or by outside specialists. The judgments can be expressed in terms of behavior exhibited, tangible outcomes of the behavior, or employee traits and skills. Performance evaluation can be improved by training evaluators, developing accurate measuring procedures, and scheduling evaluations at appropriate intervals.

REVIEW AND DISCUSSION QUESTIONS

1. Define and explain each of the following key terms: measurement deficiency, measurement contamination, halo effect, sex-role stereotype, paired-comparisons, field review, critical incident.
2. What are the relative advantages and disadvantages of using employee comparison methods?
3. Since all subjective procedures depend upon human judgment to some degree, they are likely to be susceptible to certain kinds of distortions. What are some of the potential sources of bias and errors affecting these evaluations?
4. What are some of the wide variety of uses of employee proficiency measures in organizational settings?
5. Assume that you have just been asked by your college or university to measure the teaching effectiveness of individual faculty members. You have no available direct measures and therefore must rely on subjective procedures. You want the measures to be as valid, reliable, and practical as possible. What method(s) would you choose and why?
6. Think of a job with which you have some familiarity. Outline the procedures that you would follow in developing behaviorally anchored rating scales for it.
7. Critically evaluate the current state of knowledge in the area of measuring employee proficiency. Do you think that we know a lot? In what ways do we still have to learn more?
8. Suppose you were given the assignment by a company of installing a performance appraisal program for all middle and upper level managerial jobs. What method would you use and why would you prefer it?

REFERENCES

Beach, D. S. Personnel: The management of people at work. New York: Macmillan, 1975.

Blood, M. R. Spin-offs from behavioral expectation scale procedures. Journal of Applied Psychology, 1974, 5, 513–515.

Blum, M. L., & Naylor, J. C. Industrial psychology: Its theoretical and social foundations. New York: Harper & Row, 1968.

Borman, W. C. Effects of instructions to avoid halo error on reliability and validity of performance evaluation ratings. Journal of Applied Psychology, 1975, 60, 556–560.

Borman, W. C., & Dunnette, M. D. Behavior-based versus trait-oriented performance ratings: An empirical study. Journal of Applied Psychology, 1975, 60, 561–565.

Cummings, L. L., & Schwab, D. P. Performance in organizations: Determinants and appraisal. Glenview, Ill.: Scott, Foresman and Company, 1973.

Ghiselli, E. E., & Brown, C. W. Personnel and industrial psychology. New York: McGraw-Hill, 1955.

Glueck, W. F. Personnel: A diagnostic approach. Dallas, Tex.: Business Publications, Inc., 1974.

Goodale, J. G., & Burke, R. J. Behaviorally based rating scales need not be job specific. Journal of Applied Psychology, 1975, 60 389–391.

Hollander, E. P. Buddy ratings: Military research and industrial implications. Personnel Psychology, 1954, 12, 385–393.

Kirchner, W., & Reisberg, D. J. Differences between better and less effective supervisors in appraisal of subordinates. Personnel Psychology, 1962, 15, 295–302.

Korman, A. K. Industrial and organizational psychology. Englewood Cliffs, N.J.: Prentice-Hall, 1971.

Latham, G. P., Wexley, K. N., & Pursell, E. D. Training managers to minimize rating errors in the observation of behavior. Journal of Applied Psychology, 1975, 60, 550–555.

Lawshe, C. H., Kephart, N. C., & McCormick, E. J. The paired-comparison technique for rating performance of industrial employees. Journal of Applied Psychology, 1949, 33, 69–77.

McCormick, E. J., & Bachus, J. A. Paired-comparison ratings. I. The effect on ratings of reductions in the number of pairs. Journal of Applied Psychology, 1952, 36, 123–127.

McCormick, E. J., & Tiffin, J. Industrial Psychology. Englewood Cliffs, N.J.: Prentice-Hall, 1974.

Porter, L. W., Lawler, E. E., III, & Hackman, J. R. Behavior in organizations. New York: McGraw-Hill, 1975.

Rand, T. M., & Wexley, K. N. Demonstration of the effect, "Similar to

Me," in simulated employment interviews. *Psychological Reports*, 1975, 36, 535–544.

Roadman, H. E.   An industrial use of peer ratings. *Journal of Applied Psychology*, 1964, 48, 211–214.

Schein, V. E.   Relationships between sex role stereotypes and requisite management characteristics among female managers. *Journal of Applied Psychology*, 1975, 60, 340–344.

Schultz, D.   *Psychology and industry today*. New York: Macmillan, 1973.

Smith, P. C., & Kendall, L. M.   Retranslation of expectations: An approach to the construction of unambiguous anchors for rating scales. *Journal of Applied Psychology*, 1963, 47, 149–155.

Wexley, K. N., & Nemeroff, W. F.   Effects of racial prejudice, race of applicant, and biographical similarity on interviewer evaluations of job applicants. *Journal of Social and Behavioral Sciences*, 1974, 20, 66–78.

Wexley, K. N., Sanders, R. E., & Yukl, G. A.   Training interviewers to eliminate contrast effects in employment interviews. *Journal of Applied Psychology*, 1973, 57, 233–236.

PERSONNEL SELECTION

THE MOST TRADITIONAL function performed by psychologists in industry has been the selection and placement of personnel. Since the early 1900s, industrial psychologists have been actively involved in developing better ways of putting the right person in the right job at the right time. This challenging task is based on the simple fact that individuals differ. If all individuals had the same skills, knowledge, motivation, and abilities, personnel selection and placement would be unnecessary since everyone would be identical in terms of their job proficiency. This is obviously not the case.

One of the critical aspects of any organization's effectiveness is the calibre of its personnel. Thus, it is important for every company to develop efficient ways of hiring better workers to replace those who have been terminated, promoted, transferred, or retired. In this chapter we will discuss some of the methods used for making valid selection and placement decisions.

RECRUITMENT

The method of recuitment that an organization uses will directly affect the efficiency of its selection and placement program in at least three ways. First, the recruitment method will determine the number of applicants applying for a particular position. After all, the more candidates there are for each job to be filled, the more utility selection instruments will possess. Second, it will influence how well the organization meets its obligation to hire minority group members. This will usually entail advertising in minority newspapers, sending recruiters to minority colleges and high schools, and cooperating with agencies such as the Urban League which specialize in working with the minority community (Strauss & Sayles, 1972). Third, it can affect the subsequent turnover rates of employees. Several studies have shown that when recruiters give applicants realistic expectations about a particular job by pointing out *both* the positive and negative aspects of it (i.e., "telling it like it is"), lower turnover rates result (Porter, Lawler, and Hackman, 1975). Often recruiters give applicants unrealistic expectations regarding the company and their future jobs thereby resulting in frustration, dissatisfaction, and early termination. One possible solution to this problem used by several companies is a work sample preview which gives the prospective employee a realistic picture of what will be expected of him (Wanous, 1973).

Among the many *external* sources that organizations use to actively recruit new employees are the following: (1) advertising in newspapers, radio, professional magazines, and local television; (2) visits to college and high school campuses; (3) government and private employment agencies; (4) word-of-mouth recruiting by current employees who are given incentives for doing this; (5) labor unions; and (6) professional organizations and societies. Sometimes organizations recruit *internally* by using computerized data banks which store the skills, knowledge, and abilities of each employee. When a new position becomes available the computer can survey the entire work force in a matter of minutes (Chruden and Sherman, 1972).

METHODS OF OBTAINING INFORMATION ABOUT JOB CANDIDATES

There are a large number of methods which organizations use to collect information about job candidates before deciding whom to hire. These methods differ greatly in terms of their popularity and their usefulness. In this section, we will discuss testing, biographical data, interviewing, references and letters of recommendation, peer ratings and supervisory judgments, and assessment centers. We will pay particular attention to the validity or predictive efficiency of each of these selection approaches.

Personnel Testing

CHARACTERISTICS OF A GOOD TEST. There are certain characteristics that all well-constructed psychological tests have in common, namely, standardization, norms, reliability, and validity. It is these characteristics that should be looked for in any published or tailor-made test. These factors are what set psychological tests apart from the "tests" often seen in popular magazines (e.g., "How good is your marriage?"). It should be noted at the beginning that few, if any, tests meet all of the standards set forth below. Nevertheless, they are ideals which should be striven for in all types of selection devices.

Standardization. Standardization refers to the consistency or uniformity of procedures for administering and scoring a test. If we expect to compare the scores obtained by several job applicants, then the testing conditions must obviously be identical for all of them. Otherwise, any change in the testing procedures may put certain applicants at an unfair advantage. In order to achieve this uniformity of testing conditions, the test developer must specify in the test manual the exact procedures to be followed regarding such things as time limits, oral instructions, ways of handling specific questions from examinees, test materials needed by examinees, physical testing conditions (e.g., seating facilities, illumination), and scoring procedures.

Norms. If you were informed that a job applicant got 60 problems correct on a 100-item mechanical reasoning test, this score would convey little information about the applicant's relative standing in this ability. In order to interpret this score, it must be compared with the scores obtained by a sample of similar individuals. This is accomplished by means of test norms. Essentially, norms are a distribution of test scores obtained from a large sample of persons representative of the population of applicants being considered for the job. The distribution of scores of this reference group (sometimes called a norm group) serves as a yardstick against which a job applicant's score can be compared. Does our applicant's score coincide with the average score of the norm group? Is the applicant considerably above or below average? Maybe he falls at the 90th percentile, i.e., his score exceeds the scores obtained by 90 percent of those in the norm group. An example of test norms is presented in Table 11–1.

A comprehensive guide for the evaluation of psychological tests has been published by the American Psychological Association. It is called the *Standards for Educational and Psychological Tests* (1974) and it is quite useful for any personnel administrator involved in testing. These standards are concerned with the information about validity, reliability, norms, and other test characteristics which should be reported in test manuals. Listed below are some of the more important rules adapted from the Standards regarding norms:

1. Except where the primary use of a test is to compare individuals with their own local group, norms should be published in the test manual at the time of release of the test for operational use (authors' comment: too often tests are published with no norms, only the promise that they will be available sometime in the near future).

2. Norms presented in the test manual should refer to defined and clearly described populations. These populations should be the groups to whom users of the test will ordinarily wish to compare the persons tested.

3. The description of the norm group should be sufficiently complete in

TABLE 11–1. Female Norms from the Edwards Personal Preference Schedule

WOMEN N = 4932

Score	ach	def	ord	exh	aut	aff	int	suc	dom	aba	nur	chg	end	het	agg	con	Score
28											99						28
27											98			99			27
26						99				99	96			99			26
25			99			98	99			97	91	99	99	98			25
24			98			96	98	99	99	95	87	98	98	98			24
23	99	99	96			92	97	98	98	92	79	97	96	97			23
22	98	98	94			88	95	98	98	87	72	94	94	96			22
21	96	97	90	99	98	81	93	96	98	82	64	91	90	95	99		21
20	95	94	85	98	97	73	89	94	97	75	56	87	85	94	98		20
19	92	89	80	97	96	63	84	92	95	68	47	81	79	93	97		19
18	88	83	73	95	93	54	77	88	94	59	38	76	72	91	96		18
17	83	75	65	93	89	44	70	84	91	51	31	68	64	89	93		17
16	77	66	56	89	85	35	62	78	89	43	24	60	56	87	91		16
15	70	56	46	84	79	27	52	72	85	36	18	53	47	84	87	99	15
14	60	46	38	78	72	20	42	64	80	29	13	45	39	81	83	97	14
13	50	37	30	70	64	15	32	55	76	23	9	37	32	78	78	85	13
12	40	27	24	61	54	10	25	46	71	18	6	30	25	75	71	66	12
11	30	19	19	51	45	7	18	38	64	14	4	23	20	71	64	45	11
10	21	14	14	42	36	5	12	30	56	11	3	18	15	66	55	25	10
9	15	9	9	32	28	3	8	24	49	7	2	13	11	63	46	12	9
8	9	5	6	23	20	2	5	17	40	5	1	9	7	58	38	5	8
7	5	3	4	15	13	1	3	12	32	4		6	5	53	29	2	7
6	3	2	3	9	8		1	8	22	2		3	3	48	20		6
5	1	1	1	5	4			5	15	1		2	2	42	14		5
4				2	2			2	9			1	1	37	9		4
3				1				1	4					30	4		3
2									1					24	2		2
1														17			1
0														10			0

the test manual that the user can judge whether his or her sample data fall within the population data represented by the norm group. The description should include number of cases, classified by such variables as age, sex, and educational status.

4. The number of cases on which the norms are based should be reported in the test manual. If the sample on which norms are based is small or otherwise undependable, the user should be cautioned explicitly in the test manual regarding the possible magnitude of errors arising in interpretation of scores.

5. The test manual should report whether scores vary for groups differing on age, sex, amount of training, and other equally important variables.

Reliability. One of the most important characteristics of any measuring instrument is that it gives consistent results on repeated trials. A bathroom scale would be worthless if every time you weighed yourself it gave different results. Similarly, a psychological test would not be useful if the scores obtained by examinees were not consistent or stable on successive testings. After all, when making personnel decisions we must be fairly certain that when applicant A gets a higher score on a selection test than applicant B, the difference between these two individuals would be the same if they took the test again at some other time (Ghiselli & Brown, 1955). If test scores are unstable, the value of the test for selecting the better applicant would be diminished.

No matter how ideal the testing conditions, no test is perfectly reliable. All tests are affected, to some degree, by random changes in the examinee (e.g., fatigue, access to memory, emotional strain) and the testing conditions (e.g., unexpected noises, sudden changes in the weather). Thus, before a test can be used for selection purposes, its reliability should be shown to be adequate.

There are several straightforward methods for determining reliability, three of which are briefly described below:

The *test-retest method* involves administering the same test on two different occasions to the same group of individuals and correlating the two distributions of scores. The closer the correlation is to +1.00, the more the examinees have maintained their relative position from the first to the second testing. Of course, it is important that the test manual report the time interval between the two test administrations since reliability will normally decrease as the interval is lengthened. With many psychological tests, this method is inappropriate. Since the examinees take the same test twice, the correlation is often distorted by memory and practice effects. Only tests not appreciably affected by repetition (e.g., certain perceptual speed tests and motor tests) are amenable to this method (Anastasi, 1975).

The *equivalent-forms method* is exactly the same as the test-retest approach, except that two equivalent forms of the same test are used rather than a readministration of the same test. The major advantage of this method is that it reduces the problems of memory and learning encountered with the test-retest method. The obvious disadvantage of this method is the expense involved in constructing two equivalent forms of a test—forms alike in all respects except for their specific items. Like the test-retest method, this type of reliability should always be accompanied by a statement of the time interval between testings.

The concept of reliability takes on a slightly different meaning when talking about the *split-halves method.* Here we are concerned mainly with the *internal consistency* of the test rather than with its temporal consistency. To find the split-half reliability, one administers the test once, divides the test by assigning the even-numbered items to one half and the odd-numbered items to the other, scores the halves separately for each examinee, correlates the scores earned by the examinees on each half, and boosts the correlation by means of the Spearman-Brown formula. This procedure can be found in any basic textbook on testing (e.g., Anastasi, 1975). It is quite popular because it requires only one administration of the test.

Regardless of the method used, reliability estimates should fall in the $+.80$s and $+.90$s to be considered satisfactory for selection purposes. Since the magnitude of the correlation obtained is dependent upon the particular method used, test developers should report the results of using several different methods rather than just one.

Validity. In a broad sense, validity refers to the degree to which a test actually measures what it claims to measure. The specific methods employed for determining a test's validity are numerous. Since our interests here relate primarily to personnel selection and placement, two main types of validity are especially important, namely, criterion-related validity and content validity.

Criterion-related validity is determined by correlating the scores obtained by individuals on a selection test with some available criterion (see Chapter 10) of their job performance. Thus, sales aptitude test scores might be correlated with sales figures available for a three-year period. Two kinds of criterion-related validity should be distinguished: predictive validity (also known as the "follow-up" method) and concurrent validity (also called the "present-employee" method). Of the two, predictive validity is the more convincing validity for selection purposes since it comes closer to assessing the actual power of the selection instrument for predicting subsequent job performance. In order to assess predictive validity, a test is administered to job applicants at the time of hire and correlated with criterion measures obtained at some later time (e.g., at the end of 12 months). Concurrent validity, on the other hand, is determined by administering the test to employees presently on the job and correlating their scores with currently available measures of their job proficiency. The exact procedures involved in determining predictive and concurrent validity will be discussed in greater detail in the next chapter together with the pros and cons of each method. For now, let us look at a few important rules regarding criterion-related validity adapted from the *Standards for Educational and Psychological Tests* (1974):

1. The manual should report the validity of the test for each criterion about which a recommendation is made.
2. For any type of prediction the manual should report test-criterion correlations for a variety of institutions or situations.
3. The time elapsing between the test administration and the collection of criterion data should be reported in the manual.
4. If a test is recommended for long-term prediction, but comparisons with concurrent criteria only are presented, the manual should emphasize that the validity of predictions is undetermined.
5. The criterion score should be determined independently of test scores. The manual should describe any precautions taken to avoid contamination of the criterion or should warn the reader of possible contamination.
6. The validity sample should be described in the manual in terms of those variables known to be related to the quality tested, such as age, sex, socioeconomic status, and level of education.
7. The validity of a test should be determined on subjects who are at the age or in the same educational or vocational situation as the persons for whom the test is recommended in practice.
8. When information other than the test scores is known to have an appreciable degree of criterion-related validity and is ordinarily available to the prospective test user, the manual should report the validity of the other information and the resulting multiple correlation when the new test information is combined with it.

Content validity also deserves mention because it is sometimes used for validating achievement (or trade) tests. It involves a systematic review of the test content to determine whether it adequately measures the skills, knowledge, and attitudes required by the job. The determination of this kind of validity is made on the basis of the judgment of "experts" (e.g., supervisors and managers) with regard to the appropriateness of the test content in relation to the job analysis information. From a legal standpoint, it would seem wise to make certain that an organization's selection tests possess both content as well as criterion-related validity.

TYPES OF TESTS. Although all selection devices are "tests" in a legal sense, most people typically use the word "test" to refer to psychological tests. At last count, there were over 1,200 published psychological tests on the market (Buros, 1972). There are several ways we can classify this numerous assortment of tests. They can be discussed in terms of the way they are scored (objectively or subjectively), administered (individually or to large groups of people at one time), or even the method used by the examinee to record answers (written, oral, or equipment manipulation). The most useful classification scheme for our purposes is perhaps to categorize these tests in terms of the characteristics which they purport to measure. Table 11–2 includes seven main categories of tests together with a few examples of commercially available instruments in each grouping.

Intelligence Tests. These short (12–30 minutes) and easily administered group intelligence tests have been especially developed for gross screening of lower and middle level industrial personnel. The tests may have fairly high validity for certain jobs and no validity at all for others depending upon the amount of verbal and numerical ability required to learn or perform the particular job. Unfortunately, there are those who have the erroneous impression that these tests can predict success in almost all jobs. The fact is that this kind of test has been shown to be a better predictor of success in training than for job proficiency (Ghiselli, 1973). This is probably true because many business and industrial training programs stress the same intellectual abilities as required in formal school situations. There is evidence that certain of these tests may sometimes inadvertently discriminate against minority group applicants. This possibility should be examined before any test is used for selection purposes.

Unlike the short group intelligence tests, the Wechsler Adult Intelligence Scale (WAIS) is a lengthy (over an hour) individualized test administered by a trained psychologist. Because of its administration costs, it is used primarily for selection of high-level managers.

Psychomoter Tests. Numerous jobs such as packer, assembler, mechanic, and machine operator require good arm, hand, or finger dexterity. Thus, many commercially available tests have been developed to measure speed and accuracy of motor coordination. Most of these tests are individually administered and involve the manipulation of actual apparatus. For instance, the Crawford Small Parts Dexterity Test requires the examinee to first use tweezers to insert pins in close-fitting holes, and then to place a collar over each pin. The examinee is also asked to place small screws in threaded holes and then screw them down using a small screwdriver.

The most important characteristic of psychomoter tests is their high degree of *specificity* (Anastasi, 1975). That is, the intercorrelations among these tests are so low that we can assume that each instrument is tapping a unique and very specific motor ability. Because of this specificity, it is important to:

TABLE 11–2
Examples of Some Commercially Available Employment Tests

Name of Test	Test Publisher
Intelligence	
Adaptability Test	Science Research Associates
Wechsler Adult Intelligence Scale (WAIS)	The Psychological Corporation
Wesman Personnel Classification Test ...	The Psychological Corporation
Wonderlic Personnel Test	E. F. Wonderlic & Associates
Psychomotor	
Purdue Pegboard	Science Research Associates
Crawford Small Parts Dexterity Test	The Psychological Corporation
Hand-Tool Dexterity Test	The Psychological Corporation
Minnesota Rate of Manipulation Test ...	Educational Test Bureau
Personality	
Guilford-Zimmerman Temperament Survey	Sheridan Psychological Services
California Psychological Inventory	Consulting Psychologists Press
Sixteen Personality Factor Questionnaire	Institute for Personality and Ability Testing
Edwards Personal Preference Schedule ...	The Psychological Corporation
Minnesota Multiphasic Personality Inventory	The Psychological Corporation
Interest	
Kuder Preference Record Vocational Form CP	Science Research Associates
Strong-Campbell Interest Inventory	Stanford University Press
Holland Vocational Preference Inventory	Consulting Psychologists Press
Mechanical Aptitude	
SRA Mechanical Aptitudes	Science Research Associates
Bennett Mechanical Comprehension Test	The Psychological Corporation
Revised Minnesota Paper Form Board ...	The Psychological Corporation
MacQuarrie Test for Mechanical Ability	California Test Bureau
Clerical Aptitude	
Typing Test for Business	The Psychological Corporation
Short Tests of Clerical Ability	Science Research Associates
General Clerical Test	The Psychological Corporation
Minnesota Clerical Test	The Psychological Corporation
Projective	
Thematic Apperception Tests	Harvard University Press
Tomkins-Horn Picture Arrangement Test	Springer Publishing Company
Miner Sentence Completion Scale	Springer Publishing Company

1. Make very certain that the particular commercial motor test chosen is valid for the specific job in question.
2. Use commercial motor tests as part of a large battery of selection devices rather than as a single predictor.
3. Try whenever possible to build custom-made motor tests that reproduce as closely as possible the exact movements required on the particular job. Well-constructed job sample tests can often result in higher validities than available commercial tests.

Personality and Interest Tests. The rationale underlying the use of personality and interest tests in selection is that an individual will be a more successful worker if personality and interest patterns closely resemble those of successful employees already on the job in question. Interest inventories are used primarily for vocational counseling where the emphasis is on finding the right type of work for an individual. Nevertheless, many organizations include interest tests as part of their selection batteries. The most well-known and respected of the interest inventories are the Strong-Campbell Interest Inventory (SCII) and the Kuder Preference Record Vocational Form CP. For selection purposes, an individual's SCII can be scored for a single occupation to determine how closely the applicant's interests resemble those of, let us say, successful sales managers. Most often, the inventory is used by scoring the 124 occupational scales, the 6 general occupational themes, and the 23 basic interest scales in order to determine the applicant's total interest pattern. The Strong-Campbell consists of 325 items and requires the applicant to indicate whether he or she likes, dislikes, or is indifferent to various occupations, school subjects, activities, amusements, and types of people. The examinee is also asked to contrast two activities or circumstances (e.g., *Taking a chance* versus *Playing safe*) and to decide which is more appealing, or whether the two are equally attractive. In the last section, the respondent is asked to describe personal abilities and weaknesses by answering either "Yes," "No," or "?" as to whether certain statements are an apt self-description. Until the development of the latest form (i.e., Merged Form T325), male and female examinees were treated separately in that different sets of occupational scales and norms were used. Now the same booklet and profile sheet can be employed with both sexes.

The Kuder Preference Record Vocational Form CP indicates an applicant's relative interests in ten broad interest areas rather than in specific occupations. The interest scales include: outdoor, mechanical, computational, scientific, persuasive, artistic, literary, musical, social service, and clerical. Examinees are presented with sets of three activities similar to those shown below. The respondent indicates in each set which activity he or she would like most and least (see Figure 11–1).

FIGURE 11–1
Sample Items from the Kuder Preference Record Vocational Form CP

Check Activity You Like Most
and Least in Each Triad

	Most	Least
Visit an art gallery	_____	_____
Browse in a library	_____	_____
Visit a museum	_____	_____
Collect autographs	_____	_____
Collect coins	_____	_____
Collect butterflies	_____	_____

From *Kuder Preference Record Vocational Form CP*. © 1948, G. Frederic Kuder. Reprinted by permission of the publisher, Science Reseach Associates, Inc.

Self-report personality inventories generally ask the examinee how much he "agrees" with a statement, how well the statement "describes" him, or which of several alternatives he "prefers most" (Blum & Naylor, 1968). These tests measure such traits within a person as sociability, need for achievement, and self esteem. Figure 11–2 shows a few typical questions taken from several well-known tests.

FIGURE 11–2
Sample Items from Self-Report Personality Inventories

I am an important person.   ☐ True   ☐ False

Which of these two statements is more characteristic of what you like?

A. I like to talk about myself to others.
B. I like to work toward some goal that I have set for myself.

Prefers to get up early in the morning

☐ Most like me   ☐ Least like me

Personality and interest tests have several possible limitations as selection devices, the major one being the problem of "faking." People can distort their true answers when applying for a job they really desire. To what extent individuals actually do fake their answers in the selection situation is an open question.

The validity of personality and interest tests have been summarized by Ghiselli (1973) for different occupations. Good predictions of trainability and job proficiency criteria are provided for both lower sales occupations (the sales clerk) and higher ones (the salesmen). They have also shown moderate validity for forecasting success as executives and administrators, supervisors, tradesmen and craftsmen, and vehicle operators.

Aptitude Tests. The demands of vocational selection have led psychologists to develop a large number of special aptitude tests. Unlike intelligence tests which measure one's *general* capacity to learn, these tests attempt to predict the likelihood that an applicant will be able to learn *specific* jobs. For instance, there are several commercially available tests which measure mechanical aptitude. These tests are concerned primarily with measuring mechanical reasoning ability and spatial ability. Probably the most widely used test of mechanical reasoning is the Bennett Mechanical Comprehension Test. This instrument employs pictures of common situations involving mechanical principles about which short questions are to be answered. Two sample items taken from Forms S and T of the Bennett are presented in Figure 11–3.

The Revised Minnesota Paper Form Board is a well-known measure of spatial visualization or ability. The applicant is presented with drawings of figures cut into two or more parts (see Figure 11–4) and must be able to visualize how the complete figure would appear if the pieces were put together.

FIGURE 11–3
Sample Items from the Bennett Mechanical Comprehension Test

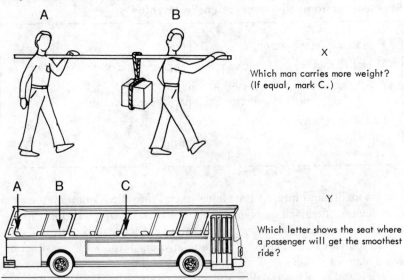

FIGURE 11-4
Sample Items from Minnesota Paper Form Board Test

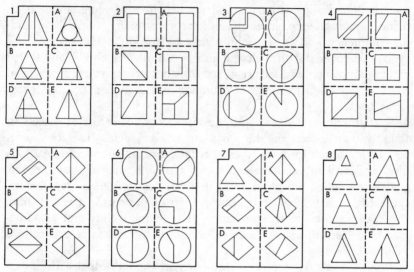

The examinee must pick the figure (from A to E) which shows how the parts will look when assembled.

There are numerous clerical tests on the market. Most of them are quite similar in measuring only one aspect of clerical aptitude, namely, perceptual speed. A good example is the Minnesota Clerical Test (see Figure 11–5). Since most clerical jobs involve a multiplicity of office skills,

FIGURE 11-5
Sample Items from Minnesota Clerical Test

> When the two numbers or names in a pair are *exactly the same*, make a check mark on the line between them.
>
> 66273894 _____ 66273984
>
> 527384578 _____ 527384578
>
> New York World _____ New York World
>
> Cargill Grain Co. _____ Cargil Grain Co.

some clerical tests combine perceptual speed with other functions necessary for clerical work. For instance, the General Clerical Test is a nine-part test dealing with name and number checking, filing, simple arithmetic, numerical error location, arithmetic reasoning, vocabulary, reading comprehension, spelling, and grammar. It is group administered and yields three overall scores: clerical aptitude, numerical ability, and verbal ability. For certain positions (e.g., secretary or clerk-typist), it is beneficial to use a general clerical test in conjunction with typing and/or stenography tests.

Spatial and mechanical aptitudes are better predictors of success in training than success on the job itself, whereas perceptual accuracy is equally important for both types of criteria. Spatial and mechanical tests give moderate to good predictions of trainability for clerical, service, trades and crafts, industrial (e.g., machine tenders), managerial, sales, protective, and vehicle occupations. Tests of perceptual accuracy have moderate validity for the prediction of both trainability and job proficiency in clerical, managerial, trades and crafts, and sales occupations (Ghiselli, 1973).

Projective Tests. Projective tests present the individual with ambiguous stimuli such as ink-blots, incomplete sentences (e.g., The thing I dislike most is . . .), or vague pictures. The underlying assumption is that these unstructured test materials will serve as a screen on which the examinee will "project" his or her dominant needs, anxieties, conflicts, and thought processes (Anastasi, 1975). A trained examiner studies the examinee's responses and makes an assessment of the individual. Originally, these tests were developed by clinical psychologists for analyzing the abnormal personality. Whether or not one favors the use of projective techniques in personnel administration, there can be no denying that they are widely used for executive selection, especially by management consulting firms.

In general, the real worth of most projective tests for personnel selection is questionable despite their apparent popularity (Kinslinger, 1966). However, there has been some indication that *certain* projective tests may possess validity. The Thematic Apperception Tests (TAT) consists of a series of cards containing vague black and white pictures. The examinee is asked to make up a story to fit each picture. When scored for such traits as need for achievement and need for power, the TAT has correlated significantly with executive success (Cummin, 1967; Wainer & Rubin, 1969). As part of an Assessment Center program (to be discussed later in the chapter), Grant, Katkovsky, & Bray (1967) administered three projective tests (one of which was the TAT) to 201 management personnel. Nine ratings were made by clinicians on each candidate based on the test protocols. The nine ratings were then correlated with salary progress seven to nine years after original assessment. Ratings on several of the variables (e.g., need for achievement, subordinate role, dependence, leadership role) correlated significantly with the criterion.

Miner (1960, 1961, 1962) has reported positive results using the Tomkins-Horn Picture Arrangement Test (PAT) for both the selection of petroleum dealer salesmen and tabulating machine operators. This test asks the individual to look at 25 sets of three pictures, arrange each set of pictures into a sensible order, and write a sentence describing each picture to tell a story. Miner (1965) has also reported three studies supporting the validity of the Miner Sentence Completion scale for predicting managerial success. This instrument consists of 40 incomplete sentences (e.g., Getting ahead . . .), but only 35 of them are actually used.

PROS AND CONS OF PSYCHOLOGICAL TESTING IN ORGANIZATIONS. It is important that one be familiar with the criticisms and retorts that have been made regarding the use of tests in industry. Critics of testing have managed to make themselves heard in many places including books, newspapers, television, and even congressional investigations. Two well-known critical books on this topic are Whyte's (1956) *The Organization Man* and *The Brain Watchers* by Gross (1962). Their main points can be summarized as follows:

1. Certain questions on personality tests pertaining to sex attitudes and personal habits constitute an invasion of privacy.
2. Tests are used to select only those individuals for executive positions who are conformists and lack individuality.
3. Employment tests are often used, either inadvertently or intentionally, to discriminate against the disadvantaged.
4. There are tests for sale by testing organizations and unscrupulous test publishers which are worthless.
5. The generally low validities of tests make them virtually useless.

What can be said in response to these criticisms? First, psychologists are concerned with protecting the privacy of job applicants. Any information an applicant is asked to reveal must be job related, otherwise, it is clearly inappropriate. Further, applicants should be told the purposes of testing as well as how the information will be used. Second, tests are designed to predict already existing criteria, not to change them. If executive success involves being a conformist, this is the kind of individual a valid test will select. As criteria change over time (as they do), the kind of applicant selected will change accordingly (Anastasi, 1975). Third, the Equal Employment Opportunity Commission (EEOC) and the office of Federal Contract Compliance (OFCC) are trying to insure that organizations properly validate their tests before using them for selection purposes. Fourth, as personnel administrators become more knowledgeable about testing and become familiar with the *Standards for Educational and Psychological Tests* published by the American Psychological Association, "fly-by-night" firms will disappear for want of clients. Finally, psychological tests can and do substantially improve the selection process, especially when they are used as part of a properly developed selection battery. They are not costly compared to other selection devices (e.g., interviews) and do not normally take much time to administer.

Biographical Data

Rarely does a person apply for a job in a large organization without being asked to complete some kind of application form as a first step in the selection process. The typical application blank contains items pertaining to the applicant's education, previous employment, military record, health, references, and such personal items as leisure time activities and debts. Most states have fair employment practice (FEP) laws which make it illegal to ask certain questions pertaining to an applicant's race, religion, sex, national origin, and age. While there are no firm guidelines on this matter, the EEOC and the OFCC may investigate items appearing on an organization's application form and recommend removal of those questions felt to be discriminatory in nature (Schultz, 1973). Interestingly, these agencies require organizations to maintain detailed records of the characteristics (i.e., race, age, sex) of their applicant population and new hires. This information can be legally collected by asking applicants to anonymously complete index cards requesting this highly sensitive information.

The major problem with conventional application forms is the haphazard way in which they are usually developed. Typically, application blanks are gathered from other companies by personnel administrators who then decide which of these items ought to be included in their own form. Rather than risking the omission of any important information, the result is an unwieldy form consisting of many irrelevant items. In fact, it is not unusual for an applicant to spend over an hour in the personnel department completing a long and irritating form. It wastes the time of both the applicant and the personnel manager. It adversely affects the public image of the organization as well.

Constructed properly, the application blank can be and often is one of the most valuable selection and placement devices. Numerous studies have shown that it can be used successfully to predict such criteria as tenure or turnover (Fleishman & Berniger, 1960; Kirchner & Dunnette, 1957), salary increase (Scollay, 1956), performance ratings by supervisors (Scollay, 1957), and research competence and creativity (Smith, Albright, Glennon, & Owens, 1961). In fact, it has been pointed out that biographical items found on typical application forms often yield higher validity than other predictors such as intelligence, aptitude, interest, and personality tests (Asher, 1972).

How should a progressive personnel department develop its application form? It is important that an application blank consist of *only* those specific items that have been empirically found to be related to future success on the job in question. The simplest method is to examine the relationship between each application blank item (e.g., number of jobs previously held) and some subsequent measure of job success (e.g., job tenure). An item is retained for use with future candidates only if a substantial relationship is found. Once the valid items are identified, each item is weighted in proportion to the magnitude of this correlation.[1] Thus, it is possible to score the blank by summing the weights of the applicant's responses to the items in much the same way that tests are scored. Two additional points need mentioning. First, one must construct separate scoring procedures for each job within an organization. After all, you would not expect the same exact items to predict job success on different jobs. Second, one must check out the validity of the blank on a sample of people separate from those originally used in developing the scoring procedure (cross-validation).

BIOGRAPHICAL INFORMATION BLANK (BIB). The BIB is an enlargement of the traditional application blank. It differs from the weighted application form in the following ways:

1. It probes into the applicant's attitudes, preferences, and values, i.e., questions are of a more personal nature.
2. It uses a multiple choice answer format (see Table 11–3 for several examples of BIB type items).
3. It is usually much longer.
4. It ordinarily does not weight items.
5. It may use statistical procedures to categorize items into factor or cluster scores.
6. It is used primarily for managerial selection.

The advantages of using biographical information items for predicting managerial effectiveness have been neatly summarized by Owens & Henry (1966). First, the method is merely an extension of the typical application blank and is likely to be more acceptable than many tests. Second, results showing which items significantly predict job behavior can aid greatly in understanding the important antecedents of managerial effectiveness. Lastly, empirical validation of biographical items against actual managerial behavior assures that only job-relevant questions will be asked of a job candidate, thereby guarding against charges of willfull discrimination against minority groups or "invasion of privacy" by tests designed to "explore the psyche."

---

[1] For an excellent discussion of how to develop weights for the application blank, read England's *Development and Use of Weighted Application Blanks* (1971). The most comprehensive catalog of life history items has been prepared by the Scientific Affairs Committee, Division of Industrial & Organizational Psychology, American Psychological Association (1966).

TABLE 11–3
Sample Biographical Information Blank Items

---

1. The place in which you spent the most time during your early life was a:
   a. Farm.
   b. Town of less than 2,000.
   c. Town of 2,000 or more but less than 10,000.
   d. City of 10,000 to 100,000.
   e. City larger than 100,000.

2. At what age did you start drinking?
   a. 12 or younger.
   b. 13 to 16.
   c. 17 to 21.
   d. 21 or over.
   e. Never drank.

3. How often do you feel self-conscious?
   a. Frequently.
   b. Occasionally.
   c. Rarely.
   d. Never.

4. Where did you get your early information about sex matters?
   a. From the "fellows."
   b. From your parents.
   c. From some member of the opposite sex.
   d. From an older friend or counselor.
   e. Didn't get any information until you were in your "teens."

5. When you first left home for school or a job, parting from your family was:
   a. Very easy.
   b. A little difficult because you were reluctant to leave.
   c. Difficult because your family was reluctant to have you leave.
   d. Very difficult because your family was very close.
   e. You have never left home.

Adapted from *A Catalog of Life History Items.* J. R. Glennon, L. E. Albright, and W. A. Owens, Chairman. Scientific Affairs Committee, American Psychological Association, Division 14. Reproduced by The Creativity Research Institute of The Richardson Foundation, June, 1966.

Employment Interviews

The employment interview is one of the most popular selection devices. A survey conducted several years ago (Spriegel and James, 1958) indicated that 99 percent of the 852 organizations queried at that time used an interview before hiring applicants. There is every reason to believe that the widespread use of the interview has not subsided since this survey and that its popularity will continue in the future. After all, even if interviewers were prohibited from participating in the making of selection decisions, there are still four duties which they would continue to perform:

> 1. He must answer fully and frankly the applicant's questions about your business, the job, and the working conditions. 2. He must convince the man he is interviewing that yours is a good firm to work for since it furnishes such and such opportunities for growth and advancement (if it does). In other words, he must be skillful in selling your firm to the applicant. 3. He must steer the applicant toward a job for which he is better suited, if there is one somewhere, lest he later discover that job and shift to it only after the firm has spent a few hundred dollars on training him. 4. Finally, the interviewer should leave the prospect, in any case, with the feeling that he has made a personal friend (Bingham, 1949, pp. 272–274).

Most personnel administrators conduct their interviews in a relatively "unstructured" manner. As the term implies, this is an unplanned, casual, and loosely organized conversation between the interviewer and interviewee. The questions asked and the evaluation of the applicant's answers vary from interviewer to interviewer and applicant to applicant. At the other extreme of the structure continuum is the patterned or structured interview in which a predetermined list of questions are asked of every person applying for a particular job.

Since 1915, hundreds of research articles have appeared in the literature on the selection interview. The most significant findings on the reliability and validity of the interview are as follows:

1. Structured interviews yield higher agreement among interviewers (interrater reliability) and have greater validity than do unstructured interviews.
2. Interrater reliability increases when interviewers are furnished with more complete job information.
3. Intrarater reliability (i.e., the extent to which an interviewer reinterviewing the same person gives the same evaluation as previously) appears to be satisfactory in most cases.
4. The interview seems to have its greatest potential for assessing the motivation to work and interpersonal competence of job applicants.

Since the 1960s, a small group of researchers have been concerned with studying the decision-making process of employment interviewers in the hope of someday improving their reliability and validity. Here are just a few of their major findings:

1. Each interviewer has a specific stereotype of the "ideal" candidate that is used as a standard in assessing actual candidates (Mayfield & Carlson, 1966).

2. Interviewers usually form biases about an applicant early in the interview (Springbett, 1958; Webster, 1964).
3. The relative importance given to various content dimensions (e.g., scholastic standing, experience, interests and activities) varies among interviewers (Hakel, Dobmeyer, & Dunnette, 1970).
4. Interviewers are more influenced by unfavorable than favorable information about an applicant (Miller & Rowe, 1967).
5. Interviewers rate applicants more favorably if the applicants are perceived as being similar to themselves (Rand & Wexley, 1975; Wexley & Nemeroff, 1974).
6. The more an interviewer talks, the more favorably the applicant is evaluated (Mayfield, 1964).
7. Interviewers are susceptible to contrast effects, i.e., their evaluations of applicants are influenced by their ratings of immediately preceding applicants (Rowe, 1967; Wexley, Yukl, Kovacs, & Sanders, 1972).
8. Interviewers are vulnerable to "halo effect"—the tendency to allow one's overall impression of an applicant to generalize across trait ratings in either a positive, negative, or neutral direction (see Chapter 10).
9. There are significant differences in nonverbal behavior (e.g., total visual interaction time) on the part of white and black applicants when interviewed by white or black interviewers (Fugita, Wexley, & Hillery, 1974). Differences in an applicant's nonverbal behavior (e.g., gesturing, smiling, tone of voice) may influence interviewer ratings (Wexley, Fugita, & Malone, 1975).

References and Letters of Recommendation

A widely used technique in selection, especially in the case of higher level personnel, involves obtaining information about an applicant from former employers or possibly co-workers. In order for any of this information to have validity, the person writing the references must have detailed knowledge of the individual's strengths and weaknesses in the former job situation and the informant must be willing to give frank and candid opinions regarding the candidate's limitations. Unfortunately, many times neither of these conditions are realized. Employers write letters of recommendation for former employees whose job skills they barely know. Most of these letters are filled with glowing descriptions of departing employees either because the former employer wants to be kind, hopes to get rid of an undesirable worker, or fears criticizing someone in writing.

Like other selection devices, letters of recommendation and references must be validated in accordance with EEOC guidelines (see the section on Equal Employment Opportunity in this chapter). What can be done by an organization to maximize its chances of having a valid reference check procedure?

1. To promote consistency across applicants, develop a scorable standardized recommendation blank rather than using unstructured letters of recommendation.
2. Determine whether or not the recommender has the knowledge and credentials to make an accurate evaluation of the applicant.
3. Make your questions as specific and behavioral as possible (e.g., How often a month was this applicant absent from work? Did the applicant ever get into overt arguments with peers?) Questions of this type would surely be better than those often used: Do you think the applicant is motivated? aggressive? personable? stable?

Peer Ratings and Supervisory Judgments

While peer ratings, sometimes called "buddy ratings" or "peer nominations," has been used extensively in military situations, other types of organizations have only recently turned to this technique. Research findings provide convincing support of its usefulness for predicting later measures (promotions and global ratings) of managerial success (Kraut, 1975; Roadman, 1964). Other studies have shown the value of peer ratings as predictors of sales performance (Mayfield, 1972; Waters & Waters, 1970). In most cases, peer evaluations are obtained from individuals during a three- or four-week training course and then correlated with subsequent measures of sales or managerial performance. The technique is also useful in identifying potential supervisory personnel within a group and is quite predictive of later performance (Weitz, 1958).

Basically, this technique involves each member's evaluation of every other group member on a certain characteristic, for example, "success as a future manager." There are two main variations of the technique. In one variation, each individual literally *ranks* all or some portion of his peers from "best" to "worst" on the characteristic being considered. The average rank received by each person is used as the individual's score. In the second variation, each individual *nominates* a specified number (e.g., five) of "high" and/or "low" peers on some characteristic. Recent research by Kaufman & Johnson (1974) suggests that negative nominations contribute little to peer rating scales and that simply the "number of positive nominations" an individual receives appears to be the most useful scoring strategy. This makes even more sense when you experience the difficulties encountered in obtaining "low" evaluations from individuals about their peers. This scoring method eliminates the frequently heard complaint that peer ratings ask a rater to "cut his buddy's throat" (Webb, 1955).

There is considerable evidence that peer ratings differ considerably from supervisory evaluations of the same employees. This is not surprising when one considers that peers and supervisors see different apects of an individual's behavior. There is also evidence to suggest that extraneous factors such as appearance, acquaintanceship, race, and friendship contaminate peer ratings less than ratings given by superiors (Gordon & Medland, 1965; Hollander, 1956, 1965; Schmidt & Johnson, 1973). What does all this mean in terms of personnel selection and placement? It suggests that the accuracy of personnel decisions such as promotions and terminations may be improved by combining ratings from several sources—supervisors, peers, and self (Kavanaugh, MacKinney, & Wolins, 1971; Lawler, 1967). The use of different types of raters reduces bias and capitalizes on the particular observational opportunities of each rating source (Miner, 1968).

Assessment Centers

The term "assessment center" refers to a standardized off-the-job procedure used to identify managerial potential for purposes of selection, placement, promotion, and/or development (MacKinnon, 1975). Although no two programs in industry are exactly alike, they all place heavy reliance upon the use of multiple methods of assessment as well as the observation of behavior in simulated situations. Here are some typical procedures included in assessment centers:

In-basket tests are situational exercises consisting of letters, memos and memoranda. The candidates being appraised are asked to pretend that these materials have accumulated in their in-baskets. They are instructed to do as much as possible toward solving the problems which the materials present. This technique is described in more detail in Chapter 14.

Manufacturing problems are games in which, for example, six candidates are given capital with which to set themselves up in business. Their task as a group is to organize their business, and buy, manufacture, and sell some product so as to make as much profit as possible. There are several time periods in the game with the cost of parts and selling prices of finished products varying from period to period.

A *Leaderless Group Discussion* (LGD) is a conference between several assessees in which no formal leader has been assigned. The discussion is often of a competitive nature in that each candidate takes a position and tries to win its adoption by the group. For example, each candidate might be asked to assume that she/he has a supervisor reporting to her/him who is qualified for promotion. The participants are told to discuss the strengths and weaknesses of each supervisor and to reach a group decision as to which one should be promoted. Sometimes, the LGD is of a cooperative nature in which each candidate is assigned a role and told to help the group make an important decision (e.g., whether or not to merge with another company).

Other procedures sometimes used are personal interviews building upon the candidate's responses to a biographical information blank. Peer ratings and self-ratings are often collected after each situational exercise. Paper-and-pencil tests of mental ability, reading, interest, and personality are often administered. Certain projective tests, often the TAT, may be used to assess the candidate's motivation for management. Assessees are typically given a writing exercise (e.g., a short autobiographical essay) and a speaking exercise to assess their oral and communication skills. Finally, some centers regard observations of behavior at coffee breaks and meals as relevant data; other centers base their evaluations solely on the formal exercises.

The number of evaluative methods used varies across centers, but the usual number is seven (Bender, 1973). The candidates spend anywhere from one to seven days at the center in groups of six or some multiple thereof. Assessments are the combined judgments of several managers two or more levels above the participants. Sometimes psychologists are also used on the assessment staff. The staff administers the individual tests and observes the candidates during each of the situational exercises. The ratio of staff members to candidates is usually about 1:2 or 1:3. Candidates are evaluated on anywhere from 10–15 qualities thought to be important for management success. A list of the qualities used by AT&T (Bray & Grant, 1966; Bray, Campbell, & Grant, 1974) is given below:

Scholastic aptitude.
Oral and written communication skill.
Human relations skill.
Personal impact.
Perception of threshold social cues.
Creativity.
Self-objectivity.
Social objectivity.
Behavior flexibility.
Tolerance of uncertainty.
Resistance to stress.
Energy.
Decision making
Need approval of superiors.
Need approval of peers.
Inner work standards.
Need advancement.
Need security.
Goal flexibility.

Primacy of work.

Bell-system value orientation.

Realism of expectations.

Ability to delay gratification.

Range of interests.

Organization and planning.

When differences in ratings occur among staff members they are discussed and resolved. The staff arrives at an overall rating of each candidate's managerial potential, and a report outlining strengths and weaknesses is prepared for the company and for the participant. Feedback is given orally and/or in writing to each participant and often involves a plan for future development.

The assessment center provides a method of evaluating individuals from various organizational functions and geographical locations in a standardized and objective manner. To the extent that the simulation exercises and procedures accurately assess the dimensions of managerial effectiveness, the center yields relevant appraisals. Many companies apparently feel they do. At the present time, more than one hundred organizations are using centers as an aid in management appraisal. Here are just a few of them: Sears, General Electric, AT&T, Penney's and Wickes Lumber.

Research studies support the conclusion that behavior observed in assessment centers can be evaluated (i.e., rated and ranked) with high interrater reliability by staff members (Greenwood & McNamara, 1967; Thomson, 1970). Overall ratings and predictions made at assessment centers have been validated against a variety of criteria: (1) job performance (performance ratings on the job for which the candidate was assessed), (2) job progress (salary increase and promotion), and (3) job potential (ratings of the probability of future progress) (MacKinnon, 1975). Despite certain methodological shortcomings, the research evidence suggests that assessment centers can be quite effective in predicting managerial success (Huck, 1973). With few exceptions, the validity coefficients have ranged from the .30s to the .60s (MacKinnon, 1975). This is particularly impressive when one compares these results to the low validities reported for most paper-and-pencil tests of leadership ability (Korman, 1966; Kerr & Schriesheim, 1974). In addition, several studies have shown the superiority of the assessment center approach as compared with conventional methods of evaluation (Campbell and Bray, 1967; Jaffee, Bender, and Calvert, 1970).

It should be noted that assessment centers can be quite inexpensive or costly depending upon their length, location, and number of participants. Byham (1971) pointed out that programs conducted on company premises can cost as little as $50, while programs at hotels may run as high as $3,000 for 12 participants. One of the major drawbacks of the assessment center approach is candidate anxiety. It is our experience that some participants come to the center with a "you bet your career" attitude. Although most people are able to handle their anxiety, there are always a few otherwise excellent candidates who cannot. It is important that the center staff be adequately trained to deal with this problem. Recently, the Third International Congress on Assessment Centers met in Quebec, Canada, and adopted a set of ethical guidelines for users of this technique. The guidelines describe minimal acceptable practices concerning organizational support for assessment centers, assessor training, informed consent on the part of participants, use of assessment center data, and validity issues.

SUMMARY

Recruitment and selection of employees are part of the process used by organizations to upgrade the quality of their membership. A selection program consists of various selection devices which are administered to applicants at the time of admission (or hiring) to predict subsequent performance.

One major type of selection device is a psychological test. The essential qualities of a good test include high reliability, high validity, standardization, and the availability of norms. Tests have been developed to measure intelligence, aptitudes, manual dexterity and motor coordination, personality traits, occupational interests, and specific job-related skills.

A selection program may also include other selection devices, such as an interview, application blank, biographical information blank, references and letters of recommendation, peer ratings, and supervisor ratings. The assessment center is a recent innovation for the selection and promotion of managers. Assessment centers usually administer a variety of selection devices to applicants, with an emphasis on situational tests such as business games, leaderless group discussions, and in-basket tests.

Each kind of selection device has certain unique advantages as well as certain limitations and disadvantages. The applicability of the selection devices and ways to improve their effectiveness were considered in this chapter. In the next chapter, we will describe the procedures used to validate selection devices and set up a selection program.

REVIEW AND DISCUSSION QUESTIONS

1. Describe or explain each of the following key terms: aptitude test, peer nominations, BIB, projective test, reliability, norms, standardization.

2. Differentiate clearly the following types of validity: content validity, predictive validity, concurrent validity, and criterion-related validity.
3. Describe how application blanks should be developed to maximize their usefulness. Contrast this procedure with how application blanks are usually constructed.
4. How would you suggest that an organization conduct its employment interviews?
5. Suppose you were thinking about ordering a certain paper-and-pencil test from a test publisher. What information about the test would you want to be included in the manual accompanying the test?
6. Discuss your general feelings about the use of psychological testing in organizations. Are you for it or against it? Defend your opinion.
7. What is your opinion regarding the use of letters of recommendation by faculty for student admissions to college and graduate schools?
8. What selection procedures would you use to select applicants for a managerial job?

REFERENCES

Anastasi, A. *Psychological testing.* New York: Macmillan, 1975.

Asher, J. J. The biographical item: Can it be improved? *Personnel Psychology*, 1972, *25*, 251–269.

Bender, J. M. What is "typical" of assessment centers? *Personnel*, 1973, *50*, 50–57.

Bingham, W. V. Today and yesterday. *Personnel Psychology*, 1949, *2*, 267–275.

Blum, M. L., & Naylor, J. C. *Industrial psychology: Its theoretical and social foundations.* New York: Harper & Row, 1968.

Bray, D. W., Campbell, R. J., & Grant, D. L. *Formative years in business: A long-term AT&T study of managerial lives.* New York: Wiley-Interscience, 1974.

Bray, D. W., & Grant, D. L. The assessment center in the measurement of potential for business management. *Psychological Monographs*, 1966, *80* (17, Whole No. 625).

Buros, O. K. (Ed.). *The seventh mental measurements yearbook.* Highland Park, N.J.: The Gryphon Press, 1972.

Byham, W. C. The assessment center as an aid in management development. *Training and Development Journal*, 1971, *25*, 10–22.

Campbell, R. J., & Bray, D. W. Assessment centers: An aid in management selection. *Personnel Administration*, 1967, *30*, 6–13.

Chruden, H. J., & Sherman, A. W., Jr. *Personnel Management.* Cincinnati: Southwestern Publishing Co., 1976.

Cummin, P. C. TAT correlates of executive performance. *Journal of Applied Psychology*, 1967, *51*, 78–81.

Fleishman, E. A., & Berniger, J.   One way to reduce office turnover. *Personnel*, 1960, 37, 63–69.

Fugita, S. S., Wexley, K. N., & Hillery, J. M.   Black-white differences in nonverbal behavior in an interview setting. *Journal of Applied Social Psychology*, 1974, 4, 343–350.

Ghiselli, E. E.   The validity of aptitude tests in personnel selection. *Personnel Psychology*, 1973, 26, 461–477.

Ghiselli, E. E., & Brown, C. W.   *Personnel and Industrial Psychology*. New York: McGraw-Hill, 1955.

Gordon, L. V., & Medland, F. F.   The cross stability of peer nominations on leadership potential. *Personnel Psychology*, 1965, 18, 173–177.

Grant, D. L., Katkovsky, W., & Bray, D. W.   Contributions of projective techniques to assessment of management potential. *Journal of Applied Psychology*, 1967, 51, 226–232.

Greenwood, J. M., & McNamara, W. J.   Interrater reliability in situational tests. *Journal of Applied Psychology*, 1967, 31, 101–106.

Gross, M. L.   *The brain watchers*. New York: Random House, 1962.

Hakel, M. D., Dobmeyer, T. W., & Dunnette, M. D.   Relative importance of three content dimensions in overall suitability ratings of job applicants' ratings. *Journal of Applied Psychology*, 1970, 54, 65–71.

Hollander, E. P.   The friendship factor in peer nominations. *Personnel Psychology*, 1956, 9, 425–447.

Hollander, E. P.   Validity of peer nominations in predicting a distant performance criterion. *Journal of Applied Psychology*, 1965, 49, 434–438.

Huck, J. R.   Assessment centers: A review of external and internal validities. *Personnel Psychology*, 1973, 26, 191–212.

Jaffee, C., Bender, J., & Calvert, D.   The assessment center technique: A validation study. *Management of Personnel Quarterly*, 1970, 9, 9–14.

Kaufman, G. G., & Johnson, J. C.   Scaling peer ratings: An examination of the differential validities of positive and negative nominations. *Journal of Applied Psychology*, 1974, 59, 302–306.

Kavanagh, M. J., MacKinney, A. C., & Wolins, L.   Issues in managerial performance: Multitrait-multimethod analyses of ratings. *Psychological Bulletin*, 1971, 75, 34–49.

Kerr, S., & Schriesheim, C.   Consideration, initiating structure, and organizational criteria—an update of Korman's 1966 review. *Personnel Psychology*, 1974, 27, 555–568.

Kinslinger, H. J.   Application of projective techniques in personnel psychology since 1940. *Psychological Bulletin*, 1966, 66, 134–149.

Kirchner, W. K., & Dunnette, M. D.   Applying the weighted application blank technique to a variety of office jobs. *Journal of Applied Psychology*, 1957, 41, 206–208.

Korman, A.   Consideration, initiating structure, and organizational criteria—A review. *Personnel Psychology*, 1966, 19, 349–362.

Kraut, A. I.   Prediction of managerial success by peer and training-staff ratings. *Journal of Applied Psychology*, 1975, 60, 14–19.

Lawler, E. E., III.   The multitrait-multirater approach to measuring managerial job performance. *Journal of Applied Psychology*, 1967, 51, 369–381.

MacKinnon, D. W.   An overview of assessment centers. Center for Creative Leadership. Technical Report No. 1, May, 1975.

Mayfield, E. C.   The selection interview: A re-evaluation of published research. *Personnel Psychology*, 1964, 17, 239–260.

Mayfield, E. C.   Value of peer nominations in predicting life insurance sales performance. *Journal of Applied Psychology*, 1972, 56, 319–323.

Mayfield, E. C., & Carlson, R. E.   Selection interview decisions: First results of a long-term research project. *Personnel Psychology*, 1966, 19, 41–53.

Miller, J., & Rowe, P. M.   Influence of favorable and unfavorable information upon assessment decisions. *Journal of Applied Psychology*, 1967, 51, 432–435.

Miner, J. B.   The concurrent validity of the PAT in the selection of tabulating machine operators. *Journal of Projective Techniques*, 1960, 24, 409–418.

Miner, J. B.   The validity of the PAT in the selection of tabulating machine operation: An analysis of productive power. *Journal of Projective Techniques*, 1961, 25, 330–333.

Miner, J. B.   Personality and ability factors in sales performance. *Journal of Applied Psychology*, 1962, 46, 6–13.

Miner, J. B.   *Studies in management education.* New York: Springer, 1965.

Miner, J. B.   Management appraisal: A capsule review and current references. *Business Horizons*, 1968, 11, 83–96.

Owens, W. A., & Henry, E. R.   Biographical data in industrial psychology: A review and evaluation. Creativity Research Institute, Richardson Foundation, 1966.

Porter, L. W., Lawler, E. E., III, & Hackman, J. R.   *Behavior in organizations.* New York: McGraw-Hill, 1975.

Rand, T. M., & Wexley, K. N.   Demonstration of the effect "Similar to Me," in simulated employment interviews. *Psychological Reports*, 1975, 36, 535–544.

Roadman, H. E.   An industrial use of peer ratings. *Journal of Applied Psychology*, 1964, 48, 211–214.

Rowe, P. M.   Order effects in assessment decisions. *Journal of Applied Psychology*, 1967, 51, 170–173.

Schmidt, F. L., & Johnson, R. H.   Effect of race on peer ratings in an industrial situation. *Journal of Applied Psychology*, 1973, 57, 237–241.

Schultz, D.   *Psychology and industry today.* New York: Macmillan, 1973.

Scollay, R. W.   Validation of personal history items against a salary increase criterion. *Personnel Psychology*, 1956, 9, 325–335.

Scollay, R. W. Personal history data as a predictor of success. *Personnel Psychology*, 1957, *10*, 23–26.

Smith, W. J., Albright, L. E., Glennon, J. R., & Owens, W. A. The prediction of research competence and creativity from personal history. *Journal of Applied Psychology*, 1961, *45*, 59–62.

Spriegel, W. R., & James, V. A. Trends in recruitment and selection practices. *Personnel*, 1958, *35*, 42–48.

Springbett, B. M. Factors affecting the final decision in the employment interview. *Canadian Journal of Psychology*, 1958, *12*, 13–22.

Standards for educational and psychological tests. Washington, D.C.: American Psychological Association, 1974.

Strauss, G., & Sayles, L. R. *Personnel: The human problems of management.* Englewood Cliffs, N.J.: Prentice-Hall, 1972.

Thomson, H. A. A comparison of predictor and criterion judgments of managerial performance using the multitrait-multimethod approach. *Journal of Applied Psychology*, 1970, *54*, 496–502.

Wainer, H. A., & Rubin, I. M. Motivation of research and development entrepreneurs. *Journal of Applied Psychology*, 1969, *53*, 178–184.

Wanous, J. P. Effects of a realistic job preview on job acceptance, job attitudes, and job survival. *Journal of Applied Psychology*, 1973, *58*, 327–332.

Waters, L. K., & Waters, C. W. Peer nominations as predictors of short-term sales performance. *Journal of Applied Psychology*, 1970, *54*, 42–44.

Webb, W. B. The problem of obtaining negative nominations in peer ratings. *Personnel Psychology*, 1955, *8*, 61–63.

Webster, E. C. *Decision making in the employment interview.* Montreal: McGill University, 1964.

Weitz, J. Selecting supervisors with peer ratings. *Personnel Psychology*, 1958, *11*, 25–35.

Wexley, K. N., Fugita, S. S., & Malone, M. P. An applicant's nonverbal behavior and student-evaluators' judgments in a structured interview setting. *Psychological Reports*, 1975, *36*, 391–394.

Wexley, K. N., & Nemeroff, W. F. Effects of racial prejudice, race of applicant, and biographical similarity on interviewer evaluations of job apcants. *Journal of Social and Behavioral Sciences*, 1974, *20*, 66–78.

Wexley, K. N., Yukl, G., Kovacs, S., & Sanders, R. The importance of contrast effects in employment interviews. *Journal of Applied Psychology*, 1972, *56*, 45–48.

Whyte, W. H. *The organization man.* New York: Simon & Schuster, 1956.

12

SELECTION DECISIONS AND EQUAL EMPLOYMENT OPPORTUNITY

RECENT federal legislation has focused considerable attention on the obligation of organizations to validate or demonstrate the job-relatedness of their selection instruments before using them. Despite the establishment of two powerful agencies to enforce this legislation, there are still companies that continue to use selection and placement devices for which there is no validity evidence. It almost goes without saying that laws and bureaucratic agencies can only do so much to bring about mass cultural change—specifically, the proper use of selection devices and the elimination of unfair discrimination against minority group members and women. Legislation must be supported by education. That is, personnel administrators and managers must be instructed in the proper procedures for validating their selection devices. Thus, the main objective of this chapter is to present the reader with the proper methods of validation. Following this, we devote our attention briefly to personnel placement, the federal guidelines on employee selection procedures, and fair employment.

DETERMINING THE CRITERION-RELATED VALIDITY OF A SINGLE PREDICTOR

In this section, we will present a step-by-step description of the procedures involved in determining the criterion-related validity of any predictor (i.e., any of the methods discussed in the previous chapter).

Step 1. Conduct a Job Analysis

A written statement describing the duties and responsibilities of a job is commonly referred to as a *job description*. It specifies what a worker does, how, why, and the circumstances under which it is done. The individual qualifications needed by an employee to carry out these duties and responsibilities is called a *job specification*. Traditionally, the process of describing work performed and specifying employee characteristics has been known as a *job analysis*. In addition to its many other applications in organizations (e.g., wage determination, training, performance appraisal), job analysis is used to determine the kinds of selection devices and criteria to be utilized in a validation study. Such an analysis may indicate, for example, that the job requires computational accuracy, mechanical reasoning ability, motor coordination, and spatial ability. Knowledge of these specifications would dictate the particular set of predictors chosen for study.

Large organizations often employ personnel specialists who are trained as job analysts; smaller companies typically use consultants for this function. Job analysts gather job information by using various methods such as observing incumbents on the job, performing the job themselves (if possible), asking incumbents to fill out checklists and questionnaires, conducting individual and group interviews, and asking incumbents to maintain diaries of their daily activities. Quite often, the *Dictionary of Occupational Titles* (commonly called the DOT) prepared by the U.S. Training and Employment Service is used as a preliminary to job analysis. It lists about 22,000 jobs and describes each one in a manner illustrated in Figure 12–1.

FIGURE 12–1
An Extract from the Dictionary of Occupational Titles

SHIPPING CLERK (clerical) II.222.587, delivery-and-order man; shipper; shipping packer. Prepares products for shipment: Counts and compares quantity and identification numbers of units against order. Assembles wooden or cardboard containers or selects preassembled containers. Inserts items into containers using spacers, fillers, and protective padding. Nails cover on wooden crates and binds containers with metal tape, using strapping machine. Stamps, stencils, or glues identifying information and shipping instructions on containers. Moves containers to shipping dock, using handtruck or overhead hoist. May weigh articles and attach postage or bill of lading. May be designated according to specialty as Freight Clerk; Reshipping Clerk.

Although these descriptions are brief and general, they familiarize analysts with the general nature of the job and its terminology before beginning their own detailed analysis. Once the job information is collected, it must be assembled in a concise and logical manner. An excellent format developed by the U.S. Training and Employment Service and used by many job analysts is presented in Figure 12–2.

FIGURE 12–2
Job Analysis Form (used by the United States Training and Employment Service)

U.S. Department of Labor   OMB 44–R0722
Manpower Administration   Estab. & Sched. No. 071–3120–423

JOB ANALYSIS SCHEDULE

1. Estab. Job Title   INFORMATION DESK CLERK, receptionist-clerk
2. Ind. Assign.   ret. tr.
3. SIC Code(s) and Title(s)   5311 Department Stores

Code 237.568

WTA Group   Information Gathering,

Dispensing, Verifying, and Related Work p. 258

4. JOB SUMMARY:

Answers inquiries and gives directions to customers, author-izes cashing of customers' checks, records and returns lost charge cards, sorts and reviews new credit applications, and requisitions supplies, working at Information Desk in de-partment store Credit Office.

5. WORK PERFORMED RATINGS:

	(D)	(P)	T
Worker Functions	Data	People	Things
	5	6	7

Work Field   282-Information Giving   231 Recording
M.P.S.M.S.   890-Business Service

DOT Title

Ind. Desig.

6. WORKER TRAITS RATINGS:

GED   1   2   (3)   4   5   6

SVP   1   2   (3)   4   5   6   7   8   9

Aptitudes   G 3 V 3 N 3 S 4 P 4 Q 3 K 4 F 3 M 4 E 5 C 5

Temperaments   D   F   I   J   (M) (P)   R   S   T   (V)

Interests   1a   (1b) (2a) 2b   3a   3b   4a   4b   5a   5b

Phys. Demands   (S)   L   M   H   V   2   3   (4) (5)   6

Environ. Cond.   (I)   O   B   2   3   4   5   6   7

FIGURE 12-2 *(continued)*

7. General Education

    a. Elementary__6__ High School__none__ Courses_____

    b. College__none__ Courses_____

8. Vocational Preparation

    a. College__none__ Courses_____

    b. Vocational Education__none__ Courses_____

    c. Apprenticeship__none_____

    d. Inplant Training__none_____

    e. On-the-Job Training____3 to 5 weeks by Credit Interviewer_____

    f. Performance on Other Jobs____none_____

9. Experience____none_____

10. Orientation____1 week_____

11. Licenses, etc.____none_____

12. Relation to Other Jobs and Workers

    Promotion: From____this is an entry job__ To____CREDIT INTERVIEWER

    Transfers: From____none_____ To____none_____

    Supervision Received____CREDIT MANAGER_____

    Supervision Given____none_____

13. Machine, Tools, Equipment, and Work Aids
Impressing Device—Small Hand-operated device, of similar construction to stapler with a nonmoving base and a moveable upper arm containing inked rollers which Impressing Device (con) are moved by a lever in the upper arm. Charge card is placed in a grove in the base, stand-up print facing up, and paper or bill positioned over card, then the upper arm is brought down and lever depressed to bring inked rollers over paper to make impress of card's imprint.

14. Materials and Products
none

FIGURE 12–2 *(continued)*

15. Description of Tasks:

   1. Answers inquiries and gives direction to customers: Greets customers at Information Desk and ascertains reason for visit to Credit Office. Sends customer to Credit Interviewer to open credit account, to Cashier to pay bills, to Adjustment Department to obtain correction of error in billing. Directs customer to other store departments on request, referring to store directory. (50%)

   2. Authorizes cashing of checks: Authorizes cashing of personal or payroll checks (up to a specified amount) by customers desiring to make payment on credit account. Requests identification, such as driver's license or charge card, from customers, and examines check to verify date, amount, signature, and endorsement. Initials check, and sends customer to Cashier. Refers customer presenting Stale Date Check to bank. (5%)

   3. Performs routine clerical tasks in the processing of mailed change of address requests: Fills out Change of Address form, based on customer's letter, and submits to Head Authorizer for processing. Files customer's letter. Contacts customer to obtain delivery address if omitted from letter. (10%)

   4. Answers telephone calls from customers reporting lost or stolen charge cards and arranges details of cancellation of former card and replacement: Obtains all possible details from customer regarding lost or stolen card, and requests letter of confirmation. Notifies Authorizer immediately to prevent fraudulent use of missing card. Orders replacement card for customer when confirming letter is received. (10%)

   5. Records charge cards which have inadvertantly been left in sales departments and returns them to customer: Stamps imprint of card on sheet of paper, using Imprinting Device. Dates sheet and retains for own records. Fills out form, posting data such as customer's name and address and date card was returned, and submits to Authorizer. Makes impression of card on face of envelope, inserts card in envelope, and mails to customer. (5%)

   6. Sorts and records new credit applications daily: Separates regular Charge Account applications from Budget Accounts. Breaks down Charge Account applications into local and out-of-town applications and arranges applications alphabetically within groups. Counts number of applications in each group and records in Daily Record Book. Binds each group of applications with rubber band, and transmits to Tabulating Room. (10%)

   7. Prepares requisitions and stores supplies: Copies amounts of supplies requested by Credit Department personnel onto requisition

FIGURE 12–2   *(concluded)*

---

forms. Submits forms to Purchasing Officer or Supply Room. Receives supplies and places them on shelves in department store storeroom.   (10%)

---

16. Definition of Terms
     Stale Date Checks—More than 30 days old

17. General Comments
     none

---

18. Analyst A. Yessarian   Date 7/25/77   Editor M. Major   Date 7/26/77

     Reviewed by____John Milton____ Title, Org.____Credit Manager____

     National Office Reviewer____W. Irving____

Judgments regarding job specifications should involve procedures which are systematic and standardized. One such procedure is to have job analysts, supervisors, and personnel specialists rate various worker trait requirements according to what extent each is needed to perform the job successfully. The job specifications for people already trained will include the amount and quality of previous work experience, whereas the specifications for untrained people will include such things as aptitudes, interests, and personality. It is quite important that the "specs" not be too broad and ambiguous (e.g., "must be a good person, hard working"), otherwise they are practically useless. In addition, there is always the danger of requiring more education and experience than the job actually requires. This can be a serious problem since it may increase salary costs, boost turnover, and interfere with compliance to affirmative action (to be discussed later).

The Position Analysis Questionnaire (PAQ) is an important contribution to the area of job analysis. The PAQ is essentially a structured job analysis questionnaire that can be used for analyzing virtually any job or position. It consists of 194 job elements (or items) arranged into six major divisions. An example of a job element in each of these divisions is shown below:

Division of the PAQ	*Example of Job Elements*
1. Information input	5. Use of visual displays (e.g., dials, clocks)
2. Mental processes	40. Analyzing information or data
3. Work output	76. Operating equipment (e.g., cranes, hoists)
4. Relationships with other persons	106. Public speaking
5. Job context	148. Civic obligations
6. Other job characteristics	165. Irregular hours

Each job element is rated in either a checklist fashion (does or does not apply) or by one of several six-point rating scales (e.g., "extent of use" of the element of the job). In practice, the PAQ can be used by job analysts, supervisors, or the workers themselves. It is computer scored and yields statistically derived dimension scores that reflect the profile of any job. It is not intended to replace conventional job descriptions in terms of characterizing the specific duties and responsibilities of the incumbent (McCormick, Jeanneret, and Mecham, 1972). This instrument has enormous potential for reducing judgmental errors in the job analysis process by making it more quantitative and objective.[1]

Step 2. Select Predictors

Once the job is analyzed, it is necessary to choose the best possible predictor, or combination of predictors (i.e., tests, application blanks, interviews) to measure the kinds of attributes necessary for success on the job. It is advisable that a properly trained industrial-organizational psychologist be consulted at this stage. This individual is qualified to develop selection devices that are tailor-made for a particular organization or to skillfully choose among the thousand or so tests commercially available.

Probably the foremost source of information on tests is the *Mental Measurement Yearbooks* edited by O. K. Buros. Published periodically, these books contain critical reviews and evaluations of over 1,200 published tests. In addition, test manuals (which can be purchased along with the test itself) as well as the research literature provide valuable data on a test's reliability, validity, standardization, and norms.

Step 3. Administer Predictor to a Sample of Individuals

Depending upon the validation approach being followed, predictor information is obtained either from job applicants or present employees.

---

[1] Position Analysis Questionnaire materials can be obtained from the University Bookstore, 360 State Street, West Lafayette, Indiana 47906.

With the predictive (or follow-up) validity approach, tests are administered to applicants at the time of hiring and put away until some later date when criterion data are available. As mentioned in the previous chapter, this is the preferred method of validation because it directly answers the important question: "Is this selection device capable of predicting subsequent behavior on the job?" Unfortunately, the predictive approach is not used as often as it should be because of two possible limitations. First, the time required to wait for criterion data and, second, the requirement that applicants be hired regardless of how poorly they scored on the predictor. In actual practice, this second problem can be partially alleviated by allowing the organization to continue choosing applicants using their current selection system. For instance, a test validation sample might not include certain individuals who were rejected because of the company's selection interview. Although this solution has certain drawbacks, it is a realistic and practical compromise.

In the concurrent (or present-employee) approach, both predictor and criterion data are obtained from present employees immediately and at approximately the same time. Although this method yields immediate results, it has certain limitations that one should be aware of:

1. Present employees represent a highly select group since those who were not satisfactory either left voluntarily or were dismissed. Thus, the predictor-criterion correlation is not representative of the correlation that one would obtain using a sample of applicants.
2. Present employees differ from the applicant sample in terms of age, experience, and the motivation to perform well on the predictor.
3. Present employees are often reluctant to take experimental tests for fear that their job security may somehow be threatened. This may occur even though the test scores are entirely anonymous.

According to the *Principles for the Validation and Use of Personnel Selection Procedures* published by the Division of Industrial-Organizational Psychology of the American Psychological Association:

> If any . . . considerations suggests that the results of a concurrent study would differ markedly from those of a predictive study, the psychologist is advised to use the predictive method or declare criterion-related research infeasible (1975, p. 6).

Step 4. Obtain Criterion Measures of Employee Proficiency

Criterion information is obtained on new or present employees depending upon the approach chosen in the previous step. For most jobs, one criterion measure will not be enough. Instead, there are a number of dimensions on which workers' success can be measured. For example, a tire builder can be evaluated not only in terms of number of tires produced, but also in terms of quality, absenteeism, tardiness, and injuries. Some of these measures will involve subjective judgments from superiors and peers while others will consist of securing data from company records (e.g., units produced). In either case, the measures chosen for use must be relevant to the job in question, reliable (or consistent), uncontaminated, and practical in terms of cost and acceptability (see Chapter 10).

Step 5. Examine Validity for Separate Groups

This step involves determining whether or not there is a statistically significant relationship between the employees' scores on the predictor and the criterion. Where technically feasible, the sample upon which the validation study is conducted should be reasonably representative of the population to which the predictor will be used. That is, the validation sample should possess minority group representation. In addition, the analyses should be done separately for various subgroups such as: (1) white male, (2) black male, (3) white female, (4) black female, (5) Spanish-surnamed male, and (6) Spanish-surnamed female. The possibility of the moderating effects of other variables besides race, sex, and ethnic group membership should also be investigated where reasonable and technically possible. For instance, the effects of such moderator variables as age and socio-economic status might also be investigated. It is important to remember that each subgroup analysis must be conducted on a sample large enough to warrant reliable results. Although the minimum sample size needed depends upon each particular organizational situation, a good rule of thumb to follow would be to have at least 30 individuals per subgroup. If this is not feasible due to company size, an approach called "synthetic validity" might be used (see Guion, 1965).

Step 6. Relate Predictor Scores to Measures of Employee Proficiency

Although the relationship between scores on a predictor and job proficiency may be presented in the form of correlation coefficients, it is understood better by nonstatisticians and laymen when expressed in the form of expectancy charts. These charts present the validity of a predictor graphically and are of two types. The *individual* expectancy chart illustrated in Figure 12–3A permits individual prediction. That is, personnel administrators are able to estimate an individual applicant's probability of being a "successful" employee by knowing his/her score range on the predictor. Of course, what "successful" means must be defined for each job before a chart can be developed. As Figure 12–3A shows, if an applicant scores between 75 and 95 on the predictor, this individual has a 30 percent chance of being successful on the particular job. The *institutional*

FIGURE 12-3
Individual and Institutional Expectancy Charts

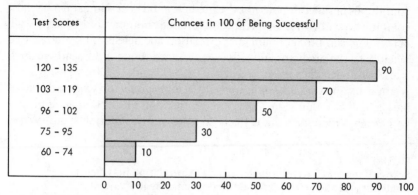

A. An Example of an Individual Expectancy Chart

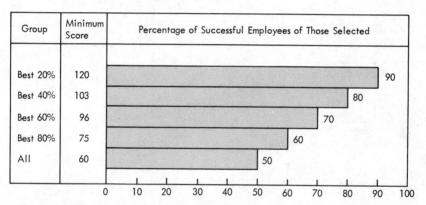

B. An Example of an Institutional Expectancy Chart

expectancy chart shown in Figure 12–3B permits the prediction of the average performance of a *group* of applicants. With such a chart, the personnel manager can predict the percentage of successful employees that would be obtained if the minimum predictor score for hiring was set at various cutoff levels. The reader should realize that if a predictor had no validity whatsoever, there would be no systematic trends in the length of the horizontal bars. The procedures for developing expectancy charts are described in Guion (1965) and Lawshe & Balma (1966).

A more effective procedure for expressing the validity of a predictor is the correlation coefficient. It gives a more precise indication of the extent of relationship between predictor and criterion scores than do expectancy charts. For this reason, correlations are commonly used in test manuals and technical reports. They are employed regardless of whether a predictive or concurrent validation strategy is followed. There are many different types of correlation coefficients available depending upon the shape of the relationship (i.e., linear or curvilinear) and the form (i.e., continuous or dichotomous) of the predictor and criterion data. The most common type of correlation employed for determining validity is the well-known Pearson product-moment correlation coefficient (r) which is used when both the predictor and criterion are continuous and linearly related. This validity coefficient varies between $+1.00$ and -1.00. A positive correlation means that an applicant with a high predictor score is likely to have a high criterion score. A negative correlation means that an applicant with a low predictor score is likely to have a high criterion score. When

FIGURE 12–4
Scatter Plots for Five Different Degrees of Correlation between a Predictor and a Criterion (each dot represents one individual)

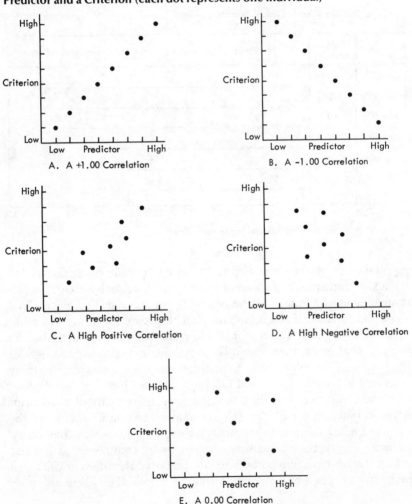

$r = 0.00$, no relationship exists between the predictor and criterion. It is important to note that the *sign* of the r is not important here, but the *size* is. The larger the r, the better the predictions will be. Figure 12–4 shows scatter plots for various degrees of relationship between predictor and criterion. Any analysis should involve information about the statistical significance of the obtained r. Traditionally, a validity coefficient is expected to be significant at the 5 percent level, i.e., the probability is less than one chance in twenty that the obtained correlation for the sample will be as large as it is if the correlation for the population from which the sample is drawn is actually zero. The specific procedures for computing the various types of correlation coefficients and testing their statistical significance can be found in any basic statistics text.

Step 7. Determining the Utility of the Predictor

Up until now, we have been considering only the statistical significance of the predictor. Another important consideration is the practical significance, or utility, of the selection procedure from the organization's point of view. Utility refers to the gain in hiring successful employees using the predictor as opposed to using no selection system or the existing one.

The easiest way to determine the utility of a predictor is to construct a scatter plot of the predictor and criterion scores. Suppose, for example, that 90 applicants had been given a predictor test and followed up until each applicant's job performance could be assessed. Figure 12–5 shows the scatter plot for the 90 individuals. The correlation between the predictor and the criterion variables (i.e., validity coefficient) is $+.75$. The heavy horizontal line is the point dividing the successful and unsuccessful

FIGURE 12–5
Scatter Plot of Job Proficiency and Test Data for 90 Individuals

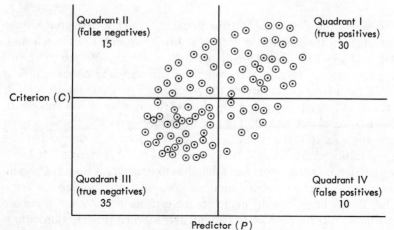

Quadrant II
(false negatives)
15

Quadrant I
(true positives)
30

Criterion (*C*)

Quadrant III
(true negatives)
35

Quadrant IV
(false positives)
10

Predictor (*P*)

workers. Those individuals falling below the line represent job failures while those above the line are job successes. The heavy vertical line is the cutoff score on the predictor which separates those individuals who will be hired from those who will be rejected. These two heavy lines split the scatter plot into four quadrants:

Quadrant I (true postives)—new employees whom the predictor indicates will do well and who subsequently succeed on the job.

Quadrant II (false negatives)—new employees whom the predictor indicates will do poorly and who subsequently succeed.

Quadrant III (true negatives)—new employees whom the predictor indicates will do poorly and who subsequently do not succeed.

Quadrant IV (false positives)—new employees whom the predictor indicates will do well and who subsequently do not succeed.

To estimate utility, the concept of base rate must be introduced. It refers to the proportion of applicants who succeed on the job if the predictor were not used to select them. It is estimated by determining the ratio of persons found in the following quadrants:

$$\text{Base rate} = \frac{\text{I} + \text{II}}{\text{I} + \text{II} + \text{III} + \text{IV}} \quad \begin{array}{l}\text{(the base rate in our sample} \\ \text{equals } 45/90 = 50\%)\end{array}$$

The utility or gain in the percentage of successful employees over and above the base rate can be determined by the following formula:

$$\text{Utility} = \underset{\substack{\text{(percentage} \\ \text{of successful} \\ \text{workers hired} \\ \text{using predictor)}}}{\frac{\text{I}}{\text{I} + \text{IV}}} \quad - \quad \underset{\text{(base rate)}}{\frac{\text{I} + \text{II}}{\text{I} + \text{II} + \text{III} + \text{IV}}} \quad \begin{array}{l}\text{(the percentage} \\ \text{improvement in our} \\ \text{example is} \\ 75\% - 50\% = 25\%)\end{array}$$

Several factors determine the functional utility of any predictor. Among them are: (1) the magnitude of the validity coefficient, (2) the selection ratio, and (3) the percentage of present employees who are successful (i.e., base rate). The nearer the validity coefficient is to either +1.00 or −1.00, the better the utility of the predictor. The selection ratio refers to the number of job openings divided by the number of job applicants. For instance, if one tests 80 job applicants and hires the top 20 among them, the selection ratio would be 20/80 = 25 percent. If one had to hire all applicants tested, the selection ratio would be 100 percent. The lower the selection ratio, the more favorable the labor market is from the organization's viewpoint since there are more job applicants than job openings. Other things being equal, predictors increase in utility when there are more applicants from which to choose, that is, when the selection ratio is low. The final factor affecting utility is the base rate. If everything else is equal, the closer the base rate is to 50 percent, the more utility the predictor will have. As the base rate becomes more extreme (e.g., 10 percent or 90 percent), the value of the predictor decreases. In other words, it is more difficult for a predictor to bring about an improvement in the calibre of the work force when the current group of employees are either extremely satisfactory or unsatisfactory.

Taylor-Russell tables (1939) provide a method of determining the gain in the percentage of satisfactory employees hired by considering the validity coefficient, the selection ratio, and the base rate. For illustrative purposes, one of their ten tables is presented in Table 12–1. Suppose you had a predictor with an $r = +.70$, you had five times as many applicants as there were openings, and only 20 percent of your present employees on the job in question are considered satisfactory. By referring to the table, you find that under these conditions you can expect that 56 percent of the applicants placed would be satisfactory instead of merely 20 percent.

TABLE 12–1
An Example of a Taylor-Russell Table
Proportion of Employees Considered Satisfactory = .20
Selection Ratio

r	.05	.10	.20	.30	.40	.50	.60	.70	.80	.90	.95
.00	.20	.20	.20	.20	.20	.20	.20	.20	.20	.20	.20
.05	.23	.23	.22	.22	.21	.21	.21	.21	.20	.20	.20
.10	.26	.25	.24	.23	.23	.22	.22	.21	.21	.21	.20
.15	.30	.28	.26	.25	.24	.23	.23	.22	.21	.21	.20
.20	.33	.31	.28	.27	.26	.25	.24	.23	.22	.21	.21
.25	.37	.34	.31	.29	.27	.26	.24	.23	.22	.21	.21
.30	.41	.37	.33	.30	.28	.27	.25	.24	.23	.21	.21
.35	.45	.41	.36	.32	.30	.28	.26	.24	.23	.22	.21
.40	.49	.44	.38	.34	.31	.29	.27	.25	.23	.22	.21
.45	.54	.48	.41	.36	.33	.30	.28	.26	.24	.22	.21
.50	.59	.52	.44	.38	.35	.31	.29	.26	.24	.22	.21
.55	.63	.56	.47	.41	.36	.32	.29	.27	.24	.22	.21
.60	.68	.60	.50	.43	.38	.34	.30	.27	.24	.22	.21
.65	.73	.64	.53	.45	.39	.35	.31	.27	.25	.22	.21
.70	.79	.69	.56	.48	.41	.36	.31	.28	.25	.22	.21
.75	.84	.74	.60	.50	.43	.37	.32	.28	.25	.22	.21
.80	.89	.79	.64	.53	.45	.38	.33	.28	.25	.22	.21
.85	.94	.85	.69	.56	.47	.39	.33	.28	.25	.22	.21
.90	.98	.91	.75	.60	.48	.40	.33	.29	.25	.22	.21
.95	1.00	.97	.82	.64	.50	.40	.33	.29	.25	.22	.21
1.00	1.00	1.00	1.00	.67	.50	.40	.33	.29	.25	.22	.21

Source: H. C. Taylor & J. J. Russell, The relationship of validity coefficients to the practical effectiveness of tests in selection: Discussion and tables. *Journal of Applied Psychology*, 1939, 23, 565–578.

Three other variables that affect predictor utility should also be mentioned: (1) the monetary costs of administering and scoring the predictor, (2) the relative costs and availability of alternative selection devices, and (3) the relative importance or value of making true positive, false negative, true negative, and false positive decisions; this must be weighted in terms of dollars and cents, public relations, social values, and so on (Anastasi, 1975).

Step 8. Reevaluation

It is important to remember that the predictive situation is a dynamic one. Jobs change, applicant populations change, organizations change, employment conditions change, and criteria change over time. What is a valid predictor today, might be outdated tomorrow. Thus, it is important that the criterion-related validity of a predictor be reevaluated periodically to make certain that it still exists. It is also possible that new innovations in psychological testing, or new social issues, may require changes in the predictors being employed.

MAKING SELECTION DECISIONS WITH A SINGLE PREDICTOR

Once we determine that the predictor's validity is both statistically and practically significant, we can use it for selection purposes by developing a prediction or regression equation. This regression equation is formulated using the predictor and criterion data from our validation sample. To illustrate the general procedure for developing this equation, consider the scatter plot in Figure 12–6A. In order to describe the relationship

FIGURE 12–6
Finding the Line Which Best Fits This Scatter Diagram

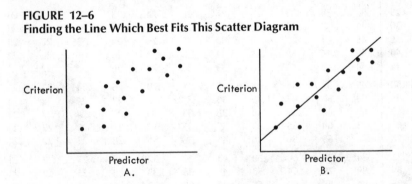

Criterion   Criterion

Predictor   Predictor
A.   B.

between the predictor and criterion scores in this scatter plot, we mathematically find the line which best "fits" these data, i.e., the line which slips in best among the set of data points (see Figure 12–6B). In most cases, this line will be a straight one in the form of the following equation:

$$C' = a + bP_1$$

where a and b are statistical weights differing in each selection situation, P_1 is a single predictor score, and C' is a predicted criterion score.

Why do we need this prediction equation if we already know the predictor and criterion scores of everyone in our validation sample? The answer is that we use the validation data to develop our prediction equation which is then used for selecting among future applicants on whom we have no job performance data. In fact, each applicant's job performance is precisely what we are attempting to predict before hiring. For instance, suppose our prediction equation is

$$C' = 8 + 3P_1.$$

If one applicant scores 30 on the predictor, her predicted criterion score will be 98 or $[8 + 3(30)]$. Another applicant with a predictor score of 45 would have a C' score of 143 or $[8 + 3(45)]$. The final choice among all applicants will depend upon the particular cutoff score chosen by the organization.

MAKING SELECTION DECISIONS WITH MULTIPLE PREDICTORS

Rarely can job success be accurately predicted using only one predictor score. Even the most simple jobs require several abilities. For this reason, most selection situations require the combining of several predictors (e.g., tests, interviews, application blanks) into a test battery. There are three main methods for combining predictive information: (1) multiple regression; (2) multiple cutoff; and (3) combining by judgment.

The multiple regression method usually involves assigning different weights to the predictors. These weights are derived by means of a fairly complicated statistical procedure which need not concern us here.[2] The prediction equations shown below would result if either two, three, or four predictors were used. The a and bs in these equations are statistical weights, Ps are predictors, and C' is a predicted criterion score.

2 predictors: $C' = a + b_1P_1 + b_2P_2$

3 predictors: $C' = a + b_1P_1 + b_2P_2 + b_3P_3$

4 predictors: $C' = a + b_1P_1 + b_2P_2 + b_3P_3 + b_4P_4$

Let us look at some concrete examples. Suppose that our multiple regression equation is

$$C' = 2 + 3P_1 + 2P_2 + 4P_3$$

[2] The reader is referred to Wiggins (1973) for a more detailed discussion of the procedures for determining prediction equations.

where, let us say P_1 is a structured interview, P_2 is a weighted application blank, and P_3 is a paper-and-pencil test. If an applicant's score on these three predictors were 10, 20, and 15, respectively, this individual's C' score would be 132 or $[2 + 3(10) + 2(20) + 4(15)]$. It is quite possible for another applicant to have an identical C' score even though his test score pattern differs substantially from the first person [e.g., $2 + 3(20) + 2(5) + 4(15)$]. These two applicants exemplify one of the major characteristics of multiple regression: it is possible for a high score on one predictor to compensate for a low score on another. If a C' score of 130 had been established as the cutoff score for hiring, both individuals would have been selected regardless of their individual test score patterns.

The multiple cut off method is a noncompensatory approach. That is, each predictor in the test battery has its own cutoff score; an applicant who does not reach the cutoff score on every single predictor will not be hired. Performing exceptionally well on one predictor (e.g., visual acuity) will not compensate for unsatisfactory performance on another (e.g., manual dexterity). This method typically involves a multiple hurdle or "survival of the fittest" strategy. Applicants are evaluated using one test at a time with certain low-scoring applicants eliminated from consideration along the way.

Probably the most widely used method of combining predictive data entails some sort of composite judgment on the part of a psychologist, a manager, or a personnel administrator. Typically, the individual pools together all the information available about an applicant, combines this information in her/his own unique way, and then makes a final subjective judgment about whether or not to hire the applicant.

What can we say about the relative advantages of these three approaches? First, research has shown that it is better to combine predictive data statistically or mechanically rather than judgmentally (Meehl, 1954, 1965; Sawyer, 1966). Second, it has been shown that sophisticated weightings of predictors using multiple regression analysis seldom yield higher validities than simply adding up the individual predictor scores (Lawshe, 1959; Trattner, 1963). Third, the multiple cutoff approach is a stringent selection paradigm. It should be used only when there is a low selection ratio and when a job analysis reveals that compensation is clearly inappropriate (e.g., an airplane pilot's job). Otherwise, a multiple regression approach (preferably without differential weighting) would seem best to follow.

CONTENT VALIDITY

The content validity of a test is the degree to which scores on it may be regarded as a representative sample of a specific content domain of which the test is a sample. If a test is to be used for selection purposes, the content domain should be defined in terms of the skills, knowledge, or behaviors required to perform the job. This content domain is determined by a careful and detailed job analysis. Unlike criterion-related validity, content validity is not generally measured statistically but rather is based on the judgments of persons highly familiar with the particular job (e.g., job incumbents, supervisors, and the test developer). These individuals determine whether the test items are an adequate sample of all the major aspects of the job in question. Although content validity is relevant to the construction of all kinds of tests, it is commonly used in evaluating achievement or trade tests (i.e., tests designed to measure how well a person has mastered a particular skill or content area) rather than aptitude or personality tests. For instance, one of the authors recently constructed a maintenance mechanic test consisting of the following parts: (1) a 20-minute blueprint reading test in which the examinee filled in the correct dimensions in each of 38 positions on a mechanical drawing; (2) a 55-minute multiple-choice test consisting of questions that measure knowledge of the trade; and (3) a 45-minute physical test requiring the examinee to assemble a gear reducer. The test is currently being used to select experienced mechanics requiring no training.

Content validity should not be confused with face validity. The latter is not really validity; it refers simply to how appropriate the test content "appears" to the examinee tested and to company officials. It is a desirable feature of tests in that it affects the examinee's motivation to do well and the organization's acceptance of the test results. Imagine, for instance, how ridiculous it would be for managers to be taking a test of quantitative ability where the questions are expressed in terms of apples or oranges rather than in terms of relevant managerial problems. Important as face validity is, it is not an essential characteristic for a test to possess before it can be used as a predictor.

PLACEMENT OF PERSONNEL

Up until now, we have devoted our attention to the problem of selection. In personnel selection the concern is with accepting or rejecting applicants for a specific job. For example, it may be that we have 10 openings for salespeople and 32 applicants. The task is to determine which, if any, of these individuals should be hired. The problem of placement or classification is considerably more complex. It involves individuals who have already been selected by the organization. The objective is to place each individual on that job where he or she will be most effective. As an illustration, an organization may have 20 different kinds of job openings and 20 people who have been hired after passing some initial screening. The question now becomes "which of the 20 jobs should each individual be placed in?" It should be obvious that one's opportunity to use a placement strategy as opposed to a selection strategy depends upon the size of the organization and the diversity of jobs available for applicant assignment (Dunnette, 1966).

There are several alternative methods of performing personnel placement. One method involves setting up regression equations which can predict an applicant's success on each of the job openings available. Our decision would then be to place each individual on that job for which he has the highest predicted criterion score. An alternative approach might involve placing an applicant on the job to which he is most similar to currently successful workers. Specifically, we can use a technique called profile analysis to compare an applicant's pattern of predictor scores (e.g., biographical data and test scores) with the average pattern of predictor scores for successful employees in each job. It is important to note that sometimes these approaches can get quite complicated and should only be instituted after cost/benefit analyses are performed.

What are some of the benefits of using a system of differential placement? First, the organization can save in recruiting costs since applicants who might otherwise be denied employment are placed somewhere. Second, since people are considered for more than one job, the selection ratio becomes more favorable. This increases the utility of the overall selection program. Finally, it fits in nicely with an organization's desire to hire all minority group members whom they may have taken the effort to recruit.

EQUAL EMPLOYMENT OPPORTUNITY

Prior to 1964, there were essentially no restrictions placed on employers regarding their hiring practices. Title VII of the Civil Rights Act of 1964 dramatically changed all that. This act, as amended in 1972, prohibits discrimination in hiring and treatment during employment on the basis of race, color, religion, sex, and national origin by an organization employing 15 or more employees 20 weeks per year. The only organizations exempt from this law are private clubs paying no income tax and religious groups hiring individuals of their own faith. To enforce this act, two government agencies have been established: (1) the Equal Employment Opportunity Commission (EEOC) which has the power to sue, and (2) the Office of Federal Contract Compliance (OFCC) which monitors contractors and subcontractors having federal contracts exceeding $10,000. Both of these agencies have, in turn, issued guidelines on proper personnel selection procedures.[3] Listed below are some of the most common questions asked about the guidelines and fair employment practices in general.

---

[3] Both sets of guidelines have been published in the *Federal Register*. See *Federal Register*, vol. 35, no. 149, August 1, 1970 for the EEOC and vol. 36, no. 77, April 21, 1971 for the OFCC Guidelines.

1. Q. What is meant by "unfair discrimination"?
    A. Unfair discrimination exists when applicants (e.g., whites and blacks) have equal probabilities of success on the job but have unequal probabilities of being hired (Guion, 1966). Figure 12–7 illus-

FIGURE 12–7
An Example of Unfair Discrimination against Black Applicants

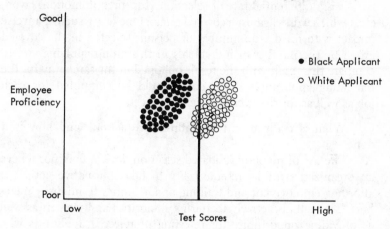

trates this: There is a significant difference between the two groups on average test score, yet no significant differences in their level of proficiency. If a cutoff score were established on the predictor test using the two groups combined, the black group would not be as likely to be hired, even though their chances of job success are essentially the same (Bartlett & O'Leary, 1969).

2. Q. What is "validation" according to the guidelines?
    A. Validation is the demonstration of the job relatedness of a selection device. Evidence of validity should consist of empirical data demonstrating that the selection device is predictive of or significantly related to job performance. Evidence of content validity may also be acceptable when criterion-related validity is not technically feasible. Content validity may also be justified with certain tests of skills or knowledge that the applicant is expected to bring to the job. Job analyses are needed to support any claims of validity.

3. Q. What kind of selection devices need to be validated according to the guidelines?
    A. All formal, scored, quantified or standardized techniques of assessing job suitability. This includes paper-and-pencil tests, interviews, special educational or work history requirements, biographical information blanks, application blanks, personal history and background requirements.

4. What is meant by "subgroup validation?"
    A.   Where technically feasible, a selection device must be validated separately for each subgroup of applicants with which it will be used (e.g., white female; white male; black female; black male; Spanish-surnamed male; Spanish-surnamed female).

5. Q.   What is adverse impact?
    A.   It is a differential rate of selection (for hire, promotion, layoff, etc.) which works against a covered group. One way to detect adverse impact is to divide the number of persons selected in the covered group by the number of individuals in this group applying and to compare this result with the result obtained in the same way for the remaining applicants. These data should be computed for each job as well as for the overall selection process.

6. Q.   What is really meant by "affirmative action" and how is it done?
    A.   The use of properly validated selection devices does not relieve an organization of its responsibility to take affirmative action in affording employment and training opportunities to minority members. This entails actively recruiting minorities and women as well as providing opportunity for retesting of rejected applicants who have obtained additional training or experience.

7. Q.   Are state employment service tests validated and permissible to use?
    A.   Their tests are validated, but there is no guarantee that their validity evidence is relevant enough for an organization's particular situation. The mere assertion from a state employment service representative that their tests are validated is not enough. Personnel administrators and managers should check with their compliance officers or with a qualified psychologist.

8. Where can I find individuals who can advise me on validation procedures?
    A.   Members of the American Psychological Association (1200 Seventeenth Street, N.W., Washington, D.C. 20036) in Divisions 14 (Industrial and Organizational Psychology) or 5 (Evaluation and Measurement) should be contacted.

9. Q.   If I decide to discontinue all paper-and-pencil testing and other formally scored devices, how will "other selection devices" be evaluated?
    A.   If there is adverse impact, the employer must either provide the same validation evidence as he would for paper-and-pencil tests, or modify selection practices to eliminate this condition.

10. Q. What about age discrimination?
     A. In 1967, the federal Age Discrimination in Employment Act
     was passed which protects people ages 49–65 against discrimination
     in hiring, wages, and discharging.

Two landmark cases have reached the U.S. Supreme Court. In the
case of *Griggs* v. *Duke Power Company*, the Court ruled that it was
illegal for Duke Power to require black laborers to have a high school
diploma and to pass the Wonderlic intelligence test and the Bennett
Mechanical Comprehension test as a condition for promotion since these
three "tests" were not shown to be job-related in this particular organizational situation. In the recent case of *Moody* v. *Albemarle Paper Company*, the Court ruled that compensatory back pay awards be made to
minorities or women denied jobs or promotions. The Court called for
"great deference" to the EEOC Guidelines, attacking Albemarle's validity
study on several points, including: (1) no job analysis was done; (2) the
criteria used were subjective supervisory rankings based on vague standards; (3) no subgroup validation was done, nor was one shown to be
infeasible; and (4) the validation involved only experienced whites in a
concurrent or present-employee approach (Sandman and Urban, 1976).

SUMMARY

The first step in developing a selection or placement program is to conduct a job analysis. Each job for which applicants will be considered
should be analyzed to determine what skills, traits, and experience are
likely to be required. Next, potential selection devices are either developed
or are obtained from appropriate sources. In order to estimate the capacity
of each selection device to predict subsequent performance, a validation
procedure must be conducted. This requires an accurate criterion of employee performance or job success. The "present-employee method" can
sometimes be used initially to identify promising selection devices. However, use of the "follow-up method" is always advisable to determine
predictive validity, even if preceded by the present-employee method. For
some kinds of selection devices, it is also useful to consider content
validity.

A selection program is more likely to be successful the higher the
predictive validity, the more favorable the selection ratio, and the closer
the base rate is to 50 percent. In determining which, if any, selection
devices to use, their relative costs and benefits for the organization should
also be considered. Once valid and economical selection devices have
been found, procedures for administering them to applicants and making
selection or placement decisions must be developed.

A major concern of organizations in establishing a selection program is equal employment opportunity. Federal legislation in the United States makes it illegal to use selection devices that discriminate on the basis of race, color, religion, national origin, sex, or age. The burden of proof is on the organization to show that selection devices do not adversely affect any population subgroup in hiring, transfer, promotion, or membership decisions. Subgroup validation and affirmative action programs may be necessary to insure compliance with fair employment laws.

REVIEW AND DISCUSSION QUESTIONS

1. What conditions affect the utility or practical significance of a selection procedure?
2. Explain why the size and not the sign of a validity coefficient is the important consideration.
3. Describe the steps that you would follow in determining the criterion-related validity of a predictor.
4. Define and explain each of the following key terms: affirmative action, selection ratio, adverse impact, job analysis, unfair discrimination, expectancy chart, job description.
5. What are the relative advantages and disadvantages of using multiple regression and multiple cutoff approaches? Under what conditions would one approach be better than the other?
6. Suppose you decided to conduct an extensive job analysis of the job of auditor for a large manufacturing organization. How would you proceed in accomplishing this task?
7. Compare and contrast the processes of personnel selection and personnel placement. How does one decide whether a test is valid and useful for each of these processes?
8. If you were responsible for your company's meeting of affirmative action goals, what would you do?

REFERENCES

Anastasi, A. *Psychological testing.* New York: Macmillan, 1975.

Bartlett, C. J., & O'Leary, B. S. A differential prediction model to moderate the effects of heterogeneous groups in personnel selection and classification. *Personnel Psychology,* 1969, 22, 1–17.

Dunnette, M. D. *Personnel selection and placement.* Belmont, Calif.: Wadsworth, 1966.

Guion, R. M. *Personnel testing.* New York: McGraw-Hill, 1965.

Guion, R. M. Employment tests and discriminatory hiring. *Industrial Relations,* 1966, 5, 20–37.

Lawshe, C. H. Statistical theory and practice in applied psychology. *Personnel Psychology,* 1959, 22, 117–124.

Lawshe, C. H., & Balma, M. J. *Principles of personnel testing.* New York: McGraw-Hill, 1966.

McCormick, E. J., Jeanneret, P. R., & Mecham, R. C. A study of job characteristics and job dimensions as based on the Position Analysis Questionnaire (PAQ). *Journal of Applied Psychology*, 1972, 56, 347–368.

Meehl, P. *Clinical vs. statistical prediction.* Minneapolis: University of Minnesota Press, 1954.

Meehl, P. E. Seer over sign: The first good example. *Journal of Experimental Research in Personality*, 1965, 1, 27–32.

Principles for the validation and use of personnel selection procedures. Division of Industrial and Organizational Psychology, American Psychological Association, 1975.

Sandman, B., & Urban, F. Employment testing and the law. *Labor Law Review*, January 1976, 38–54.

Sawyer, J. Measurement and prediction, clinical and statistical. *Psychological Bulletin*, 1966, 66, 178–200.

Taylor, H. C., & Russell, J. T. The relationship of validity coefficients to the practical effectiveness of tests in selection: Discussion and tables. *Journal of Applied Psychology*, 1939, 23, 565–578.

Trattner, M. H. Comparison of three methods for assembling aptitude test batteries. *Personnel Psychology*, 1963, 16, 221–232.

Wiggins, J. S. *Personality and prediction: Principles of personality assessment.* Reading, Mass.: Addison-Wesley, 1973.

13

DESIGN AND EVALUATION
OF TRAINING PROGRAMS

"TRAINING" AND "DEVELOPMENT" are terms referring to planned efforts designed to facilitate the acquisition of relevant skills, knowledge, and attitudes by organizational members. The two terms, however, are not entirely alike in meaning. Development focuses more on improving the decision-making and human relations skills of middle and upper level management, while training involves lower level employees and the presentation of a more factual and narrow subject matter (Campbell, Dunnette, Lawler, and Weick, 1970).

Surveys indicate that over 90 percent of private corporations have some type of formalized training (Goldstein, 1974). It has also been reported that management may spend as much as 10 percent of their payrolls on training and development activities (Bass and Barrett, 1972). There are at least five major reasons for its widespread popularity. First, personnel selection and placement by themselves do not usually provide organizations with new employees skillful enough to meet the demands of their jobs adequately. Many of these people must learn new skills, attitudes, and knowledge after they are hired. Second, there is mounting government pressure on modern organizations to train minority group members, women, individuals over 45 years of age, and the hard-core unemployed. Third, experienced employees must sometimes be retrained because of changes in their job content due to automation, advances in computer technology, promotions, and transfers. Fourth, management is aware that effective programs can result in increased productivity, decreased absenteeism, reduced turnover, and greater employee satisfaction. Fifth, some organizations, unfortunately, adopt a particular training technique simply because "everyone else is doing it." A new "supertechnique" appears with a group of people extolling its virtues and with only a few empirical studies supporting it. The new technique is widely used until there is backlash, another new fad appears, and the cycle begins again (Campbell, 1971).

IDENTIFYING TRAINING NEEDS

The first phase in the instructional process must involve a *systematic* assessment of the organization's training needs. Too often training programs are a sheer waste of company time and money because they get their start in somewhat the following offhand manner:

> "John," said the vice president of personnel to his training director, "I hear that both Tolake Sporting Goods, Inc., and Fairland Sports Corp., have been sending a lot of their management people to Maine for three days of Binks training. The rumor is that they think it does their people a lot of good. I definitely think we should send some of our managers up there to see how they like it."

It makes no sense to institute an expensive training program simply to "keep up with the Joneses." Instead, the assessment of training needs should involve three kinds of analyses: organization, job, and person analysis (McGehee & Thayer, 1961).

Organization Analysis

Organization analysis deals with the question, "Where is training needed in this organization?" This analysis requires determining the short- and long-term goals for the organization as a whole, as well as for its various divisions, departments, and sections. Beyond this, one needs to estimate how closely these goals are being achieved by using cost accounting indices such as labor costs, utilization of machinery and equipment, and cost of materials. Of course, one must realize that not all inefficient operations can be dealt with by means of training. It could be that such nontraining factors as faulty equipment, inefficient work procedures, and low wages are the cause of the problems. In these cases, the problems might better be alleviated by purchasing new equipment, redesigning jobs, or modifying wages and salaries.

Analyzing organizational climate is important for training since the existing climate, especially the employees' attitudes toward organizational change, will largely affect a program's success. Further, as a result of analyzing its climate, an organization may realize that it needs to bring about certain changes in itself in order to reduce employee turnover and absenteeism. The climate of an organization is a function of its individual members' perceptions of the relevant stimuli, constraints, and reinforcement contingencies that govern their behavior (Campbell et al., 1970). One of the best measures of the prevailing organizational climate is the Survey of Organizations, a machine-scored, standardized instrument developed by the University of Michigan's Institute for Social Research. As currently developed, this questionnaire accesses certain critical dimensions of organizational climate (e.g., communication flow, motivational conditions, decision-making practices), managerial leadership, peer behavior, group processes, and satisfaction.

Another aspect of organization analysis is concerned with determining *how many* people need to be trained immediately and in the near future for each job classification. This is determined by conducting a manpower inventory similar to the one presented in Figure 13–1. What can be said

FIGURE 13–1
A Manpower Analysis of One Job Classification

1.	Number of employees in the job classification: 37
2.	Number of employees needed: 38

3.	Age levels:	29	33	45	47	50	51	53	55	63
	No. per age group:	2	8	7	10	3	2	2	1	2

			Level	
	Factors	*Satisfactory*	*Questionable*	*Unsatisfactory*
4.	Skill	32	2	3
5.	Knowledge	33	3	1
6.	Attitude	36	1	0
7.	Performance	33	2	2

8. Skill and knowledge levels for other jobs:

Classification	*Number*	*Jobs*
No other jobs	33	x
One other job	3	Job Z, Dept. Y
Two or more other jobs	1	Job Z, Dept. Y; Job A, Dept. B

9–11. Potential replacements and training time:

Outside Company	*Within Company*	*Training Time*
0	1	Less than 1 week
0	1	3 weeks to 6 weeks
10	0	12 weeks to 16 weeks

12.	Training time on job for novice: 12 to 16 weeks
13.	Rate of absenteeism (Two year average): 2.3%
14.	Turnover (Two year period): 5 employees; 13.5%
15.	Statement of job specifications

Adapted from W. McGehee and P. W. Thayer, *Training in Business and Industry* (New York: John Wiley & Sons, 1961), p. 35.

about this hypothetical department's training needs based upon its manpower analysis?

Job Analysis

Job analysis answers the question, "What must a trainee be taught in order to perform a job effectively?" Its purpose is to provide information about the duties involved in performing the job; the manner in which each duty should be performed; the skills, knowledge, and attitudes required to do the job well; and standards of performance (e.g., a worker must produce 25 nondefective "pedukes" in six hours). Some of the better methods of collecting job information have previously been discussed in Chapter 11.

Person Analysis

Person analysis deals with the individual employee. It attempts to answer the question, "*Who* needs training and what kind?" First, we determine how well each employee is doing his/her job by using supervisory evaluations (see Chapter 10), job-knowledge tests, and company production records. Second, we determine what specific skills, knowledge, and attitudes an unsatisfactory employee needs to learn in order to be brought to a satisfactory level of performance. This second step is obviously time consuming and costly since it requires a complete diagnosis of each individual's strengths and weaknesses using various achievement tests, observational measures, and situational procedures. It is therefore important to decide whether it is better from a cost/benefit to train unsatisfactory employees or to transfer or terminate them and train new applicants for their positions.

Comments on Identifying Needs

It is obvious that the three kinds of analyses described above require a lot of time and energy to conduct. It is not something that a single individual in an organization can complete overnight. These analyses, to be effective, take the combined efforts of many specialists (e.g., job analysts, manpower analysts, cost accountants) carefully collecting information over several years. It should be an ongoing process since organizations are continually changing in terms of their jobs, products and services, climate, and so forth. The three analyses must be conducted simultaneously because they interrelate so highly with one another. In our opinion, the approach presented here is the most sophisticated and comprehensive one at the present time. Finally, one must remember that the organization is an open system and that there are various outside social, political, economic, and geographical factors that may affect its training needs.

PRINCIPLES OF LEARNING

Since the basic foundation of all training and development is human learning, it is important for us to agree on a comprehensible definition of this rather complex phenomenon. Learning can be defined as a relatively permanent change in behavior that occurs as a result of experience or practice (Bass and Vaughn, 1966; McGehee and Thayer, 1961). When we say that an individual has learned something, we are not talking about temporary changes in behavior due to such factors as drugs, fatigue, lapses in attention, or lack of motivation. Rather, we are referring to observable changes that remain intact over fairly long periods of time. The process of learning cannot be seen directly. It can only be inferred whenever an individual's job behavior or test performance shifts from one level to another as a result of going through certain experiences. Of course, we realize that it is possible for an individual to learn something, yet show no overt behavior change. Unfortunately, one would not know the person learned unless one could detect a change in performance.

Over the years, psychologists have expended considerable effort in studying the process of learning in both humans and animals. Although there is still a great deal they do not know, experimental psychologists have uncovered certain principles of learning that are applicable to organizational training and development. We believe that a knowledge of these principles can be helpful in designing training programs and in choosing among alternative training methods. These principles should be regarded as "guiding principles" and not "laws." They should be applied cautiously with full cognizance of the type of trainees, the training material, and the organization in which training takes place. Many of these learning principles have been incorporated into the design of successful training programs.

Size of the Unit to Be Learned

Should one try to teach the entire task at each practice session (i.e., whole method) or is it more efficient in the long run to teach individual segments of the total task at each session and as the trainee begins mastering each subtask begin the process of combining them (i.e., part method)? Imagine for a moment a task consisting of three separate subtasks, A, B, and C. Whole and part training schedules would take place as follows:

	Training Session			
	1	2	3	4
Whole training	A+B+C	A+B+C	A+B+C	A+B+C
Part training	A	A+B	A+B+C	A+B+C

It has been shown that the relative effectiveness of these two strategies depends upon two aspects of the task to be learned: task complexity and task organization. Task complexity refers to the difficulty of each of the subtasks comprising the total task. Task organization refers to the degree of interrelationship among the set of subtasks. For highly organized tasks, the whole method seems to be superior to the part method. Part training, however, is superior to the whole method when task organization is low. These statements are especially true as the complexity of the subtasks increase (Blum and Naylor, 1968).

Now let's look at a few examples to clarify these points. Imagine how ridiculous it would be to teach someone to drive a forklift truck or automobile using part learning. Individual lessons would have to be devoted to such things as starting the engine, steering, braking, backing up, and shifting. Since the skills required here are highly interrelated, a whole training method is preferred. On the other hand, suppose you wanted to train someone to be a maintenance electrician. Here, training sessions would have to be devoted to such specific topics as tachometers, reading schematic drawings, pyrometers, D.C. motors, thermocouples, and wiring. It would be virtually impossible to teach all tasks at each training session; the skills and knowledge required would have to be progressively built-up over time.

Meaningfulness of the Material

Material is learned easier and remembered better when it is meaningful for the trainees. By meaningfulness we mean material rich in associations and easily understood (McGehee and Thayer, 1961). There are at least six ways that training materials can be made more meaningful.

1. At the start of training, provide the trainees with a bird's-eye view of the material to be presented. Knowing the overall picture and understanding how each unit of the program fits into it facilitates the acquisition of each element and the training as a whole (Kolasa, 1969).

2. Present the material using a variety of examples familiar to the trainees.

3. Organize the material so that it is presented in a logical manner and has meaningful units.

4. Split the material up into meaningful chunks rather than presenting it all at once.

5. Use terms and concepts that are already familiar to the trainees.

6. Use as many visual aids as possible to augment theoretical materials.

Transfer of Training

Transfer of training refers to whether or not learning in a training situation facilitates performance in a subsequent job situation. The following three transfer possibilities exist:

Positive transfer. Learning in the training situation results in better performance on the job.

Negative transfer. Learning in the training situation results in poorer performance on the job.

No transfer. Learning in the training situation has no effect on job performance.

Obviously, the goal of all organizational training is to bring about positive transfer. Listed below are a few guidelines adapted from Ellis (1965, pp. 70–72) for facilitating positive transfer:

1. *Maximize the similarity between the training situation and the work situation.* For example, if a machine operator is eventually going to work in a noisy environment with a great deal of distractions, then sometime during training the trainee should be given practice in producing under conditions of noise and interruptions. In general, the trainee must learn the job in a setting which contains many of the elements which will be experienced in the work environment.

2. *Provide adequate experience with the tasks during training.* Extensive practice with the tasks during training increases the likelihood of positive transfer, whereas less practice may lead to negative or no transfer. Of course, it is difficult to specify exactly how much practice is needed since it depends greatly on what is being taught. A good rule of thumb, however, would be to give trainees as much practice as possible, especially on those tasks or topics known to be critical for the mastery of the job.

3. *Provide for a variety of stimulus situations when teaching concepts or skills.* When teaching a trainee a concept it is best to present several examples of instances which represent and do not represent the concept. Similarly, when teaching a skill, the trainee should be given an opportunity to practice the skill in varying conditions.

4. *Label or identify important features of the task.* Labeling helps the trainee distinguish between important features of the task. An illustration of the use of this principle can be seen in training someone to operate an industrial boiler. Each part of the boiler is given a label (e.g., water pump) as well as each step of the firing procedure (e.g., pilot lighting, purging the firebox).

5. *Make sure that the trainee understands general principles.* The likelihood of positive transfer is increased when the trainee understands the general principles underlying what is being taught. In the course of teach-

ing a particular subject, such as statistics, trainees will have a difficult time applying what they have learned if they have merely memorized formulas and techniques. It is important that they comprehend the principles and assumptions involved. The trainer sould insure this level of learning by checking periodically to discover if trainees do understand general principles.

Motivation

Even a student with a great deal of ability will master little if he/she is disinterested in what is being taught. Similarly, for an employee to benefit from training, there must be some degree of motivation or desire to learn on the individual's part. In fact, it can be assumed that for every learning situation there is some optimal level of motivation (Bass and Vaughn, 1966); it is essential that the trainee's motivation not be too low (i.e., lethargic and bored) or too high (i.e., overly tense or fearful).

Granted that motivation is vital to learning, what are some of the ways of motivating trainees? Consider the following suggestions:

1. Trainees should be made aware of the instrumentality of the training. That is, it is important that they understand how participating in the training program will facilitate their attainment of valued outcomes (e.g., promotions, raises, desired jobs) in the future. The training program should be preceded by an orientation session to discuss the utility of the program from the trainees' vantage point.

2. The goals and objectives of the training must be clearly conveyed to the trainees at the start of training.

3. All material presented must be meaningful and relevant to the trainees' jobs.

4. Immediate knowledge of results in the form of trainer's comments, test scores, and productivity measures should be provided during the course of training.

5. Trainees learn quicker and easier if rewarded for correct behavior immediately after it is performed. Delays in reinforcement can lead to the strengthening of some other irrelevant behavior which may occur after the correct response. A trainee learning to build a radial tire, for example, will do better if the trainer rewards appropiate behaviors soon after they occur rather than several days later.

6. It is best to provide continuous reinforcement (rewarding the individual for every correct response) while the behavior is initially being learned. Once the behavior is fairly well established, a partial schedule of reinforcement (rewarding the individual for only some correct responses) is useful since it makes the behavior more resistant to extinction (or forgetting).

7. The trainer may "shape" the employee's behavior. Shaping refers to the process of reinforcing any behavior which approximates the behavior the trainer wishes to generate while failing to reinforce all other responses. Step by step, closer and closer approximations to the desired behavior are required on the part of the trainee before reinforcement is administered. In this way, the trainee does not have to perform the desired behavior immediately, but can perform different behaviors which begin to approximate the goal response.

8. The final goal of "completing the program" should be supplemented with periodical subgoals during training such as paper-and-pencil quizzes, work sample tests, and trainer evaluations. The trainee may derive pleasure from the feeling of completing each unit of material and, consequently, look forward to proceding to the next one.

Patterns of Learning

"Learning curves" are used to indicate how a trainee's rate of learning varies as a function of continued practice. Figure 13–2 illustrates four

FIGURE 13–2
Four Curves Occurring Regularly in Employee Training

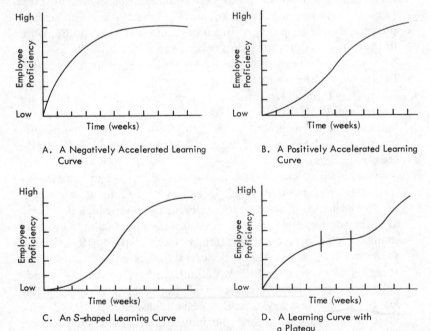

A. A Negatively Accelerated Learning Curve

B. A Positively Accelerated Learning Curve

C. An S-shaped Learning Curve

D. A Learning Curve with a Plateau

Adapted from B. M. Bass and J. A. Vaughn, *Training in Industry: The Management of Learning* (Belmont, Calif.: Wadsworth Publishing Company, Inc., 1966).

curves which occur with some regularity in employee training (Bass and Vaughn, 1966). These curves have been smoothed out; in actuality, learning curves are jagged and irregular. Knowledge of learning curves is important since they provide trainers with some understanding of the pattern in which new skills are developed. They emphasize the important fact that individuals differ considerably in their patterns of learning. Some trainees learn faster, some begin training with more expertise, others are capable of higher terminal levels of performance, still others are barely capable of improving at all regardless of how much practice they are given. It is important that trainers realize and take into consideration these individual differences in trainability. It seems likely that any training program or educational system which is not sensitive to the individual needs of trainees can reach only modest degrees of success.

During the course of learning some trainees will exhibit what is called a "plateau." Notice for a moment learning curve "D" in Figure 13–2. Can you see how despite additional training trials there does not appear to be any improvement in performance? For some reason it seems that the trainee has temporarily stopped learning. It is essential that the trainer realize that the trainee has not reached the final level of performance and that continued practice will again bring about improvement; otherwise, training will be prematurely stopped. It is also important that the trainer motivate the learner at this time of frustration and discouragement. This may involve applying extra incentives, explaining to the trainee that plateaus are often "par for the course," providing additional feedback, and encouraging the trainee not to lose hope.

Knowledge of Results or Feedback

It is important that individuals be given knowledge of results or feedback regarding the adequacy of their efforts during training. Trainees should be told when, how, and why they have done something correctly or incorrectly (Wexley and Thorton, 1972). Feedback, whether in the form of verbal praise, tangible rewards, censure, penalties, or performance measurement, serves the dual function of motivating the trainee to learn and providing information about performance. Imagine how difficult and boring it would be for trainees to learn some skill (e.g., playing tennis) if they had no feedback whatsoever about how they were doing. Without a trainer's specific comments regarding the accuracy of their performance, it would not be long before they would discontinue learning.

Feedback should be timed so that it is provided as soon as possible after the trainee's performance. In this way, the information can be used immediately to either alter or strengthen the individual's actions. Additionally, the specificity or amount of feedback provided must be appropriate to the particular capabilities of the learner. Too much feedback at once can lead to confusion, frustration, and performance decline on the part of the trainee. Likewise, too little feedback can result in similar outcomes. It appears that for each task and each trainee there is an optimum level of feedback specificity which should be provided. It is essential that trainers be aware of this inverted-U relationship when designing training programs (see Figure 13–3).

FIGURE 13–3
Hypothesized Relationship between Specificity of Feedback and Amount of Learning

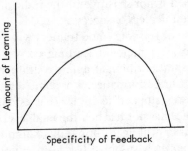

Adapted from Blum and Naylor, 1968.

Massed or Distributed Practice Sessions

What is the best way to schedule practice sessions? If, for example, you decided to give trainees eight hours of practice, which of the following schedules would be best to use?

One eight-hour nonstop session.

Four hours a day for 2 days.

Two hours a day for 4 days.

A half-hour a day for 16 days.

In essence, the question being raised is whether it is better to practice something "all at once" or whether the practice periods should be stretched out over time. In general, the literature suggests that distributed practice periods interspersed with reasonable rest periods is usually the favored technique over massed sessions for the learning and retention of motor (e.g., operating a lathe) and verbal (e.g., memorizing safety rules) skills. Therefore, in this case, it would be best to schedule practice sessions for a half-hour a day for 16 days. It should also be considered that distributed practice requires a longer period of time to complete.

Active Practice and Repetition

Whether a trainee is learning a new motor skill or studying a new subject it is generally agreed that the greater the opportunity for practice and repetition of whatever is being taught: (1) the better it will be learned, and (2) the less easily it will be forgotten. Thus, it is important that training programs be designed so that individuals are given adequate opportunity to practice new motor skills so that correct responses are well ingrained. When studying a new subject (e.g., accounting), the trainee makes implicit responses rather than observable ones. Nevertheless, here too, the trainee must be given time to rehearse overtly and covertly the knowledge being learned (McGehee and Thayer, 1961).

Overlearning

Overlearning refers to giving the trainee continued practice even after the task has been performed correctly several times. By providing thorough learning, the following benefits can result: (1) trainees will be better able to positively transfer what they have learned to their jobs; (2) trainees will be more likely to maintain performance on their jobs during periods of emergency and added pressure (for example, professional athletes who have thoroughly overlearned their sport are more likely to perform effectively despite such things as unfavorable weather conditions and monetary pressures); and (3) trainees will be less likely to forget what they have learned. In providing overlearning, the trainer must be willing to extend the length of the training program while realizing that, in the long run, it will pay off.

Some Additional Learning Principles

It should be noted that there are those who question the relative usefulness of these traditional learning principles. For instance, according to Robert Gagné (1962), a well known learning psychologist, these principles can seldom be applied in the design of military and industrial training. He presented instead three new principles of training design which he believes are more applicable and more important than the traditional learning principles. The Gagné principles are as follows: (1) identify the tasks that comprise a final performance; (2) insure that each task is achieved; and (3) sequence the learning so as to insure the maximum transfer from one subtask to another.

EVALUATING TRAINING AND DEVELOPMENT PROGRAMS

Everyone agrees that it is important to evaluate the effectiveness of training and development programs. Despite this consensus, few programs are currently being evaluated correctly (Catalanello and Kirkpatrick, 1968). Too many industrial training programs are evaluated solely on the basis of how well participants liked the program. One must be skeptical of these evaluations since participants' reactions to training programs are generally favorable regardless of the length or content of the program. This is especially true when the training is held at an attractive resort area away from everyday work. When a company really wants to know how much its training efforts contribute to the achievement of organizational goals, it must conduct a controlled experimental study using relevant criteria such as behavioral observations, productivity, absenteeism, and turnover. Only through rigorous evaluation studies will management be able to determine whether its training efforts are yielding a favorable return on investment. With so much at stake, why has evaluation of training been such a neglected area? We can only speculate by offering the following reasons:

1. Some managers are reluctant to evaluate something that they have already convinced themselves and their superiors is worthwhile. After all, the evaluation could prove to be quite embarrassing!
2. Many training directors do not have the necessary skills to conduct rigorous evaluation research. Rather than hiring a consultant who has been trained in experimental design and statistical analyses, they do what little they can.
3. Some companies are involved in training, not because of any real conviction that it works, but because their competitors are doing it or their unions are demanding it.
4. Some training programs are extremely difficult to evaluate because the behaviors taught are extremely complex and ambiguous (e.g., T-group training for high level managers).
5. After spending huge amounts of money on the training itself, some organizations are reluctant to spend even a dollar more on evaluation.
6. Some managers see training as a function which requires little knowledge or skill. They have no conception of the sophisticated experimental and statistical techniques available for assessing training effectiveness.

According to McGehee and Thayer (1961), the evaluation of training has two main aspects. The first is that of determining whether the behavior changes brought about by the training program contributes to the achievement of organizational objectives. The second involves comparing various training techniques to determine if any one or combination of techniques are superior for the purpose of achieving the desired results. To deal with these two problems, the evaluation process must involve the use of several measures of training effectiveness and an experimental design that allows us to conclude with assurance that any success is due to the training itself and not to some other cause. In the next two sections we will discuss measures of training effectiveness and then touch briefly on a few useful experimental designs.

Measures of Training Effectiveness

The effectiveness of training programs should be evaluated in terms of four types of outcomes, namely, *reaction, learning, behavior,* and *results* (Kirkpatrick, 1959). The initial step in the evaluation process involves measuring *reaction,* that is, how well the trainees liked the program. This entails determining first what you want to find out from the trainees, and then designing a form so that their answers are anonymous and easy to tabulate and score. They should also be permitted to write in additional comments not covered by your questions. The comments sheet shown in Figure 13–4 illustrates this type of reaction form. Although a favorable reaction on the part of trainees is important because it helps to insure organizational support for any program, it does not guarantee that learning has taken place.

Learning refers to the principles, facts, and techniques that were absorbed by the trainees. Knowledge of principles and facts is measured by paper-and-pencil tests similar to those used in college courses. The following are two items that might be used in a test for measuring knowledge of industrial pipefitting:

1. What type of gasket material would you use on a cold water line? (a) composition; (b) rubber; (c) paper; (d) cork.
2. Up to what pressure can you use forged steel pipe fillings? (a) 150 pounds; (b) 300 pounds; (c) 800 pounds; (d) 2,000 pounds.

The following personal experience described by Kirkpatrick (1967, pp. 100–101) is the best way of introducing step three *(behavior):*

> During the week I was particularly impressed by a foreman named Herman from a Milwaukee company. Whenever a conference leader asked a question requiring a good understanding of human relations principles and techniques, Herman was the first one who raised his hand. He had all the answers in terms of good human relations approaches. I was very impressed and I said to myself, "If I were in industry, I would like to work for a man like Herman." It so happened that I had a first cousin who was working for that company. And oddly enough Herman was his boss. At my first opportunity, I talked with my cousin, Jim, and asked him about Herman. Jim told me that Herman might know all the principles and techniques of human relations, but he certainly did not practice them on the job. He performed as the typical "bull-of-the-woods" who had little consideration for the feelings and ideas of his subordinates. At this time I began to realize there may be a big difference between knowing principles and techniques and using them on the job.

FIGURE 13–4
Example of a Form Used to Measure Trainee Reaction

ASTD INSTITUTE

Leader_____ Subject_____

Date_____

1. Was the subject pertinent to your needs and interests?
   ☐ No   ☐ To some extent   ☐ Very much so

2. How was the ratio of lecture to discussion?
   ☐ Too much lecture   ☐ OK   ☐ Too much discussion

3. Rate the trainer on the following:

		Excellent	Very Good	Good	Fair	Poor
A.	How well did trainer state objectives?					
B.	How well did trainer keep the session alive and interesting?					
C.	How well did trainer use the blackboard, charts, and other aids?					
D.	How well did trainer summarize during the session?					
E.	How well did trainer maintain a friendly and helpful manner?					
F.	How well did trainer illustrate and clarify the points?					
G.	How was the trainer's summary at the close of the session?					

What is your overall rating of the trainer?
   ☐ Excellent   ☐ Very good   ☐ Good   ☐ Fair   ☐ Poor

4. What would have made the session more effective?

_____

_____

_____

_____

_____
Signature (optional)

Adapted from D. L. Kirkpatrick, "Evaluation of Training," in R. L. Craig and L. R. Bittel, (eds.), *Training and Development Handbook* (New York: McGraw-Hill Book Company, 1967), p. 90.

The appraisal of on the job behavior should be gathered from as many qualified sources as possible such as the trainee's superiors, immediate peers, and subordinates. This appraisal should be made several months after training in order to give the individual adequate opportunity to put into practice what has been learned. Several of the performance appraisal techniques presented in Chapter 10 can be used in the evaluation of behavior (e.g., weighted checklists, forced-choice checklists, behavioral expectation scales, and critical-incident checklists).

The last step deals with an important question: What were the tangible *results* of the program in terms of such things as reduced cost, improved quality and quantity of production, and decreased absenteeism. Unfortunately, in many cases, these cost-related measures are either impossible to obtain or contaminated by so many other factors so as to make them virtually useless. In these situations, the training analyst must resort to evaluations in terms of reaction, learning, and behavior. Whichever measures are used, their reliability, validity, and practicality should be seriously considered.

Experimental Designs and Analysis

In this section we will present a few examples of the numerous experimental designs that have been used to assess the effects of training on learning, behavior, and results. As we shall see, these designs differ a great deal in terms of their rigorousness and, consequently, their value. We mentioned earlier that most evaluation research is done poorly. One reason for this is the weak designs employed. Presented below are three *pre-experimental* designs which are used quite often in organizations but are, in fact, unacceptable. In presenting the designs, an X will represent the exposure of a group to training, T_1 the pretest, T_2 the posttest, and R the random assignment of individuals to separate treatment groups.

Design 1.	Measures after training without a control group.		X	T_2
Design 2.	Measures before and after training without a control group.	T_1	X	T_2
Design 3.	Measures after training with a control group.		X	T_2
				T_2

Design 1 has no value at all. There is no way to measures changes in performance since no pretest was administered prior to training. Design 2 permits us to assess changes but we have no idea whether the T_1–T_2 differences are due to training or to extraneous factors such as maturation processes within the trainees, exposure to the pretest or specific events occurring within the organization between the pretest and posttest in addition to the training. Without a control group, one can never be certain what brought about the changes. Design 3 uses a control group but is still weak. Even if we found a difference in performance between the trained and untrained groups, we have no assurance that these two groups were comparable in knowledge of the subject being taught prior to the training program.

A recommended design is one that entails a training group and a control group, both of which are measured before and after training. In this design, equivalency of groups is achieved by randomly assigning individuals (e.g., with a toss of a coin) to the two conditions. Although this design cannot be said to be perfect, it controls for most extraneous factors and is feasible in most organizations.

R	T_1	X	T_2	Before and after
R	T_1		T_2	training with control group

In a nutshell, this analysis tells whether or not the trained group showed a significantly greater gain in performance than did the control (untrained) group. If the training program proves to be successful, what should be done for those individuals in the control group? The control group can now be trained and measured subsequent to their learning. In this way, the results obtained from training group two can corroborate the results gotten with the first training group.

The use of two or more control groups permit even more sophisticated experimental designs (Campbell and Stanley, 1966). Unfortunately, these designs are usually not feasible in most organizational settings.

Some Recommendations

Before ending this discussion of training evaluation, there are several general comments that should be made:

1. Do not assume a training or development program is effective because of "hearsay" or because it worked in other organizations. Always evaluate it in your organization.
2. Plan your evaluation of the training program at the same time the program is being developed, not after it is finished.
3. Make certain the measures used to evaluate the training program are reliable, valid, free of contamination, and practical.
4. It is not enough to prove that a change in behavior is statistically significant. You should also determine the practical significance or util-

ity of the training from the organization's viewpoint by comparing the benefits with the costs.

5. Examine the relationship between the effectiveness of the training program and other aspects of the organization such as its selection and placement system.

6. Examine the effectiveness of training over time (e.g., six months after the trainees have returned to their jobs) to make certain that its effects hold up.

A SPECIAL TRAINING PROGRAM: THE HARD-CORE UNEMPLOYED

The passage of Title VII of the 1964 Civil Rights Act has brought about dramatic effects on the hiring and training of increasing numbers of minority group members (e.g., Afro-Americans, Mexican-Americans, American-Indians), women, the physically disabled, and the aged. In response to this law, some organizations have made efforts to hire and train those underprivileged individuals in our society labeled "hardcore unemployed" (HCU). It is difficult to precisely define the term "HCU" because the specific criteria applicants must meet for entrance into HCU training programs varies between organizations. Nevertheless, the typical HCU individual is a member of a minority group, has been unemployed for more than a year, has never received intensive skill training, and has a sixth-grade education with a third-grade reading level and a fourth-grade math level (Adelberg, 1969). Moreover, he/she is usually under 22 years of age and of a poverty level specified by the Department of Labor (Goodman, Salipante, and Paransky, 1973). It is obvious from these characteristics that the training and retaining of the HCU is an enormous challenge.

One of the main objectives of all HCU training efforts is to provide minority group members with the skills and attitudes that will allow them to adapt to the predominant culture which is employed, better educated, of a middle-class socioeconomic level, and values the work ethic (Friedlander & Greenberg, 1971). In order to accomplish this socialization process, most programs have focused on some combination of the following three areas of training (Goldstein, 1974):

1. *Remedial Education.* This consists of such subject areas as basic English and math, written communication, speech, vocabulary, and reading.

2. *Specific Job Skills.* This consists of training in such skills as auto repair, retail selling, welding, typing, and grocery store clerking.

3. *Motivational and Attitude Factors.* This consists of topics such as how to conduct oneself in an interview, the importance of attendance and punctuality, acceptable work attitudes, grooming, and personal hygiene.

Several articles have appeared in the literature on training the HCU. A review of these articles reveals that few programs have had any demonstrable utility (Goldstein, 1974). There is little indication that training improves the retention or performance of the HCU worker despite large expenditures of money by private companies and the federal government.

What can an organization do to improve the effectiveness of its HCU training? The four suggestions discussed below should be kept in mind when designing HCU training programs:

1. The work effectiveness and retention of the HCU depends upon the amount of supportiveness of the organizational climate in which he/she is placed (Friedlander & Greenberg, 1971). Several studies have shown that the perceived supportiveness by the HCU worker of the first-level supervisor and peers greatly affects the HCU's work behavior (Beatty, 1971; Quinn, Fine, and Levitin, 1970). The implication of this finding for our purposes is that organizations must improve the social climate in which HCU workers find themselves by training and orienting the supervisors and co-workers who will most frequently come into contact with them. As an example, one of the authors recently completed an orientation session with supervisors and co-workers before initiating a three-year on-the-job training program for minority group workers. Listed below are some of the topics discussed during these small group orientation sessions:

The company's policies regarding the hiring and training of minority group members.

Stereotypes held by the supervisors and co-workers about minority group people.

Fears and stereotypes held by the trainees regarding the supervisors and workers.

Strengths and weaknesses of the trainees.

Methods of handling specific problems (e.g., tardiness, absences) that may arise.

2. Research findings indicate that HCU trainees are more willing to conform to middle-class socialization attempts from black than white counselors (Goodman et al., 1973).

3. There are significant individual differences among HCU workers that are often overlooked. For example, several studies have reported a greater dropout rate for younger HCU workers during training; higher job retention for females than males; higher turnover rates for unmarried HCU workers; and higher retention rates for those born in the rural South as opposed to the urban North (Goodman et al., 1973). The important point here is that these individual differences should be taken into account when designing HCU training programs. Surely, a young unmarried male

from the urban North would have to be dealt with differently (e.g., level of pay, supervisory support, nature of the job, counselor-trainee interactions) than an older married female from the rural South.

4. In order for the program to be successful, the HCU trainee must believe that his/her participation in the training leads to more desirable rewards or outcomes than not being in training (Goodman et al., 1973). This implies that the training program must place its trainees in jobs which are perceived by them as leading to valued outcomes (e.g., high wages, interesting work, opportunity for future advancement, etc.). Unless trainees can expect these behavior-reward contingencies, they will see the training program as just another futile exercise leading nowhere and, therefore, drop out.

SUMMARY

Personnel training is the process whereby employees learn the skills, knowledge, attitudes, and behaviors necessary to perform their jobs effectively. Development is training designed to improve the decision-making and human relations skills of managers. Most organizations have some form of training and development program. Such programs are a major means of improving employee performance and satisfaction. Some organizations also conduct special programs to train "disadvantaged" and "hard-core unemployed" persons, and these programs involve some unique problems.

The first step in designing a training or development program should be the identification of training needs. This entails an organization analysis, a job analysis, and a person analysis. These analyses should be part of an ongoing program of manpower planning and human resource administration.

To be conducted successfully, any training or development program should take into consideration certain fundamental principles of learning. Traditional learning principles include: whole and part learning, meaningfulness of subject matter, transfer of training, trainee motivation, individual differences in learning patterns, knowledge of results, active practice, repetition, and overlearning. Some newer learning principles involve identification of task elements and optimal sequencing of these elements during training.

Training and development programs should be evaluated systematically to insure that they are effective and economical. The evaluation process should use an experimental design that indicates whether changes are due to the training rather than to some other cause. Several kinds of criterion variables should be used, including: trainee reactions, acquisition of knowledge, change in actual trainee job behavior, improvement in trainee performance, and the economic utility of the training program.

REVIEW AND DISCUSSION QUESTIONS

1. Describe or explain each of the following key terms: organization analysis, person analysis, learning, negative transfer, part training, overlearning, shaping.
2. How should an organization systematically determine its training needs?
3. Why do some trainees exhibit a plateau in the course of learning?
4. Why has the evaluation of training programs been such a neglected area in some organizations?
5. Certain principles of learning can be very useful in designing training and development programs. Describe in detail the *three* principles which you believe are most applicable for improving the training process.
6. The hard-core unemployed face unique problems in the world of work. What are these problems and how can they be overcome?
7. What new psychological principles does Gagné argue for?
8. Design a study to determine whether a training program for improving the interpersonal skills of managers is effective. Be specific in explaining your experimental design and your measures.

REFERENCES

Adelberg, M. Industrial training of the hard-core unemployed. *Personnel,* 1969, *46, 22–27.*

Bass, B. M., & Barrett, G. V. *Man, work and organizations: An introduction to industrial and organizational psychology.* Boston: Allyn and Bacon, 1972.

Bass, B. M., & Vaughn, J. A. *Training in industry: The management of learning.* Belmont, Calif.: Wadsworth Publishing Co., 1966.

Beatty, R. W. First and second level supervision and the job performance of the hard-core unemployed. Paper presented at the meeting of the American Psychological Association, Washington, D.C., September 1971.

Blum, M. L., & Naylor, J. C. *Industrial psychology.* New York: Harper & Row, 1968.

Campbell, D. T., & Stanley, J. C. *Experimental and quasi-experimental designs for research.* Chicago: Rand McNally, 1966.

Campbell, J. P. Personnel training and development. *Annual Review of Psychology.* Palo Alto, Calif.: Annual Reviews, 1971.

Campbell, J. P., Dunnette, M. D., Lawler, E. E., III, & Weick, K. E., Jr. *Managerial behavior, performance, and effectiveness.* New York: McGraw-Hill, 1970.

Catalanello, R. F., & Kirkpatrick, D. L. Evaluating training programs—the state of the art. *Training and Development Journal,* 1968, *22, 2–9.*

Ellis, H. C. *The transfer of learning.* New York: Macmillan, 1965.

Friedlander, F., & Greenberg, S. Effect of job attitudes, training, and organization climate on performance of the hard-core unemployed. *Journal of Applied Psychology*, 1971, 55, 287–95.

Gagné, R. M.   Military training and principles of learning. *American Psychologist*, 1962, 17, 83–91.

Goldstein, I. I.   *Training: program development and evaluation*. Monterey, Calif.: Brooks/Cole Publishing Co., 1974.

Goodman, P. S., Salipante, P., & Paransky, H.   Hiring, training, and retaining the hard-core unemployed: A selected review. *Journal of Applied Psychology*, 1973, 58, 23–33.

Kirkpatrick, D. L.   Techniques for evaluating training programs. *Journal of the American Society of Training Directors*, 1959, 13, 3–9, 21–26; 1960, 14, 13–18, 28–32.

Kirkpatrick, D. L. Evaluation of training.   In R. L. Craig and L. R. Bittel (Eds.), *Training and Development Handbook*. New York: McGraw-Hill, 1967.

Kolasa, B. J.   *Introduction to behavioral science for business*. New York: Wiley, 1969.

McGehee, W., & Thayer, P. W.   *Training in business and industry*. New York: Wiley, 1961.

Quinn, R., Fine, B., & Levitin, T.   Turnover and training: A social-psychological study of disadvantaged workers. Unpublished paper, Survey Research Center, University of Michigan, 1970.

Wexley, K. N., & Thornton, C. L.   Effect of verbal feedback of test results upon learning. *The Journal of Educational Research*, 1972, 66, 119–121.

14

TRAINING METHODS AND MANAGEMENT DEVELOPMENT

WHEN designing training programs, there is a large variety of methods and techniques from which to choose. In this chapter, we have tried to give the reader a feel for the range of training methods that are currently being used by organizations. These techniques incorporate some of the principles of learning discussed in the previous chapter.

In reviewing the methods, we have grouped them according to whether they are typically carried out on- or off-the-job site. Of course, some of them are used in both circumstances. The off-the-job methods have been subdivided further into information presentation techniques and simulation methods (Campbell, Dunnette, Lawler, & Weick, 1970). Each method is described together with its advantages and disadvantages and the research evidence bearing on its effectiveness. When there is little or no research data supporting a method, we are not hesitant about pointing this out. In fact, it is hoped that the reader will come away from this chapter with the realization that considerably more research is needed in this area. At the present time, relatively little is known about which training and development method is best for what, whom, or when.

OFF-SITE METHODS

Information Presentation Techniques

Information presentation techniques include those approaches which try to modify the skills, knowledge, and attitudes of trainees without requiring them to participate in any simulated practice away from the job and/or actual practice on the job itself.

LECTURE. Considered in relation to the traditional learning principles, the lecture method appears weak. There is little opportunity for active practice, reinforcement, overlearning, knowledge of results, or transfer of learning. In addition, because all people involved must receive the same exact training, the method cannot readily adapt itself to individual differences among trainees in their motivation, abilities, personality characteristics, and so on. Probably for these reasons and others, the lecture method has been downgraded and underestimated by authors (e.g., Bass and Vaughn, 1966; Korman, 1971; McGehee and Thayer, 1961) and by training directors alike. Table 14–1 summarizes the results of a survey conducted to determine how training directors of Fortune's largest 500 corporations rate nine different training methods for achieving each of six training objectives (Carroll, Paine, & Ivancevich, 1972). In general, the results show that the lecture with questions is ranked as *least* effective of all the nine training methods.

A review of the literature reveals that the bias and negative attitude toward the lecture method may not be completely warranted. In general, the research shows that the lecture is more effective for the acquisition of knowledge and has more participant acceptability than training directors believe (Carroll et al., 1972). For example, in reviewing studies comparing programmed instruction to conventional lectures in industrial situations, it was concluded that most studies show neither statistically or practically significant differences in favor of either approach when immediate learning and retention are considered (Nash, Muczyk, and Vettori, 1971). Similarly, reviews of studies comparing the lecture and group discussion (Buxton, 1956; Dietrick, 1960; Stovall, 1958; Verner and Dickinson, 1967) have shown them to be equally effective methods for acquisition of knowledge by college students. Several studies have even shown that some managers prefer the lecture to the more nondirective group discussion approach (House, 1962; Mann and Mann, 1959). Thus, it appears that the lecture can be an effective and, we might add, economical method of conveying information to sizeable groups of trainees.

On the negative side, studies have shown that the lecture method by itself is not as effective as others such as role playing or case study for changing attitudes, developing problem solving skills, or improving interpersonal competence (Carroll et al., 1972). Using the lecture by itself in an attempt to achieve these training objectives is a sheer waste of time and money. The authors know of too many managers who have attended a company-sponsored lecture on such topics as "human relations" or "participatory management" and have left the lecture with no idea how to apply what they have learned to their jobs.

TELEVISION AND FILMS. Contrary to popular opinion, there is substantial evidence to suggest that there are no significant differences in learning achieved using audio-visual devices such as TV and films instead of con-

TABLE 14–1
Ratings of Training Directors on Effectiveness of Alternative Methods for Various Training Objectives

Training Method	Knowledge Acquisition Mean	Mean Rank	Changing Attitudes Mean	Mean Rank	Problem-Solving skills Mean	Mean Rank	Interpersonal Skills Mean	Mean Rank	Participant Acceptance Mean	Mean Rank	Knowledge Retention Mean	Mean Rank
Case study	3.56[b]	2	3.43[d]	4	3.69[b]	1	3.02[d]	4	3.80[d]	2	3.48[e]	2
Conference (discussion) method	3.33[d]	3	3.54[d]	3	3.26[c]	4	3.21[d]	3	4.16[a]	1	3.32[f]	5
Lecture (with questions)	2.53	9	2.20	8	2.00	9	1.90	8	2.74	8	2.49	8
Business games	3.00	6	2.73[f]	5	3.58[b]	2	2.50[e]	5	3.78[d]	3	3.26[f]	6
Movie films	3.16[g]	4	2.50[f]	6	2.24[g]	7	2.19[g]	6	3.44[g]	5	2.67[h]	7
Programmed instruction	4.03[a]	1	2.22[h]	7	2.56[f]	6	2.11[g]	7	3.28[g]	7	3.74[a]	1
Role playing	2.93	7	3.56[d]	2	3.27[e]	3	3.68[b]	2	3.56[c]	4	3.37[f]	4
Sensitivity training (T-group)	2.77	8	3.96[a]	1	2.98[e]	5	3.95[b]	1	3.33[g]	6	3.44[f]	3
Television lecture	3.10[g]	5	1.99	9	2.01	8	1.81	9	2.74	9	2.47	9

a. More effective than methods ranked 2 to 9 for this objective at .01 level of significance.
b. More effective than methods ranked 3 to 9 for this objective at .01 level of significance.
c. More effective than methods ranked 4 to 9 for this objective at .01 level of significance.
d. More effective than methods ranked 5 to 9 for this objective at .01 level of significance.
e. More effective than methods ranked 6 to 9 for this objective at .01 level of significance.
f. More effective than methods ranked 7 to 9 for this objective at .01 level of significance.
g. More effective than methods ranked 8 to 9 for this objective at .01 level of significance.
h. More effective than method ranked 9 for this objective at .01 level of significance.

Adapted from S. J. Carroll, F. T. Paine, & J. M. Ivancevich, "The Relative Effectiveness of Training Methods: Expert Opinion and Research," *Personnel Psychology,* 25, (1972), 495–509.

ventional live lectures. In one major review of 393 studies comparing the amount learned in TV courses and conventionally taught courses there were no significant differences found in 65 percent of the comparisons. Of the remaining comparisons, 21 percent favored the television approach while 14 percent favored live lectures (Schramm, 1962).

Television and films offer unique advantages over live lectures and should seriously be considered under the following circumstances:

1. There is a desire to illustrate how some event or procedure should be conducted over time. For instance, demonstrations of welding, soldering, cooking, and electrical wiring could be facilitated with the use of film or TV. Close-ups of apparatus and manual techniques, stop action, instant replay, and slow motion are options not available with live lecture.

2. There is a need to represent events that cannot be created in the lecture (e.g., open heart surgery).

3. The training is going to extend organization-wide and it is far too costly and time consuming to ask the same instructors to travel from plant to plant or to assemble the trainees in one place. Instead, copies of the same TV tapes or films can be mailed to all plants at one time.

CONFERENCE (DISCUSSION) METHOD. The conference method is essentially a small group discussion in which the leader plays a neutral role providing guidance and feedback. The participants take an active role in the discussion and get feedback regarding their individual actions and attitudes from the other participants and the leader. The purpose of the planned meeting is for the group to discuss a particular topic selected by the leader or by the participants themselves (Campbell et al., 1970).

The object of the conference method is basically threefold (McCormick & Tiffin, 1974): (1) developing the decision-making and problem-solving skills of personnel; (2) presenting new and sometimes complicated material; and (3) changing or modifying attitudes. It is often used in organizations to teach such things as effective communication, general approaches to problem solving and decision making, sales training, safety education, and supervisory human relations.

According to training directors, the conference method is superior to the lecture in modifying attitudes (Carroll et al., 1972). Their opinion is well confirmed by several research studies showing that the discussion method is more effective than the lecture in changing adult behavior (Bond, 1956; Butler, 1966; Levine and Butler, 1952; Lewin, 1958; Silber, 1962). On the other hand, at the present time there is no research supporting the claim that the discussion method leads to a better understanding of new information or that it improves decision-making and problem-solving skills.

One problem with this method is its restriction to small groups and, therefore, its high cost. Nevertheless, this method of training incorporates active participation, reinforcement, and immediate knowledge of results. Its effectiveness depends greatly on the discussion leader's skill, education, and personality (Bass and Barrett, 1972). An untrained discussion leader can easily make a successful conference into an authoritarian lecture resulting in participants resisting all attempts to modify their behavior.

PROGRAMMED INSTRUCTION. Programmed instruction (PI) is a training approach consisting of the following basic characteristics: (1) the training material is broken up into discrete steps or frames; (2) these frames are ordered in a logical sequence which typically progresses from the simple to the complex; (3) at the end of each frame the trainee is asked to give a response which assesses his knowledge of the material in that frame; and (4) the trainee is given immediate feedback regarding the correctness of the response made. If the response is correct, the learner proceeds to the next frame; if the response is incorrect, the trainee's progress is held until the correct response is exhibited.

Incorporated into these elements of PI are many of the principles of learning we have discussed earlier.

1. Immediate reinforcement—a trainee is permitted to proceed to the next frame when the answer is correct.
2. Individual differences—each trainee proceeds independently at own particular pace.
3. Active practice—trainees actively respond by answering questions, making decisions, and solving problems.
4. Knowledge of results—trainees are told the correctness of their responses immediately.
5. Meaningfulness of material—the units of information are "programmed" in the most comprehensible sequence for the subject matter at hand.

Several varieties of PI methods are currently being used in organizational settings (e.g., teaching machines and programmed books). An example of these programmed materials is presented in Figure 14–1.

What can be concluded about the effectiveness of this training approach? Nash, Muczyk, and Vettori (1971) reviewed the results of over 100 studies using PI in industrial and academic situations. They concluded that the major advantage of PI is that it almost always reduces training time. Trainees can be taught the same amount of information as other methods in about one third the time. However, contrary to many hopes and expectations, PI procedures do not appear to improve training performance in terms of immediate learning or retention over time compared to conventional methods.

The costs of developing PI materials are substantial. It is not unusual for a new industrial program to cost anywhere from $50,000 to $150,000,

FIGURE 14–1
An Example of Programmed Instruction

Directions: Beside the first frame place a strip of heavy or dark paper which covers the left-hand margin. Read the first frame and write your answer in the space provided; then slide the paper downward just enough so that the correct answer is exposed. After insuring that your answer(s) to the first item is correct, complete the second frame. Repeat this procedure throughout the program.

1. Programmed instruction involves several basic principles of learning. One of these, called the principle of *small steps*, is based on the premise that new information must be presented in _____ steps.

 small

2. The learner gradually acquires more and more information, but always in _____ _____ .

 small steps

3. Because active readers generally acquire more knowledge than passive readers, programmed instruction also is based on the principle of *active participation*. Writing key words as one is reading involves the principle of _____ participation.

 active

4. While reading a book, an uninterested learner may slip into a passive state and discover that he cannot recall what he has just "read." In using programmed instruction the learner is prompted to remain alert by writing the key words, thus utilizing the principle of _____ _____ .

 active
 participation

5. In these two techniques of programmed instruction, information is presented in _____ _____ , and occasionally key words are missing, thus requiring the learner's _____ _____ to complete the statements.

 small steps

 active
 participation

6. A third principle, *immediate knowledge*

FIGURE 14–1   *(continued)*

knowledge

immediate
of results

immediate knowledge of
results

small steps

active
participation; immediate
knowledge of results

review

small
steps

of results, is illustrated when a professor returns quiz papers to his students at the end of the class in which they were written. These students receive almost immediate _____ of results.

7. If a student makes an incorrect response at any point in programmed instruction, he discovers his mistake because the correct answer may be seen immediately after the frame, before the next one is considered. Thus, in programmed instruction, the learner receives _____ knowledge _____ _____.

8. Notice that in programmed instruction, unlike the evaluation of term papers, "immediate" does not mean a week or even a day but rather a few seconds. The reader of the program is continuously informed concerning his progress; he receives _____ _____ _____ _____.

9. Let us review the three techniques of programmed instruction already considered. By means of _____ _____, the reader learns new material, which he acquires through _____ _____ followed by _____ _____ _____ _____.

10. At this point, the fourth principle, *review,* already is apparent to the reader. Since new information may interfere with the recall of previously acquired information, earlier material is periodically repeated in programmed instruction. Thus programming techniques also involve the principle of _____.

11. On Sundays many coaches show their players movies of Saturday's game. Each play is seen in slow motion, a procedure which suggests the technique of _____ _____. As the films are shown, various team members are asked to make comments about the plays. This pro-

FIGURE 14–1   (concluded)

active participation	cedure requires _____ _____ on the part of the players. The coaches do not wait until the middle of the next week to show the films because the play-
immediate knowledge of results	ers profit most from _____ _____ _____ _____. Sometimes the movies are shown two or three times before the next practice and often a single play is rerun several times. This procedure is similar to the pro-
review	gramming technique of _____.
	12. List the four programming techniques below:
small steps	1. _____
active participation	2. _____
immediate knowledge of results	3. _____
review	4. _____

Adapted from N. L. Munn, L. D. Fernald, Jr., and L. Carmichael, *Introduction to Psychology* (Boston: Houghton Mifflin, 1972), pp. 249–250.

especially when it is fairly complex and involves hardware (Nash et al., 1971). The crucial question for any organization contemplating PI is whether the costs involved in the purchase and/or development of PI materials will be returned in the savings in training time. This, of course, will depend upon several factors such as number of people to be trained, the type of PI installation proposed, and amount of training needed for each individual.

COMPUTER-ASSISTED INSTRUCTION. One of the newest developments in instructional methodology is computer-assisted instruction. An individual interacts directly with a computer by means of electronic typewriters, pens that draw lines on cathode-ray tubes, and devices that present auditory material (Goldstein, 1974). The computer is capable of assessing the trainee's progress and adapting to his particular needs by virtue of its remarkable storage and memory capacities.

At the present time, it is difficult to reach any definite conclusions regarding the applicability of computer-assisted instruction due to the small number of studies that have been conducted. Most research on this method has been carried on in academic institutions. Until recently, little use was made of computer-assisted instruction in industrial, military, or government organizations.

T-GROUP (OR SENSITIVITY) TRAINING.   One of the most widely used management development techniques is known variously as T-group (*T* for "training") training, sensitivity training, and laboratory education. The popularity of this method largely stems from the discouragement many organizations have experienced when attempting to improve the interpersonal behavior of managers using such conventional informational presentation techniques as lectures and conferences. These organizations send their managerial personnel to either the National Training Laboratories (NTL), university institutes, or consulting firms for sensitivity training.

Although the objectives of T-group training have been stated differently by various people (e.g., Argyris, 1964; Bradford, Gibb and Benne, 1964; Schein and Bennis, 1965), its goals have been neatly summarized by Campbell, Dunnette, Lawler, and Weick (1970, p. 239) as follows:

Goal 1:   To give the trainee an understanding of how and why he acts towards other people as he does and of the way in which he affects them.

Goal 2:   To provide some insight into why other people act the way they do.

Goal 3:   To teach the participants how to "listen," that is, actually hear what other people are saying rather than concentrating on a reply.

Goal 4:   To provide insights concerning how groups operate and what sorts of processes groups go through under certain conditions.

Goal 5:   To foster an increased tolerance and understanding of the behavior of others.

Goal 6:   To provide a setting in which an individual can try out new ways of interacting with people and receive feedback as to how these new ways affect them.

Some T-groups put more emphasis on the goals of enhancing an individual's self-awareness and sensitivity to other persons while other programs concern themselves more with emphasizing the trainee's understanding of group processes. Regardless of the particular emphases sought, most T-groups have similar processes and structural characteristics. The excerpt below provides a good description of the typical T-group procedure:

At the fifth meeting the group's feelings about its own progress became the initial focus of discussion. The "talkers" participated as usual, conversation shifting rapidly from one point to another. Dissatisfaction was mounting, expressed through loud, snide remarks by some and through apathy by others.

George Franklin appeared particularly disturbed. Finally pounding the table, he exclaimed, "I don't know what is going on here! I should be paid for listening to this drivel? I'm getting just a bit sick of wasting my time here. If the profs don't put out—I quit!" George was pleased; he was angry, and he had said so. As he sat back in his chair, he felt he had the group behind him. He felt he had the guts to say what most of the others were thinking! Some members of the group applauded loudly, but others showed obvious disapproval. They wondered why George was excited over so insignificant an issue, why he hadn't done something constructive rather than just sounding off as usual. Why, they wondered, did he say their comments were "drivel"?

George Franklin became the focus of discussion. "What do you mean, George, by saying this nonsense?" "What do you expect, a neat set of rules to meet all your problems?" George was getting uncomfortable. These were questions difficult for him to answer. Gradually he began to realize that a large part of the group disagreed with him; then he began to wonder why. He was learning something about people he hadn't known before. ". . . How does it feel, George, to have people disagree with you when you thought you had them behind you? . . ."

Bob White was first annoyed with George and now with the discussion. He was getting tense, a bit shaky perhaps. Bob didn't like anybody to get a raw deal, and he felt that George was getting it. At first Bob tried to minimize George's outburst, and then he suggested that the group get on to the real issues; but the group continued to focus on George. Finally Bob said, "Why don't you leave George alone and stop picking on him. We're not getting anywhere this way."

With the help of the leaders, the group focused on Bob. "What do you mean, 'picking' on him?" "Why, Bob, have you tried to change the discussion?" "Why are you so protective of George?" Bob began to realize that the group wanted to focus on George; he also saw that George didn't think he was being picked on, but felt he was learning something about himself and how others reacted to him. "Why do I always get upset," Bob began to wonder, "when people start to look at each other? Why do I feel sort of sick when people get angry at each other?" . . . Now Bob was learning something about how people saw him, while gaining some insight into his own behavior (Tannenbaum, Weschler, & Massarik, 1961, p. 123).

The controversy over the effectiveness of this approach during the past 20 years can be described as heated. Critics of T-group education (e.g., House, 1967; Odiorne, 1963), have made the following comments:

1. Not a single piece of research has been reported which proves that T-groups change the effectiveness of trainees back in their organizations. This is inconsistent with the business and money-making world in which we live.

2. There are no selection standards for admittance. Any person with the registration fee can attend. The manager may already be sensitive and aware, in fact he may be too sensitive for his particular kind of organization and subordinates.

3. There are anecdotal reports of individuals having serious emotional

breakdowns and needing psychiatric care as a result of participating in T-groups. As Kirchner (1965, p. 212) states:

> Do we really want to rip off the "executive mask," which hides from the individual his true feelings, desires, and knowledge of self? Most people have taken many years to build up this "mask" or to build up their psychological defenses. While it can be enlightening to find out that nobody loves you and that some people think you have undesirable traits, this can also be a very shocking experience to individuals and not necessarily a beneficial one.

4. In most labs, the trainers have only a vague notion of how to conduct their groups. They have little idea of the objectives of individual sessions, and are unable to do any careful planning so that progressive stages of development will occur. They are also not professionally qualified to deal with these emotional learning sessions that deliberately induce anxiety, interpersonal feedback, and experimentation with new modes of behavior.

5. Not only are the trainees unaware of what the outcomes of training will be; but, since there are no controls and anything can happen, the trainers are too.

6. The objectives of T-group training are often stated in such vague terminology as developing the manager "to feel" . . . "to relate" . . . "to understand" . . . "to be sensitive." Little behavioral terminology is used to describe what the trainees will do, do differently, or stop doing as a result of training.

7. Since the effectiveness of the method has not yet been proven and possible damages may be severe, it is unethical to offer T-groups on a commercial basis and to make claims about its beneficial effects on management practices.

8. It is an invasion of personal privacy and not rightfully within the domain of organizations, consulting firms, and business schools.

9. Even if T-group training could result in more considerate, sensitive, and supportive managers, there is no guarantee that these characteristics are beneficial in all organizational contexts.

10. Organizations coerce their members into attending T-groups. It is not uncommon among organizations to administer training to entire departments or divisional units. Superiors often "suggest" to subordinates that they attend.

In defense of laboratory education, Argyris (1963) has provided the following facts about T-group training as he sees them.

1. More research has been conducted on T-group education than all other management development programs combined.

2. Psychotic breakdowns at NTL is no more frequent than in the population at large. Out of over 10,000 cases, there have been only four trainees who have had nervous breakdowns, and all of these people had previous psychiatric histories.

3. In order for someone to become an NTL trainer, he/she must have completed an approved graduate training (usually a Ph.D.) program. The individual is then put through a rigorous three-month training program which entails participating as a member of a laboratory program, conducting labs under the supervision of a senior faculty member, attendance at special meetings, and final approval by one's peers.

4. At NTL, the staff usually meets for three days, several months before each lab to plan it and develop assignments to work on back at home. Later on, another few days are spent on additional planning.

5. Lab training at NTL does have objectives. Before every laboratory, hours are spent discussing these objectives.

Putting this controversy aside, what conclusions can be reached about the effectiveness of T-group training as a result of research evidence? First, the evidence is reasonably convincing that T-group education does bring about changes in the "back home" behaviors of participants. There is still some problem specifying the exact nature of these changes since they seem to differ for various individuals. Despite this, it does appear that many of the group changes found in studies are in line with some of the main objectives of T-group training, namely, increased sensitivity, more open communication, and more flexibility in role behavior (Campbell & Dunnette, 1968). At the present time, these behavior-change studies form the main evidence supporting the organizational utility of laboratory training. Unfortunately, there is no convincing evidence that these behavior changes result in any tangible profits for the organization.

In our opinion, if T-group training is to be utilized in organizations, the following is needed:

1. Voluntary participation and withdrawal of all participants.

2. Careful selection, training, and licensing of T-group leaders.

3. Screening of participants by means of qualified judges and/or psychometric instruments. This screening must take into consideration the individual's emotional state, need for this type of training, and back home situation.

4. Clarification of the training objectives in behavioral terms.

5. Continued research to study the effectiveness of this approach using both behavior and results measures (see Chapter 10).

BEHAVIOR MODELING. One of the most prevalent ways we all learn social behavior is by observing and imitating models. Think about how much of your adult behavior results from childhood imitations of your parents. Goldstein and Sorcher (1974) have incorporated modeling principles into a supervisory development program for improving the competence of managers in handling subordinates. The training begins with a discussion of leadership behavior in order to establish what a supervisor does in behavioral terms. Next, a series of "modeling displays" or videotapes is shown to the trainees. Each videotape is introduced by a high credibility figure, preferably the model's boss, who defines the kinds of behavior to be modeled during the tape. The model's boss also makes certain concluding statements after each videotape so as to provide additional reinforcement for the model's behavior. The trainees then respond to the modeling display in terms of how well they felt the model handled the situation. This phase of the program is followed by role-playing exercises, in which the target behaviors are "tried on" by the trainees. In the last stage of the program, the trainees are asked to describe how they felt during the role-playing and how the situation was handled. The more adaptive behaviors are verbally reinforced during this phase by the trainee's colleagues and by the trainer. Participants learn, for example, that it is important to maintain a subordinate's self-esteem, that most problems cannot be solved at a single confrontation or meeting, and that it is important to make employees feel you are concerned with their success.

Evidence on the effectiveness of behavior modeling training in organizations has been reported by Goldstein and Sorcher (1974). In one study, the voluntary quit rate of new, young employees from disadvantaged backgrounds was substantially reduced by conducting parallel modeling programs for these employees and their supervisors. In another study, the results showed that average performance was significantly higher for subordinates supervised by supervisors who had participated in a behavior modeling program, as compared to a control group of untrained supervisors. The authors believe that behavior modeling is a potentially useful method of management development, but that more research is needed before any definitive statements can be made about its overall usefulness.

Simulation Methods

Simulation is an approach which replicates certain essential characteristics of the real world organization so that trainees can react to it as if it were the real thing and, consequently, transfer what has been learned back to their jobs. Employees can learn to operate complex equipment (e.g., airplanes, boilers) free of danger to themselves and co-workers, practice emergency procedures before they are exposed to danger on their jobs, try out new interpersonal behaviors in a relatively safe psychological climate, and practice new behaviors and receive immediate knowledge of results (Goldstein, 1974).

EQUIPMENT SIMULATORS. Sometimes it is too costly, inefficient, or just plain dangerous to teach an individual or team of individuals motor skills while on the job itself. In these cases, facsimilies of the equipment are set up away from the actual work situation with hazards removed, pressure for results minimized, individualized feedback increased, and opportunity for repeated practice provided. The trainee does not have to worry about damaging expensive company equipment (assuming that the simulator is less expensive than the actual equipment), slowing down the normal productive process, or being embarrassed by making errors in the presence of future co-workers.

Listed below are several examples of equipment simulators currently being used by organizations. Two things should be noted. First, they range from simple mock-ups to computer-based simulations of complete environments. Second, some are utilized to train single individuals while others are used for team training.

Machine mock-ups for training press and lathe operators.

Automobile simulators for driver education.

Airplane cockpits for training pilots and flight crews.

Thirty-foot utility poles with special safety harnesses for training telephone company personnel.

In designing simulators, it is important to facilitate positive transfer of training by having a close correspondence between the simulator and the actual work situation. Simulators must possess both physical fidelity (representation of the essential physical components of the job) and, even more importantly, psychological fidelity (representation of the essential behavioral processes necessary to do the job). There are no shortcuts to obtaining fidelity. It can be achieved only through careful analyses, testing, and retesting (Goldstein, 1974). Because of this, skill development via simulators is usually quite an expensive undertaking. An organization must seriously consider the cost/benefit ratios before attempting to develop equipment simulators.

CASE STUDY. The case study method was initiated at the Harvard School of Business and involves presenting a trainee (typically a manager or supervisor) with a written description of an actual or hypothetical organizational problem. The trainee is given time to study the case privately and to prepare a solution. Then, the individual meets with other trainees and as a small group (e.g., 5–10 people) they discuss the various solutions proposed and attempt to answer questions such as "What basic managerial principles underlie this case?" "How might this problem have been avoided?" "What should be done to prevent this situation from reoccurring?" The kinds of problems used vary in length and difficulty depending upon the skill and experience level of the trainees involved.

This method has the following intended purposes: (1) to show that there is usually no single or easy solution to complex organizational problems; (2) to show how rarely two trainees view a case in exactly the same way and arrive at the same solution; (3) to help trainees discover for themselves certain managerial principles; and (4) to help them develop their skills in diagnosing organizational problems. How closely these objectives are met depends greatly upon the skill of the trainer who must encourage the participation of all trainees and emphasize the discovery of underlying principles rather than quick solutions.

Critics of this technique point to its inability to teach general principles and its lack of guided instruction concerning the inferences that trainees draw from their case discussions (Campbell et al., 1970). Nevertheless, survey results indicate that the case method is considered by training directors to be the best method of developing problem-solving skills (Carroll et al., 1972). Unfortunately, research on the effectiveness of this method of training is limited in number and restricted to college populations. The research that has been done suggests that: (1) business games lead to higher performance than case studies on such measures as final written examinations and standardized cases (McKenney, 1962; Raia, 1966); (2) trainees may grow tired of case study after being exposed to it for a while (Castore, 1951) and find other methods more involving and interesting; and (3) there is more evidence showing that role playing develops problem-solving skills than there is evidence for the case study method.

ROLE PLAYING.   Instead of just presenting a problem for discussion, role playing requires the trainees to play out the parts of various characters in the case. Participants are told to imagine themselves in the situations created for them by the trainer and to try to take on the feelings and attitudes of the people they are pretending to be. Once the role playing is begun, interactions among participants are spontaneous. A critique session follows immediately after their playing of the problem. Some trainees find it difficult to "get into" their roles at first because they feel self-conscious or because they tend to overact. With proper orientation by the trainer, this usually disappears after a short while.

There are several variations of the role playing method. The two most widely used are role reversal and multiple role playing. In role reversal trainees who have differences of opinion are asked to exchange roles. For example, supervisors and union stewards, superiors and subordinates, or even two opposing managers reverse roles in order to give them the feel of experiencing and solving problems from viewpoints other than their own. Hopefully, differences in opinions will be reduced by making each person more aware of the other's needs and attitudes. It has been demonstrated that when a person is forced to verbalize opinions opposite to his/her own and defend these opinions to others, the individual's own private attitudes are modified in the direction of the role being played (Janis & King, 1954; Janis & Mann, 1965). This is true regardless of how much the trainee is satisfied with his/her role playing performance (King and Janis, 1956). The important point here seems to be that the trainee privately shifts attitudes so that they are consistent with what he/she is saying (Kelman, 1953).

In multiple role playing a large number (usually 20–30) of trainees are divided into small groups of five or six persons each. The trainer presents a problem which each of the subgroups is asked to role play. Following the role playing within groups, the entire group of trainees are reassembled to share and compare their experiences (Maier and Zerfoss, 1952). It should be noted that multiple role playing is quite economical since large groups of individuals can be trained at the same time. In addition, the various teams can be given systematically different directions (unknown to them), so that the effects of these differences will be dramatically revealed during the final discussion session (Bass & Barrett, 1972). For instance, different communication networks might be established in each of the groups resulting in some rather distinct differences in problem solutions and member satisfactions between groups.

More evaluative information is urgently needed on role playing. At the present time, role playing has been shown to be effective in studying small group leadership skills (Maier, 1953; Maier and Hoffman, 1960; Maier and Maier, 1957), increasing sensitivity to the motivation of others (Bolda & Lawshe, 1962), improving interviewing skills (Van Schaack, 1957), enhancing ability to develop innovative solutions to human relations problems (Solem, 1960), and modifying attitudes (Culbertson, 1957). The method provides opportunity for practice and does a good job of bridging the gap between "knowing" and "doing" so seldom seen with other management training approaches.

Two problems with this method deserve mention. It is true that it provides the trainee with both immediate reinforcement and knowledge of results. However, since trainees receive feedback primarily from the other role playing participants rather than from the trainer, it is possible for a trainee to behave inappropriately from an organizational viewpoint and still be reinforced for this behavior by the others. Second, managerial personnel have indicated only fair acceptance of this method of training (Bolda and Lawshe, 1962). In light of these problems, the authors would recommend that role playing be used in collaboration with other management development methods such as appraisal feedback, goal setting, case study, and lecture.

MANAGEMENT GAMES. Games are used today in industrial, government, and educational organizations. They are found in management development programs, business school courses, and the military. Imperial Oil has a game for training managers of service stations; the Pillsbury Company has one to train top level managers in new divisionalization and decentralization policies; the air force has a game developed for them by the Rand Corporation in which players must schedule aircraft expenditures, personnel, parts, and equipment; universities such as Stanford and UCLA offer thousands of students the opportunity to participate in a wide variety of business games. The objectives of most games are to:

1. Teach general management skills such as decision making, setting of priorities, long-range planning, and effective use of time, personnel, and equipment.
2. Convey information about how various parts of a complex organization operate and interact.
3. Provide an appreciation of the range of factors that must be considered in making wise decisions.
4. Experience the consequences of making decisions which are either too hasty, slow, risky, or conservative.
5. Realize the importance of dealing effectively with others.

It would be helpful at this point to give a brief description of a typical management game for the benefit of those readers who have not yet participated in one. The basic procedures of play are similar for most existing games. The following general description of management games by Kibbee et al. (1961) is based on the Remington Rand Univac Marketing Game:

> The game session begins with a briefing. At this time the instructor describes for the participants the type of company they are about to manage, the economic environment, the general nature of the products, and the competitive forces they will face. The scope of their authority, the functions to be filled, the decisions to be made, and the information they will receive are all discussed. In addition the mechanics of play, the purpose of the exercise and the manner in which it relates to the entire educational program are covered.
>
> After the briefing the participants meet with the other members of their management team. In a typical game, involving perhaps forty to fifty executives, there might be six teams each with seven or eight members. The management teams determine their organization, set objectives, decide on the short- and long-range plans necessary to achieve these objectives, and introduce necessary controls and procedures. Typical organizational structures evolve, with presidents, vice-presidents, etc. In addition to the obvious desire to maximize net profit, other objectives will be set concerning share of market, stabilized production, inventory control and personnel policies.
>
> Games are played in periods, each period being a day, week, month,

quarter, or year, depending on the particular game. The Univac Marketing Game takes place in months. The participants have already received operating reports for December and begin by making decisions for January. A variety of other pertinent information, such as a case history, sales forecast, and reference material on operating costs, production facilities and shipping times is provided. Usually all companies begin in the same condition.

The teams make decisions for January, these are processed by the computer, and operating reports for January are then returned. In most game sessions, management has about a half hour in which to make decisions. Play continues for a simulated year.

In the Univac Marketing Game, each company manufactures one product. All are competing in three regions comprising a common market. The managers set price, spend money on advertising, hire and fire salesmen, set salesmen compensation rate, set production level, engage in special market research projects, etc. The operating reports show the sales obtained, the net profit achieved, and an accumulated year-to-date net profit.

Management is trying to achieve the largest possible net profit, and the team that obtains the greatest accumulated profit is often called the "winner." Good performance in a management game, however, as in a real business, is dependent on many factors such as return on investment, share of market, personnel policies, and the numerous aspects of the company which determine whether it will continue to succeed.

While the participants are busily engaged in operating their companies, other people are observing their performance. Some of these may be guests or visitors, but others may have been specifically selected to follow the proceedings so as to be able later to provide feedback on the human interactions evidenced. These observers may themselves be members of the training course, or may be specially invited social scientists. In some cases elaborate facilities are available for observing and recording the actions of the participants.

At the end of the game play, which may well simulate from six to sixteen months, a discussion session takes place. This "critique" session is held to focus attention on the lessons which were to be taught. The participants have the opportunity of reviewing their performance, discussing management principles with other members of the group, and receiving feedback from the game administrator and observers. Very often the critique takes the form of a report to the "board of directors" and is guided along specific channels by a previously prepared check list. (*Management Games: A New Technique for Executive Development* J. M. Kibbee, C. J. Craft, and B. Nanus [New York: Reinhold Publishing Corporation, 1961], pp. 4–6.)

Games may be quite complex, or, as in the case of those used in assessment centers (see Chapter 11), extremely simple. In some games, computations are made manually or by electronic calculator; in other games, the complexity of the model requires that the results be analyzed and fed back to the trainees by computer. In these computer-based games, a larger number of realistic variables (e.g., strikes, delays of raw materials, new competition, shortages of labor) can be introduced.

There are several advantages of management games. They provide trainees with the opportunity to learn from experience without actually suffering the real life consequences of poor decisions. They compress time thereby providing trainees with many years of management experiences in just a few short days. The games are also intrinsically motivating for the participants due to their realism, the dynamic nature of play, and the immediacy and objectivity of the feedback.

This technique is not without its limitations. Sometimes participants become too motivated and concerned with "beating the system" that they fail to comprehend the principles of management being taught. Others have complained that the method stifles creative approaches to solving problems and that it is too costly compared with other management development techniques. Finally, little scientific research has been done thus far to investigate the effectiveness of this technique. Most of its current popularity stems from its face validity and the persuasiveness of its advocates.

IN-BASKET TECHNIQUE. This method consists of presenting a trainee with a description of a manager's job which he or she is to pretend to assume. Then the person is presented with a "basket" full of letters, memoranda, requests from subordinates, operating statements, customer complaints, and the like. These materials are intended to simulate the kinds of problems an administrator might experience on a given day of work. The trainee is told to solve the problems by working through the in-basket items in the time allotted. The trainee is permitted to plan meetings, issue memoranda, draft letters, delay action, delegate decisions, and determine priorities. Rather than merely indicating what he/she "intends" or "hopes" to do, the trainee is required to actually "take action." Once the time limit (usually one to three hours) is reached, the trainee fills out a form which gives him an opportunity to explain why he took the actions he did. Finally, a critique session is held which permits the trainer and a small group of trainees to evaluate and interpret each trainee's responses. The discussion usually centers around some of the following issues:

Taking versus deferring action.

Ability to consider all the alternatives before making decisions.

Interpersonal relations with peers.

Setting correct priorites.

Ability to see the larger picture.

Acting independently versus seeking advice from superiors.

Incidence and detrimental effects of hasty decisions.

Courteousness to subordinates.

Interpersonal relations with superiors.

Amount of work output completed.

What can one say about the effectiveness of the in-basket technique as a training method? Some of its main advantages are its: (1) acceptability to trainees, (2) inexpensiveness, (3) ease of use with large numbers of people, and (4) amenability to numerical scoring, if desired. Unfortunately, the utility of the in-basket technique for training remains undetermined (Goldstein, 1974). In our opinion, there are four main issues needing attention.

1. Does the trainee transfer the skills learned on the in-basket to the job itself?
2. How should the critique session best be conducted?
3. Should the in-basket be scored subjectively or quantitatively?
4. Do we need to construct an in-basket for each managerial position to insure transfer of learning, or, can we develop general in-baskets which can be used to train all managers?

ON-SITE METHODS

On-the-Job Training (OJT)

One of the oldest and most widely used methods of training consists of assigning new employees to experienced workers and supervisors. Typically, the experienced worker is told by a superior to "break in this new trainee" or "teach Mary your job." The trainee is expected to learn the job by watching the experienced employee and by working with the actual machinery and materials that will be used once the formal training is completed. The skilled worker is expected to provide a good model with whom the trainee can identify and to take time out from his regular duties to guide the new employee.

The approach offers certain advantages, one of which is its economy. Trainees learn while actually producing, thereby partially paying the costs of their instruction. There is no need to establish any off-site training facilities or to hire professional trainers. In terms of the learning principles, the method facilitates positive transfer since the training and actual work situations are almost identical. It provides active practice and immediate knowledge of results. The trainees learn by doing and can know almost immediately whether or not an error has been committed. This feedback can come from the trainer, co-workers, or from seeing defective units.

While OJT can work, often it turns out to be a terrible mistake! This usually happens when an organization uses it to avoid the necessity of designing systematic training programs. Too often, OJT is implemented by simply telling an individual to "train John" with little concern for the trainer's willingness or ability to train someone else. We offer the following suggestions for implementing effective OJT programs.

1. The technique must be chosen in the first place because it is actually felt to be the best strategy for training the particular skills needed.
2. The choice of trainers should be based upon their ability to teach and their desire to take on this added responsibility. Trainers will not necessarily be the most competent and experienced employees; these characteristics do not guarantee that a person has the ability to teach the job to somebody else.
3. Those skilled workers chosen as trainers should be trained in the proper methods of instructions (i.e., use of reinforcement, knowledge of results, distributed practice).
4. Trainers should be convinced that the training of new employees in no way threatens their current job security, seniority, pay level, or shift status.
5. The individuals serving as trainers should realize that this added responsibility will be instrumental in obtaining certain rewards.
6. Adequate evaluation of the trainee's progress needs to be made and fed back to the trainees frequently using reliable and valid measures.
7. Learning must take precedence over production, especially during the early stages of training.
8. There must be careful planning of the stages of learning by the trainer and staff training specialists.
9. Trainers and trainees should be carefully paired so as to minimize any differences in background, language, personality, attitudes, or age which may inhibit communication.
10. Trainees should be rotated to compensate for weaker instruction by some trainers and to expose each trainee to the specific know-hows of various workers.
11. It must be made clear to trainers that their new assignment is by no means a chance to get away from their own jobs and "take a vacation."
12. The organization must realize that there is a possibility that production may be slowed down, equipment damaged, and some defective products made.
13. The trainer must be made to realize the importance of close supervision in order to avoid trainee injuries.
14. OJT should be used in conjunction with other training approaches such as programmed instruction, lectures, and films.

Apprenticeship

Organizations that employ skilled tradesmen such as carpenters, plumbers, masons, printers, and sheetmetal workers may develop journeymen by conducting formal apprenticeship programs. The typical apprenticeship lasts anywhere from two to five years. It includes on-the-job training supplemented with about 144 or more hours per year of related classroom instruction held typically in the evenings at local high schools. The majority of apprentices attend these classes on their own time without pay. Each apprentice is usually given a workbook consisting of reading materials, tests to be taken, and practice problems to be solved. The workbooks permit the students to work at their own individual pace. The classroom instructors are either regular daytime vocational school teachers or skilled craftsmen (i.e., journeymen or supervisors). Many of them use class time for presenting lectures, giving demonstrations, conducting class discussions about actual work experiences, inviting outside speakers, presenting films, or providing skill practice (Strauss, 1968). For example, the school portion of an apprenticeship program for pipefitters might include local building codes, shop arithmetic, blueprint reading, and hydraulics. In general, apprentices learn how to do the work on the job, and learn the facts of their trade in the classroom.

In recent years, apprenticeship training has been the target of much criticism from civil rights groups and from manpower experts. Among the major criticisms have been that they racially discriminate and show preferential treatment for relatives and friends.

It may be surprising to learn that apprenticeship is not a prevalent method of learning skilled trades in this country. In a typical year only about 30,000 people complete apprenticeship programs and gain entry into journeymen status. The majority of skilled tradesmen get their training informally on nonunion, rural, or industrial jobs. These individuals are admitted to the union as skilled tradesmen (not journeymen) without any formal apprenticeship training (Strauss, 1971).

Job Rotation

A frequently used on-site training method is called job rotation. Trainees are placed in different jobs in different parts of the organization for a specified period of time. They may spend several days, months, or even years in different company locations. In this way, they gain an overall perspective of the organization and an understanding of the interrelationships among its departments or divisions. The method is often used with college graduates who have only a vague idea about where in the organization they want to work. Job rotation helps them to sharpen their career objectives before settling on a permanent position. Rotation is used also to develop company managers for higher level executive positions by exposing them to a wide range of experiences in a relatively short span of time.

Probably the major drawback of this method is the fact that it is time consuming and expensive. One wonders whether it is really worthwhile from a cost/benefit standpoint. To maximize its effectiveness, trainees must be placed in company locations where they receive maximum feedback, reinforcement, and monitoring of their performance by competent and interested trainers.

THE RELATIVE ADVANTAGES OF ON- AND OFF-SITE METHODS: A SUMMARIZATION

The major advantage of on-site training is that the problem of transfer of learning is basically eliminated. Trainees learn the job skills, knowledge, and attitudes in the exact physical and social environment in which they will work once formal training is completed. The methods require no special equipment or space. Further, trainees produce while learning thereby minimizing training costs. The most likely disadvantage of on-site training may be that employees acting as trainers are either not capable of or not interested in providing trainees with favorable learning experiences. This can be a particularly serious problem when certain employees are asked to train minority group members and do so half-heartedly!

The most obvious advantage of off-site training is that it provides an environment conducive to learning away from everyday job pressures. For this reason, most management development programs are conducted away from the job setting. Another off-site benefit is the potential use of outside resource people such as retired executives, university faculty, and consultants who have expertise in particular subject areas. Its major drawback is the transfer problem. Too often trainees learn new facts and principles at lectures, workshops, and conferences but have no idea how to apply what they have learned back on their jobs.

The choice between using on-site versus off-site methods depends upon the job, the employees being trained, and the desired results (i.e., improved problem-solving skills, increased sensitivity, etc.). It is safe to say, however, that in most situations a combination of the two approaches would be most beneficial.

METHODS FOR MANAGEMENT DEVELOPMENT

Management development programs became popular in the late 1940s and early 1950s. Prior to their establishment, individuals were responsible for obtaining their own managerial skills by working in their jobs or through whatever other learning experiences they could somehow avail themselves of. Since World War II, management development programs have become an accepted and well-established personnel function in most larger firms and in many smaller ones as well. With the rapidly occurring technological and sociological changes confronting organizations today, it is essential that managers not let their jobs outgrow them. The problem of obsolescent executives can be avoided by organizations exerting continuous pressure on their managers to continue their self-development.

Although management development and organization development (see Chapter 15) overlap greatly, the two areas are different. Organization development is an organization-wide effort designed to increase organizational effectiveness and health by changing such things as structure, cultural norms, climate, intergroup collaboration, motivation, and managerial strategy (Beckhard, 1969). Management development is a narrower concept concerned mainly with improving the effectiveness of individual managers (Strauss and Sayles, 1972).

Many of the conventional training methods presented in the previous section have some value as management development techniques—lectures, conferences, laboratory (T-group) training, case study, role playing, business games, in-baskets, and rotation. These methods have been used for training in a wide variety of subjects including: human relations, problem-solving, decision-making, company policies and practices, communications, and supervision. The emphasis in this section will be on some of the more common on-the-job and off-the-job techniques used primarily in management development programs.

Junior Boards

The concept of the junior board of directors, or "multiple management" as it is sometimes called, was introduced by Charles P. McCormick in 1932 at the McCormick Company in Baltimore. The purpose of these boards is to permit promising junior executives to experience some of the problems and responsibilities faced by high-level managers in their company. The board is ordinarily permitted to study any problems faced by the organization and to make recommendations to the senior board of directors (i.e., the official board elected by the stockholders). The junior board serves in an advisory capacity since the senior board is under no obligation to accept its recommendations. Junior board members get experience in aspects of the business outside their own specialty as well as practical experience in group decision making and teamwork (Beach, 1975).

Understudy Assignments

Some organizations assign their management trainees as understudies to senior executives. An understudy relieves the superior of some duties, thereby learning the superior's job and the superior's unique methods for handling it. As mentioned previously, the benefits that the trainee derives from this type of on-the-job learning depends upon the willingness and ability of the superior to teach effectively. Understudy assignments insure that the organization will have trained personnel immediately available to take over certain key positions as managers vacate them due to retirement, promotions, or transfers.

Performance Appraisal Interviews

In some companies subordinates are never told how they have been evaluated by their superiors. Consequently, many of them never really know where they stand with their bosses. As one engineer commented, "The only time I know that my manager thinks I'm doing a good job is when my wife—who does our banking—tells me that I've gotten a raise." Fortunately, many companies today conduct evaluation interviews. These interviews between workers and superiors are usually conducted once or twice a year and serve two purposes: (1) they enable each subordinate to get feedback as to how he or she is doing in the opinion of the boss, and (2) they give the manager and subordinate an opportunity to discuss how the subordinate can improve his or her performance. These interviews can be an effective management development approach if handled properly. It is generally agreed that the superior should refrain from criticizing subordinates since criticisms lead to defensiveness (e.g., denial of shortcomings, blaming others); assume the role of helper or coach rather than judge; and allow the subordinate to participate in the setting of future performance goals (Meyer, Kay, and French, 1965; Wexley, Singh, and Yukl, 1973).

Coaching

The term "coaching" as used here refers to effective managers assisting certain of their subordinates to perform their management duties and responsibilities more effectively. Unlike evaluation interviews which are formal and scheduled, coaching occurs on an informal and day-to-day basis. The manager who coaches a subordinate answers questions, explains why things are done the way they are, suggests ways the subordinate can develop further, shows approval and disapproval, and makes certain the subordinate meets the proper people so that the job can be learned easiest. Coaching is most effective when the incumbent manager "models" the correct behaviors being taught. In addition, good coaching requires that superiors build on their trainees' strengths, provide them with frequent and immediate feedback on how they are doing, give them enough authority to make some of their own decisions and mistakes, assign specific and reasonably difficult goals (Hillery and Wexley, 1974), focus attention on subordinates' work achievements rather than on their personality traits, seek their opinions whenever feasible, and use concrete behavioral examples when reviewing their performance.

Rational Manager Training

Rational Manager Training (Kepner and Tregoe, 1965) is designed to improve a manager's skill in rational problem analysis and decision making. A group of managers grapples with the problems and decisions of a simulated organization. During each exercise, each manager is assigned a specific role (e.g., production manager, sales manager) and is given background information about the particular organization's problems. Trainees have their own offices, talk to one another on the telephone, and conduct meetings to solve the problems. When the group of trainees have used up the time allotted to them for working on a particular exercise (regardless of whether they have solved the problem or not), they return to their conference room for a critical evaluation of their performance by the course leader. They examine the assumptions they have made and the ways they have used the information available to them. These feedback sessions expose them to some of their own inadequate methods of thinking about problems and decision making.

Universities and Corporate Institutes

One of the most frequently used methods of management development are the various programs offered by colleges and universities. Probably the best known of these programs is Harvard Business School's Advanced Management Program. It lasts for 13 weeks and is designed for top-level managers. Included in the program are case study courses dealing with such topics as business policy, finance, human behavior in organizations, and labor relations. In addition to these residential programs in which managers live for awhile on campus, numerous universities offer series of lectures on such special topics as decision making, leadership, communication, and so on.

A few very large organizations such as General Motors, General Electric, and Pepsi-Cola have developed their own corporate institutes. These institutes offer special in-house programs for their managerial personnel.

MANAGEMENT DEVELOPMENT PROGRAMS: A SUMMARIZATION

What can one conclude about the effectiveness of management development programs? The research literature has been reviewed elsewhere by Campbell et al. (1970). Their general conclusions seem to be the following:

Managers can be taught to be more supportive, to allow subordinates more participation in decision making, to show concern for subordinate welfare, and to communicate effectively. There is little direct evidence, however, showing that such managers have higher producing groups.

T-group training appears to induce behavior changes that are transferable to the job situation. There is some confusion as to the specific nature of these changes. The effects seem to be unpredictable in that the training affects each trainee differently. Also, the effects of these behavior changes on performance have not been determined.

The small number of studies dealing with the effects of training on teaching problem-solving and decision-making skills have yielded disappointing results.

Research comparing the combined efforts of two or more methods are too few to warrant any generalizations.

Despite these somewhat gloomy conclusions, we are optimistic about the future potential of management development. It seems that more eclectic approaches combining several procedures such as positive reinforcement and goal-setting (Wexley and Nemeroff, 1975) or positive reinforcement and behavior modeling (Robins and Wexley, 1975) are needed. It also seems important to pay attention to two additional things: (1) how individual differences interact with the particular training methods used, and (2) how the particular organizational environment or climate interacts with the effects of training.

REVIEW AND DISCUSSION QUESTIONS

1. Define or explain each of the following key terms: in-basket, multiple role playing, role reversal, computer-assisted instruction, psychological fidelity, case study, behavior modeling.
2. What are the advantages and disadvantages of using programmed instruction in industrial training programs?
3. Describe each of the following methods for developing managers. Compare them with each other, and indicate which you prefer and why: understudy assignments, junior boards, university programs.
4. Compare and contrast the relative effectiveness of on-the-job and off-the-job training methods.

5. Discuss the effectiveness and applicability of T-group education in organizations.
6. Assume you have been asked by an organization to set up an on-the-job training program for jet engine mechanics. What would you do to maximize the effectiveness of this training?
7. Formulate an outline of a training program for a job with which you are familiar. Length and costs of the program are not important here. Make certain to choose the most appropriate methods for your particular training objectives.
8. What kinds of research breakthroughs would you like to see accomplished in the area of training methods and management development during the next ten years?

REFERENCES

Argyris, C. A brief description of laboratory education. *Training Directors Journal*, 1963, *17*, 4–8.

Argyris, C. T-groups for organizational effectiveness. *Harvard Business Review*, 1964, *42*, 60–74.

Bass, B. M. & Barrett, G. V. *Man, work and organizations: An introduction to industrial and organizational psychology.* Boston: Allyn and Bacon, 1972.

Bass, B. M., & Vaughn, J. A. *Training in industry: The management of learning.* Belmont, Calif.: Wadsworth Publishing Company, 1966.

Beach, D. S. *Personnel: The management of people at work.* New York: Macmillan, 1975.

Beckhard, R. *Organization development: Strategies and models.* Reading, Mass.: Addison-Wesley Publishing Company, 1969.

Bolda, R. A., & Lawshe, C. H. Evaluation of role playing. *Personnel Administration*, 1962, *25*, 40–42.

Bond, B. W. The group discussion-decision approach: An appraisal of its use in health education. *Dissertation Abstracts*, 1956, *16*, 903.

Bradford, L. P., Gibb, J. R., & Benne, K. D. *T-group theory and laboratory method.* New York: Wiley, 1964.

Butler, J. L. A study of the effectiveness of lecture versus conference teaching techniques in adult education. *Dissertation Abstracts*, 1966, *26*, 3712.

Buxton, C. E. *College teaching: A psychologist's view.* New York: Harcourt Brace, 1956.

Campbell, J. P., & Dunnette, M. D. Effectiveness of T-group experiences in managerial training and development. *Psychological Bulletin*, 1968, *70*, 73–104.

Campbell, J. P., Dunnette, M. D., Lawler, E. E., III, & Weick, K. E., Jr. *Managerial behavior, performance, and effectiveness.* New York: McGraw-Hill, 1970.

Carroll, S. J., Jr., Paine, F. T., & Ivancevich, J. J. The relative effectiveness of training methods—expert opinion and research. *Personnel Psychology*, 1972, 25, 495–510.

Castore, G. F. Attitudes of students toward the case method of instruction in a human relations course. *Journal of Educational Research*, 1951, 45, 201–213.

Culbertson, F. Modification of an emotionally held attitude through role playing. *Journal of Abnormal and Social Psychology*, 1957, 54, 230–233.

Dietrick, D. C. Review of research. In R. A. Hill, A *comparative study of lecture and discussion methods*. Pasadena, Calif.: The Fund for Adult Education, 1960, 90–118.

Goldstein, I. I. *Training: Program development and evaluation*. Monterey, Calif.: Brooks/Cole Publishing Company, 1974.

Goldstein, A. P., & Sorcher, M. *Changing supervisor behavior*. New York: Pergamon Press, Inc., 1974.

Hillery, J. M., & Wexley, K. N. Participation effects in appraisal interviews conducted in a training situation. *Journal of Applied Psychology*, 1974, 59, 168–171.

House, R. J. An experiment in the use of management training standards. *Journal of The Academy of Management*, 1962, 5, 76–81.

House, R. J. T-group education and leadership effectiveness: A review of the empiric literature and a critical evaluation. *Personnel Psychology*, 1967, 20, 1–32.

Janis, I. L., & King, B. T. The influence of role playing on opinion change. *Journal of Abnormal and Social Psychology*, 1954, 49, 211–218.

Janis, I., & Mann, L. Effectiveness of emotional role-playing in modifying smoking habits and attitudes. *Journal of Experimental Research in Personality*, 1965, 1, 84–90.

Kelman, H. C. Attitude change as a function of response restriction. *Human Relations*, 1953, 6, 185–214.

Kepner, C. H., & Tregoe, B. B. *The rational manager: A systematic approach to problem solving and decision making*. New York: McGraw-Hill, 1965.

Kibbee, J. M., Craft, C. J., & Nanus, B. (Eds.). *Management games: A new technique for management development*. New York: Rhinehold Publishing Corporation, 1961.

King, B. T., & Janis, I. L. Comparison of the effectiveness of improvised role playing in producing opinion changes. *Journal of Human Relations*, 1956, 9, 177–187.

Kirchner, W. K. Book review of A. J. Marrow's *Behind the executive mask*. *Personnel Psychology*, 1965, 18, 211–212.

Korman, A. K. *Industrial and organizational psychology*. Englewood Cliffs, N.J.: Prentice-Hall, 1971.

Levine, J., & Butler, J. Lecture versus group decision in changing behavior. *Journal of Applied Psychology*, 1952, 36, 29–33.

Lewin, K. Group decision and social change. In E. E. Maccoby, T. M. Newcombe, & E. L. Hartley (Eds.), *Readings in Social Psychology*. New York: Henry Holt, 1958, 197–211.

Maier, N. R. F. An experimental test of the effect of training on discussion leadership. *Human Relations*, 1953, 6, 161–173.

Maier, N. R. F., & Hoffman, L. R. Using trained developmental discussion leaders to improve further the quality of group decisions. *Journal of Applied Psychology*, 1960, 44, 247–251.

Maier, N. R. F., & Maier, R. A. An experimental test of the effects of developmental vs. free discussions on the quality of group decisions. *Journal of Applied Psychology*, 1957, 41, 320–323.

Maier, N. R. F., & Zerfoss, L. R. MRP: A technique for training large groups of supervisors and its potential use in social research. *Human Relations*, 1952, 5, 177–186.

Mann, J. H., & Mann, C. H. The importance of group tasks in producing group-member personality and behavior change. *Human Relations*, 1959, 12, 75–80.

McCormick, E. J., & Tiffin, J. *Industrial psychology*. Englewood Cliffs, N.J.: Prentice-Hall, 1974.

McGehee, W., & Thayer, P. W. *Training in business and industry*. New York: Wiley, 1961.

McKenney, J. L. An evaluation of a business game in an MBA curriculum. *Journal of Business*, 1962, 35, 278–286.

Meyer, H. H., Kay, E., & French, J. R. P., Jr. Split roles in performance appraisal. *Harvard Business Review*, 1965, 43, 123–129.

Nash, A. N., Muczyk, J. P., & Vettori, F. L. The relative practical effectiveness of programmed instruction. *Personnel Psychology*, 1971, 24, 397–418.

Odiorne, G. S. The trouble with sensitivity training. *Training Directors Journal*, 1963, 17, 9–20.

Raia, A. R. A study of the educational value of management games. *The Journal of Business*, 1966, 39, 339–352.

Robins, G. L., & Wexley, K. N. Modification through modeling and reinforcement in leaderless groups. *The Journal of Psychology*, 1975, 91, 87–91.

Schein, E. H., & Bennis, W. G. *Personal and organizational change through group methods: The laboratory approach*. New York: Wiley, 1965.

Schramm, W. Mass communication. *Annual Review of Psychology*, 1962, 13, 251–284.

Silber, M. B. A comparative study of three methods of effecting attitude change. *Dissertation Abstracts*, 1962, 22, 2488.

Solem, A. R. Human relations training: Comparisons of case study and role playing. *Personnel Administration*, 1960, 23, 29–37.

Stovall, T. F. Lecture vs. discussion. *Phi Delta Kappan*, 1958, 39, 255–258.

Strauss, G.   Apprentice-related instruction: Some basic issues. *The Journal of Human Resources*, 1968, 3, 213–236.

Strauss, G.   Union policies toward the admission of apprentices. In S. M. Jacks (Ed.), *Issues in labor policy: Papers in honor of Douglas Vincent Brown.* Cambridge, Mass.: MIT Press, 1971.

Strauss, G., & Sayles, L. R.   *Personnel: The human problems of management.* Englewood Cliffs, N.J.: Prentice-Hall, 1972.

Tannenbaum, R., Weschler, I. R., & Massarik, F.   *Leadership and organization: A behavioral science approach.* New York: McGraw-Hill, 1961.

Van Schaack, H., Jr.   Naturalistic role playing: A method of interview training for student personnel administrators. *Dissertation Abstracts*, 1957, 17, 801.

Verner, C., & Dickinson, G.   The lecture, an analysis and review of research. *Adult Education*, 1967, 17, 85–100.

Wexley, K. N., & Nemeroff, W. F.   Effectiveness of positive reinforcement and goal setting as methods of management development. *Journal of Applied Psychology*, 1975, 60, 446–450.

Wexley, K. N., Singh, J. P., & Yukl, G. A.   Subordinate personality as a moderator of the effects of participation in three types of appraisal interviews. *Journal of Applied Psychology*, 1973, 58, 54–59.

15

ORGANIZATION DEVELOPMENT

ORGANIZATION DEVELOPMENT (OD) is a relatively new field which is rapidly changing as a result of new knowledge. Thus, there is some disagreement among authors and practitioners about the nature and scope of OD. In fact, there is no single definition of OD with which everyone would agree. Therefore, instead of merely presenting a long list of OD definitions offered by numerous experts in this area, it would seem more worthwhile for us to examine some of the common characteristics of *most* OD efforts.

CHARACTERISTICS OF ORGANIZATION DEVELOPMENT

1. *It involves a total organizational system.* As Beckhard (1969) points out, this does not necessarily mean that the entire organization must be involved. Rather, OD can be initiated in any subsystem which is relatively free to determine its own plans and future (e.g., a fairly autonomous plant of a multiplant organization).

2. *It views organizations from a systems approach.* The organization is seen as an interdependent set of integral component parts. The practitioner realizes that when one part of the total system is changed in some way, it will have multiple effects on other parts of the system. The practitioner also thinks in terms of multiple rather than single causes of organizational events (French & Bell, 1973).

3. *It is supported by top management.* Top management must show a definite commitment and awareness of the OD effort.

4. *The services of a third-party change agent is often used.* As French & Bell (1973) point out, the agent may be a member of the organization, but should be external to the particular organizational subsystem initiating

the OD effort. It is interesting to note, however, that there is a growing tendency to use internal change agents (Huse, 1975). This issue is a controversial one with little evidence as to which approach is better.

5. *OD is a planned effort.* It entails a systematic diagnosis of the organization, a detailed plan for improving the current state of affairs, and a mobilization of the resources needed to carry out the program (Beckhard, 1969).

6. *It is intended to increase organization competence and health.* A competent organization is one which is both effective and efficient (Huse and Bowditch, 1973). Organizational effectiveness is the degree to which an organization reaches its goals and objectives; organizational efficiency refers to the amount of resources the organization requires to produce its outputs. Although the two concepts are highly interrelated, they are distinct. After all, it is quite possible for an organization to be efficient but not effective or vice versa (Etzioni, 1964).

Other authors, most notably Beckhard, prefer to speak in terms of organizational health. In Beckhard's view, a healthy organization is one which manages its work toward established goals; is properly organized; makes decisions by and near the sources of information; rewards (and punishes) managers and supervisors according to their performance; has communications which are relatively undistorted; minimizes win/lose conflicts between individuals and groups; has a high clash of ideas about tasks and projects, but little clash over interpersonal difficulties; is an "open system"; and attempts to help each person and organizational unit maintain its integrity as well as grow.

7. *It uses behavioral-science knowledge.* An OD intervention is based on knowledge and technology obtained from various areas of the behavioral sciences: leadership, communication, motivation, goal setting, learning, intergroup relations, small group behavior, conflict management, attitudes, organizational structure, and interpersonal relations.

8. *It is a relatively long-term process.* It often takes several years to bring about a meaningful and lasting organization change. For example, grid organization development (discussed later in this chapter) may take five years to complete.

9. *It is an ongoing process.* The OD process is a continuous and dynamic one. The practitioner must be capable of modifying or changing strategy in midstream as a result of emerging problems and organizational events. There are continual ups and downs in the process, but the change agent must "hang in there."

10. *It mainly focuses on changing the attitudes, behavior, and performance of organizational groups or teams rather than individuals.* However, as we shall see later, some interventions are directed at individuals.

11. *It relies primarily on experiential as opposed to didactic learning.* Although OD may involve the imparting of factual knowledge by means

of lectures and group discussions, it relies heavily on organizational members actually experiencing, experimenting with, and reflecting on new forms of behavior.

12. *It uses an action research intervention model.* The key aspects of the model include collecting research data about an ongoing system by the change agent, making preliminary diagnosis, feeding back and discussing these data with the client group, joint action planning by the agent and client, action, and rediagnosis. This model will be discussed in greater detail later in the chapter.

13. *It emphasizes the importance of goal setting and planning activities.* One of the major features of OD programs is teaching individuals and groups how to set measurable and realistic goals and how to translate these goals into action.

It would also be helpful to understand also what OD is *not*. OD is *not* management development. Management development is concerned specifically with improving the skills, knowledge, and attitudes of individual managers. Although an OD effort might possibly involve management development, it would do so only as a part of its larger objective of improving the competence or health of the units comprising the total organization (Beckhard, 1969). The term OD should not automatically be associated with sensitivity training or participating in a Managerial Grid seminar. Instead, there are a variety of different approaches that can be used in OD depending upon the particular organization's needs. Finally, OD differs from most other methods of organizational change in which a consultant studies an organizational situation and makes recommendations. The OD practitioner does not make recommendations in the traditional sense but, instead, works hand-in-hand with the organization to assist it in its attempt to survive and remain competent in a world of rapid technological and cultural change.

HISTORICAL BACKGROUND

The history of organization development can be traced back to two related but different sources. One source, laboratory or T-group training, emerged in 1946 when Kurt Lewin and his staff formed the first T-group workshop. It involved community leaders who were brought together to discuss problems and were later given an opportunity to react to feedback about their individual behavior. As a result of this experience, Lewin and his associates believed that individuals could learn from their own interactions by participating in unstructured, small-group (called T-group) situations. Their early work led to the establishment of the National Training Laboratories (NTL)—Institute for Applied Behavioral Science at Bethel, Maine in the late 1940s. During the 1950s, many of the NTL trainers became increasingly involved in providing managers in business and industry with T-group training. Since then, T-groups have been quite popular in a wide variety of organizations. The second source also stems from the early work of Lewin, this time in survey research and feedback. As an illustration of this approach, the Detroit Edison Company was given a company-wide employee and management attitude survey beginning in 1948 (Mann, 1962). During the next few years, meetings were held separately with nonsupervisory employees, first- and second-line supervisors, and various levels of management in order to feed back information about each work group's attitudes regarding their supervision, promotional opportunities, job satisfaction, and so on. This was the first of many research studies still continuing today by the Institute for Social Research at the University of Michigan on the effects of survey research feedback. Today, OD applications emerging from one or both of these sources can be seen in many kinds of organizations throughout the world (e.g., industrial, police departments, churches, public schools) (French & Bell, 1973).

ASSUMPTIONS OF OD INTERVENTIONS

Most of the assumptions and values basic to organization development interventions are in concordance with the humanistic theories of such individuals as McGregor, Likert, Argyris, Maslow, Bennis, and Schein. French & Bell (1973) have made these OD assumptions explicit by classifying them into those relating to people as individuals, as group members, and as members of total organizations. Listed below is a summarization of some of these underlying assumptions.

As Individuals

1. Most individuals desire personal growth and development when placed in a supportive and challenging work environment.
2. Most individuals are capable of making a greater contribution to their organizations than their organizations are willing to permit. Organizations often squelch their member's constructive actions (e.g., participation in decision making, providing suggestions) by either not rewarding them or penalizing them.

As Group Members

1. One's work group is extremely important in determining feelings of competence and satisfaction.
2. Most people want to be accepted by and get along well with their work group. These work groups can be made more effective if individuals work together more cooperatively.

3. The formal leader of a work group cannot possibly perform all of his/her leadership functions at all times. Hence, group members must help the leader by sharing in leadership functions.
4. Suppressed feelings adversely affect the functioning of groups and organizations. Group climate should be one of increased "openness."
5. The level of interpersonal trust and support is much lower in most organizations than is desirable.

As People in Organizational Systems

1. Most managers in organizations are members of overlapping work groups. A manager's behavior in both groups is extremely important in affecting the interrelationships between them.
2. Whatever happens in one subsystem of an organization (e.g., changes in technology, personnel, goals) will affect and be affected by other parts of the total organization.
3. Resolving conflict in such a way that one party wins triumphantly and the other loses severely may be realistic and appropriate in some situations, but is not healthy for the organization in the long run for solving most organizational problems.
4. Improved performance due to OD efforts needs to be supported and maintained by appropriate managerial changes in other subsystems of the organization such as performance appraisal, training, personnel selection and placement, and communication.

CHANGE PROCESSES AND STAGES

Organizational development efforts are directed at bringing about some planned change in order to increase organizational competence. The basic change model underlying most OD interventions is known as "action research." Action research is a series of steps or activities that is used in actual practice for bringing about desired changes. Figure 15–1 presents a diagram of the events involved in action research. Two things are evident from this figure: first, action research is a cyclical, ongoing process; and second, it consists of the following five key stages:

1. *Problem perception.* The process begins when a powerful key executive realizes that the organization has one or more problems and persuades others in the organization that a behavioral-scientist consultant should be contacted. Some of the many problems an organization may be experiencing include poor communication, intergroup conflicts, poor planning and goal setting, low motivation on the part of employees, poor team effectiveness, and poor managerial style.
2. *Collection of data and preliminary diagnosis.* The consultant gathers information about the ongoing system by using face-to-face inter-

FIGURE 15–1
Diagram of the Specific Steps of the Action Research Model for Organization Development

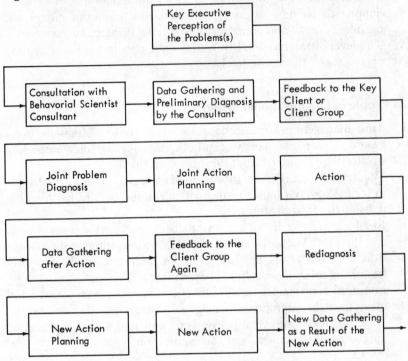

Adapted from W. French, "Organization Development Objectives, Assumptions and Strategies," *California Management Review,* 12 (1969), p. 26.

views, structured or unstructured questionnaires, observations of individuals or groups in action, and company performance records. Based on these data, the practitioner arrives at certain hypotheses or hunches about possible courses of action that should be followed.

3. *Feedback and joint diagnosis.* All relevant information obtained by the consultant is shared with the client group usually at some informal group meeting. The consultant is careful to protect all sources of information by not divulging their identity. The practitioner and the client group then jointly diagnose the situation and discuss whether there exists any real problems worth alleviating.

4. *Joint action planning and action.* First, the consultant and the client group jointly agree on the objectives of the OD program and how these objectives are to be attained. Next, the actual program is put into action.

5. *Data gathering, feedback, and rediagnosis.* Data is gathered after

action has been taken and once again fed back to the client group by the consultant. This usually leads to a rediagnosis, the taking of new action, and so on.

There are several important aspects of this change model which should be noted. First, it is a scientific approach in that it includes a systematic examination of the program's effects on the organization. Second, it is not committed or restricted to any particular type of OD intervention. It can be used with any OD technique or approach depending upon the particular results of the diagnostic process. Third, it reduces resistance to change on the part of the individuals involved by taking into account their needs and beliefs as well as having them participate in the diagnoses.

VARIETIES OF OD INTERVENTIONS

An OD intervention is any set of structured activities that selected target groups or individuals are asked to participate in for the purpose of organizational improvement (French & Bell, 1973). There are many different varieties of OD interventions and, consequently, many different kinds of classificatory schemes that have been suggested. We prefer to classify OD interventions according to the size of the organizational unit (i.e., individual, dyads/triads, teams and groups, intergroup relations, total organization) involved as the target. Figure 15–2 presents a classification of several of the many types of interventions currently in use. Notice that some interventions are listed in more than one category since they are used at various levels in an organization.

Life and Career Planning Interventions

One of the newer types of OD interventions focuses on helping individual organizational members plan their life and career goals. Individuals differ greatly in how they make career decisions. Numerous factors such as childhood experiences, social class, nonwork activities, values, attitudes, educational level, and job experiences can influence career aspirations. A single factor such as the challenge an individual experiences during the first-year in a career can have a substantial impact on career plans as well as commitment to an organization (Berlew & Hall, 1966).

Life and career planning interventions are particularly meaningful for individuals who have given little thought about their future, who feel that they are stagnating in their current position, who are experiencing a forced demotion, who are thinking about making some sort of career change, or who no longer have any upward (only lateral) mobility. Generally, the program deals simultaneously with an individual's overall life aims as well as specific career orientations. The importance of this

FIGURE 15–2
Classification of OD Interventions (according to size of organizational unit)

Organizational Unit	*Types of Interventions*
Individuals	Life and career planning. Grid OD phase 1. Role analysis technique. Coaching and counseling.
Dyads/Triads	Grid OD phases 1, 2. Process consultation.
Teams and Groups	Survey feedback. Grid OD phases 1, 2. Role analysis technique. Team building—family groups. Process consultation.
Intergroup Relations	Survey feedback. Grid OD phase 3. Process consultation.
Total Organization	Survey feedback. Management by objectives. Grid OD phases 4, 5, 6. Scanlon plan.

Adapted from W. L. French, & C. H. Bell, Jr., *Organization Development—Behavioral Science Interventions for Organization Improvement* (Englewood Cliffs, N.J.: Prentice-Hall, 1973), p. 107.

type of career counseling from the organization's point of view can be seen by the high turnover figures reported. Studies of college graduates indicate that five years after graduation more than half of them change organizations with some even changing occupations (Porter, Lawler, & Hackman, 1975). Studies of nonmanagement personnel show similar trends. Although much of this turnover is unavoidable, some of it can be reduced by helping individuals to formulate realistic life and career goals as well as plans for achieving them. Sometimes this intervention can cause an individual to leave an organization if he realizes that he is not going to get what he wants from it.

The life and career planning exercises used focus on the individual's past, present, and future. These interventions last anywhere from one day to an entire week. Participants first work on the exercises individually and then discuss their data in small groups of about 10–15 people. The exercises include such activities as writing a hypothetical obituary about yourself, describing a fantasy day, responding to the question, "Who am

I?" and preparing a career/life inventory of important experiences you have had and would like to have in the future.[1]

Grid Organization Development

Robert Blake and Jane S. Mouton have designed one of the most thorough programs of organization development. Grid® organization development is a six-phase program lasting anywhere from three to five years. It begins by examining individual managerial behavior and style and then systematically widens its focus to the team or group, to intergroup relations, and finally to the total organization. The program utilizes a variety of problems, questionnaires, and exercises which allow individuals and groups to identify their own strengths and weaknesses. All phases of the program are conducted by the organization's own members who have been trained in grid methodology.

Basic to Grid OD is Blake and Mouton's (1964) concept of leadership best described as "the managerial grid." As shown in Figure 15–3, there are two basic dimensions for describing the behavior of individual managers: *concern for production and concern for people.* The first dimension, comparable to the concept of "initiating structure" described by the Ohio State leadership studies (see Chapter 8), is shown on the horizontal axis of the grid. Concern for people is comparable to the concept of "consideration." Figure 15–3 shows that concern for production and concern for people can range from low (1) to high (9) yielding 81 (i.e., 9 × 9) possible kinds of managerial leadership styles and orientations. For instance, it is possible for a manager to show a high concern for production while showing little concern for people (i.e., a "9,1" manager). Another manager may have a low concern for production and a high concern for people (1,9). The manager with a 5,5 orientation shows an intermediate concern for both production and people. For Blake and Mouton, the most desirable manager is the 9,9 individual who exhibits simultaneously a high concern for production and people. Their OD intervention *assists* management in changing toward a 9,9 approach which cannot be fully attained without certain improvements and changes in the total organizational system.

Let us look briefly at the six phase program typically employed by Blake and Mouton (1968):

PHASE ONE: THE GRID SEMINAR. Several teams are formed, each consisting of five to nine managers who come together for an entire week.

---

[1] These exercises are representative of those attributed to Herbert A. Shepherd. For more information see French & Bell, *Organization Development*, pp. 144–46 and E. F. Huse, *Organization Development and Change*, pp. 266–69.

FIGURE 15–3
The Managerial Grid

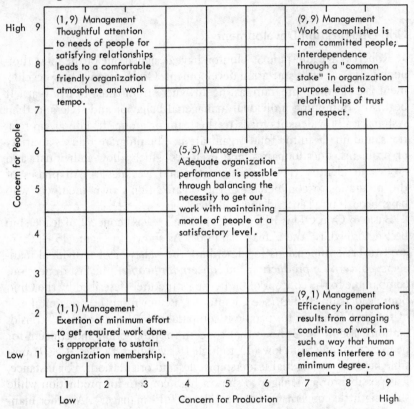

Source: R. R. Blake and J. S. Mouton, *The Managerial Grid* (Houston: Gulf Publishing Company, 1964), p. 10. Reproduced by permission.

Ideally, each team consists of members representing different departments, divisions, and levels within the organization. During this phase, participants assess their own grid styles, develop team action skills, work at achieving unobstructed communication within their teams, develop problem-solving and critiquing skills, and learn to analyze the culture of their team and of the existing organization using grid concepts. During this stage, all managers in the organization learn all theories of the Grid as well as the 9,9 theory.

PHASE TWO: TEAM DEVELOPMENT. Week-long seminars are held again, this time with actual work teams (i.e., a manager and subordinates). As with phase 1, this stage is conducted away from the job setting and begins with top level management participation. The objective is to perfect teamwork by having each team analyze and improve its problem-solving, planning, goal-setting, and communication skills. In addition, each manager is given feedback as to his individual and team behavior; this allows each person to see himself as team members do.

PHASE THREE: INTERGROUP DEVELOPMENT. Teams having important working relations with one another come together in pairs to create better cooperation and coordination. Key members on each team work together to discuss the key elements that would be needed if an ideal relationship existed between them (e.g., "the other team would allow us to use their computer facilities"). Joint discussions are then held between the key members of both teams to share ideas. After that, each team works separately to develop action steps to move toward the ideal situation which the two groups jointly defined.

PHASE FOUR: DEVELOPING AN IDEAL STRATEGIC CORPORATE MODEL. The top management group, consisting of the head of the organization and those reporting directly to him, are charged with the task of designing an ideal strategic corporate model. This model defines exactly what the organization would be like if it were truly perfect. The team convenes for a week to discuss such things as organization structure, advertising strategies, marketing procedures, financial planning, and so on. It may take the team as long as a year to develop the final model. As the model progresses, it is discussed with subordinate managers to get their evaluations and commitment.

PHASE FIVE: IMPLEMENTING THE IDEAL STRATEGIC MODEL. Implementing the model involves the following: (1) designing logical subunits of the organization which are fairly autonomous (e.g., product lines, profit centers, geographical areas); (2) appointing planning teams to each subunit to study how the subunit can be moved more in line with the ideal strategic model; (3) appointing a coordinator to serve as a resource person for the various planning teams; (4) establishing an additional planning team which designs a headquarters and evaluates whether the supervision and services provided by the headquarters to the subunits are justified; possibly some of these services (e.g., developing investment capital) might be more efficiently handled within the subunit itself.

PHASE SIX: SYSTEMATIC CRITIQUE. The final phase is an extremely important one. It involves a systematic critiquing and evaluation of the change program. Quantitative measurements should be taken at the beginning of the program as well as during and after each stage. This phase will indicate what progress has been made, what obstacles still exist, and what directions should be taken in the future.

The major evidence cited to support grid OD is a study by Blake, Mouton, Barnes, and Greiner (1964). It involved all 800 managers and technicians in a 4,000-member division of a large petroleum company. The firm experienced a considerable rise in profits, increase in productivity per worker-hour, and decrease in costs while the grid program was in effect. Other improvements attributed to the program were increased frequency of meetings among managers, changes in criteria for management appraisals, increase in number of transfers within the plant (i.e., greater flexibility), increased emphasis on teamwork and problem solving, and a pronounced shift toward 9,9 values. The results of this research, however, must be viewed with caution. Since no control or comparison group was used, we have no way of knowing whether factors (e.g., changes in the economy) other than the OD intervention caused the improvements. Some measures were quite subjective and anecdotal and many of them were not collected both before and after the intervention as they should have been. Therefore, considerably more evidence is needed before any definitive statements can be made.

Process Consultation

Process consultation is a difficult concept to describe because it cannot be linked with any particular kind of OD intervention. Instead, it involves a skilled third party (consultant) coming into an organization to help individuals and groups diagnose and solve their own problems using various kinds of interventions. The best source on the concept of process consultation is a book by Edgar H. Schein (1969) who defines it "as a set of activities on the part of a consultant which helps the client to perceive, understand, and act upon process events which occur in the client's environment" (p. 9). According to this definition, the consultant does not offer an organization "expert advice" or "look them over" much the way a doctor looks over a patient. Instead, the consultant works jointly with the members of the organization to diagnose the problem, help them learn to see problems for themselves, and be actively involved in generating a remedy.

Schein presents a broad categorization of some of the OD interventions which a process consultant might use:

1. *Agenda-Setting Interventions.* The purpose of this type of intervention is to make the group more aware of its own internal processes by:
   a. Holding special "process analysis sessions" after regular business meetings to direct the group's attention to such issues as its communication patterns and leadership styles.
   b. Having the group complete a post-meeting reaction form (see Figure 15–4), tabulate their own data, and discuss the results.
   c. Helping the group to analyze and improve its agenda-setting procedures.
   d. Setting up meetings away from the office to explore interpersonal processes within the group.
   e. Presenting to the group relevant elements of theory about individuals, groups, and the management process.

FIGURE 15–4
Sample Form for Analyzing Group Effectivness

A: Goals

Poor   1   2   3   4   5   6   7   8   9   10   Good

Confused; diverse;   Clear to all; shared
conflicting; indifferent;   by all; all care about
little interest.   the goals, feel
                                               involved.

B: Participation

Poor   1   2   3   4   5   6   7   8   9   10   Good

Few dominate; some   All get in; all are
passive; some not   really listened to.
listened to; several
talk at once or
interrupt.

C: Feelings

Poor   1   2   3   4   5   6   7   8   9   10   Good

Unexpected; ignored   Freely expressed;
or criticized.   empathic responses.

D: Diagnosis of group problems

Poor   1   2   3   4   5   6   7   8   9   10   Good

Jump directly to   When problems arise
remedial proposals;   the situation is care-
treat symptoms   fully diagnosed before
rather than basic   action is proposed;
causes.   remedies attack basic
                                               causes.

E: Leadership

Poor   1   2   3   4   5   6   7   8   9   10   Good

Group needs for   As needs for leadership
leadership not met;   arise various members
group depends too   meet them ("distributed
much on single   leadership"); anyone
person or on a few   feels free to volunteer as
persons.   he sees a group need.

F: Decisions

Poor   1   2   3   4   5   6   7   8   9   10   Good

Needed decisions don't   Consensus sought and
get made; decision made   tested; deviates appre-
by part of group; others   ciated and used to
uncommitted.   improve decision;
                                               decisions when made
                                               are fully supported.

FIGURE 15–4   *(continued)*

G: Trust

Poor	1	2	3	4	5	6	7	8	9	10	Good

Members distrust one
another; are polite,
careful, closed,
guarded; they listen
superficially but in-
wardly reject what
others say; are afraid
to criticize or to be
criticized.

Members trust one
another; they reveal
to group what they
would be reluctant
to expose to others;
they respect and use
the responses they
get; they can freely
express negative
reactions without
fearing reprisal.

H: Creativity and growth

Poor	1	2	3	4	5	6	7	8	9	10	Good

Members and group
in a rut; operate
routinely; persons
stereotyped and rigid
in their roles; no
progress.

Group flexible, seeks
new and better ways;
individuals changing
and growing; crea-
tive; individually
supported.

Adapted from E. H. Schein, *Process Consultation: Its Role in Organization Development* (Reading, Mass.: Addison-Wesley, 1969), pp. 42–43.

2. *Feedback of Observations or Other Data.* This intervention consists of the consultant feeding back observations or interview results to either individuals or groups. This is only an appropriate intervention when the group or the individuals have indicated a readiness to hear this feedback.

3. *Coaching or Counseling of Individuals or Groups.* The giving of feedback to either individuals or groups inevitably leads to the question, "How can I (or we) change to achieve better results?" At this point, the consultant becomes a counselor or coach. According to Schein, the consultant's role should become one of helping the individual or group to evaluate various alternative courses of action. At no time, should the consultant give the client advice; the role must be a nondirective one.

4. *Structural Suggestions.* The consultant helps the client to generate solutions to structural problems such as how work should be allocated, how communications should be altered, or how committees should be reorganized. The consultant can help the client to assess the consequences of different alternatives, or suggest alternatives which have not been considered.

Survey Feedback

Survey feedback is a systematic method of collecting data about a total organization, feeding back these data to groups at all levels within the organization, and asking these groups to use the information as a basis for planning and taking corrective action. This technique originated in 1947 at the University of Michigan. Today, the University of Michigan's Institute for Social Research (ISR) is the largest provider of the survey feedback method. Thus, let us examine the steps involved in their approach.

1. Top level management must be involved in the initial planning.
2. The Survey of Organizations questionnaire is administered anonymously to all organizational members. The current 1974 edition of the Survey of Organizations yields the measures shown in Figure 15-5.

FIGURE 15-5
Measures Found on the Survey of Organizations Questionnaire

Organizational Climate	*Leadership*
Technological readiness	Managerial support
Human resources primacy	Managerial goal emphasis
Communication flow	Managerial work facilitation
Motivational conditions	Managerial team building
Decision-making practices	Peer support
Lower level influence	Peer goal emphasis
	Peer work facilitation
Group Process	Peer team building
Motivation	*Satisfaction*
	Satisfaction with company
Job Characteristics	Satisfaction with supervisor
Job challenge	Satisfaction with job
Task variety	Satisfaction with pay
Autonomy	Satisfaction with work group
Identity	Satisfaction with progress to date
Feedback	Satisfaction with future progress

Source: J. Taylor and D. Bowers, *Survey of Organizations: A Machine-Scored Standardized Questionnaire Instrument* (Ann Arbor: Center for Research on Utilization of Scientific Knowledge, Institute for Social Research, University of Michigan, 1974).

Also included in the questionnaire are questions measuring respondent demographic characteristics and several questions measuring supervisory needs. Finally, space is included for an organization to add some of its own questions. Shown in Figure 15-6 are two items

FIGURE 15–6
Sample Items from the Survey of Organizations Questionnaire

To what extent are you clear about what people expect you to do on your job?
1. To a very little extent.
2. To a little extent.
3. To some extent.
4. To a great extent.
5. To a very great extent.

All in all, how satisfied are you with your supervisor?
1. Very dissatisfied.
2. Somewhat dissatisfied.
3. Neither satisfied nor dissatisfied.
4. Fairly satisfied.
5. Very satisfied.

---

taken from the latest edition containing 105 items as well as answer spaces for up to 58 additional questions.
3. The ISR computer analyzes the results. Separate tabulations are provided for each group and for each higher level of responsibility within the organization. In addition, ISR provides a diagnostic report describing principal strengths and problems in the organization.
4. A consultant feeds back the information to individual managers, starting at the top of the organization and proceeding down.
5. Each manager meets with subordinates to interpret the data and make corrective action plans. The consultant attends all the meetings to help the group relate the data to its own specific situation and set action goals.

The effectiveness of survey feedback is supported by research results reported by David Bowers of the Institute for Social Research. This research is probably the most comprehensive and elaborate evaluation of OD interventions to date. Bowers (1973) analyzed data from nearly 15,000 white- and blue-collar respondents in 23 organizations in which various OD interventions were carried out. Four types of interventions (survey feedback, two varieties of process consultation, and T-group training) were compared with each other and with two control groups in which there was no systematic change attempt. The dependent variables for evaluating the interventions were changes in organizational climate, leadership behavior, and job satisfaction. In general, the results showed that survey feedback was usually more effective than the other three kinds of interventions.

It should be noted that many organizations are effectively using survey feedback methodology without the assistance of ISR. These organizations have found it quite advantageous to develop and use their own tailor-made survey questionnaires.

Team Building Interventions

An organization's competence depends greatly on the ability of its individuals to work effectively in teams. This is especially true today as organizations must deal with increasingly complex technological problems that can no longer be handled by single individuals. Thus, improving the effectiveness of various teams within organizations is one of the most important functions performed by OD specialists. Some interventions are directed at family groups (a permanent team consisting of a superior and several subordinates) while others are directed at special groups such as temporary teams created to tackle specific tasks, ad hoc committees, and newly formed groups. The interventions are usually focused on one or more of the following objectives: (1) clarifying role expectations and obligations of team members, (2) improving superior-subordinate or peer relations, (3) improving problem solving, decision making, resource utilization, or planning activities, (4) reducing conflict, and (5) improving organizational climate.

Let us now briefly examine a few of the more widely used team intervention strategies:

ROLE ANALYSIS TECHNIQUE (RAT). This technique is designed to improve team effectiveness by clarifying the role obligations of each team member and explicating what others expect in terms of fulfilling particular roles. The intervention consists of a structured series of meetings in which each individual lists the specific duties and responsibilities of the job with the help of peers, lists what is expected from others, learns what others expect from the individual, and leaves the program with a written summary of the individual's complete team role. This strategy is particularly useful with newly formed teams but can also be helpful with family groups in which role ambiguity exists.[2]

FAMILY GROUP DIAGNOSTIC MEETING. The primary purpose of this intervention is to identify a team's problems (if any), not to solve them. Typically, a team leader and an OD consultant agree that this approach would be beneficial; they then discuss it with the group members to get their reactions. If everyone agrees to proceed, the consultant schedules a

---

[2] See I. Dayal and J. M. Thomas, "Operation KPE: Developing a New Organization," *The Journal of Applied Behavioral Science*, 4 (1968), pp. 473–506 for a description of how this technique was used to clarify top management roles in a new Indian organization.

half- or full-day team meeting away from the work situation itself. Prior to the meeting, the consultant asks each member to think about such questions as: Can this team be more effective than it is? What are we doing correctly and incorrectly? Are we getting along and communicating with one another as well as we should? The consultant often interviews some or all of the members before the general meeting. At the meeting, all the diagnostic information is shared among the team members. They identify and discuss their problem areas and attempt to generate *preliminary* action steps. One of these action steps may be the scheduling of a "family group team-building meeting."

FAMILY GROUP TEAM-BUILDING MEETING. This intervention is somewhat similar to the family group diagnostic meeting in its general sequence of events. However, unlike the previous method, it has the goal of improving team effectiveness by deciding upon the action steps to be taken (i.e., "who is to do what") in order to solve problems. The group meeting typically lasts two or three days instead of just a day or less. Usually, more than one group meeting is needed to insure that the intended changes take place and remain stable over time. Despite the term "family," this technique can be used with either family or special groups.

A case example of a team development intervention is provided by Schmuck, Runkel, & Langmeyer (1969). Their program was aimed at improving the organizational functioning of a junior high school faculty by improving its problem solving, openness, and ease of interpersonal communication. The intervention sought to increase the effectiveness of the faculty as a whole, not individual development. It involved almost the entire staff of the school, including secretaries, the head cook and head custodian, as well as the faculty and administrators. The program was started just prior to the academic year and continued periodically until February.

The consultant invited all 54 trainees to verbalize the frustrations they experienced in the school. Three problems emerged as being most significant, namely, insufficient role clarity, failure to draw on staff resources, and low staff involvement and participation at meetings. Three groups were then formed, each to work through a problem solving sequence to reduce one of these problems. Each of these groups arranged for the entire staff to break into subgroups to participate in various simulation and discussion exercises (e.g., communication, decision making, nonverbal behavior). The researchers reported a number of observable, although anecdotal, changes within the school after the intervention (for example, improved relations between principal and staff and less mistrust among teachers). In addition, they compared their results with conditions in other schools. Using questionnaire data they concluded that members of their experimental school were more supportive of their principal, had more effective faculty meetings, made many more innovations in solving problems, were more willing to share new ideas, and were more willing to take risks to improve their teaching effectiveness.

Although many organizations are currently experiencing team building interventions, there is little empirical research evidence on their effectiveness. Although they "sound" impressive, this is no substitute for rigorous evaluation.

Management by Objectives

Management by objectives (MBO) is an OD approach which has been widely adopted by a number of organizations during the past decade. This approach rests on the following key elements:

1. Setting measurable, concrete performance goals.
2. Subordinate participation in the setting of goals.
3. Periodic performance review sessions to discuss goal accomplishment.
4. Organizational commitment to the program.

Organizations which have used this approach refer to it variously as "management by objectives," "work planning and review," "management by results," and so on.

The approach is generally credited to Peter Drucker (1954) who stressed the importance of each manager, from the top to the bottom of the organization, establishing objectives for his department or unit. Drucker emphasized that these objectives must be consistent with the overall purpose of the organization and that every manager should participate in the establishment of the objectives of the next higher unit. Douglas McGregor (1960) also supported the use of an MBO approach, although his conception of it differed somewhat from that of Drucker. McGregor advocated MBO as a better method of appraising managerial performance than traditional procedures since MBO involved superior-subordinate agreement on job duties, mutual goal setting, specific action plans for achieving goals, self-appraisals, and the discussion of the self-appraisals with a superior.

Listed below are the steps (adapted from Carroll & Tosi, 1973) which are involved in the MBO process.

Step 1. Ask top management to develop organizational objectives and programs to achieve them. These objectives must be stated concretely otherwise organizational units will not know how they can contribute to goal achievement. An objective such as "be the *best* in our industry" is obviously not clear enough. The term "best" must be operationalized in terms of productivity, market penetration, profitability, and so on.

Step 2. Have the top corporate executive meet with all immediate subordinates (e.g., heads of major divisions and departments) to communicate these objectives and plans.

Step 3. Have each department head, based on the information presented in Step 2, develop goals, actions, and performance measures for his or her particular organizational unit. These goals are then discussed and agreed upon in a private meeting with the top corporate executive.

Step 4. Ask each department head to meet with immediate subordinates to communicate these goals. Once subordinates understand the commitments made, each subordinate prepares a set of goals and action plans for self and his/her unit which later is discussed and agreed upon with the department head. The process then continues down the organizational hierarchy.

Step 5. Have intermediate review sessions to review all individual and unit performance in terms of established goals and performance. These sessions should be held on a frequent basis between a single manager and a single subordinate. The meeting should review progress, identify and solve any problems blocking goal attainment, and revise the goals if necessary. The sessions should also be used to provide positive (e.g., praise and recognition) and negative feedback.

Step 6. A final review session should be conducted between superior and subordinate to determine which goals were successfully reached and how.

ADVANTAGES AND DISADVANTAGES. There are several advantages of MBO. Managers learn what is expected of them by their superiors, know the standards by which their performance will be judged, and are made more aware of their organization's objectives. The program induces managers to interact more with their people which results in more effective communication and more accurate feedback to subordinates. An MBO program brings about the identification of problem areas, improves organization planning and the organization of work, and forces the setting of specific target dates.

Despite its advantages, there are several problems in implementing MBO programs which occur. Some managers complain that it involves an excessive amount of paperwork. There are also those who find it inconsistent with their ordinary managerial style to allow subordinates to participate in goal setting. Some managers do not know how to develop or use performance objectives and must be given special training. It is difficult to develop and measure goals for certain jobs such as executive vice president or certain job components (e.g., developing one's subordinates). Thus, there tends to be heavy stress on only measurable goals at the expense of unmeasurable ones. Moreover, during a period of rapid change, goals established one day may be outmoded the next. Finally, there is the problem of interdependent jobs in which it is meaningful to set team goals but not individual goals.

Ivancevich (1974) recently used objective measures of employee performance to evaluate an MBO program in a manufacturing company.

The performance of production departments in three plants was compared. One plant had an MBO program for supervisors which included encouragement and support from top management in the form of letters, memos, telephone conversations, and meetings. The second plant had an MBO program that was not given encouragement and support by top management. The third plant did not have an MBO program and served as a control condition. Only the production department in the first plant had a sustained improvement in quantity and quality of performance over the course of the three year study. In addition, there was a significant decrease in absenteeism and grievances in this one plant.

Ivancevich also compared the performance of marketing departments in the three plants. Unlike the production workers, sales people in the two plants with an MBO program were involved in the goal-setting process along with their supervisors. The results indicated that sales performance improved in both MBO programs, but there was no improvement in the plant without an MBO program. For a review of other studies evaluating MBO programs, the reader is referred to Latham and Yukl (1975).

The Scanlon Plan

This approach was first proposed in the 1930s by Joseph Scanlon, a union leader in a steel mill facing the prospect of going out of business.[3] After the success of Scanlon's intervention in this plant, he went on to become a top officer in the United Steelworkers Union and, a few years later, a lecturer at the Massachusetts Institute of Technology. Throughout his career, Scanlon publicized his plan which consists of two basic mechanisms: (1) a new suggestion system for insuring that all organizational members have an opportunity to participate in decision making, and (2) an equitable system of providing rewards for increased productivity.

The participation system involves two types of committees. In each department a *production committee* is established consisting of one management representative (usually the supervisor of the department) and one or more nonmanagement representatives elected by the people who work in the department. The committee encourages people to make suggestions to improve productivity and meets periodically (every two to four weeks) to discuss these suggestions. The production committee either puts the suggestion into effect immediately or, if the suggestion requires large expenditures of money or interdepartmental cooperation, passes it to a *screening committee*. This committee is composed of top management and an equal or greater number of elected nonmanagerial personnel

---

[3] Parts of this section are drawn from C. F. Frost, J. H. Wakeley, and R. A. Ruh, *The Scanlon Plan for Organization Development: Identity, Participation, and Equity* (East Lansing: Michigan State University, 1974), chap. 1.

(sometimes union leaders). This committee meets once a month to decide on all suggestions sent to it by the production committees and to determine whether a bonus is to be paid for the previous month's production. All decisions made by this committee are made by consensus so as to avoid any domination by management.

The equity system is designed to reward everyone (i.e., hourly workers to top management) in the company based on the productivity of the *total* organization. Although each organization establishes its own unique Scanlon plan ratio (bonus computation formula), bonuses are usually tied to the total cost of compensating personnel compared to the total sales value of whatever the organization produces. To establish a baseline ratio, the organization reviews its efficiency during the past three to five years. Once this ratio is established, bonuses are paid whenever monthly productivity exceeds the ratio. While each employee receives the same percentage bonus (e.g., 2 percent increase in wages or salary), the actual dollars each person takes home depends on his or her base pay. One percent of a vice president's monthly salary will be more than 1 percent of an hourly worker's. Thus, Scanlon plan equity depends greatly on the equity of the company's regular wage and salary system.

Despite its 40-year history, there have been few well controlled quantitative studies on the effectiveness of the Scanlon plan. Most of the research has consisted of descriptive or qualitative analyses of the experiences of a small number of organizations. These studies have typically reported: (1) improved labor-management relations, (2) increased acceptance of change, (3) more favorable attitudes toward the company and management, and (4) increased productivity and employee earnings. On the other hand, several companies have reported unfavorable results leading to the abandonment of the plan. Recent research has shown that management attitudes toward employees and participative decision making may mediate the retention of the Scanlon plan in an organization (Ruh, Wallace, and Frost, 1973). This finding, coupled with the finding that employees often see the plan as providing less than desired opportunities for participation in decision making, point to needed changes in future implementations of the approach (Goodman, Wakeley, and Ruh, 1972).

CONDITIONS FOR MAXIMUM OD EFFECTIVENESS

Previous research and experience suggest certain conditions which contribute to the maximal success of the OD process.[4] Let us briefly look at some of the distinguishing features of effective OD programs:

---

[4] For further discussion on the conditions contributing to optimal success in OD, see W. L. French, and C. H. Bell, Jr., *Organization Development: Behavioral Science Interventions for Organization Improvement* (Englewood Cliffs, N.J.: Prentice-Hall, 1973), chap. 14.

1. There is a realization on the part of key personnel that there are certain organizational problems that must somehow be alleviated.
2. There is commitment and support for the OD effort by top management in the organization.
3. An action research model (preliminary diagnosis, data gathering, feedback, and action planning) is followed. Unfortunately, there are some practitioners who use only those interventions which they know best, regardless of the diagnosis made.
4. The OD consultant (either internal or external) is honest and consistent with the client. In addition, the consultant lives up to whatever he or she professes. For instance, a change agent calling for openness must model these behaviors for the client.
5. The change agent keeps everyone concerned informed about what is happening, and why. This minimizes everyone's fears and suspicions regarding the purposes of the program.
6. The initial intervention is a highly successful one causing other subunits within the organization to request the same treatment.
7. The external change agent reduces the organization's dependency by developing internal resource people who can take over once the change agent leaves.
8. There is a continuous monitoring of the results by the consultant to insure that the organizational changes remain stable over time.
9. The OD agent acknowledges management's effective practices in the past rather than acting as though "nothing was right around here until I was brought in."
10. The OD consultant does everything possible to prevent certain high level managers from interfering with the OD efforts. Interference by a threatening, autocratic-type manager can reverse several months of painstaking OD work.

SUMMARY

In this chapter we have examined the major characteristics of the change programs referred to as organization development. These change programs are broader in scope than the training techniques discussed in Chapter 14 or the motivational techniques described in Chapter 5, although an OD program may include training techniques such as T-groups or motivational techniques such as job enrichment. The general objective of OD is to improve the problem solving, communication, leadership, and conflict-resolution processes of an organization.

An OD program is usually a long-range, large-scale effort rather than being limited to one small subunit of the organization. The targets of the change effort are usually groups rather than individuals, but changes in the attitudes, diagnostic skills, and interpersonal competence of individual employees are also expected to occur. The assumptions underlying OD programs reflect an optimistic, positive view of human nature. People are assumed to have drives toward psychological growth and to be capable of positive change in personality and values. It is also assumed that the effectiveness of groups can be improved by expression of emotions, openness of communication, and participation by members in decision making.

The basic tactic used in organization development is some type of intervention. The major OD interventions include life and career planning, Grid OD, process consultation, survey feedback, and team building. Management by objectives and the Scanlon plan are large-scale change programs that may also be regarded as a form of OD. Although research on OD programs is still limited, a beginning has been made in discovering the conditions for maximizing their effectiveness.

REVIEW AND DISCUSSION QUESTIONS

1. Define or explain each of the following key terms: action research, survey feedback, process consultation, role analysis technique, family group team-building meeting, survey of organizations, managerial grid.

2. What is the difference between organization development and management development?

3. What are the advantages and problems that sometimes characterize management by objectives?

4. What assumptions about people are implicit in organization development?

5. Discuss the sources of people's resistance to change and what OD interventions must do to overcome this resistance if they are to be effective.

6. What arguments can be made for and against the use of the Scanlon plan?

7. What are the ideal organizational conditions for implementing successful OD interventions?

8. Assuming you are a high-level manager, would you advocate the use of life and career planning interventions in your organization? Do you think that they are beneficial from a cost/benefit point of view?

REFERENCES

Beckhard, R. *Organization development: Strategies and models.* Reading, Mass.: Addison-Wesley, 1969.

Berlew, D. E., & Hall, D. T. The socialization of managers: Effects of expectations on performance. *Administrative Science Quarterly*, 1966, *11*, 207–223.

Blake, R. R., & Mouton, J. S. *The managerial grid.* Houston: Gulf Publishing Co., 1964.

Blake, R. R., & Mouton, J. S. *Corporate excellence through grid organization development.* Houston: Gulf Publishing Co., 1968.

Blake, R. R., Mouton, J. S., Barnes, L. B., & Greiner, L. E.   Breakthrough in organization development. *Harvard Business Review*, 1964, *42*, 133–155.

Bowers, D. G.   OD techniques and their results in 23 organizations: The Michigan ICL study. *Journal of Applied Behavioral Science*, 1973, *9*, 21–43.

Carroll, S. J., Jr., & Tosi, H. L., Jr.   *Management by objectives: Applications and research.* New York: Macmillan, 1973.

Drucker, P.   *The practice of management.* New York: Harper and Bros., 1954.

Etzioni, A.   *Modern organizations.* Englewood Cliffs, N.J.: Prentice-Hall, 1964.

French, W. L., & Bell, C. H., Jr.   *Organization development: Behavioral science interventions for organization improvement.* Englewood Cliffs, N.J.: Prentice-Hall, 1973.

Goodman, R. K., Wakeley, J. H., & Ruh, R. A.   What employees think of the Scanlon plan. *Personnel,* 1972, *49,* 22–29.

Huse, E. F.   *Organization development and change.* St. Paul, Minn.: West Publishing Co., 1975.

Huse, E., & Bowditch, J.   *Behavior in organizations: A systems approach to managing.* Reading, Mass.: Addison-Wesley, 1973.

Ivancevich, J. M.   Changes in performance in a management by objectives program. *Administrative Science Quarterly,* 1974, *19,* 563–574.

Latham, G. P. & Yukl, G. A.   A review of research on the application of goal setting in organizations. *Academy of Management Journal,* 1975, *18,* 824–845.

Mann, F.   Studying and creating change. In W. Bennis, K. Benne, and R. Chin (Eds.). *The planning of change: Readings on the applied behavioral sciences.* New York: Holt, Rhinehart and Winston, 1962.

McGregor, D.   *The human side of enterprise.* New York: McGraw-Hill, 1960.

Porter, L. W., Lawler, E. E., III, & Hackman, J. R.   *Behavior in organizations.* New York: McGraw-Hill, 1975.

Ruh, R. A., Wallace, R. L., & Frost, C. F.   Management attitudes and the Scanlon plan. *Industrial Relations,* 1973, *12,* 282–288.

Schein, E. H.   *Process consultation: Its role in organization development.* Reading, Mass.: Addison-Wesley, 1969.

Schmuck, R., Runkel, P., & Langmeyer, D.   Improving organizational problem solving in a school faculty. *Journal of Applied Behavioral Science,* 1969, *5,* 455–482.

indexes

AUTHOR INDEX

SUBJECT INDEX

This book has been set in 10 point and 9 point Electra, leaded 2 points. Part numbers are 48 point Optima and part titles are 24 point Optima. Chapter numbers are 42 point Weiss Series I and chapter titles are 24 point Optima Semi Bold. The size of the type page is 26 by 45½ picas.